A CULTURAL HISTORY OF HAIR

VOLUME 1

A Cultural History of Hair
General Editor: Geraldine Biddle-Perry

Volume 1
A Cultural History of Hair in Antiquity
Edited by Mary Harlow

Volume 2
A Cultural History of Hair in the Middle Ages
Edited by Roberta Milliken

Volume 3
A Cultural History of Hair in the Renaissance
Edited by Edith Snook

Volume 4
A Cultural History of Hair in the Age of Enlightenment
Edited by Margaret K. Powell and Joseph Roach

Volume 5
A Cultural History of Hair in the Age of Empire
Edited by Sarah Heaton

Volume 6
A Cultural History of Hair in the Modern Age
Edited by Geraldine Biddle-Perry

A CULTURAL HISTORY OF HAIR

IN ANTIQUITY

VOLUME 1

Edited by Mary Harlow

BLOOMSBURY ACADEMIC
LONDON • NEW YORK • OXFORD • NEW DELHI • SYDNEY

BLOOMSBURY ACADEMIC
Bloomsbury Publishing Inc,
1359 Broadway, New York, NY 10018, USA
Bloomsbury Publishing Plc, 50 Bedford Square,
London, WC1B 3DP, UK
Bloomsbury Publishing Ireland,
29 Earlsfort Terrace, Dublin 2, D02 AY28, Ireland

BLOOMSBURY, BLOOMSBURY ACADEMIC and the Diana logo are trademarks of Bloomsbury Publishing Plc

First published in Great Britain 2021
Paperback edition published 2022

Copyright © Bloomsbury Publishing, 2022

Mary Harlow has asserted her right under the Copyright,
Designs and Patents Act, 1988, to be identified as Editor of this work.

Series design: Raven Design
Cover image: Krater depicting a girl washing her hair © DEA / G. DAGLI ORTI / Getty Images

All rights reserved. No part of this publication may be: i) reproduced or transmitted in any form, electronic or mechanical, including photocopying, recording or by means of any information storage or retrieval system without prior permission in writing from the publishers; or ii) used or reproduced in any way for the training, development or operation of artificial intelligence (AI) technologies, including generative AI technologies. The rights holders expressly reserve this publication from the text and data mining exception as per Article 4(3) of the Digital Single Market Directive (EU) 2019/790.

Bloomsbury Publishing Plc does not have any control over, or responsibility for, any third-party websites referred to or in this book. All internet addresses given in this book were correct at the time of going to press. The author and publisher regret any inconvenience caused if addresses have changed or sites have ceased to exist, but can accept no responsibility for any such changes.

A catalogue record for this book is available from the British Library.

A catalog record for this book is available from the Library of Congress.

ISBN:	HB:	978-1-4742-3201-2
	HB set:	978-1-4742-3212-8
	PB:	978-1-3502-8532-3
	PB set:	978-1-3502-8751-8
	ePDF:	978-1-3500-8790-3
	eBook:	978-1-3500-8791-0

Typeset by Integra Software Services Pvt. Ltd.

To find out more about our authors and books visit www.bloomsbury.com
and sign up for our newsletters.

CONTENTS

LIST OF FIGURES	vi
GENERAL EDITOR'S PREFACE	xii
Introduction *Mary Harlow*	1
1 Religion and Ritualized Belief *Mary Harlow and Lena Larsson Lovén*	15
2 Self and Society *Katherine A. Schwab and Marice Rose*	31
3 Fashion and Adornment *Kelly Olson*	47
4 Production and Practice *Janet Stephens*	65
5 Health and Hygiene *Lydia Matthews*	85
6 Gender and Sexuality *Mary Harlow*	97
7 Race and Ethnicity *Marguerite Johnson*	111
8 Class and Social Status *Susan Stewart*	129
9 Cultural Representations *Glenys Davies*	145
NOTES	162
BIBLIOGRAPHY	205
CONTRIBUTORS	219
INDEX	222

LIST OF FIGURES

INTRODUCTION

I.1 Ancient Greek hairstyles from *The Mode in Hats and Headdress: A Historical Survey* by R. Turner Wilcox (first published by Charles Scribner's Sons, New York, 1945; reprinted by Dover Publishing, New York, 2008), p. 16 — 5

I.2 Ancient Roman hairstyles from *The Mode in Hats and Headdress: A Historical Survey* by R. Turner Wilcox (first published by Charles Scribner's Sons, New York, 1945; reprinted by Dover Publishing, New York, 2008), p. 24 — 6

I.3 The mosaic of Roman matron, at her toilette, Bardo National Museum, Tunis. Photo: eFesenko / Alamy Stock Photo — 12

CHAPTER ONE

1.1 Detail of Apollo from the west pediment of the Temple of Zeus at Olympia. Photo: Erin Babnik / Alamy Stock Photo — 17

1.2 Head of Apollo from Museum of Aphrodisias. Photo: DEA / G. DAGLI ORTI via Getty Images — 18

1.3 *Mummy Portrait of a Youth* (150–200 CE), encaustic on wood, 20.3 × 13 cm (8 × 5.12 in.). The J. Paul Getty Museum, Los Angeles, CA — 19

1.4 *Votive Relief to Demeter and Kore* (425–400 BCE), marble, 53 × 53 × 3.9 cm (20.87 × 20.87 × 1.54 in.). The J. Paul Getty Museum, Los Angeles, CA — 21

1.5 Statue of a Vestal Virgin in the Roman Forum in Rome. Photo: Georges DIEGUES / Alamy Stock Photo — 25

1.6 Augustus *capite velato*. D-DAI-ROM-0328_F5.jpg — 26

1.7 *Ara Pacis* frieze showing the procession of priests, with figure with covered head on right. Photo: Mary Harlow — 27

1.8 Late sixth century BCE terracotta loutrophoros (ceremonial vase for water). Metropolitan Museum of Art, New York, NY. Funds from various donors, 1927. Acc. No. 27.228 — 28

CHAPTER TWO

2.1 Tetradrachm of deified Alexander III, the Great (360–281 BCE), obv Alexander the Great, rev. Athena Nikephoros. Mount Holyoke

LIST OF FIGURES vii

  College Art Museum, South Hadley, MA. Gift of the Estate of Nathan Whitman   33

2.2 Portrait head of Augustus (25–1 BCE), marble, 39 × 21 × 24 cm (15.35 × 8.27 × 9.45 in.). The J. Paul Getty Museum, Los Angeles, CA   33

2.3 Portrait of a young girl (first quarter of first century CE). Yale University Art Gallery, New Haven, CT. Maitland F. Griggs, B.B., 1896, Fund 1995.80.1. Photo: Yale University Art Gallery   35

2.4 Attic white ground cup interior with frenzied maenad, Brygos Painter (ca. 490 BCE). Antikensammlungen, Munich, 2645   36

2.5 Stele of Hegeso. National Archaeological Museum, Athens. Photo: Erin Babnik / Alamy Stock Photo   37

2.6 *Gemma Augustea*. Kunsthistorisches Museum, Vienna. Photo: Granger Historical Picture Archive / Alamy Stock Photo   37

2.7 Dying Gaul. Photo: Heritage Image Partnership Ltd / Alamy Stock Photo   39

2.8 Onesimos (Greek (Attic), active 500–480 BCE) and Euphronios (Greek (Attic), active 520–480 BCE), Attic red-figure cup fragment (ca. 500–490 BCE), terracotta, 10 × 11.2 × 2 cm (3.94 × 4.41 × 0.79 in.). The J. Paul Getty Museum, Los Angeles, CA   40

2.9 Caryatid A. © Acropolis Museum. Photo: Socrates Mavromates   42

2.10 Attic red-figured stamnos, group of Polygnotos. Antikensammlungen, Munich   43

CHAPTER THREE

3.1 Kouros. Photo: Deutsches Archäologisches Institut—Rom. D.DAI.ROM 62.8   48

3.2 Ancient Greek kouros. National Archaeological Museum, Athens. Photo: Realy Easy Star / Salvatore Pipia / Alamy Stock Photo   48

3.3 Apollo from west pediment, Olympia. Photo: Ancient Art and Architecture / Alamy Stock Photo   50

3.4 Proto-Attic Nessos vase with a mustachioed Herakles (before 625 BCE). Photo: Deutsches Archäologisches Institut—Athens. National Museum of Athens. Inv. No. 1002. D-DAI-ATH-NM-5313   51

3.5 Grave stele of a little girl (ca. 450–440 BCE), marble. Metropolitan Museum of Art, New York, NY. Fletcher Fund, 1927. Acc No. 27.45   52

3.6 Funeral stele of young woman ("Giustiniani Stele"), classical Greece (ca. 460 BCE), from the island of Paros, Greece, marble, h. 143 cm (56.2 in.). Inv. Sk 1482. Photo: Juergen Liepe. Art Resource: ART 180483   53

3.7 Adult Greek woman. Photo: D-DAI-ATH-NM-4602   53

3.8 Bust of Augustus. Erbach, Germany. Photo: Deutsches Archäologisches Institut Koln. DAI G. Fittschen-Badura Fitt 72-03-09 (http://arachne.uni-koeln.de/item/marbilder/7774622) — 56

3.9 Marble portrait bust of Antoninus Pius (ca. 138–161 CE). Metropolitan Museum of Art, New York, NY, Fletcher Fund, 1933. Acc. No. 33.11.3 — 56

3.10 Portrait head of Constantine (ca. 325–370 CE), marble. Metropolitan Museum of Art, New York, NY. Bequest of Mary Clark Thompson, 1923. Acc No. 26.229 — 57

3.11 Portrait of the Empress Faustina the Younger, wife of the emperor Marcus Aurelius (ca. 161–180 CE), marble. Metropolitan Museum of Art, New York, NY. Gift of Shelby and Leon Levy, 1986. Acc. No. 1986.40 — 60

3.12a Fonseca Bust. Photo: G. Fittschen-Badura. Cap81-26-02_16304,12 (http://arachne.uni-koeln.de/item/marbilder/8304888) — 61

3.12b Fonseca Bust, rear view. Photo: G. Fittschen-Badura. Cap73-75-08_16304,25 (http://arachne.uni-koeln.de/item/marbilder/8304415) — 61

3.13 Woman in a wig. Musei Capitolini, Rome. Photo: D-DAI-ROM-65.1891 — 62

CHAPTER FOUR

4.1 Hair structure and histology. © Janet Stephens — 66

4.2 A strong forehead cowlick. Portrait head of Pompey the Great, Roman, early imperial period (first half of the first century CE), marble. Ny Carlsberg Glyptotek, Copenhagen. IN 773 — 67

4.3 Standard curl patterns. © Janet Stephens — 68

4.4 Two identically dressed mid-second-century tower hairstyles. Model on left has waist length, high density, medium textured hair, model on right has shoulder-blade length, average density, fine textured hair. © Janet Stephens — 70

4.5 Modern reproduction ancient hairdressing tools: (1) comb; (2) gold needle and woolen thread, bone needle; (3) wooden hair bodkins; (4) woolen ribbon; (5) unguent; (6) *calamistrum* curling wand; (7) *forfex* shears; (8) convex glass mirror. © Janet Stephens — 72

4.6 Bronze mirror (early fourth century BCE), Etruscan. Metropolitan Museum of Art, New York, NY. Gift of Henry G. Marquand, 1897. Acc. No. 97.22.16 — 72

4.7 Hercules knot. Head of a male votary (late sixth to early fifth centuries BCE), limestone, Cyprus. Metropolitan Museum of Art, New York, NY. The Cesnola Collection, purchased by subscription, 1874–76. Inv. No. 64.51.2632. Photo: OASC — 74

LIST OF FIGURES

4.8 Bronze razor. Metropolitan Museum of Art, New York, NY. Acc No. X21.131 — 76

4.9 Gold hairnet, Roman period. Museo Nazionale, Rome. Photo: Heritage Image Partnership Ltd / Alamy Stock Photo — 78

4.10 Roman mummy portrait of a woman with a jeweled garland (ca. 60–70 CE). Metropolitan Museum of Art, New York, NY. Inv. No. 19.2.6. Photo: OASC — 79

4.11 Syrian style turban in funerary relief of Aththaia, daughter of Malchos, Roman (Palmyra, Syria) (150–200 CE). Museum of Fine Arts, Boston, MA. Funds donated by Edward Perry Warren in memory of his sister. Inv. No. 22.659. Photo: © 2018 Museum of Fine Arts, Boston — 79

4.12 Natural colors, levels and corresponding tones of the stages of lightening. © Janet Stephens — 80

4.13 Barber cutting a man's hair (archaic period, ca. early fifth century BCE), terracotta, Greece (Boiotia, Tanagra). Museum of Fine Arts, Boston, MA. Inv. No. 01.7784. Photo: © 2018 Museum of Fine Arts, Boston — 82

CHAPTER SIX

6.1 Older man titillating younger man. Brygos painter (500–475 BCE). © Ashmolean Museum, Oxford, 1967. 304 — 100

6.2 Tondo of red-figure kylix in the manner of Onesimos (ca. 500 BCE). David M. Robinson Memorial Collection, University of Mississippi and Historic Houses — 105

6.3 Attributed to the Dinos painter, bell-krater (mixing bowl for wine and water): Eros with two women; three cloaked men (not visible) (ca. 430–420 BCE), red-figure, terracotta, 30.3 × 30.8 cm. Harvard Art Museum / Arthur M. Sackler Museum at Harvard University, Cambridge, MA. Anonymous loan, 9.1988. Photo: Imaging Department. © President and Fellows of Harvard College — 105

CHAPTER SEVEN

7.1 Artemision bronze. Statue depicting God Zeus or Poseidon, severe style, detail (460 BCE). National Archaeological Museum, Athens. Photo: PRISMA ARCHIVO / Alamy Stock Photo — 112

7.2 Figure of a Celtic warrior, early Roman period, terracotta. © Ashmolean Museum, University of Oxford — 118

7.3 *The departure of Memnon for Troy* (550–525 BCE), black-figure vase. Royal Museums of Art and History, Brussels — 120

7.4 Alabastron, showing "Ethiopian and Amazon" (ca. fifth century BCE). Staatliche Museum, Berlin. Inv. No. 3382. © bpk Antikensammlung, SMB / Johannes Laurentius — 121

7.5 Etruscan pottery mug in the form of the head of a black slave, Etruria (fourth century BCE). Photo: © Ashmolean Museum, University of Oxford   122

7.6 Rembrandt, *The Conspiracy of Claudius Civilis*. Nationalmuseum, Stockholm. Photo: PAINTING / Alamy Stock Photo   124

7.7 Relief from the Sebasteion of Aphrodisias showing Claudius victorious over Britannia. © New York University Excavations at Aphrodisias (G. Petruccioli)   125

7.8 Mausoleum of Halicarnassus, detail of Amazon warrior in defeat. Photo: Ali Kabas / Alamy Stock Photo   126

CHAPTER EIGHT

8.1 Mosaic of theater masks. Capitoline Museums. Photo: B.O'Kane / Alamy Stock Photo   130

8.2 Fonseca Bust. Photo: B. Malter DAI Mal615-10_16304 (http://arachne.uni-koeln.de/item/marbilder/8304610)   133

8.3 Bone pin. Roman Cypriot (first to fourth centuries CE), 10.6 cm in length. Metropolitan Museum of Art, New York, NY, The Cesnola Collection. Purchased by subscription, 1874–75. Acc. No. 74.515206   134

8.4 Toilette scene from Neumagen. Image © GDKE / Rheinisches Landesmuseum Trier. Photo: Th. Zühmer   135

8.5 Late Roman republican statue, holding ancestor busts. Photo: D-DAI-ROM-2001.2076   137

8.6 Funerary relief of Sextus Maelius Stabilio, Vesinia Iuncunda, and Sextus Maelius Faustus. North Carolina Museum of Art, Raleigh. Purchased with funds from the State of North Carolina, 79.1.2   139

CHAPTER NINE

9.1 Bust of Marcus Aurelius. Vatican Museum, Rome. Photo: DAI-ROM-96Vat2081   146

9.2a Portrait of Matidia. Capitoline Museum, Rome. Photo: B. Malter DAI-ROM Mal2005-04_16577,01 (http://arachne.uni-koeln.de/item/marbilder/4147914)   146

9.2b Back view of Matidia. Capitoline Museum, Rome. Photo: B. Malter DAI-ROM Mal2005-06-16577,03 (http://arachne.uni-koeln.de/item/marbilder/4147916)   147

9.3 Detail of a bronze statue of Trebonianus Gallus (emperor 251–253 CE). Metropolitan Museum of Art, New York. Rogers Fund, 1905. Acc. No. 05.30   147

LIST OF FIGURES xi

9.4 Mummy Portrait of a Young Woman (ca. 170–200 CE), tempera on wood, 34.9 × 21.3 cm. The J. Paul Getty Museum, Los Angeles, CA — 148

9.5 Detail of the marble figure of an old seer from the East pediment of the Temple of Zeus at Olympia (c. 460 BCE). Photo: D-DAI-ATH Hege – 0321. Arachne 34462 — 149

9.6 Mummy portrait of old woman (Roman period: date uncertain). British Museum, 1980.0921.1. © Trustees of the British Museum — 150

9.7 Head of the marble statue known as the 'Rampin Horseman' (ca. 550 BCE). Louvre Museum, Paris. Photo: Superstock/Alamy Stock Photo MFA — 152

9.8 Attic red-figure psykter with revelling satyrs by Douris (ca. 500–470 BCE). Brish Museum. ©Trustees of the British Museum — 153

9.9 Coin portrait of Otho: obverse of an aureus, 69 CE. © Andreas Pangerl, www.romancoins.info. Published in "Portraits—500 years of Roman Coin Portraits," Munich, 2017 — 154

9.10 Attic red-figure calyx crater with Herakles wrestling the giant Antaios by Euphronios (ca. 510–500 BCE). Louvre Museum, Paris. Photo: DAIR 54.142R. — 156

9.11 Coin portrait of Nero: obverse of an aureus, 64-66 CE. © Andreas Pangerl, www.romancoins.info. Published in "Portraits—500 years of Roman Coin Portraits," Munich, 2017 — 157

9.12 Terracotta antefix with the head of Medusa (mid-5th century BCE): from the Heraion, Samos, in Samos Museum. Photo: D-DIA-STH-Samon 5371 — 159

GENERAL EDITOR'S PREFACE

A Cultural History of Hair offers an unparalleled examination of the most malleable part of the human body. This fascinating set explores hair's intrinsic relationship to the construction and organization of diverse social bodies and strategies of identification throughout history. The six illustrated volumes, edited by leading specialists in the field, evidence the significance of human hair on the head and face and its styling, dressing, and management across the following historical periods: antiquity, the Middle Ages, the Renaissance, the Age of Enlightenment, the Age of Empire, and the Modern Age.

Using an innovative range of historical and theoretical sources, each volume is organized around the same key themes: religion and ritualized belief, self and societal identification, fashion and adornment, production and practice, health and hygiene, gender and sexuality, race and ethnicity, class and social status, representation. The aim is to offer readers a comprehensive account of human hair-related beliefs and practices in any given period and through time. It is not an encyclopedia. *A Cultural History of Hair* is an interdisciplinary collection of complex ideas and debates brought together in the work of an international range of scholars.

Geraldine Biddle-Perry

Introduction

MARY HARLOW

In the later fourth or early fifth century CE, a neo-Platonist philosopher, warrior lord and reluctant bishop, Synesius of Cyrene, wrote a treatise on baldness. This work both praised and parodied an earlier *Encomium on Hair* by the first–second century orator, Dio Chrysostom. Synesius' treatise typifies the writing of the educated elite of his time. Despite ostensibly being part of a Christian world, Synesius expressed his eruditeness by an extensive knowledge of the traditional "pagan" classics. *On Baldness* expresses many of the commonly held opinions of hair and multiplicity of meanings associated with it in antiquity. Synesius began his defense of baldness when he was "wounded to the heart when the terrible thing happened and my hair began to fall off"[1] and was anxious about "What wrong doing have I committed that I should appear more unsightly to the fair sex?"[2] Synesius quotes from Dio's *Encomium* wherein Dio complains about his own matted and knotted hair and praises those who make "a cult of their hair" even keeping a reed in it with which to comb it when they are at leisure. These men, for both authors only address male hair, will not even sleep with their hair on the ground. Dio refers to the mythical Greek heroes whom Homer praises for their hair: Achilles for his fair hair; Menelaus for his blond locks; Hector for his dark hair; and Odysseus with black hair curling "like the flower of the hyacinth."[3]

Synesius' response to Dio's encomium is as playful as it is learned and literate. He openly acknowledges the rhetorical games that both Dio and he use to manipulate audience reactions to their speeches.[4] He begins by comparing hairy animals to bald intelligent ones:

> And just as man is the most intelligent, and at the same time the least hairy of earthly beings, conversely it is admitted that of all domestic animals, the sheep is the stupidest, and this is why he puts forth his hair with no discrimination, but thickly bundled together. It would seem that there is a strife going on between hair and brains, for in no one body do they exist at the same time.[5]

Having stressed intelligence, the treatise then begins a catalogue of positive attributes of baldness. Listing Diogenes, Socrates, and Silenus, he argues that all philosophers, the wisest of men, are bald, indeed if a man is not bald he is unlikely to be wise. The divine elements of nature that are revealed to man are spheres which are bald and while simpler souls may dwell in a hairy head, a wise soul will find a sphere, a bald head, in which to live.[6] In order to address the images of gods with luxurious hair, Synesius argues that the plastic arts are the least truthful but rather play to the opinions of the ignorant masses who admire external things, such as a full head of hair.[7] Bald people are healthier, which is why the champion of medicine, Asclepius, is represented correctly by the Egyptians as bald.[8] He continues, referencing Herodotus' observations on the bones of Medes and

Egyptians, that bald skulls are stronger than hairier ones. This is further supported by the antics of a strong man in the theater, who can butt rams, crack vases, and bear hot pitch on his bald skull, so in the event of disaster, bald men could always earn a living as street performers![9]

Synesius knows that cultural practice and custom can influence how men wear their hair, and that the rules are different for women:

> always and in every place it has been thought a beautiful thing for each woman to make the care of her hair a most serious affair. The woman does not exist, nor has even existed, who has submitted her head to a razor, unless on account of some ill-omened and horrible calamity.[10]

In this sense, Synesius, argues nature and custom are in harmony as no woman would ever display baldness if it occurred. Men, on the other hand, can actually assist nature and reach the ideal situation of baldness by using the razor.[11] Synesius adds more and more well-known examples to prove his point: the long-haired Spartans of Thermopylae did not survive the battle; the Persians defeated Alexander but seizing the hair and beards of his troops; warrior helmets, which cover the cranium in emulation of baldness are the most terrifying.[12] Towards the end of the treatise, Synesius critiques Dio's readings of Homer and his heroes, refuting them one by one. He does agree, however, that Homer was right in suggesting that adulterers and seducers come from the type of men who care for their hair, and that long hair is clear evidence of effeminacy and deviant sexual behavior in men.[13] In his conclusion Synesius argues that Dio cannot be taken seriously and here gives away part of the game by arguing that "the rhetorician has made it evident that rhetoric is merely a hair-dressers' art," having, with his discourse, drenched the heads of the hairy with perfumed oil. Bald men, on the other hand, make up the worthy in society, they are priests, prophets, generals, school masters, and guardians of youth, and possess a superiority of intelligence.[14] Finally, Synesius concludes in the hope that after reading his treatise, "wearers of long hair are put to shame and that they adopt at least a rather moderate and restrained cropping of their hair, and if it inclines them to congratulate those who need not the barber, they need not thank me for this."[15]

Synesius was writing at a time when hair for men was often cropped quite short, at least among the elites of the later empire, of which he was a member; and the debate about women veiling was a hot topic in Christian discourse.[16] Synesius was a highly educated individual, with experience of living in both Constantinople and Alexandria, one the imperial capital and the other a renowned, cosmopolitan center of learning. He had visited Athens and may have been initiated into the Eleusinian Mysteries while there. He existed, like many of his age, across the divide between Christianity and paganism. His neo-Platonic leanings meant he had absorbed the works of the classical canon, and his training had taught him how to make persuasive and flattering speeches. It is important to understand *On Baldness* in this context but also to recognize the humor, parody, and arguably comic defensiveness of the piece. Above all, *On Baldness* is a good example of the problems we face when interpreting ancient sources discussing hair, be they written or visual.

Synesius' speech is one of the longest surviving pieces of writing which address hair behavior in the ancient world.[17] Such works are very rare in the corpus of surviving ancient literature as elite writers stood in a complex position when it came to care of the self. As readers of this volume will discover, in antiquity, both men and women trod a fine line between looking elegant, well-groomed, and attractive, and either underdoing or overdoing attention on their appearance. Rarely does writing directly address personal appearance as *On Baldness* appears to do. The genre of any written source needs to be taken into account as a key element of any interpretation, and this is a superior piece of rhetoric. Synesius was an accomplished speaker with a reputation that led to him performing an oration in front of the Emperor Arcadius in Constantinople; he knew the tricks of his trade. A good rhetorician knew how to appeal to different sections of his audience, to allow them to feel that both he and they were part of a shared culture. Hence, the very starting point of addressing Dio Chrysostom—an orator so renowned he earned the epithet "golden tongue" (Chrysostom). Synesius established a link between himself and one of the great orators of the past, and re-enforced their shared learning (and, by implication, that of his audience) with the references to Homeric heroes scattered throughout the speech. Thus, *On Baldness* is about much more than addressing male hair loss. It is about showing off the author's ability to turn a subject (male grooming) which is normally perceived negatively to a positive; about showing off his knowledge of the classics; his ability to refute another's arguments; his power to entertain; and arguably, give a topic that might be considered low-brow, high-brow attention. Synesius' rather overdefensive approach has both erudition and humor. So, while we cannot take it at face value, it remains, with circumspection, a gift for our purposes as it expresses many of the commonly held notions of the symbolic and social meanings of hair and baldness. Several chapters in this volume address attitudes to hair loss which Synesius covers, demonstrating that across the centuries, this has been a matter of anxiety for men and is, as he says in his introduction, to do with their attractiveness to others, particularly women. At the same time, all the evidence from antiquity needs the type of contextualization and circumspection that we need to give to reading Synesius.[18]

The study of hair and hairstyles in antiquity has traditionally formed a part of research into other aspects of the physical appearance of the body. Hair is taken into account in studies of dress and adornment, in studies of gender, and of the body, often with a focus on the evidence provided by various visual media. It has rarely been given the attention which it receives in this volume.[19] Several reasons account for this gap in research, one of which is the vast time span "antiquity" encompasses. This volume covers a period which saw the rise of the Greek city states and the development of what is commonly known as "classical" Greek art, philosophy, and drama; the absorption of much of the Greek world and the eastern Mediterranean into the Hellenistic empires after the death of Alexander the Great; the rise and spread of Roman imperialism which in turn absorbed many of the Hellenistic states and much of northern Europe; and finally, the spread of Christianity across the Roman Empire. It is a chronological period that runs from approximately 600 BCE to 800 CE. Traditionally these periods are named and divided as follows: archaic (776 BCE–480 BCE), classical (480 BCE–323 BCE), Hellenistic (323 BCE–146 BCE), Roman republic (509 BCE–27 BCE), Roman Principate/Empire (27 BCE–284 CE), and late antiquity (284 CE–600 CE) but obviously dates are not definitive and there is much blurring of cultural and political events across "periods." However, this periodization will help readers who do not have in-depth knowledge of antiquity to anchor their readings. Together with a broad timescale, antiquity also covers a vast geographical area that reaches from Scotland, to North Africa, to Egypt and the near East, including most of modern Europe in between. It includes a huge number of different peoples, tribes, languages, and cultures, all of which had their own hair behavior and styles which did not remain static over time. The frame of antiquity is vast and complex, and here we are only attempting to address cultures which fall within the influence of the Roman Empire at it largest extent. The question is how we approach this enormity without falling into generalizations.

To provide some framework for this huge cultural conundrum that constitutes and ancient world, this introduction presents some of the defining elements which hold the period, the cultures, and the volume together. At the outset it is important to understand that most of these cultures shared a social and political hierarchy that privileged the male over the female. Women were rarely given active political power, although they might exert political pressure in other more subtle ways; and they were almost always subordinate to men in any given situation. For much of antiquity, across most of the cultures studied for this volume, patriarchy in its many forms, was the dominant system of power. Ancient Greek, Roman, Jewish, Christian, and Celtic societies were highly gendered and these relationships—of power and gender—were often expressed in the language of hair. Male and female hairstyles were often diametrically opposed, most commonly noticeable in terms of length, and control of the hair was a reflection of social control—between the sexes, the classes, and even between citizens and noncitizens. The way the hair was worn, could, like dress, express inclusivity and exclusivity; it could symbolize belonging to a particular group in terms of sex, of age, status, of class, religious leanings, and ethnicity—and any mix of these categories. The subtle interrelationships between these categories are often hard to decipher and define given the nature of the ancient source material.

The wide extent of the geographical area and chronological periods covered by this volume is further complicated by the nature of the evidence. By far the majority of the visual and written evidence which survives is a product of elite society. This relatively small section of society could both afford to commission artworks and were literate enough to articulate thinking in writing, but they offer limited explicit commentaries on the physical appearance of their societies. As noted above, Synesius' treatise was an exception. The elite made up a tiny percentage of the population in the ancient world, yet they are the most articulate and it is their voices which, by and large, are heard across the centuries. In addition to this, given the nature of the societies from which they emerge, the voices we hear are predominantly male. This is a constant that needs to be uppermost in the mind when analyzing and examining the ways we might think about hair, particularly female hair, in ancient societies.

It is relatively easy to take a selection of visual sources from antiquity and identify a series of "hair stereotypes" in which gender, status, and age are the dominant signs: slaves will often be portrayed as smaller than other more significant figures and they might have long hair, like a child, or more rarely in iconography, shaved heads; girls and boys might wear their hair long but this style might change during the transitions to adulthood—young men might cut their hair, young women bind it up or cover it. Overall men tend to have simpler hair arrangements, whether worn short or long, while women might be portrayed with more exotic and complicated coiffures. Baldness might indicate intelligence, as Synesius would prefer, but it could also signify old age and boorishness. Body hair too can be slipped into an apparently simple dichotomy of hairiness equating to masculinity and thus a lack of body hair being associated with femininity. Synesius would again argue against this dominant idea, with his claim that intelligence cannot reside in a hairy body. In tune with Synesius, hairy bodies are rarely portrayed in ancient art, unless trying to describe wildness or otherness. In sculpture even hypermasculine gods are often portrayed as smooth skinned with perhaps ornately carved or molded pubic hair.[20] Their cephalic hair, on the other hand, is often shown beautifully coiffed.

Associations of idealized masculine and feminine beauty tend to follow similar lines. Hair becomes part of the discourse of physical appearance which grants meaning to the body and helps create identity.[21] There are, however, always exceptions to the rules, and in antiquity these are often identified in Sparta, as readers will discover.[22] It is these inherent contradictions in ideologies, together with the ability of ancient authors and artists to play with such contradictions that are the minefield the authors of this volume have picked their way through.

Earlier research on hair in antiquity recognized the links between class, status, and ethnicity, but has taken a relatively descriptive approach, primarily noting changing hairstyles as part of a discourse of *cultus* and fashion, and to note a passing of time with some hair arrangements associated with particular periods. Coiffure is often used by art historians to date a particular figure.[23]

FIGURE I.1 Ancient Greek hairstyles from *The Mode in Hats and Headdress: A Historical Survey* by R. Turner Wilcox (first published by Charles Schribner's Sons, New York, 1945; reprinted by Dover Publishing, New York, 2008) p. 16.

FIGURE I.2 Ancient Roman hairstyles from *The Mode in Hats and Headdress: A Historical Survey* by R. Turner Wilcox (first published by Charles Scribner's Sons, New York, 1945; reprinted by Dover Publishing, New York, 2008), p. 24.

In the second half of the twentieth century scholars of the ancient world began taking a more theoretical approach to the study of sexuality, women, the body, and dress and appearance, following work done in other fields such as literary criticism, anthropology and sociology, and cultural history. Taking a lead from some of this more recent scholarship on the body in antiquity, the chapters in this volume look beyond the decorative and descriptive nature of hair to examine its symbolic representations. We follow some of the most influential research which directly addresses the subject of hair in antiquity. The list is not extensive, but too long to include here in any detail, and readers will find, among numerous others, the following authors repeatedly cited:

Elizabeth Bartman, Howard Eilberg-Schwartz, Molly Myerowitz Levine, David Leitao, Mireille Lee, Maria Elisa Micheli, and Anna Santucci. Like the contributors to this volume, these authors come from a range of backgrounds: classics, ancient history, art history, archaeology, and most use a complementary range of evidence from texts and visual and material culture.

The authority of these scholars is enhanced by the ways in which they have addressed, implicitly and explicitly, the psychological and anthropological approaches which have reappraised the role of hair in the construction of the individual and of society since the early twentieth century. In my summary below I am indebted to the work of Howard Eilberg-Schwartz whom I follow here.[24] Influenced by Freud, early psychoanalytic thought saw the head and the hair as phallic symbols, imbuing both with sexual and erotic meaning. For Freud, a symbolic association between upper and lower body saw the upper body as the nexus for the expression of the repressed desires of lower body, and in extreme conditions, the cutting of the hair could be viewed as a symbolic castration. Freud explained the decapitation of Medusa as an articulation of castration anxiety in the male. Depictions of Medusa with a wide gaping mouth and lolling tongue and writhing snakes as hair (see Figure 9.12) would, in Freud's view, remind the male viewer of female genitals, particularly those of his mother. In the 1930s and 1950s, Charles Berg used the work of Freud, together with ethnographic parallels, to argue that all hair behavior was an expression of castration anxiety, for men and for women.[25] He accepted Freud's ideas of the tension between the upper and the lower body and argued that touching and playing with the hair on the head, an act which could take place in public, was symbolic of other acts of touching which could not.[26]

Anthropologists entered the discussion from the 1930s and while there was some consensus on the erotic symbolism inherent in hair and hair behavior, there was also a move away from the notion that this was always a subconscious association. In studying a range of societies, anthropologists noted the hair symbolism that was often a key part of transition or rites of passage rituals such as initiations, marriage, and mourning. They also noted the use of hair in magic. In the still seminal "Magical Hair," Edward Leach attempted to bring together the psychoanalytical and anthropological approaches. He used a range of ethnographic examples including Hinduism in India and Buddhism in Sri Lanka. One of his conclusions was that hair behavior in these communities could be categorized as follows: long, unkempt hair signified unrestrained sexuality, while short, partially shaven, or covered hair signified a controlled or restrained sexuality, and finally that a shaved head symbolized celibacy, an active denial of sexuality. In this view, hair behavior symbolized sexual desire, rather than castration anxiety. Leach moved away from the idea that hair behavior is solely part of the subconscious and argued that ways in which an individual might control their hair could be a conscious decision about their self-identity.[27] Leach's notion that such symbols might always be public was questioned, as was the extension of his threefold relationship between hair and sexual behavior as other ethnographic parallels produced different results. Mary Douglas and C. R. Hallpike argued strongly that rather than reflecting desire, hair behavior is more symbolic of social control or social deviance. In this thinking, cutting the hair or shaving the head (monks, prisoners, soldiers) signified those who were constrained or controlled by social rules and norms, while long or unkempt hair signified those who stood outside social control. It is, perhaps, no coincidence that this thinking in the West coincided with the appearance of beatniks and hippies who were partly identified (and are still stereotyped) by their hair behavior.[28] More recently it has been accepted that while such rules are useful as a way of thinking, not all societies conform to such definitions. Indeed, in the 1980s Gannath Obeyesekere, for instance, identified female Hindu ascetics who grew their hair long and matted but were celibate. Obeyesekere argued that the dreadlocks of these women were in fact phallic symbols, signifying their "marriage" to the god, reigniting the debate between psychoanalysis and anthropology.[29] Later in the same decade Anthony Synnott modified the theories of Leach and Hallpike by developing a theory of oppositions in which three premises are understood: opposite sexes have opposite hair; head hair and body hair are opposite; opposite ideologies have opposite hair.[30]

Synnott's oppositions acknowledge the inherent difference in symbolism that accrues to the linked but separate zones of head (cephalic) hair, facial hair, and body hair. It takes gender difference as a starting point and recognizes that norms for men and women often stand in opposition. It also takes into account that within any given society or culture, many different kinds of hair symbolism and hair behavior might exist depending on the gender, social, religious, cultural, and ideological position of an individual or group.[31] His theories acknowledged the danger of universalism and recognized that hair behavior could change over time and symbolize different things to different groups at the same time in the same culture. Synnott's categories can be mapped on to the ancient evidence with more ease than those of psychoanalysis, simply because of the nature of the evidence. Many of the chapters in this volume deal implicitly or explicitly with the concept of opposition as this was a common way by which ancient philosophers and thinkers conceptualized the world, particularly in terms of gender.[32] It was the norm in the ancient world for hair to differ between the sexes. It was not a universal rule, and the nature of the difference in hair may change over time, but the concept generally holds good. Moments when it is inverted, such as the cropping or shaving of the Spartan bride's head, were noted as unusual, even by commentators in antiquity.[33] Several chapters here discuss the nature of masculinity and femininity and how this was defined at particular times and in particular places. For men who might, as Synesius did, experience hair loss, it was not so much head hair but facial hair which defined them. The first appearance of facial hair was often a marker of an imminent change of status for a boy and associated with transition rituals in both Greece and Rome.[34] Beards appear to go in and out of fashion in the ancient world but retain an association with wisdom, age, and gravitas. In ancient Greece beards are commonly depicted on all types of men, from warriors to philosophers, but a change comes with the iconography of Alexander the Great, who was depicted as youthful and clean-shaven.[35] In the Roman world the clean-shaven look was preferred until the time of Hadrian in the mid-second century CE, when his fondness for Greek culture was expressed in his luxuriant beard. After this time the depiction of facial hair, as beards or a form of ancient "designer stubble," become common in imagery again, until the early fourth century.[36] While hairiness is closely associated with masculinity in antiquity, as we have noted above, very little body hair is actually depicted in ancient art. It is in fact in discussions which denigrate depilation that we understand that hairiness is to be preferred in ideology if not in reality.[37] Again, the notion of definition by opposition gives modern scholars an insight into the ancient mindset.

If some hair behaviors were common among men, then the norm for women tended to be the opposite. In antiquity the discourse surrounding women and female behavior is inextricably linked with the discourses of gender and power. It is written by men and exposes the social tensions that must have existed between (male) ideals of female behavior and appearance and the social realities of everyday experience, as well as women acting as agents of their own identity and appearance. Women were considered to be more interested in matters of the body and physical appearance than men, but in a male-dominated world this tendency towards beautification should be put to the service of their menfolk. Women should appear as decorous but modest appendages to their fathers or husbands. In terms of hair behavior this was expressed in different ways: in Athens respectable citizen women were required to cover their hair once they married, whereas in Rome, while they may cover their heads when in public, the survival of some very ornate coiffures in portrait busts suggest that hair was a status marker of some significance. The ideal woman was also, as far as we can tell, smooth skinned but the evidence for the removal of body hair is again complicated by matters of class and status. Discussions of female beauty often occur in contexts of erotic poetry or comedy and, if women are named, they are thought to be courtesans, not respectable wives. However, as a hairy woman was a subject for derisory verse in both Athenian and Roman culture, we assume that feminine beauty was the opposite to masculine hairiness. Indeed, a second-century CE physician, Galen, could write that:

> The hair of the beard not only protects the cheeks but serves to ornament them. For a man seems more stately, especially as he grows older, if he has a good covering of hair everywhere. Women only needed hair on her head for protection and ornament and not elsewhere.[38]

Given the gendered nature of ancient societies, it is no surprise that this is one of the dominant categories by which hair is articulated and which in turn articulates hair. Taking gender as a category of analysis extends Synnott's categories of opposition and forms a useful focus of interpretation for antiquity. There is little doubt that the hair was a locus of eroticism in ancient society. The very ideology of covering a woman's head assumes that there is something dangerous about both her hair and her glance. Similarly, certain male hair behaviors are imbued with erotic connotations, in ancient Athens, for example, the fuzz of the first growth of beard was considered highly attractive and sensuous to other men.[39] At the same time, men who paid too much attention to their hair risked being accused of effeminacy.

As stated earlier, one of the problems with the ancient sources, particularly when combined with the psychoanalytic approach, is that women are denied an active role. We rarely hear women's voices in the ancient sources and as both Freud and Berg were interested in the fear of castration, women are in danger of being passive actors in hair behavior. The Synnott approach provides some room for maneuver, but we are still faced with sources that talk about women, not women talking about themselves. However, it is women's hair and head coverings that are by far the most elaborate in antiquity. Women were obviously actors in their own lives despite being controlled, to varying degrees, by men, by custom, and by tradition. Convention demanded that "respectable" women were constrained in public life and little talked about so the women we do hear of are either of the very high elites and ruling classes—Hellenistic queens or the wives of Roman emperors, for example—or those at the other end of the social spectrum, the courtesans and mistresses. Such women, of course, might be of lower class than the elites but high on the erotic spectrum. The hair of each group might reflect their status as bound by convention, veiled and/or bound hair, albeit in complex coiffures, or loose flowing locks that advertised sexual availability. But even courtesans and mistresses understood how to "look" respectable. Several of the chapters in this volume deal with the complexity of multifaceted identities, in the polyvalent symbolism of hair, including its ability to be used as disguise and deception.

Hair was also one of the descriptors that ancient authors used to identify noncitizens, outsiders, and foreigners, who, like women, were often passive actors in citizen discourse. Citizenship was a central part of the individual's identity in antiquity, and was often linked to family and status group, so it was in the interests of insiders (ancient authors and artists) to consolidate a sense of belonging by stressing the difference of those who were outsiders, even though they may live (more or less comfortably) alongside each other. The geographic spread of the classical and late antique worlds included many different peoples and cultures and there was considerable interaction between these cultures. Those living in the cosmopolitan cities of the Roman Empire—Rome, Constantinople, Athens, Alexandria, Palmyra, Antioch, Marseilles, to name but a few— and on the borders, were well aware of the variation in look and hair behavior that others brought to the mix, but still they enjoyed exploiting the literary and visual conceit of "otherness." At the same time there was a great thirst for information about other peoples as the fifth-century BCE *Histories* of Herodotus and first-century CE geographer Strabo attest.[40]

All evidence from the ancient world needs to be contextualized. The example of Synesius, used as an opening to this introduction, demonstrates how genre and rhetoric shaped the structure of any piece of literary writing. In interpreting descriptions of hair in ancient written sources, readers may be dismayed by the number of caveats authors attach to any individual example or genre, but understanding the assumptions an author might make of his audience are key to interpreting meaning. Many ancient authors presume a certain amount of learning in their audience by making implicit references to earlier parts of the classical canon or to mythological stories, drawing on a shared culture that a modern reader might not be fully aware of.

Visual material needs to be deconstructed in similar ways to ascertain the relationship between context, form, and iconography, and between the artist, the commissioner of the piece, and the viewer. Images are used by the authors of this volume in order to portray particular hair arrangements, generic hairstyles for particular groups, and sometimes to examine the practicalities and mechanics of arranging hair. At the same time they are employed to discuss symbolic use of hair as part of a discourse which might express status, class, gender, modesty, authority, etc. Like written sources, images communicate a multiplicity of meaning which often need careful decoding. Sculpture makes up the "bread and butter" of the evidence, providing historians with carefully carved styles from which can be created a catalogue of changing fashion (e.g. Figures I.1 and I.2). They can also, in combination with literature, enhance knowledge of the person portrayed. The innovative portraiture of Alexander the Great, for instance, was consciously taken up by the young emperor Augustus, creating a new hairstyle which was emulated by members of his family. The visual links between the Julio-Claudians in their portraiture enhanced the notion of political legitimacy and dynasty, as well as emphasizing ideas of a new world order expressed in a very different image from that of the previous veristic, warts-and-all style of late Republican Rome.[41]

Looking at images always raises the issue of the relationship between any piece of art and social reality. Augustus's image remained youthful and idealized to the end of his life (see Figure 3.8), although we hear from Suetonius that in old age:

> He could not see very well with his left eye. His teeth were wide apart, small and ill kept, his hair was slightly curling and inclined to golden; his eyebrows met. His ears were of moderate size, and his nose projected a little at the top and then bent slightly

inward ... He was short of stature ... but this was only noticeable when a taller person stood beside him.

So perhaps not as ideally handsome as his portraiture suggests.[42] The tendency to privilege youth is also apparent in Greek vase painting—a media which is deceptively seductive in it apparent reproduction of "reality." From around 500 BCE in some genre scenes, such as the departing warrior, men are shown beardless in defiance of reality. Andrew Stewart argues that for the adult male Athenian spectator, any image of a youth offers promise of the future but also of homoerotic desire which was part of the structure of male life.[43]

At times literary sources and imagery appear to come together to create a coherent discourse. The art and commentary of *cultus* is a case in point. The care of the self and the attention to physical appearance, including hair dressing, are perceived primarily as an aspect of women's lives in antiquity, a notion that is confirmed by both texts and iconography. Images of women at their toilette form part of the iconography of fifth- to fourth-century BCE Athens, as much as that of the Roman period from first century BCE to fifth century CE—and, despite changes in emphasis, this is a remarkable continuity. Within this spectrum, however, there are notable differences and we should not be seduced into thinking that continuity implies an easy relationship between image and reality. In Greek vase painting, for instance, images of women, dressed and undressed, attending to their bodies, faces, and hair form a large body of material. The question is, as with the "youthening" of warrior figures, how far such images are representations of daily life or "genre" scenes; do they display mythological or divine women (Aphrodite at her toilette, for instance) or real women; and, if they display "real women," are they courtesans rather than respectable wives and daughters? There are other questions that need to be asked of vase paintings too, such as the type of vase a scene is painted on, and where on the vase it is placed: was this a vase that would have be used for male symposia, or as a funerary offering? How might the function of the vase dictate the content of decorative iconography, and how might this combination have been perceived by contemporary viewers? Scholars differ as to how far such imagery can give access to the lives, habits, and practices of "real" women in fifth- and fourth-century Athens, or at least access to ways in which their lives might be imagined.[44]

Similar images of women attending to their physical appearance appear in different visual and literary media throughout our period. Several authors here discuss the Hegeso monument from classical Athens (Figure 2.5) and the toilette scene from Neumagen (Figure 8.4).[45] In the Roman and early Christian world the moralizing discourse which criticizes both men and women for paying too much attention to the self is at odds with poetry where female beauty is often carefully cultivated. In each genre hair behavior is employed to amplify the artist's or the writer's ends.[46] Images in art tend to present a more positive attitude, and follow a relatively continuous programme of representation across the empire. In the fourth and fifth centuries CE the ornate, sliver casket, known as the Projecta casket, now in the British Museum, shows the young woman on her way to the baths and seated, surrounded by attendants, fixing her hair. A similar iconography is found in a mosaic floor from North Africa, dating to the early fifth century (Figure I.3).[47]

Authors in this volume differ as to how they use vase paintings and other visual material as evidence for hairstyle and behavior. To the extent that there is a shared approach, it is that imagery is at least representative of themes or overarching constructs and ideals. The appearance of toilet articles and accoutrements, may, for instance, signal an attention to the self, and the presence of mirrors may add the symbolism of reflective thought,

FIGURE I.3 The mosaic of Roman matron, at her toilette, Bardo National Museum, Tunis. Photo: Alamy H81BHX.

but certainly a snapshot of boudoir etiquette. It may also be a reflection of an artist's knowledge of the canon and as such, imaginary. As Gloria Ferrari has so succinctly put it, we still need "to make distinctions: between reality and representation and between the representation of reality and that of fiction."[48] One thing we should not do is isolate hair in the way that it appears in the earlier catalogues illustrated above.

Images and texts contain many layers of meaning, and present different meanings to different audiences. As the authors contributing to this volume come from a range of different academic backgrounds (art historians, archaeologists, ancient historians, and classicists, and one practicing hair dresser) their approaches tend to favor their central disciplines, but all have stepped outside their comfort zones in order to embrace the subject matter and the broad spectrum of antiquity as defined by this volume. The evidence selected by the contributors is relevant to the themes of particular chapters and when a single piece of evidence serves a number of agendas, this has been left to stand, both as an example of the varied ways in which scholars might interpret the evidence and to emphasize the interlinked nature of the themes that form the chapter headings in this series.

The interests of each author, or set of authors, has also dictated the content of the chapters with regard to the time frame of the volume. Given the nature of the evidence, the cultures given most attention are classical Athens, often with a side glance at Sparta (fifth to fourth centuries BCE); imperial Rome with nods towards the Hellenistic kingdoms and earlier Rome (ca. 300 BCE to 300 CE); and finally Jewish and early Christian practices (ca. first century BCE to fifth century CE). These periods overlap and intertwine but they take account of some of the major political changes in the Mediterranean in this time frame, and their consequences for Europe, North Africa, and the Near East.

The pattern of Bloomsbury Cultural Histories is that each volume in a collection contains the same chapter headings, so readers can if they wish read a single chapter on, say, Race and Ethnicity or Class and Social Status across a time frame from archaic Greece to the twenty-first century within the series. Some of the chapter headings are more relevant to some periods than others and it has inspired many of the authors in this volume to "think outside the box" and gather together information on attitudes to hair from diverse sources and rethink what we know about hair behavior in antiquity.

CHAPTER ONE

Religion and Ritualized Belief

MARY HARLOW AND LENA LARSSON LOVÉN

In the ancient world, religion was an integral part of the everyday. Religious and ritual practice was not confined to a single day of the week, or a specific area, it was embedded in every part of life and action. Ancient Greeks and Romans lived in a world full of gods who could choose to either protect or harm individuals or whole communities. They were appealed to, appeased, worshipped, and honored in a range of rituals, festivals, and secret mystery cults which operated on both a public and a private level. Worship could take the form of large, public festivals which might involve animal sacrifice, drama, processions, and feasting which affirmed the community, or could simply be a private, personal offering such as a small gift of grain to a particular god at a small altar in one's own home. Sanctuaries to the gods were placed in cities, such as on the Acropolis in Athens and on the Capitol in Rome, where they might form part of a temple complex. They could also be found at in the agora and fora of ancient towns, at crossroads, at corners, by rivers and water generally; temples and sanctuaries were also placed in the countryside, often in quite remote areas such as mountains, or in areas associated with particular deities or events. Small shrines to local gods are found across the ancient world in both urban and rural settings. Put very simply, ancient religion was about performing the appropriate rituals to keep the gods on side, and as such it was both a state and an individual affair. An individual took part in these rituals on his or her own, or as part of a family, or part of the community, or in groups divided by age and/or sex. For the ancients, the supernatural was ever-present and everywhere. To the modern eye, which tends to have a very different view of religion, ancient beliefs and practices are often perceived negatively as "superstition" or "magic." In antiquity, "magical" practices were very much part of the religious everyday from the arcane and dangerous curses sworn to cause harm to the seemingly more mundane amulet used to ward off evil.

In many cultures, hair itself, hair practices, and behavior surrounding hair signify a complex of intertwined, culturally specific markers of gender, of age status, of ethnicity, of sexual status, of belonging, or of exclusion. The hair's potential for manipulation and its ability to constantly replenish itself allow it to serve as dedications, as metonymic symbols, as charms, and sympathetic magic.[1] Hair, or lack of it, can cover a multiplicity of meanings: a shaved male head, for instance, may represent punishment or slavery in one context, or devotion to a particular deity in another. In a woman a shaved head may mark her as a bride in Sparta, as a slave in Rome, or as an extreme ascetic in early Christianity—it may also, of course, also be a practical cure for head lice![2] In all these cases, apart from the head lice, the head and hair act as symbol for the social and/or ritual situation of the individual. The control of hair, or indeed, its opposite, wild, uncontrolled hair, are useful symbols for the expression of rites of passage, the movement from one status to another,[3] or to express moments of heightened emotion and crisis. It is in these contexts that we commonly observe the ritual use of hair in ancient society. Similarly, in a religious context, a priest or priestess may possess a particular hairstyle in order to place them outside the ordinary and into the sacred realm. Many of the ritual practices of antiquity have origins in the mythical past which have been translated into the social and religious customs of society. This chapter examines ways in which the male and female head and hair are integrated and manipulated into the ritual behavior of ancient societies

HAIR AND AGE-RELATED RITUALS

Hair is a very clear marker of biological and physiological stages of life; the growth of secondary hair accompanies puberty for both males and females, and at the other end of life, thinning or graying hair is also common to both sexes while complete hair loss and baldness is more common in men. The transition into adulthood is one of the most significant stages of life in most cultures and it is no surprise to find it hedged with rituals, many of which involve the most obvious physical markers of change, hair. Moving from adolescence to adulthood can involve a number of stages and might depend on the rank and status of the individual's family in society and, in antiquity, would certainly differ in the cases of boys and girls.[4]

Ancient Greek culture in the period this volume covers has many examples of boys and men growing their hair, or particular locks of hair and cutting it as part of cult practice or in fulfilment of a vow, but as David Leitao has argued, as hair grows naturally, "a normal practice can become invested with particular power and symbolism if done in a ritual context. It blurs the boundaries between the everyday and ritual space."[5] It is this blurring of boundaries and the embeddedness of Greek religion into every part of life that makes ritual hair practices hard to identify unless ancient authors specifically discuss them. Growing hair also takes time, and if grown to fulfil a particular vow, it is unclear whether the individual is in a liminal state while the hair is growing, with the growing being part of the ritual, even though he is presumably going about his daily business. Again, there is a mingling of ritual and the everyday, or rather, ritual forms part of the everyday.[6] That said, "growing hair for the god" was a common practice in the Greek world and appears to happen at a number of occasions and ages, but it was a public part of the male entry into adult life in many Greek states. Several gods were associated with male maturation rituals, including Herakles, Dionysos, Hermes, and Apollo. Apollo is often associated with the ideal of youth, and in iconography can be recognized by his long, boyish hair and beardless face (Figure 1.1).

In classical Athens, an important event in the lives of citizen boys was the ceremony by which they entered their father's phratry. For citizen boys, the enrolment into the phratry was essential to secure inheritance rights. This traditionally happened during the annual festival of the Apatouria. On the third day of the festival, the Koureotis, consisting of a number of ceremonies took place marking different stages in the life course, depending on the individual concerned. For boys just entering the phratry, an animal sacrifice was accompanied by ritual hair cutting (*koreion*) which marked the first part of the boy's transition into adulthood. This was a public ceremony, performed in front of other members of the group and established a young man's credentials for entering full citizen

RELIGION AND RITUALIZED BELIEF

FIGURE 1.1 Detail of Apollo from the west pediment of the Temple of Zeus at Olympia. Photo Alamy BNMD7Y.

life and its responsibilities, and perhaps took place for a cohort of boys aged between fourteen and eighteen.[7] Other Greek states had similar ceremonies in which hair cutting accompanied rites of passage rituals.[8] After these ceremonies the boys had short hair which set them apart from younger members of society. It is unclear exactly how the hair on these youths might look, it might never have been cut since birth, or it may be that particular locks were never cut, while the rest of the head conformed to local styles. The specially grown locks are known by a number of terms (*skollos, konnos, mallos, krôbylos*) and in iconography it appears they could be topknots, sidelocks, backlocks, and even, as in Figure 1.2 of Apollo from Aphrodisias, frontlocks.[9]

FIGURE 1.2 Head of Apollo from Museum of Aphrodisias. Photo Alamy CW5DYN.

Plutarch tells the story of Theseus who went to Delphi to celebrate his coming of age and cut off just the front locks of his hair. This style was subsequently named *Theseis* after him and, according to Plutarch writing in the early second century CE, recalled the heroic, war-like, Homeric Abantes who were famed for close fighting and cut their hair to deny the enemy a chance to hold on to it.[10]

Pausanias, a second century CE author with a great interest in the local cults of provincial Greece collected a number of examples, many of which were no longer extant in his own time. He noted a dedication of a boy who cut his hair for the river Kephisos,[11] and recorded that at Corinth boys no longer cut their hair for Medea's daughters or wore black clothes:[12] David Leitao has collected examples from across the Greek world which demonstrate the range of contexts in which hair might be dedicated, and the performative potential of these dedications which can highlight family relationships, primarily fathers and sons, but also mothers and sons, and brothers. And, that almost all of the examples appear to be in the context of coming-of-age rituals.[13]

In Pharonic and Greco-Roman Egypt some young boys are shown with shaved heads and "Horus lock." Horus was the son of Isis and Osiris and a symbol of youth. The wearing of the lock may simply indicate youth, but it can also suggest dedication or devotion to Horus, and has been interpreted as offering protection to the child. In Figure 1.3, dating to the mid to late second century CE, a young boy is shown with his head shaved, apart from two tufts of hair at the front and the Horus lock, decorated with a gold pin. Unfortunately as this is a portrait of the child after his death, his Horus lock could not protect him from the ever-present dangers to life in antiquity.[14] Jane Draycott's recent study of votive offerings highlights the Egyptian practice noted by Herodotus of parents shaving a child's hair and making a dedication in gold of silver, equivalent to the weight of the hair. This ritual continued into the Roman period.[15]

FIGURE 1.3 *Mummy Portrait of a Youth* (150–200 CE), encaustic on wood, 20.3 × 13 cm (8 × 5.12 in.). The J. Paul Getty Museum, Los Angeles, CA.

In the Roman world, while children are traditionally shown with longer hair, the cutting of cephalic hair is not such a key element in the male transition to adulthood; in contrast, the focus is on the first real shaving of the beard. The appearance of facial hair in young men also marked the beginning of a new stage of life and the emergence of sexuality. Greek culture saw the first downy growth of young men as particularly attractive and erotic and for male lovers this marked the beginning of the end of acceptable homosexual relationships. The appearance of a full beard and shaving marked the arrival of adulthood in which the man would become the active lover rather than the passive beloved.[16]

In the Roman world the shaving of the first beard was not done until a full beard could be grown. So adolescents with downy facial hair formed a particular social group, not yet full adults. These "beardless" youths could still be subject to immoral influences and behave recklessly.[17] As their facial hair grew and matured, so the young men were expected to behave more like responsible adults, but until they could shave their first beards their position in the adult world was insecure. The young Octavian, who became the Emperor Augustus, was leading troops to avenge his adoptive father, Julius Caesar, by 43 BCE at the age of nineteen, despite the fact that he did not shave his first beard until 39 BCE. To compensate for his perceived youthfulness he aligned himself with Apollo, the youthful, beardless, and long-haired god, and perhaps for political expediency, Octavian remained clean-shaven after his first shave, retaining the association with Apollo. Octavian's first shaving of the beard was accompanied by some ritual, and he granted all citizens a festival at public expense.[18] The young emperor Nero, another great showman, accompanied his first shave with a sacrifice of bullocks, and placed the shavings in a golden box adorned with pearls and dedicated it to the Capitoline gods.[19] Nero possessed a family cognomen of Ahenobarbus, meaning bronzed beard, which, in the family mythology, was granted to an ancestor who had his cheeks stroked by the Dioscuri after the Battle of Regulus in 496 BCE.[20] While in reality social behavior does not necessarily change with social expectations or with hair growth, a young man was treated differently once his beard was shaved. Martial complains that his *paedagogus* (chaperone) would still not let him behave like an adult, even though his girlfriend complains about his now prickly lips.[21] One particular festival at Rome, the Lupercalia, involved specifically young men who had passed the time of their first shave. As part of this festival, two young men were anointed with the blood of sacrificed animals (goats and a dog) and dressed in goatskins. After they had feasted together with other youths and leading magistrates the naked, or semi-naked, *luperci* ran through the city striking women with thongs made from the skin of the sacrificed goats.[22] In the *Fasti*, Ovid interprets the actions of the Lupercalia as part of a fertility ritual, recalling that after the mythical Rape of the Sabine women no children were produced. The goddess Lucina suggested as a remedy to "Let the sacred he-goat go in to the Italian matrons," words which were interpreted by an augur and the ritual of the Lupercalia created.[23] The festival involved young bearded men or men who had taken their first shave, demonstrating their fertility by running naked, by striking young women who were also at an age at which they could become pregnant; ritually replaying the violence of the rape of the Sabines. The run of the *luperci* marked a change in the life course of the young man, an end to uncontrolled sexual desire, and an acceptance of the adult responsibilities.

The cutting of hair or shaving of the beard were among the common rites-of-passage rituals for young men and recognize that life course transitions can occur over relatively long periods of time; a young girl on the other hand entered the adult world on the day of her marriage, when she moved from being a daughter to being a wife. In most Greek and Roman contexts this transformation was marked by a change in hairstyle and often also by headdress.

Figure 1.4 shows mother and daughter deities Demeter and Kore, where the age and status difference between the two women is illustrated not only by their posture and body shape—the more mature Demeter sits, while the slender Kore stands behind her mother—but also by hairstyle: the younger Kore wears her hair in a simple ponytail, while Demeter's hair is bound up and decorated with a crown (*polos*).

Most societies had prenuptial rites of some description which involved dedicating "girlish" items such as toys to a goddess prior to marriage but there is little reference to female hair cutting in this context. Pausanias writing in the second century CE does, however, record two rituals from Greece. One is at Megara in Attica where, before their marriage, young girls brought pitchers to the memorial of Iphinoe, daughter of Alkathous who died a virgin, and also cut a lock of their hair as a dedication. Pausanias likens this ceremony to one in Delos where young girls cut their hair as dedications to Hekaerge and Opis.[24] It is hard to establish if this ritual was regularly undertaken either in the past or in Pausanias' own time.

Figure 1.4 *Votive Relief to Demeter and Kore* (425–400 BCE), marble, 53 × 53 × 3.9 cm (20.87 × 20.87 × 1.54 in.). The J. Paul Getty Museum, Los Angeles, CA.

In the Roman world it is equally hard to know how common some of the recorded rituals were. A Roman wedding, for instance, could take place with very little ceremony, but authors who record such events list a series of rituals which a bride might be engaged in prior to and during her wedding. It was the bride who was the focus on the wedding day while the groom played only a minor role, and indeed could be absent altogether. Marriage was the most important change in a young female's life, and in a traditional Roman wedding both the dress and the coiffure of the bride would be in an archaic style. The woolen dress was to be woven by the bride herself and the hair was parted and plaited into six braids. A spear, *hasta caelibaris*, would be used to arrange the coiffure which was fastened with woolen fillets, *vittae*, and crowned by a garland.[25] The head/hair and the face of the bride was then covered by a veil in a bright orange-red color, the *flammeum*.[26] The hairstyle and some clothing details in the bridal outfit reappears in the public dress and coiffure of the Vesta priestesses (see below).

OTHER RITUALS INVOLVING HAIR

Not all hair offerings are part of a controlled process of growth and cutting in which the dedication is clearly planned in advance, nor are they always part of growing-up rituals. In Greek drama the visual theater of a hair offering is often used to heighten the tension of the narrative and to give weight to the ritual action. In the *Ajax*, Sophocles presents a highly charged scene after the hero, Ajax, has been killed and there is a danger that his body will be claimed and defiled by the enemy. The bleeding corpse of Ajax occupies the stage and, in order to protect both it and Ajax's young son, Eurysaces, and his wife, the child is told to kneel by the body of his father, holding ritual locks of hair cut by Teucer, Ajax's kinsman, from his own head and from Eurysaces and Tecmessa:

> Boy, come here and, standing close by, clasp as a suppliant the father who begot you. Sit there in supplication, holding a lock of mine and one of hers and thirdly one of your own, a store of instruments of supplication! And if any of the army tries to drag you by force away from this corpse, may that man perish out of the earth without burial, evilly as befits an evil man, with the seed of all his house cut off, even as I now cut this hair! Hold him, boy, and guard him! Let no one move you, but throw yourself upon him and keep hold. And do you men not stand around like women, but render aid, until I return from taking care of this grave, even if everyone forbids it.[27]

Albert Henrichs has identified this action as unique in Greek ritual as the hair cutting serves a multiplicity of ritual purposes: it acts first as a supplication, but also as a funerary offering from those closest to the deceased, and, as significantly in this context, as a "curse reinforced by sympathetic magic."[28] The action is aimed not only at protecting the corpse of Ajax until he can be buried but also at protecting his wife and son, now apparently bound by some supernatural link to the dead body. In the actions of Eurysace's supplication, Sophocles is endowing the dead body of Ajax, which is in real danger of being denied burial, with supernatural powers, justifying his transformation into mythical cult hero.[29]

In another drama, described by Molly Myerowitz Levine as "perhaps the most famous and complex hair scene in Western literature,"[30] Aeschlyus presents the hero Orestes returning home and cutting two locks of hair at the tomb of his father, Agamemnon, who had been murdered by his wife, Clytemnestra, on his return from the Trojan Wars. In this third play of the trilogy, which retells the myth, Orestes finally avenges his father. He dedicates two locks of hair, the first to the river Inachus, the second for his dead father.[31] The dramatic positioning of this ritual, in the opening prologue of the play, sets the tone for the subsequent action. It identifies Orestes as now an adult and at the same time identifies him with his father.[32]

In his *Guide to Greece*, written in the second century CE, Pausanias recalls visiting the shrine of Asclepius at Titane, near Corinth where the statue of the goddess Hygeia could not be seen "all that easily for the masses of women's hair" left as dedications.[33] Like the dedications at graves, or in other sacred places, these offerings assume something in return from the god. There is an expectation of reciprocity: the hair might be part of a request for protection, a cure or help of some kind from the dedicant to the god, on the assumption of divine intervention. The closer the hair was to the object of dedication perhaps the more evocative the plea.[34]

In another tale, retold over the centuries, Berenice, wife of King Ptolemy III of Egypt, vowed to dedicate a lock of her hair if her husband returned safe home from war. On his return, Berenice dedicated a lock of her hair at the Temple of Artemis-Arsinoe at Zephyrium. This story was originally told by Berenice's contemporary, the Hellenistic poet Callimachus, and then retold some two centuries later by the Latin poet Catullus. In Catullus' poem the hair narrates her own story, recalling how she was whisked from the altar, first into the sea and then up into the heavens, where now she remains as a constellation. In Callimachus' poem, the court astronomer claims that he recognizes the lock of hair in the group of stars between Leo and Virgo. In Catullus, the lock bewails her fate, and the oils and perfumes which were used to adorn her, and asks that Berenice and other chaste women look to the skies and pour perfumes in her honor, a ritual that should ideally take place before the bridal night. Catullus makes the lock of hair serve as a signifer of separation: the lock pines for Berenice as Berenice pined for her new husband. In both versions the life story of the lock of hair is also used to exemplify themes of marriage and sexuality with the associations of dedication to Aphrodite in Callimachus and the stressing of preconsummation rites in Catullus.[35]

The power of hair to act as metonym or substitute for an individual in a form of sympathetic magic is evident across our period. In antiquity people would often write wishes and curses on small pieces of lead, which were then folded or rolled up and left somewhere pertinent. The placing could depend on the nature of the curse or love spell, and on the god appealed to; the tablets (*defixiones* pl.) have been found in burial contexts, buried beneath the ground in sanctuaries, thrown down wells, or fixed to temple walls. Some attack thieves, threatening dire consequences for those who have stolen clothes from the baths, others target opponents in court cases, or simply call down a curse on their neighbors, or solicit the help of the gods in causing the object of the plea to fall in love. In a survey of *defixiones*, D. R. Jordan has identified several with hair attached which appear to be love charms, and presumably the attached hair was somehow acquired from the intended lover/victim.[36] Literary texts provide some evidence that this was thought to make the spell stronger. In one of Lucian's *Dialogues of Courtesans*, a witch advises a courtesan that in order to make an effective spell which will bring her lover back to her, she must provide something belonging to the man "such as clothing, or boots or a few of his hairs."[37] Similarly in Apuleius' *Metamorphoses*, the young serving woman, Photis, collects the hair clippings of a young man her witch mistress is in love with, from the barber's shop. She is caught by the barber who threatens her with the magistrates.[38] Other examples, however, are certainly not love charms. One, addressed to the god Typhon, curses a certain Tyche and mentions her hair rolled up in the *defixio*. Among other demands the dedicator asks the deity:

> As I have written down here the names and they grow cold, so, too let the body and the flesh and the muscles and the bones and the members and the bowels of Tyche, whom Sophia bore, grow cold, that she may no longer rise up, walk around, talk, move about, but let her remain a corpse, pale, weak, paralysed, chilled until I am taken out of the dark air, rather let her grow exhausted and weak until she dies.[39]

This desire to do a particular individual harm is characteristic of curse tablets which are often very specific in their focus, and an intriguing insight into the personal element in the relationship between the individual and the divine. In these examples the hair stands as an element of sympathetic magic and works as a link between the individual and the power of the deity, it relies on the idea that it can stand for the individual. In being wrapped around the lead it can also work as a binding charm, a very powerful part of any curse.

In the early Christian period hair was considered powerful if it came from the head or body of a saint. The association of power and spirituality residing in the bodies of holy persons was transformed into the cult of saints and relics in late antiquity, when hair along with other body parts became sought after to enhance the sanctity of holy places. All relics were also considered to have the potential to heal miraculously and there is some evidence of hair, allegedly belonging to a saint, being given to those seeking help from "holy" men.[40] The link between religion, magic, and the body remained strong throughout the early Middle Ages.

HAIR REGULATIONS IN RITUAL CONTEXTS

Rules survive from some ancient cults which prescribe the appearance, clothing, and footwear required when in the sacred precincts of the god. These rules vary from cult site to cult site and vary between deities. The regulations often specify what type of clothing can be worn, and commonly rule against the wearing of leather shoes and belts. In terms of hair, women are often required to wear their hair unbraided and men to have their heads uncovered. Many of the cult regulations may have been concerned with controlling excessive competition between devotees but the point about unbound hair carries with it associations with the supernatural as notions of binding and knotting are common to magical spells. Loose or unbraided hair is also a reversal of what is expected of women in everyday life, so hair behavior marks out the movement between sacred and profane space.[41]

At Andania, in the Peloponnese, a very long inscription records the clothing regulations of the cult when it was revived in 92 BCE. These address both priest and initiates, male and female. Women are not allowed headbands or braided hair; in processions women priests wore a white felt cap and during the Mysteries the male board of ten wore purple headbands. First-time initiates at the Mysteries wore a tiara which was replaced by a laurel wreath after initiation, marking as an outward symbol the change they had undergone. Anyone found in breach of the many regulations had to pay a fine or dedicate the offending clothing or headdress to the goddess.[42] Other cults and religious processions often have a similar prohibition on bound or braided hair.[43] Ovid tells us that women pray to Juno Lucina when in childbirth and when a pregnant woman goes to the shrine she should "unbind her hair before she prays, in order that the goddess may gently unbind her teeming womb."[44] A similar recommendation with more practical ends, was also given by the doctor Soranus in his *Gynecology* for women in labor.[45]

One particular priesthood for whom we do know something about appearance is the Vestal Virgins. Vestals held a particular place in the Roman hierarchy of priesthoods. They were priestesses in their own right which was one of very few accepted public roles for Roman women, but their lives were restricted and controlled, and supervised by the Pontifex Maximus (chief priest). Their unique position was visually demonstrated by their clothes and hairstyle. In sculptural representations they are shown wearing a particular hairstyle, the *sex crines*. However, this is a hairstyle that is mentioned only once in the extant literature: "Brides are adorned with six braids (*sex crines*), because this was the most ancient style for them. Which indeed the Vestal Virgins also use, whose chastity for their own men [lacuna] brides."[46] The *sex crines* appear to be braided from a center parting. In representations of brides, the head is covered by the bridal veil, the *flammeum*, so it is not clear if they commonly wore this hairstyle. The association between brides and Vestals is not difficult to understand, both had to be virginal while at the same time being associated with fertility and the guarding of the hearth, the symbol of life (Figure 1.5).

The bride's fertility, chastity, and loyalty to her family guaranteed the integrity of the household, while the continued virginity and chastity of the Vestal guaranteed the integrity of the state. The initiation of the Vestal used wording similar to that of the archaic, traditional Roman wedding with the Pontifex Maximus saying, "Thus beloved, I seize you."[47] When

FIGURE 1.5 Statue of a Vestal Virgin in the Roman Forum in Rome. Photo: Alamy Image ID: GPBC90.

performing her ritual duties the Vestal wore a short veil, the *suffibulum*, which is described as a white veil with a praetextate border, that is, a purple border which symbolizes protective power. The *suffibulum*, as it appears in sculpture, was worn so that the *sex crines* are on view, and falls over the shoulders to be fastened by a fibula on the chest.[48] Under the *suffibulum*, a white *infula*, a fillet (ribbon) of unspun wool, was wound around the head, with the ends hanging in long loops (*vittae*) falling over the shoulders. Both these additional headdresses, the veil and the *infula*, signified protection and identified the individual as inviolate and ritually pure.[49] The dress and the hair of Vestal Virgins are exceptional and marked them out as occupying a very different ritual and social space to other women.

When Roman men are taking part in religious rites, and certainly when sacrificing, the common practice was to cover their heads by using the excess fabric in the toga or mantle.

This practice, *capite velato* (with veiled head, see Figure 1.6), was used both in public and in domestic cults and, according to Livy (59–17 BCE), male head covering was an old tradition in Roman cult practices which marked the participation in rituals and the worship of the divinity. The normal male cult practice of using part of the toga is illustrated on the Altar of Peace (*Ara Pacis Augustae*) in Rome, dedicated by the Senate ca. 13 BCE (Figure 1.7). Here a procession, led by the emperor, is represented. Those who are about to perform a sacrifice have their heads covered. Also in the procession are a

FIGURE 1.6 Augustus *capite velato*. D-DAI-ROM-0328_F5

FIGURE 1.7 *Ara Pacis* frieze showing the procession of priests, with figure with covered head on right. Photo: Mary Harlow.

group of men with special headgear, the *galerus* and *apex*. These are the *flamines*, Roman priests of high status devoted to the service of one particular god in central public cults, *sacra publica*.[50]

The most important priest of this group was *the flamen Dialis*, the high priest of Jupiter and with a lifelong cult assignment he was a powerful person in Roman state religion, his head gear was white (*albogalerus*).[51] The wife of the *flamen Dialis*, the *flaminica*, was not a priestess in her own right but more of an assistant to her husband. Her status required a special dress and a hair arrangement that identified her specific position. Her hair was arranged in a *tutulus*, which was a coiffure of a conical form plaited with purple bands as signs of her status and position.[52] Ancient sources also mention a clothing detail, a *rica*[53] (which has been interpreted by some as a veil of the same sort as was used by the Roman bride, a *flammeum*).[54] In some cults, however, it was common practice for priests to perform the sacrificial rituals with an uncovered head, *aperto capite*, according to *sacra ritu Graeco*. This was done in the cults to Saturnus, Hercules, and Apollo, and at some later point it appears to have also included the cult of the goddess Ceres.[55]

MOURNING RITUALS

Mourning rituals are also played out in hair behavior. In Greek literature, beginning with Homer, behavior at funerals is often highly emotional, expressing overwhelming grief in very physical acts. At the funeral of the Trojan hero Hector, we see his mother,

Hecabe, and his wife, Andromache, throwing off their headgear and tearing their hair; they also beat their heads and breasts.[56] Women might also lacerate their faces and necks with their fingernails as well as crying out and wailing. Men, in Homer, are not exempt from showing excessive sorrow. On the death of Patroclus, Achilles poured dust in his hair and head, and tore at his hair.[57] This tradition of expressing grief went back to prehistoric times as is illustrated by the standard scenes representing funerals and depicted regularly in Greek geometric vase painting. The scenes on the loutrophoros in Figure 1.8 show the ceremonies that precede the funeral: the laying out of the body (the *prothesis*) surrounded by mourning women and the procession when the dead body is transported from the home to the grave (the *ekforà*). Both men and women took part in the ceremonies and to express grief and mourning visually the women are shown with both their hands placed on the head, or beating their heads. They may also have cut their hair as a sign of mourning. On the other side of the vase, men also walk in procession, with only right arms raised.

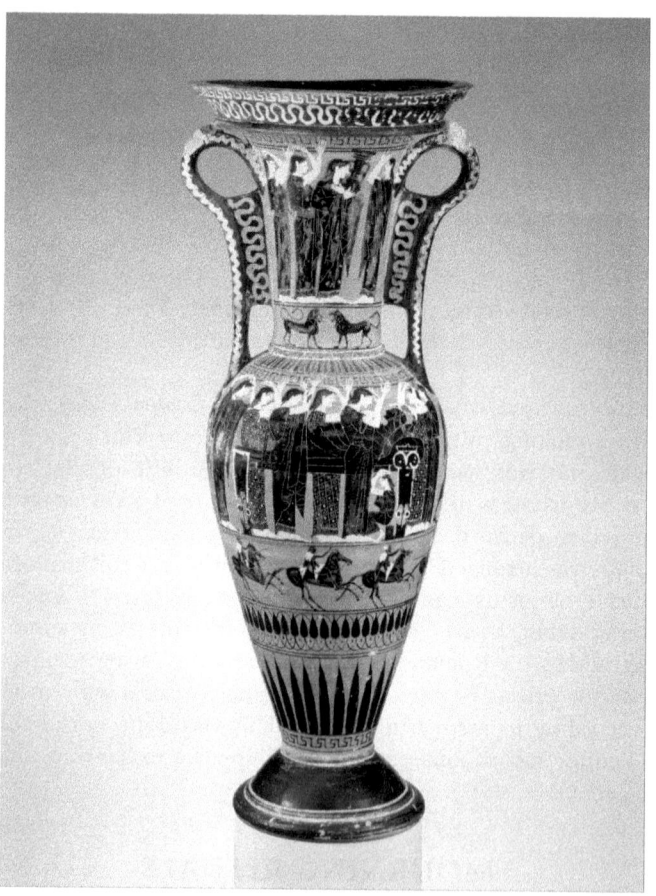

FIGURE 1.8 Late sixth century BCE terracotta loutrophoros (ceremonial vase for water). Metropolitan Museum of Art, New York, NY. Acc. No. 27.228. Funds from various donors, 1927.

In Athens, excessive mourning behavior was legislated against by Solon (sixth century BCE) but the iconography of mourning in black-figure vases and plaques continued to show women with their hair loose or cut, and their hands to their heads—a ritual behavior that continued into the Roman period and is still part of mourning in some cultures today. The ancient world in the main allowed women to express themselves more forcefully at funerals than men, as women were considered to be naturally less able to control their emotions. Men, on the other hand, were expected to show more moderation than Achilles, but they too expressed their grief by covering their heads. This inversion of normal practice—men who are normally bare-headed cover their heads and women who are normally veiled expose theirs—is a general principle which holds good for most funerary practices in antiquity, Greek or Roman. It is a clear demonstration that rituals surrounding death stand outside normal behavior and time.

This apparent role reversal at funerals was also noted by Plutarch, writing in the second century CE. In his *Roman Questions* he asked:

> Why do sons cover their heads when they escort their parents to the grave, while daughters go with uncovered heads and hair unbound?

> Is it because fathers should be honoured as gods by their male offspring, but mourned as dead by their daughters, that custom has assigned to each sex its proper part and has produced a fitting result from both? Or is it that the unusual is proper in mourning, and it is more usual for women to go forth in public with their heads covered and men with their heads uncovered? So in Greece, whenever any misfortune comes, the women cut off their hair and the men let it grow, for it is usual for men to have their hair cut and for women to let it grow.[58]

Plutarch's discussion, written to explain Roman practices to a Greek audience rather assumes that men go about with uncovered heads, while women are commonly veiled, at least when out in public. The veiling of Roman women is a much discussed area and will be picked up in later chapters in this volume.[59]

JEWISH AND CHRISTIAN PRACTICES

The Jewish and Christian religious authorities viewed hair and hair practices in a slightly different way to traditional Greek and Roman religions. Traditional Greco-Roman religious prescriptions and behaviors concerning hair were primarily concerned with not offending the gods and performing rituals in the most efficacious manner. Jewish and Christian authorities were equally concerned with the proper performance of rites and rituals but they added a strong moral and gendered dimension in which hair behavior and control were seen as part of the inner character and outward expression of the probity of the individual. The way hair was worn and controlled could express religious identity in a much more overt manner than in most traditional ancient religions. At the same time, both Jewish and Christian attitudes were framed by ancient Mediterranean gender values and the different roles and anxieties surrounding male and female hair behavior are evident in the opinions of their various authorities. While we cannot know to what extent any Jewish or Christian individuals adhered to these rules concerning appearance, their very existence reflects a desire to create a visible Jewish or Christian identity in their societies. For the most part the instructions on appearance conform to traditional Greco-Roman views in that they are framed in particular ways for men and women.[60] Mary

Rose D'Angelo has argued that both Judaism and Christianity adhere to the link between the head and the genitals in seeing the exposure of a woman's head to anyone but her husband as a sexual violation.[61] She cites several examples which are part of the discourse in the early centuries CE across the Mediterranean from Paul's letter to the Corinthians, to Rabbinic texts, to Tertuallian, which all deal with how and when a woman should be veiled.[62] These texts all deal with the covering of women's heads in public, with particular reference to behavior required in the temple and the church, rather than ritual behavior of hair itself.

CONCLUSION

Hair played an important part in traditional Greek and Roman religion primarily because of its inherent properties as a detachable part of the body. As such it could act as a symbol or metonym for the individual. Growing hair for the gods, or publicly cutting it in a ritual context connected the individual with the divine and established a reciprocal relationship between the two. The public nature of dedications, particularly at times of rites of passage, also demonstrated the social persona of the dedicant and their family to the wider community. The power of hair to act as a symbol is also demonstrated by the rules and regulations about its control at life course events, cult sites, and for particular priesthoods. The association of hair with the body remained even when the hair was cut. This link is clear in the fact that hair was considered a valuable votive offering. This same power could be used to different ends in magical practices where the power of the hair could be used to charm or harm its original owner. In the early medieval period the hair of holy men and women took on their sanctity and was preserved for its value and power as a relic, where again it was often used to heal.

ACKNOWLEDGMENTS

We would like to thank Glenys Davies for her insight and constructive comments on this chapter, and to the anonymous reviewer for comments on structure. We would also refer readers to Jane Draycott "Hair Today, Gone Tomorrow: The Use of Real, False and Artificial Hair as Votive Offerings," in *Bodies of Evidence: Ancient Anatomical Votives Past, Present and Future* edited by Jane Draycott and Emma-Jayne Graham (2017) which only appeared towards the end of the production of this volume and which will provide an enhanced perspective on this chapter.

CHAPTER TWO

Self and Society

KATHERINE A. SCHWAB AND MARICE ROSE

INTRODUCTION

Self is generally defined as the condition of an individual's existing, together with a combination of characteristics that distinguish the individual from others.[1] This chapter will examine the role of hair (or its absence) as a mutable part of the body that defined various aspects of ancient Greeks' and Romans' individual and collective self-identities.[2]

The work of sociologist Anthony Synnott provides a useful frame for this inquiry into hair, self, and society. He codified a system of internally and externally regulated oppositional meanings for hair that he recognized specifically in mid to late twentieth-century American/Canadian/British cultures, yet they can be applied to ancient Greek and Roman societies.[3] For this chapter, the relevant oppositions are: men and women groom head and body hair in opposite ways (e.g. when women wear long hair, men wear short; when women have elaborate hairstyles, men have simple), and opposing social ideologies feature opposing choices with regard to hair (e.g. in antiquity male philosophers rejecting urban society wore long, ungroomed hair in contrast to the conventional short-haired fashion), as do "opposite states" (e.g. mourning, when head and facial hair were changed from how they were usually worn).[4]

In the "Hair and Identity" section, we consider gender, age, leadership qualities, and morality. "Hair as Social Organization" addresses how hair indicated one's role within or outside society, including marital status and profession. "Materialization of Power" looks at hair as symbol of authority and foreign-ness, and its manipulation as punishment. "Hair Practice and Cultural Milestones" examines how hair cutting, styling, and accessorizing were linked to birth, adolescence, marriage, warfare, and death.

HAIR AND IDENTITY

Whether or not it was cut or grown long, exposed or veiled, hair was an essential means of communicating a person's identity in ancient Greece.[5] Hair texture, from loose waves to tight curls, formed a distinctive characteristic of Greek identity which, in turn, was strongly contrasted with portrayals of non-Greeks. As such, Greek hairstyles were an essential component of how people recognized one another and understood who they were within society. With a majority of finds from ancient Athens, we have a better idea of Athenian attitudes, especially from the classical period, than elsewhere, due in large part to the preservation of sculptures and vase paintings. A number of recent studies reveal the significance of hair and its arrangement to mark gender, age, and rites of passage across the life course.[6]

It is perhaps noteworthy that Greek maidens reveal more of their hair, often worn long, as a sexually appealing feature. Maidens shown with abundant hair include the many sixth century BCE Athenian Acropolis *korai* dedications and grave markers, as well as the preserved figures of Philippe and Ornithe, from the elaborate Genelaos family dedication on Samos, whose hair length and thickness are conspicuous.[7] These sixth century BCE maidens are shown at what was an optimal time in their adolescence when their sexuality and fertility were portrayed as ideal for marriage. While abundant long hair described the ideal for these maidens, in reality such hair had far more to do with genetics than elite status and associated nutrition. Even in elite families, boys received better nutrition than girls.

Adolescent boys were clean-shaven and wore their hair long, only to grow a beard and cut their hair shorter upon reaching maturity. The god Apollo remained an eternal adolescent by maintaining long hair and smooth cheeks. In contrast, Zeus, the father of the gods, is always shown with a full beard and thick well-groomed hair. His brother Poseidon often had more tousled hair, probably to evoke the wild sea and his role as earth-shaker. Hair rituals, growing and cutting for dedication were both sides of the act for a god, for youths in Greek society were complex and multilayered because they needed to account for family status, gender, age, social class, transition point, cults to associations in clubs and organizations, etc., each with its own initiation expectations.[8] On reaching maturity beards were grown and the long head hair was cut shorter. Hairstyles could be used to evoke political statements as well as reflecting fashion trends. One such example is laconizing hairstyles—higher status youths in Athens wore their hair in the Spartan style in the late fifth century BCE as a rebellion against their parents' generation and the ongoing Peloponnesian war. Spartan warriors grew their hair long and groomed it carefully before battle. Tresses were expected to look good, especially if one died on the battlefield.[9]

The great diversity of the Roman Empire means that its inhabitants would have known a range of hair colors and textures, worn in a variety of styles. Despite—or because of—these possibilities for variety, certain head and facial hairstyles were considered appropriate for men and women of particular identities. Although specific styles came in and out of favor, hair was always an important part of the Roman notion of *cultus*—the cultivation of the body and the self which included dress and grooming. The attention which an individual devoted to *cultus* could indicate both morality and degree of civilization.[10] An important distinction was hair worn in its natural state versus hair that was manipulated in some way, including coloring, cutting, combing, and controlling by various means.[11]

Head hair length played a large role in representing Roman gendered identities.[12] Women after adolescence were expected to wear their hair long (but off their necks and shoulders) (Figure 2.3).[13] Boys' short hairstyles would continue into adulthood for most civilized Roman men. In a rare ancient first-person account of hair loss, philosopher Synesius of Cyrene's treatise on baldness protests his hair loss by calling it a "terrible thing," and asks what he did to deserve being so unattractive to women, showing not only the perceived importance of hair to an appearance of virility to the opposite gender, but also that making emotional connections to one's hair is not a modern phenomenon.[14]

Imperial portraiture used the degree of the hair's fullness to communicate information about the emperors' personal identities and their reigns. For instance, until the end of his life, the emperor Augustus' (32 BCE–14 CE) portraiture depicted him as having abundant, wavy hair with curling locks on his forehead, imitating the iconography of Alexander the Great and thus, by implication, emulating his qualities of heroic leadership (Figures 2.1 and 2.2; see also Figure 1.6).[15]

SELF AND SOCIETY

FIGURE 2.1 Tetradrachm of deified Alexander III, the Great (360–281 BCE), obv. Alexander the Great, rev. Athena Nikephoros. Mount Holyoke College Art Museum, South Hadley, MA. Gift of the Estate of Nathan Whitman.

FIGURE 2.2 Unknown. Portrait head of Augustus (25–1 BCE), marble, 39 × 21 × 24 cm (15.35 × 8.27 × 9.45 in.). The J. Paul Getty Museum, Los Angeles, CA.

Portraits of later emperors recalled the fullness and style of Augustus' hair to show familial links (e.g. busts of his great-grandson Caligula, 37–41 CE), or similar imperial strength (e.g. Constantine I, 306–337 CE).[16] In contrast, Vespasian's (69–79 CE) portraiture featured Republican-style verism, including baldness, to emphasize the return to "traditional" Roman values after the disaster of Nero's suicide and the 68–69 CE civil war.[17] Hadrian (117–138 CE) and the Antonine emperors (138–192 CE) who followed him were depicted with full, curly hair, which probably reflected their hair's true texture while communicating youthful virility in the manner of Augustus. Caracalla (198–217 CE) began a trend of emperor portraits displaying clipped hair evocative of soldiers, again a style which reflected the trend of empire at this point in time (see Figures 3.9, 3.10, 9.1, and 9.3).[18]

Length and neatness of facial hair, or its removal, were important components of Roman male *cultus* and masculinity, and also identity relating to the wearer's native culture and religion.[19] Jewish men, for example, followed religious law and custom and did not shave.[20] After several clean-shaven emperors, Hadrian's choice of growing a short curly beard was part of a widespread fashion trend probably associated with beards becoming markers of masculinity and masculine virtues.[21] In this period, long beards and balding heads similar to images of Greek philosophers could communicate both manliness and intellect.[22] Shaving now became associated with excessive adornment and effeminacy. This concept was echoed by early Christian writers who saw shaving as sinful emasculation.[23]

For Roman women, if and how hair was dressed played a crucial role in identity formation, especially regarding virtue and status.[24] The regulation of a woman's long hair—as opposed to its being unbound—represented her decorum and chastity, as hair was considered to be erotically charged.[25] There is little evidence for women in Roman society choosing to cut their hair, the exception being Christian ascetic women who shaved their heads or cut their hair short, probably in a renunciation of worldly society.[26]

One example of a style that was used to communicate different aspects of Roman and female identity is the *nodus*.[27] This native Roman style was adopted by Augustus' sister Octavia and his wife Livia, possibly to emphasize their Roman-ness in contrast to the popular Hellenistic styles associated with the enemy Egyptian queen, Cleopatra.[28] Imperial women used the *nodus* to demonstrate familial and dynastic connections. When non-imperial women in the late first and early second centuries wore the *nodus*, it was symbolic of its wearer's modesty and chastity, because Livia was considered an exemplar of female virtue. In Figure 2.3, a portrait of an unidentified girl, the *nodus* likely expressed her suitability as a future bride and mother, as well as her elevated social status. When worn by freedwomen and by women in provinces, the *nodus* communicated membership in Roman society, and an active choice to adapt to the now dominant culture.[29]

HAIR AS SOCIAL ORGANIZATION

Much of the social organization of hair in the ancient Mediterranean related to the patriarchal views and structures of Greek and Roman societies. Hair was considered to be an important locus of female sexuality; the control of the hair, therefore, was seen as necessary for those who felt threatened by the possibility of unrestrained female sexuality.[30] Art and texts written by men (including satires, epitaphs, and moralizing tracts) present models of acceptable appearance and behavior that included references to

FIGURE 2.3 Portrait of a young girl (first quarter of first century CE). Yale University Art Gallery, New Haven, CT. Maitland F. Griggs, B.B. 1896, Fund 1995.80.1. Photo: Yale University Art Gallery.

hair for men and especially for women. Married women were cautioned in male-penned literary sources to cover their hair to protect their modesty and prevent male attention.[31] In the first century CE, Valerius Maximus reported that the Republican statesman Sulpicius Gallus divorced his wife because she left the house without a head covering.[32] This is undoubtedly a cautionary tale but it demonstrates normative attitudes to female appearance in public. Physical attractiveness was considered a virtue, and differentiating oneself from foreigners was important; yet male writers criticized grooming regimens (of both men and women) as superficial, deceptive, and a waste of time and resources.[33]

Control of hair length, arrangement, and style were all contributing factors to social organization in ancient Greek society. Greek convention displayed opposing traits for those standing outside of societal norms, whether in mythic space or daily life. The most distinctive example of this opposition is the maenad, a follower of Dionysos (Figure 2.4). Her ecstatic state was signified, in part, by unbound hair flying around as freely as her flowing dress. Unbound, uncontrolled, or unarranged hair was associated with categories on the fringes of society.[34]

In contrast to the mythological maenad and emblematic of differences in status in real life, the grave stele of Hegeso (Figure 2.5) shows servant and mistress in a quiet domestic scene preparing for the day by selecting jewelry from a box.[35] Both females wear their hair covered, but the hair wrap is different to designate status. Hegeso, the seated woman, wears her thick wavy hair bound up in a *sakkos*, a wrapped style with cloth to partially cover and hold her long hair gathered in a bun. A delicate and thin veil covers part of her

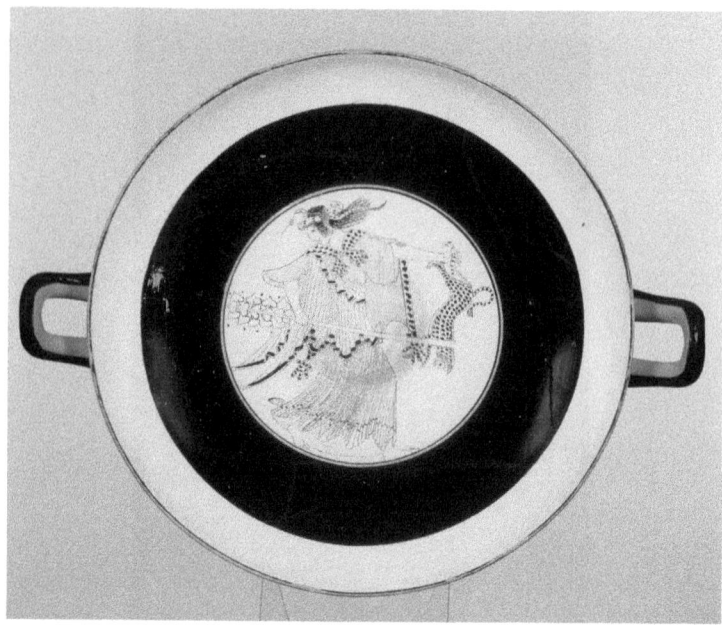

FIGURE 2.4 Attic white ground cup interior with frenzied maenad, Brygos Painter (ca. 490 BCE). Antikensammlungen, Munich, 2645.

head and is faintly visible in the background near her bun and profile. The servant wears a snood, to cover her hair and to keep it out of her face while she goes about her daily tasks. The female servant wears a long-sleeved chiton associated with foreign (barbarian) dress. In this instance, the servant holds a small box or *pyxis* containing jewelry while Hegeso lifts up a piece. Their relationship, while intimate, is separated by their actions, clothing, and how they wear their hair. The servant's appearance, from snood to long-sleeved barbarian dress, is frequently included in the iconography of Athenian grave stelai. Servant and mistress share domestic space while living within separate spheres of Athenian class and status.[36]

As in Greece, for ancient Romans the degree to which hair was groomed communicated information about its wearer's situation within or without society. Close-cropped hair was the hallmark of soldiers, as illustrated on victory monuments like the Columns of Trajan and Marcus Aurelius, and as worn by Germanicus on the *Gemma Augustea* (Figure 2.6).

Very long hair on men could describe barbarians.[37] On public monuments and private artworks like the gem, fighting and captive figures are shown by their long, messy hair to be non-Roman enemies.[38] Philosophers and farmers were also represented with long, unkempt hair as indicative of their existing outside the urban social structure.[39] Lengthy, matted hair was a mark of early Christian male hermits, not only representing their lack of *cultus*, gender and societal liminality, and similarity to Jesus and the Nazarenes, but also symbolizing to their followers the hermits' liminal existence between earth and heaven.[40] Long but neat hair was worn by some Roman priests.[41]

Similar to Greek culture, long, loose hair on a woman had a variety of connotations with regards to social identity, usually associated with the individual existing outside society permanently or temporarily, and closeness to nature.[42] Loose hair characterized barbarians,

SELF AND SOCIETY 37

FIGURE 2.5 Stele of Hegeso (ca. 410–400 BCE). National Archaeological Museum, Athens. Photo: Erin Babnik / Alamy Stock Photo.

FIGURE 2.6 *Gemma Augustea* (early 1st century CE). Kunsthistorisches Museum, Vienna. Photo: Granger Historical Picture Archive / Alamy Stock Photo.

maenads, Amazons, and sorceresses in art and texts (Figure 2.6).[43] On specific occasions, Roman matrons were shown or described with unbound hair; these included childbirth and mourning, or when engaged in gestures of supplication or gratitude.[44]

Roman expectation of respectable women's covering their hair is debated, and probably depended on geographical and religious customs. Jewish women, for example, had to wear veils.[45] It was likely common practice for most women in Greece and the Near East to cover their heads when out in public.[46] Although several surviving texts by both pagan and Christian men tell women to cover their hair in order to signify modesty and married status, the degree to which such advice was followed does not seem to be great in Italy and western provinces.[47]

MATERIALIZATION OF POWER: CRIME AND PUNISHMENT, SOCIAL INCLUSION, AND MARGINALIZATION

During his lifetime and for centuries following, portraits of Alexander the Great wore a distinctive hairstyle and clean-shaven face, in sharp contrast to the beard worn by his father Philip II and earlier political and military leaders. The dramatic change inaugurated by Alexander would mark his achievements and those of his successors, who chose this visual association to further their own reputations. Even the addition of ram's horns, symbolic of the Egyptian god Ammon to bestow divine status, was perpetuated by his Greek successors (see Figure 2.1).[48]

Alexander's short-cropped tousled hairstyle included a cowlick at his hairline, which created curling locks of hair framing his face.[49] Added to this hairstyle is the novelty of a clean-shaven face.[50] This combination generated a new image of a powerful Greek military and political leader. Alexander began the clean-shaven fashion in 331 BCE before going into battle with the Persian king. It must have been a surprise following centuries of political and military leaders wearing a beard. The decision to shave seems to be associated with Alexander's emulation of Greek heroes, especially Herakles, and his own quest of an ideal heroic image both youthful and beardless.[51] To that end, Alexander committed his men to shaving their beards in support of their commander before battle. This proved a turning point in the history of beards, which largely disappeared from the faces of political leaders until Hadrian revived the style in the second century CE.

Greek rulers after the death of Alexander in 321 BCE selected variants of his portrait in profile more than any other image for the coins they issued. Distribution of coins guaranteed awareness across a wide region of the Mediterranean, Asia Minor, and Central Asia, and a means of establishing or confirming legitimate rule.[52] Among these rulers is King Lysimachus of Thrace, who exemplifies and perpetuates the deified Alexander. The obverse of a Thracian coin of Lysimachus (Figure 2.1), 305 BCE, shows Alexander adorned with the ram's horns of Ammon.[53] This continuous use of one image established or perpetuated legitimacy during the Hellenistic period. Alexander's portrait finds further life in the Roman Julio-Claudian dynasty, especially with portraits of the emperor Augustus (see Figures 1.6, 2.2, and 3.8).[54]

Portraits of Augustus incorporate the clean-shaven face and a visual reference to Alexander's unique hairstyle, including the arrangement of locks of hair framing the forehead caused by a cowlick. Augustus was masterful in his use of recognizable imagery, and it was no accident that his selection of Alexander the Great for a clean-shaven face and tousled hairstyle was used to forge his own achievements and legacy with a military leader from the Greek past.[55]

In contrast to social inclusion and power, exemplified by images of Alexander the Great, Greek society was acutely observant of non-Greek peoples. Hair was an immediate and recognizably identifying marker of a foreigner, as can be seen in the Pergamene victory monument. This large group sculpture commemorated victory by showing the defeated Gauls and, at the same time, exalting the victor's status. As part of the Pergamene monument, the Trumpeter (Dying Gaul, see Figure 2.7) received distinctive treatment in the carved hair: thick tufts project outward from the scalp now with tips cut off.[56] The Trumpeter's facial hair is exclusively a mustache, no beard, which was unknown as a combination in Greek art. Part of this group monument included a standing male Gaul committing suicide while holding up the arm of a dead female. The male's hair is mid-length hanging in clumps, contrasting with the female's hair, which has been cut abruptly to chin length marking her defeat. In this victory monument head and facial hair emphasize the defeated enemy as outside Greek society.

One of the more astonishing images relates to a story from Herodotus, who recounts a Scythian tradition of cutting the enemy's scalp, an image of which may appear on an Attic red-figured cup fragment in Malibu (Figure 2.8).[57] A Greek warrior wears a scalp on his helmet, bowl-cut just as Herodotus has described it. The scalped hair texture is coarse and straight, unlike the warrior's thickly textured hair bursting through openings in his helmet.[58] Perhaps no other example brings such divergent hair textures in close proximity, sharpening the difference between what is known and familiar as Greek with what is unfamiliar and barbarian.[59]

The Roman Republic and Empire did not mandate hairstyles as a manifestation of its power, although individuals were well aware of hair's symbolic potential. Some aspects

FIGURE 2.7 Dying Gaul (marble copy of bronze original, ca. 230–180 BCE). Photo: Heritage Image Partnership Ltd / Alamy Stock Photo.

FIGURE 2.8 Onesimos (Greek (Attic), active 500–480 BCE) and Euphronios (Greek (Attic), active 520–480 BCE), Attic red-figure cup fragment (ca. 500–490 BCE), terracotta 10 × 11.2 × 2 cm (3.94 × 4.41 × 0.79 in.). The J. Paul Getty Museum, Los Angeles, CA.

of female hairstyling can be interpreted as reflecting the power of Roman men, and women's subjugation to them. The controlled and confined nature of some female hairstyles may have stemmed from the patriarchal fear of women's sexuality and desire to symbolically control it.[60] No evidence supports the popular contemporary assertion that prostitutes were required to shave their heads.[61] Paul's pejorative reference to a woman's shaved head (1 Cor. 11:5) probably alludes to a punishment for adultery. This punishment was cited by Tacitus (in reference to Germans), and in a text formerly attributed to Dio Chrysostom which reports that adulteresses in Cyprus had their hair cut off.[62]

Female slaves—especially blonde slaves from the northern provinces—would have their heads shorn, and the hair would be made into wigs for Roman women.[63] Art often depicts Roman soldiers pulling conquered peoples' hair, as in the *Gemma Augustea* (Figure 2.6) and the Column of Marcus Aurelius. The long, loose hair of barbarians was proof of their lack of *cultus*, and a visual justification of Roman domination. The imagery makes a vivid statement of non-Roman identity and Roman power through evoking the pain associated with this action.[64]

Foliate wreaths and diadems worn in the hair materialized a role of power for their wearers.[65] The Senate and Roman people granted the right to wear wreaths as symbols of victory, as originally worn in Greek athletic competitions. Julius Caesar often wore the *corona triumphalis*, made of laurel leaves, in public after he was awarded the privilege, although this might have been to cover his receding hairline.[66] The oak-leaf *corona civica* was awarded to soldiers for saving a citizen's life in battle by killing an enemy.[67] Pliny describes the grass crown, made of grass and flowers from the battlefield and awarded to a commander who saved a legion.[68] Other crowns included the mural crown and the naval crown. Imperial portraits from the empire's eastern provinces depict jewels within the leaves.[69] Foliate wreaths, both vegetal and imitated in gold, came to symbolize authority, and were sometimes given to emperors by conquered rulers. For empresses, crowns did not become a signifier of imperial rank on portraiture until Empress Flacilla in the late fourth century.[70] Early in the empire, Roman leaders avoided gold diadems and were criticized if they did wear them, because of their associations with Hellenistic monarchs. In contrast, in late antiquity, Constantine I (ca. 306–337 CE) made the jeweled diadem part of the emperor's official regalia.[71] The length and beauty of the diadem's *pendilia* (jewels hanging from the crown) symbolized the emperor's strength.[72]

HAIR PRACTICE AND CULTURAL MILESTONES (BIRTH, DEATH, MARRIAGE)

Cultural milestones in ancient Greece were closely tied to the practice of growing and cutting hair, with specific and separate traditions developed for boys and girls in childhood, adolescence, and adulthood. Parents controlled the length, appearance, and decision to cut hair for their children. Locks of hair were carefully grown and later cut as dedications and thank offerings to mark major transitions within the course of life. In Greek society these specific moments succeeded in keeping the family bound together as well as binding the individual to the society as a whole.

Greek children often grew and wore braids that would be later cut and dedicated to a divinity as a thank offering of protection, as discussed in Chapter One.[73] The same concept was repeated, as if crossing a threshold while leaving childhood behind, when girls would sometimes dedicate a short braid, in addition to toys and clothing, to a goddess prior to their weddings.[74] This lock more typically would be grown from the hairline and worn in a fishtail braid, as some of the Caryatids wear.[75]

Upon marriage, Spartan brides shaved their heads as part of the rituals.[76] In contrast, the Athenian bride kept her hair and followed several steps in preparation for her marriage, from washing (see Figure 2.10) to binding up her hair for the wedding. Once the hair was bound, she would wear a crown or *stephane* over which she would place a special wedding veil. The veil was worn to cover the bride's face until she was introduced to the groom. Examples in Greek art tend to show the bride's face revealed as she meets the groom.[77] In mythological representations Hera is often shown wearing her veil pulled to the side in the *anakalypsis* gesture, perpetuating her status as bride of Zeus. An Athenian bride was expected to look her best by wearing the most splendid clothing and accessories to enhance her sexual appeal to the groom. This included partly concealing her hair in modesty while still drawing attention to it with veil and *stephane*.[78] At least in Athens, the transition from childhood to bride served as a means of reintegrating the female within the fabric of society where her identity becomes wife and eventual mother.

On the Athenian Acropolis, the unique hairstyles worn by the *korai* (maidens) or Caryatids from the south porch of the Erechtheion allude to the past (Figure 2.9). Their hairstyles, intentionally old-fashioned by 430–420 BCE when these figures were carved, are worn in combination with the peplos and shoulder-pinned back mantle to form a unique combination. These stone maidens represent maidens from elite Athenian families

FIGURE 2.9 Caryatid A (ca. 430–420 BCE). © Acropolis Museum. Photo: Socrates Mavromates.

who were given the privileged position to lead a religious procession.[79] On the brink of a major life transition, these elite maidens are leaving behind childhood and entering marriage where their roles as bride, then wife and mother will weave them back into society with this new adult identity. Perpetuating a distinctive old-fashioned hairstyle supports the idea of social control, using a unique and specific Athenian identity and tradition and served as a symbolic means of connecting the current generation with those from the past.[80] The Erechtheion maidens' status on the brink of marriage is further emphasized by the central fishtail braid extending back from their forehead to disappear under the capital crowning the head. The hair texture for each of the six *korai* varies widely, from loose waves to tight curls, and is ideal for the massive fishtail braid worn down the back of each figure. Hair texture in this case is inextricably connected to the resulting hairstyle—the braid and organization of hair worn by these maidens are enhanced by their richly textured hair.[81]

FIGURE 2.10 Attic red-figured stamnos, group of Polygnotos (ca. 440 BCE). Antikensammlungen, Munich.

The prominence of these *korai* or Caryatids on the Athenian Acropolis gave rise to their fame, which generated a cultural memory—a means of forging continuity and associations across centuries while the original meaning changes.[82] Of all the Greek female imagery, it is the Erechtheion *korai* who generated a link from Greece to Rome, in some ways similar to the hairstyle of Alexander the Great perpetuated by Augustus discussed above.

The use of the "Caryatids" in the Roman Forum of Augustus was explained by Vitriuvius, a contemporary of Augustus. He claimed that the statues were the women of Caryae, enslaved as punishment for the town's betrayal of Greece during the Persian wars.[83] A selection of "Caryatids" adorning the Forum of Augustus, intended as exact replicas of the Athens group including the fishtail braid, were emulated again at Hadrian's Villa at Tivoli more than a century later, again at a time when a Roman emperor had strong ties to Athens. In reality, the Roman variants of the Erechtheion hairstyles were modified and lacked the details found in the source group.

Similar to girls, boys also cut their hair during childhood as dedicatory offerings. They grew their hair long during adolescence, sometimes cutting the front of the hairstyle while allowing the back hair to grow long.[84] Occasionally, a substitute for the real hair is dedicated, as with a painted terracotta braid at Corinth.[85] A larger dedication, with the inscription preserved on a Thessalian marble sculpture of the fourth century BCE, shows two prominent and exquisitely carved fishtail braids, a gift to Poseidon by two brothers.[86]

In some instances warriors cut locks of their hair before battle, as attested on two lekythoi: MMA and Cleveland lekythoi, both of which likely refer to the *Seven Against Thebes* by Aeschylus, where the warriors tied their locks of hair to a chariot with the hope of being the one who would return alive. The rulers of the Seleucid dynasty, for instance, grew short beards to be cut and dedicated in anticipation of a successful military campaign, hence the alternating appearance of clean-shaven cheeks and short beards on Seleucid coinage.[87]

One famous account describes the unusual odyssey of thick, long locks of light colored hair adorning the head of Berenike II. Her husband Ptolemy III considered her beautiful hair a desirable attribute. When he left Alexandria to lead a battle in Syria, Berenike II prayed to a goddess for his safe return. She promised to cut off her long hair if her husband returned alive. Upon his safe return she fulfilled her promise and dedicated her cut hair in the temple. When Ptolemy discovered her action he rushed to the temple with the priest, but the lock(s) of her hair had disappeared. The story, first described by Callimachus, whose poem survived in fragments and later preserved by the Latin writer Catullus, was written from the point of view of the lock of hair. It provides an explanation for the presence of the constellation known as Berenice's Lock.[88]

In the mortal realm, hair was a tangible display for both males and females in the state of mourning, again marking a transition as discussed above with children. In the Greek world, the inverse of normative behavior provided the outward sign. Women tossed aside their veils to expose their cut, torn, or disheveled hair, whereas men might cover their head with part of their himation.[89] At times, even intentionally exposed patches of bared scalp became an outward sign of mourning. When Romans mourned, they dressed in opposition to the societal norm, including their hair—women's was unbound and unkempt, and men who were normally clean-shaven grew a beard to show grief.[90] Propertius' cited practice of a lover's dedicating a lock of hair at a beloved's tomb likely was not common, as there is no epigraphic or other evidence to support this behavior in the Roman world.[91]

Few formal hair rituals associated with Roman pagan, Jewish, or Christian rites of passage are recorded, but because the empire was so large and multicultural, it is likely that local practices existed for which no information survives. Soranus (first–second centuries CE), a medical writer from Ephesus, wrote a treatise advising that pregnant women should unbind their hair during childbirth for health reasons, as they should also unbind their garments and relax their bodies by taking frequent warm baths.[92] Adult women who converted to Christianity unbound their hair before their baptisms, a ritual that was equated to rebirth.[93]

Most pagan evidence for the use of hair to mark cultural milestones is in relation to boys' coming of age and to female behavior at weddings, for which traditions also likely varied. Literary sources mention that a young man's entrance to manhood was marked not only by his donning of the *toga virilis*, but also by a shave and dedication of the clippings to a god followed by a festive celebration (as recorded for Augustus, Caligula, and Nero), although how widespread the practice was among ordinary Romans is not known.[94] A bride's hair was parted with a spear before the wedding, and she wore a veil called a *flammeum*. During the wedding, both bride and groom may have worn floral wreaths which connoted beauty and celebration.[95] There is evidence that crowns, probably floral, were worn by Roman Christian and Jewish couples at their weddings as well.[96]

CONCLUSION

Ancient Greek and Roman societies maintained an acute awareness of identity by gender, age, class, or status through their hair. Even though the span of time and geography is extensive, identity formation is closely aligned with how much hair is revealed and how it is worn. In both cultures there is a strong sense of identification within the society in contrast to those people inhabiting realms outside of it. Given the breadth of time and space, it is remarkable to see how successful these societies were in perpetuating traditions and their meanings for identity formation both for the individual and for collective self-identities. Oppositional meanings, defined and developed by Anthony Synnott, have provided a means of examining the surprisingly consistent practices with hair in ancient Greek and Roman cultures to highlight difference between genders, age from childhood through adulthood, and status within society. In some instances examples from ancient Greece carry over into the Roman sphere, such as the Erechtheion *korai* or "Caryatids," with their complex hairstyles and portrait iconography of Alexander the Great, where their fame and legacy suited the new Roman usage. More typically, the use of hair (head and facial) assumes specific connotations for the culture and society it serves, and for those who wear it.

CHAPTER THREE

Fashion and Adornment

KELLY OLSON

Like fashion and dress, hair can be situated as a fundamental part of "the means by which bodies are made social and given meaning and identity."[1] Hair is ascribed a special status in many cultures because of its unique qualities: a part of the body which is highly visible, straightforwardly manipulated by shaving, curling, cutting, and binding, and easily supplemented by wigs and hairpieces.[2] All of these qualities make it an excellent indicator of youth and age. Furthermore, its perceived erotic value meant that it was subject to social control by covering, cutting, or binding.[3] Thus in general, boys and girls in the ancient world wore their hair long, and as they approached adulthood, it was cut, braided, or bound in some way. The other main subject of this chapter, the relationship of hairstyle trends to wider fashion, is difficult to track in antiquity, given the complex nature of the evidence and the lack of comprehensive surveys of ancient hairstyles, but certain fashions may be noted.

HAIR IN HOMER AND THE ARCHAIC PERIOD (800–480 BCE)

There was a "significant iconography of hairstyles" in the Bronze Age and early Greek period.[4] And by certain hair colors, lengths, and styles, the Greek poets depicted "youth or age, beauty or ugliness, nobility or baseness."[5]

The basic premise of age-related hairstyles in Greek antiquity seems to be that all or part of the hair was grown out long, to be cut off (or partially cut off) at a specific time.[6] Thus there is a clear progression from "less hair" during childhood to ever "more hair" once the girls and boys reach puberty.[7] Although textual evidence does not specify which part of the hair was to be grown long, Plutarch's *Theseus* states the front hair was cut off and the rest left long.[8] Abantes, in the *Iliad*, wears his hair short in front and long in the back in a similar fashion;[9] Hector sports this hairstyle too, although it is not seen in vase painting.[10] The *Theseus* is a late text—but its description of hair does correspond with archaic visual evidence. Greek *kouroi* (see Figures 3.1 and 3.2) sport short curls across the forehead and long hair hanging down the back, with or without shoulder-locks in front (the "Daedalic style").

Though the wig-like form of many Daedalic coiffures can be explained as orientalizing or Egyptianizing, short front hair/long back hair cannot be, as this was uncommon in the Near East and Egypt.[11] In the late archaic period (the early fifth century) "the iconographical distinction between the uncut hair of pre-adolescent males and the short front hair of adolescents and adults becomes emphasized."[12] Even grown-up bearded gods have short front hair and long back hair. Thick, luxuriant hair marked young warriors,

FIGURE 3.1 Kouros. Deutsches Archäologisches Institut—Rom. D.DAI.ROM 62.8.

FIGURE 3.2 Ancient Greek kouros. National Archaeological Museum, Athens. Photo: Realy Easy Star / Salvatore Pipia / Alamy Stock Photo.

and the usual epithet is *karē komoōntes*: "long-haired," and applied to both Greeks and Trojans:[13] "Euphorbus had hair like the Graces', bound tightly with gold and silver."[14]

We do not hear much about female hair fashions in Homer, likely because noblewomen went veiled (*krêdemnon, kalyptrē, kalymna*).[15] Nausicaa and her handmaidens have beautiful braids or ringlets (they have removed their hair coverings).[16] In Semonides, long hair and fancy hairstyles are for aristocratic women who had money, leisure, and access to slave-labor.[17] *Korai* statues depict a variety of hairstyles, and most styles seem to be enhanced through the use of wigs and hairpieces. Abundant hair was likely a source of prestige and pride for a young woman, a natural treasure "that she need only arrange more inventively than another to surpass the other in the perennial contest of women's looks."[18] The uncut or cut front hair of *korai* could indicate age differences, as it probably did in males, but there is no literary evidence to support this.[19] It is also unfortunately impossible to tell when looking at a hairstyle in ancient Greek art whether the hair has been cut because of adherence to a ritual tradition or because it was the fashion.

CLASSICAL GREECE: MEN (CA. 480–400 BCE)

Hairstyles also marked age in classical Greece. Thucydides noted that old men ("until recently") fastened their long hair with golden grasshopper pins, to him a sign of Ionian luxury.[20] This may have been the *krōbylos*, "a twisted mass of long hair ... fastened with a headband in the back of the head at the nape of the neck."[21] While distinctions in hairstyle between older and younger men are mentioned in fifth- and fourth-century literature, they are not identifiable in vase paintings: all men have the same short hair.[22] Older men in visual sources, however, are sometimes recognizable by their baldness, receding hairlines, or gray or white hair and beards.[23] Grave *stelai* of fourth-century Attika generally show older men with longer hair.[24] In the early classical period the uncut front hair of boys is sometimes shown knotted over the forehead.[25]

There was supposedly an age pattern in male hairstyles in classical-era Sparta as well. At the age of twelve the boy's head was shaved, and when he had graduated from the *agela* system at around age twenty, the youth was permitted to grow his hair long.[26] This model is corroborated by artistic evidence to an extent.[27] Aristotle was of the opinion that free Spartan males wore their hair long because menial tasks are harder to do with long hair;[28] Lycurgus maintained that long hair would have made men look taller, more dignified, and more terrifying.[29]

Besides a general trend towards shorter hair in visual sources, fashions in male hairstyles are difficult to positively chart for the classical age. We can say that later *kouroi* wear shorter hairstyles (as in Figure 3.3), "sometimes achieved by rolling or plaiting the hair, [and] binding the braids along the hairline,"[30] perhaps reflecting the increasing popularity of athletics after 550 BCE.[31] From the sixth century onwards, most Greek males began to wear shorter hair (with longer hair for some divinities).[32] "By the fifth century, barbershops were popular gathering places for men ... a source of gossip and news. ... Implements such as shears, tweezers, combs, and mirrors are common finds in all periods."[33]

Literary sources of the period do, however, mention one trend in male hair in the late fifth and early fourth centuries BCE, although the form this hairstyle took is a matter of some debate. Young men of Athens (the *meirakia* and the *neoi*) were apparently fond of "laconizing," or affecting Spartan dress, and hair was part of the fashion.[34] Long "Laconian" hair for men was a trend disapproved of by Aristophanes, as to him it denoted everything from luxuriousness to a fondness for passive homoeroticism to a love

FIGURE 3.3 Apollo from west pediment, Olympia. Photo: Ancient Art and Architecture / Alamy Stock Photo.

of horses.[35] Long/laconizing hair on young men may have been seen in any number of different ways: as rebellious, old-fashioned, or sissy (Lysias was of the opinion that "one should not hate a man because he wears his hair long").[36] But other men sported it too: the elderly Bdelykleon in Aristophanes' *Wasps* is associated with two types of Spartan styles: a long unkempt beard and long cephalic hair. Letaio believes mention of long "Spartan" hair on men in literary sources actually references the *krobylos* style.[37]

The use of artificial dyes and hairpieces does not seem to have been conventional practice in classical Greece.[38] Wigs are mentioned by Xenophon as a common Median fashion, and in Greek literature are used by males disguising themselves as women,[39] but otherwise not referred to as commonplace items for men.

Beards were considered to be a mark of adult masculinity, both in vase painting and in literature.[40] The age at which males were able to grow a beard, however, was probably not until their early twenties.[41] (The first beard was often erotically charged; more facial hair signified coming maturity and a change in status from *eromenos* to *erastes*.[42]) Since it was not the custom for Greek men to appear clean-shaven, "a Greek image of a man without a beard … is [therefore] an image of a man not yet able to grow one."[43] Beards in fact may have been assumed for practical reasons: in modern experiments, shaving with a bronze blade and water took forty-five minutes.⁴⁴ In Greece, bearded warriors are represented as early as the twelfth-century BCE warrior vase; in Attic black-figure vases men display a profusion of facial hair (for instance, a bearded Apollo and a mustachioed Herakles appear on the Proto-Attic Nessos vase, see Figure 3.4).⁴⁵ Body hair also indicated boy and man, not usually in evidence on vase paintings, although it may have been painted on in sculpture.⁴⁶

FIGURE 3.4 Proto-Attic Nessos vase with a mustachioed Herakles (before 625 BCE). Photo: Deutsches Archäologisches Institut—Athens. National Museum of Athens. Inv. No. 1002. D-DAI-ATH-NM-5313.

CLASSICAL GREECE: WOMEN (CA. 480–400 BCE)

Mireille Lee has noted that hair also functioned as an indicator of age for women in ancient Greece.[47] In artistic evidence, there is a clear progression in feminine hairstyles from girlhood to adult womanhood: three classical grave *stelai* show this quite clearly. In one, a young girl wears her hair long down her back and the front in a topknot (Figure 3.5), in the second a teenaged *parthenos* wears her hair bound up with some strands emerging (Figure 3.6),[48] and the adult woman has a *sakkos* or snood and a veil

FIGURE 3.5 Grave stele of a little girl (ca. 450–440 BCE), marble. Metropolitan Museum of Art, New York, NY, Fletcher Fund, 1927. Acc No. 27.45.

FASHION AND ADORNMENT 53

FIGURE 3.6 Funeral stele of young woman ("Giustiniani Stele"), classical Greece (ca. 460 BCE), from the island of Paros, Greece, marble h. 143 cm. Inv. Sk 1482. Photo: Juergen Liepe. Art Resource: ART 180483.

FIGURE 3.7 Adult Greek woman. Photo: D-DAI-ATH-NM-4602.

(Figure 3.7). Older women on grave *stelai* sometimes have shorter locks, possibly to denote their thinning hair.[49]

In literary evidence, specific hairstyles are rarely described in detail.[50] Athenian women did wear head coverings, and veils underwent a series of fashionable changes that can be traced in the visual sources.[51] A shoulder-length veil, which Lloyd Llewellyn-Jones has termed the shoulder-veil or *shaal*-veil (from modern Arabic), dates from 750 BCE.[52] The cloak or *himation* could form a veil by lifting up part to drape around the head, and this came into fashion in the late sixth century BCE.[53] The voluminous *pharos* could achieve this as well. The *shaal*-veil makes a comeback between 520 and 420 BCE (having been ousted for the larger *himation* and *pharos* veils in the preceding centuries) and is found on all types of women: flute-girls, goddesses, and citizens.[54] These veils fall in multiple short folds around the neck and shoulders and are sometimes spangled with stars or dots.[55] The *shaal*-veil falls from favor around 420 BCE, to be replaced by the *kolpos*-veil (formed from an overfold of the dress), and longer types of veil. Face-veils, which cover the head and neck, become more popular towards the end of the classical period.[56]

There were no professional hairstylists for women, who maintained their own hairstyles with the help of slaves. Images of hairstyling are quite rare despite the many general toilette scenes on pots.[57] Women depilated body hair by means of singeing and plucking.[58] In Aristophanes, an old woman is "tweezed and plastered," a reference to pubic hair or eyebrows.[59]

THE ETRUSCANS (CA. 750–150 BCE)

Fashion trends for five centuries of Etruscan hair have been exhaustively detailed by Larissa Bonfante, and it is her work that I follow here.[60] In the seventh century, men wore short bobbed hair, bluntly cut just below the ears and combed straight back.[61] In the sixth century, the trend was towards longer hair; some men wore their long hair in ringlets; this was popular from 525 BCE onwards.[62] Around 520 BCE, short hair on men again began to be popular, and coexists with long hair. In the early years of the fifth century, both men and women wear short curls framing the face (in the Tomb of the Leopards, 475 BCE).[63] Two archaic styles for men from Greece persisted longer in Etruria, down to the early fifth century BCE: the *speira*, "formed by rolling the hair around a metal *torulus* or ribbon,"[64] and the *krobylos* style.[65] In the Hellenistic period, Etruscan men still wore short hair, although sometimes we see the "lion's-mane" style of Alexander.[66] Beards were worn in Etruria in the seventh and sixth centuries BCE, but in the late sixth century we begin to see some clean-shaven men. And from about 500 BCE on, beardless is the fashion (although older men still wear them). Bonfante believes that beards go completely out of style in the Mediterranean by the end of the fourth century, due to Alexander's influence.[67]

Women's hair in Etruria in the seventh century was characterized by the "back braid": the hair combed smoothly back behind the ears and braided in a single thick plait hanging down the back, reaching below the hemline of the back mantle and fanning out "in a fringe at the end, below round clasps or fasteners."[68] The back braid may be clearly seen on terracotta statuettes and bucchero figurines, going out of fashion in the early sixth century.[69] We can pinpoint other hairstyles of the seventh century: firstly, the fashion of wearing a lock of hair hanging down over each shoulder in the front ("Syrian curls," "Hathor locks"), together with a back braid (which scholars connect with Near Eastern models).[70] Thick braids hanging down each shoulder as far as the waist were popular in the late seventh and early sixth century; long spiral or corkscrew curls with a back braid appear on the Cinerario Gualandi (625 BCE at the earliest). Spiral hair holders of gold or bronze "testify to the popularity of the fashion among Etruscan women at this time (seventh and early sixth century)."[71] The front curls/back braid style soars in popularity in the first half of the sixth century, likely under Greek influence.[72] By 550 BCE the preference had changed to wearing two or three curls on each side.[73]

In the late sixth century Etruscan women wore their long hair loose or up in a *tutulus* (this was by far the more characteristic hairstyle for women in the late sixth/early fifth century).[74] It was created by dividing the hair, piling it high into a bun, and binding it with purple fillets of wool.[75] It was a hairdo conical in shape and likened to a boundary stone (*meta*), thought to derive from the helmet shape of the *flamen*. It had died out completely by 480 to 470 BCE.[76]

From 500 BCE on, women wore their hair either short or long and wavy, often tucked up into a Greek-style *sakkos* or in the *krobylos* style, and "never appear without some kind of diadem or headband."[77] In the Hellenistic period (third to second centuries BCE), women wear their hair loosely brushed back and held in place with a ribbon, with three locks hanging over the shoulders.[78]

ANCIENT ROME: MEN (200 BCE–200 CE)

Hair could also indicate age in Roman antiquity: young boys sometimes had long hair, a style which was also (problematically) associated with sexually available slave boys, *delicati* kept for erotic pleasure.[79] Such slaves were termed *capillati*, or otherwise described with long or curly hair,[80] an instance of metonymy standing in for juridical or sexual status.

The visual sources for trends in hairstyles for men have been neatly summarized by Elizabeth Bartman and Alexandra Croom.[81] Generally speaking, throughout Roman antiquity hair is short and men are clean-shaven. In the late first century CE most men had their hair trimmed short on the crown; during the next few decades, a simple straight hair cut with forehead bangs was popular (Figure 3.8).[82] In the Antonine and Severan periods (ca. 96–235 CE) longer hair on the crown was the norm and sometimes a full beard (on which see below and see Figure 3.9). Other trends of shorter duration may also be noted. In the later second and early third centuries CE, a receding hairline or bald head indicative of the "intellectual look," was suddenly popular. While no doubt common in real life, it was rare in artistic works until the later portraits of Marcus Aurelius (d. 180 CE).[83] The late third and early fourth centuries saw a deliberate return to an Augustan hairstyle, perhaps because emperors then wished to be associated with the Augustan ideal and not with the Tetrarchs (see Figure 3.10).[84]

Men's hair followed that of the emperor to a certain extent,[85] but it was less acceptable for men to wear wigs or hairpieces. Thus men may have imitated an emperor's hairstyle, but it would not usually be possible for followers to achieve (for example) the same degree of curl. In addition, few would have seen the emperor in person, and would be dependent on portraits and coins for a hairstyle.[86] Apropos of this, Bartman has noted that modern scholars do not characterize Roman men who change their hairstyles as "frivolous" (as women often are) but as savvy cultural actors, believing it showed allegiance to the emperor (which helped advance their careers) or visualized cultural values.[87]

The literary sources often castigate men who sport fashionable hairstyles or beards as effeminate. Cicero accuses Gabinius of using a curling iron.[88] Julius Caesar was "somewhat overnice in the care of his person, being not only carefully trimmed and shaved, but even supposedly having superfluous hair plucked out."[89] Plutarch relates how the dictator used to scratch his head with one finger and arrange his hair with nicety.[90] The statesman

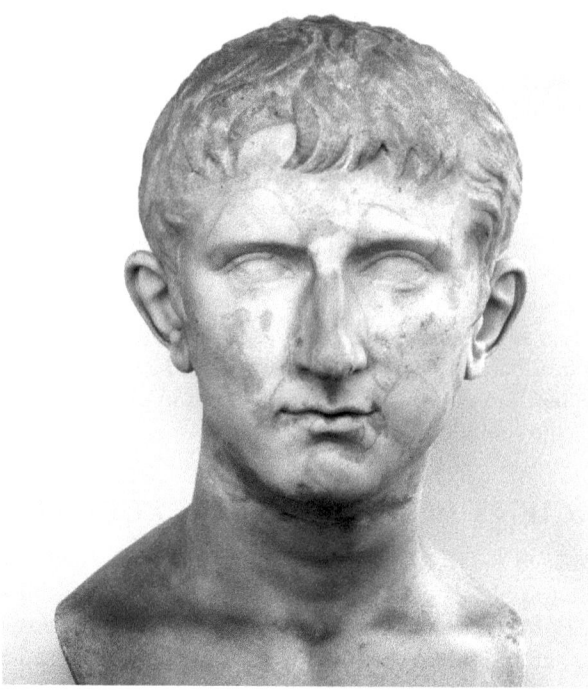

FIGURE 3.8 Bust of Augustus. Erbach, Germany. Photo: Deutsches Archäologisches Institut Koln. DAI G. Fittschen-Badura Fitt 72-03-09.

FIGURE 3.9 Marble portrait bust of Antoninus Pius (ca. 138–161 CE). Metropolitan Museum of Art, New York, NY, Fletcher Fund 1933. Acc. No. 33.11.3.

FIGURE 3.10 Portrait head of Constantine (ca. 325–370 CE), marble. Metropolitan Museum of Art, New York, NY. Bequest of Mary Clark Thompson, 1923. Acc. No. 26.229.

Maecenas' hair was described as "ringlets dripping with perfume."[91] Suetonius states that the emperor Nero had curly hair and let it grow long when he went to Greece.[92] In Martial, a man called Charmenion is scornfully described as "smart" with his curled hair.[93]

Unfortunate fashions in hair were furthermore often the hallmark of young men. In the mid-first century CE, the elder Seneca complained that young men were effeminate, transfixed by song and dance, and accustomed to braiding their hair.[94] The younger Seneca wrote "you are familiar with the young dandies, brilliant in beard and hair, complete from the book-box; you can never expect from them any strength or any soundness."[95] Martial, speaking in the voice of a young man, complains that his old chaperone/tutor disapproves of his self-presentation (Tyrian purple garments and pomaded hair), saying, "your father never did that."[96]

Even though fashionable hairstyles were often labeled as young or effeminate, it is clear that fashionable hair was an important part of being a sophisticated male city dweller. The elegiac poet Tibullus stated attractively coifed men were attractive to women: "whoever dresses his hair with art (*colit arte capillos*)."[97] In Martial, "a beautiful man (*bellus homo*) curls his hair and arranges it carefully." Elsewhere, he portrays a man with curly hair (*crispulus*), be-ringed fingers and smooth thighs who chatters into a married lady's ear and presses her chair; his appearance and behavior, says Martial, obviously indicate that he is her lover.[98] Unguents in the hair were also appealing to the opposite sex,[99] and were a sign of urbanity and status. Cicero described the politician Piso as unsophisticated and unfashionable, "with hair so dreadful (*capillo ita horrido*), that at Capua … he looked as though he meant to carry off the Seplasia with him."[100] Too little concern with personal appearance brought ridicule: the poet Horace at least speaks slightingly of one such man, the object of derision for a bad haircut, a tattered undertunic, and a toga sitting badly and askew.[101] Elsewhere a man is scorned for having a country haircut.[102] Martial painted Truth as "rustic and dry-haired" (*siccis rustica Veritas capillis*), and reports that some hair unguents could be smelt all over the theater.[103]

Both sexes used false hair.[104] The *galerus*, *galerum*, or *galericulum* was a half wig or hairpiece, used to supplement one's own hair (worn by Nero); and the *capillamentum* a full wig (Caligula assumed one on his nightly sprees).[105] The *corymbion* seems to have been a curled wig.[106] The vain emperor Otho because of his thinning hair "wore a wig so carefully fashioned and fitted to his head that no-one suspected it."[107]

Trends may also be noted in male facial hair. Roman senators apparently wore their beards long in the fourth century BCE,[108] but generally speaking clean-shaven was the norm from the republic into the first few decades of the first century. Suetonius states that Otho used to shave every day and smear his face with moist bread, beginning the practice with the appearance of the first down, so as never to have a beard.[109] Contrary to much modern scholarship on the subject, Hadrian did not in fact introduce the wearing of the beard among upper-class Romans. Beards are visible as early as 43 CE on the *Ara Pietatis Augustae*; and portraits of Nero from the mid-first century sport a slight beard as well.[110] Bearded Romans are also in evidence on Flavian monuments and the Column of Trajan.[111]

In addition, some facial hair trends were the province of young men: long sideburns and moustache (or a narrow beard) seem to have been a youthful hairstyle; in the third century, young men wore a mustache until they progressed to a full beard.[112] In the first century, Seneca detested the way young show-offs trimmed their facial hair:

> You note this tendency in those who pluck out or thin out their beards, or who closely shear and shave the upper lip while preserving the rest of the hair and allowing it to grow ... and who never design to do anything which will escape general notice; they endeavor to excite and attract people's eyes.[113]

Roman citizen males did not usually depilate their body hair, as this was a practice associated with women, male slaves who were penetrated sexual partners, and effeminates. There is some evidence, however, that depilation may have been the fashion of dandies in upper-class circles.[114] The elder Seneca complained that young men in his day were "plucked and pumiced" (*vulsis atque expolitis*); and in Martial, one Labienus depilates his chest, shins, arms, and genitals "for his mistress."[115]

ANCIENT ROME: WOMEN (200 BCE–200 CE)

Bartman has noted abundant hair could categorically only be worn by women in their prime, as hair loses strength and abundance as it ages;[116] and female hairstyles in Rome were also structured along age lines. Some young girls are portrayed in artistic evidence with hair hanging loose; mature women tend to have it braided and pinned up.[117] Sometimes a girl's hair was worn in the "melon hairstyle" (*Melonenfrisur*), that is, twisted back from the crown in sections and wound into a bun at the back of the head. "In portraits it generally indicates that the subject is not yet married."[118] While it is true that *generally* the hairstyles of young girls in Roman art tend to be simpler than their older counterparts' "architectonic" styles, it is also true that there is no one hairstyle common to all young girls in the visual evidence, no matter what time period one is considering. The funerary altar of Iunia Procula from Rome, for example, which dates to the Flavian period, shows a fashionably coiffed eight-year-old.[119] While such fashions in hair may hearken to a familiarity with Hellenistic styles,[120] it may also be that girls of a certain class, in the years before they were married, were adorned both to emphasize their status and their family's status within Roman society, and in the hope of attracting a suitor.[121]

Although these cannot be detected on statues, literary sources also mention fillets in the hair of the young girl. Propertius states that *vittae* bound the young girl's hair.[122] Valerius Flaccus tells us that Medea before her flight "kissed for the last time her virgin fillets."[123] Nonius, quoting Varro, writes that young girls before they married "went bare-headed, with hair combed and bound with *vittae*."[124] One scholar believes that girls' *vittae* were woven into a braid down the back, and the braid itself was tied with a fillet,[125] but there is nothing to indicate this particular girls' hairstyle either in artistic or in literary evidence.

There is some evidence in Roman art for the ornamentation of young girls' hair with jewels. George has noted that the girl on the south frieze of the *Ara Pacis* is wearing, as well as the *lunula*, three gems on her brow, possibly pearls.[126] On the north frieze the young girl wears pearls or gems on her forehead.[127] The girl on the Sertoriii relief has pearls interspersed amidst her curls. Ancient authors speak of veiling the head out-of-doors only in relation to married women (thus demonstrating the sexual significance of veiling),[128] and indeed little girls in funerary reliefs do not wear the *palla* over their heads.

Broad changes in Roman women's hairstyles over several centuries have been helpfully catalogued by Alexandra Croom.[129] In the Roman republic, the most popular hairstyle for women was called the *nodus* hairstyle, remarkably long-lived (see below). This was a style in which the hair at the front of the head is rolled into a knot (the *nodus*), and then braided or twisted in a tight strand down the back of the head. The hair at the sides is waved or loosely twisted into a chignon at the back of the head, incorporating the braid.[130] This style first appears on a coin of Fulvia, wife of Mark Antony, in 43 BCE, but was soon taken up by Octavia (his next wife) and appears on coins and in portraits of the 30s BCE, sometimes with loose tendrils of hair escaping to lie on the woman's neck, just below her ears.[131] The fashion was also adopted by Augustus' daughter Julia and his wife Livia, who was portrayed with several variants on the "*nodus*" coiffure.[132] This hairstyle was succeeded by a style in which the knot of hair at the front disappeared but women continued to wave bands of hair around the face and draw it into a low bun. From 38 to 64 CE, hair was worn short and curled in front, and hanging down behind or in a chignon, as in the portraits of Agrippina Maior.[133] Over the next century or so, hair rose higher up in front in a high diadem of curls secured in the back by braids wound into a bun (see Figures 4.4, 8.2, and 9.2a and b). This is the best-known of Roman hairstyles and almost certainly utilized false hair and hair stitching,[134] but oddly is not found on coins depicting empresses of this period.[135] The empress Faustina, who died in 141 CE, sported a new hairstyle that was very different from what had gone before: her hair was braided and folded into a bun which sat right on top of the head.[136] Her daughter Faustina the Younger sports nine changes of hairstyle throughout her official portraiture, from a flat bun on top of the head to a bulky style with waves around the face, possibly because she was following fashion (or perhaps it was some kind of response to dynastic politics?) (see Figure 3.11).[137]

Towards the end of the second century CE, the hair around the face drooped down to the neck before being fed back into a chignon; in the early third century the hair at the sides rises back up off the neck before being plaited and rolled into a bun at the back.

It is often stated by modern scholars that Roman hairstyles were the subject of swiftly changing innovation, based on passages such as that written by Ovid, who advised that rather than following the latest fashion in hairdressing, women should style their hair based on the shape of the face or their personality type—and thus hanging loose, braided, up in a knot, even in disarray (*ars casum simulat*).[138] He adds there are more fashions in hair than acorns on a tree, and each day adds a new *ornatus*.[139] Scholars have noted that there is really no way of tracking this rapid succession of fashions in hair, as the visual evidence presents a variety of hairstyles worn by different women and not by one individual over time.[140] Croom, in fact, asserts that as our extant hairstyles depict change

FIGURE 3.11 Portrait of the Empress Faustina the Younger, wife of the emperor Marcus Aurelius (ca. 161–180 CE), marble. Metropolitan Museum of Art, New York, NY. Gift of Shelby and Leon Levy, 1986. Acc. No. 1986.40.

over five centuries, any woman may have worn the same style for thirty years.[141] In addition, some hairstyles seem have been remarkably long-lived, such as the *nodus* hairstyle, a coiffure that began in 43 BCE, was taken up by the women of Augustus' family, and was sported by Livia (if we can believe the visual sources) until her death in 29 CE.[142] Are we to conclude from this that fashion in hair had not changed in decades? Or that by refusing to change their (official) hairstyle, the women of Augustus' house were also signifying their adherence to tradition, their sexual chastity and circumscribed political power, and the secure nature of Augustus' reign?[143] The infamous "Flavian Lady" (Figure 3.12a and b), another interesting example, actually dates not from the late first century (69 CE) but from the Trajanic/Hadrianic period (98–138 CE), which means the woman wears a hairstyle thirty years out of date.[144] Is it meant as a generational marker, or perhaps an expression of cultural identity?

False hair was known and used by women, naturally colored or dyed. Because curling tongs (the *calamistrum*, heated up in a brazier or fire)[145] and hair dyes could seriously burn the hair and scalp and cause hair loss, women found thin or scorched hair a problem; in extreme cases, false hair was resorted to.[146] Sometimes the hair for wigs and hairpieces was taken from foreigners: when Corinna's hair was ruined by *sapo* (a substance used to dye the hair), she wears a wig, described by Ovid as "captive tresses."[147] "The best wigs were thought to be of German hair, as a host of references testify."[148] Black hair for wigs and hairpieces (*capelli Indici*) was so sought after that customs dues had to be paid on it at Rome.[149] Wigs and hairpieces were generally bought near the Porticus Philippi, in front of the temple of Hercules and the Muses,[150] and were popular products.[151] But wigs had to be positioned with care: Ovid writes with derision of a woman who put her false hair on awry when his unlooked-for arrival was announced.[152] Ovid in general does not approve of wigs or hair dyes: he expects that Corinna will be embarrassed at having to wear a wig,[153] and expresses surprise that such things can be bought so openly.[154] The *caliendrum* was a woman's headpiece made of false hair.[155] Messalina reportedly wore a blonde *galerus* on her nightly visits to the brothels.[156] The high architectural hairstyles worn by women in the late first to mid-second centuries almost certainly utilized false

FASHION AND ADORNMENT

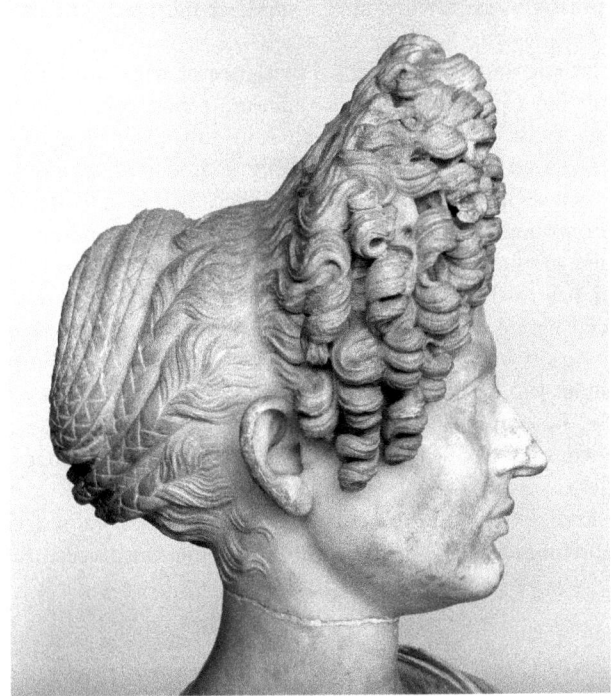

FIGURE 3.12a Fonseca Bust. Photo: G. Fittschen-Badura. Cap81-26-02_16304, 12.

FIGURE 3.12b Fonseca Bust, rear view. Photo: G. Fittschen-Badura. Cap73-75-08_16304, 25.

hair for extra impressiveness: for instance, a separate hairpiece of curls glued or sewn to a backing.[157]

We also have artistic and archaeological evidence of wigs and hairpieces. Twists and braids of false hair have been found in Roman-era female graves.[158] Chemical analysis of one such, a large twist of false auburn hair found in a fourth-century woman's grave at York, determined that the hair was probably coated with hair dye.[159] By the early third century the wig seems to have acquired cachet, as it is in evidence in many female portraits, even on women who clearly have thick, abundant natural hair. A wig may clearly be discerned on the sitter in Figure 3.13.

Since the sitter has thick curly long tresses, no recession of the hairline, and clearly no need of artificial hair, "we conclude that she wore a wig by choice."[160] Bartman has noted that "most wigs in antiquity were made of human hair and fashioned with a level of beauty and craftsmanship largely unobtainable today";[161] however, even if a wig looked demonstrably false, Roman women may not have found this a problem. The very artifice of a hairpiece or wig may have marked status and wealth, and perhaps was an objective of a woman's toilette.

Intriguingly, there exist about twenty-five statues of women from the Antonine and Severan periods which were made with detachable hairpieces, possibly so that the

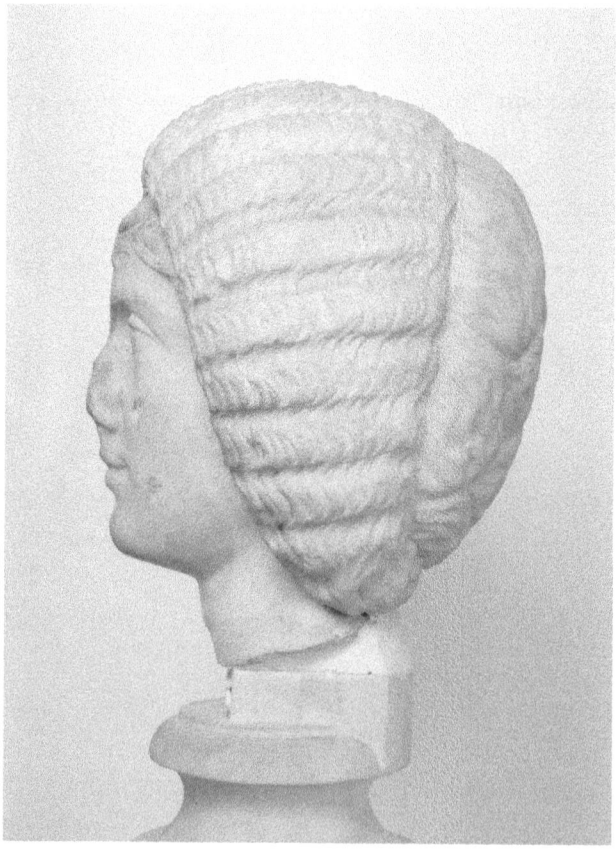

FIGURE 3.13 Woman in a wig. Musei Capitolini, Rome. Photo: D-DAI-ROM-65.1891.

subject's hair could be kept looking up to date with new marble coiffures.[162] Some scholars argue against this, stating that the portraits are funerary (and a deceased sitter no longer has a need to keep up with fashion in hairstyles), and that it would not have been an easy task to carve a new wig to fit exactly.[163] In addition, Bartman names the potential for change seen by modern scholars in such hairpieces as part of a set of essentializing assumptions about female behavior.[164] She offers no alternative explanation, however, beyond noting that if the hair was of a different stone than the bust it would be a (quite expensive) way to make a startling contrast between the hair and the face; possibly the objective. I would argue, however, that this effect could be achieved with paint; the ability of the hair to be detached from the bust must be part of the justification for its presence. A portrait bust would be on display, viewed by friends and family, and if a fashionable appearance was necessary to a woman's status in antiquity there seems no reason to my mind why this essential part of her persona would cease to exist after her death.

LATE ANTIQUITY

Christian women were ideally supposed to keep their heads covered inside as well as outside the house;[165] still, elaborate female hairstyles were denounced by Christian authors. Firmly located in the anti-cosmetic tradition, Tertullian (late second century CE) favored simple hairstyles which did not involve curling, primping, or otherwise torturing tresses, and disapproved of wigs, hairpieces, and heavy rolls of hair.[166] He felt that any amendment of the Gods' handiwork implied finding fault with it, and Tertullian exhorted women to banish away from their free head "this slavery of ornamentation."[167] Conversely, however, he complains elsewhere that matrons had thrown away distinctive hair ornaments (the *crepidulum*), and high wigs (the *caliendrum*) so that their high status was now invisible.[168]

Clement of Alexandria (ca. late second century CE) also was of the opinion that Christian women should not use wigs and artificial locks of hair.[169] In addition, he warned that women wearing wigs or hair extensions might not themselves receive a priest or bishop's blessing (i.e. the laying on of hands), as the blessing might mistakenly consecrate "the woman whose hair she wears."[170] In Claudian (late fourth century), a mother binds up her young daughter's hair with jewels.[171] The fourth- or fifth-century Jerome also disapproved of elaborately curled hairstyles, of wigs and hairpieces, inasmuch as they are worldly and do not aid in a woman's salvation, and approves of Christian women who deny their daughters hair ornaments.[172] It may have been difficult for women to imitate an empress' hairstyle in late antiquity as increasingly the imperial family used elaborate headdresses and diadems: thus the ladies of Theodora's fifth-century court keep their hair covered with hoods.[173]

CONCLUSION

Youth and age were indicated in antiquity by hairstyle, binding, and cutting. Owing to the complexity of the evidence a thorough examination of hair trends in ancient Greece and Rome has not yet been attempted; still, I have tried to note some developments here. In addition, while the Greeks of the classical period seem not to have worn wigs or hairpieces, the ancient Romans certainly made use of false hair, and *cultus* (personal care) was not restricted to the young or the unmarried because of its properties as a social marker. Hair's abundance or lack, its visible absence or presence, and the way it was worn, was essential to self-presentation in antiquity. "Hair's physiological properties and symbolic representations, regulations and rituals are … a fundamental part of any culture" because of hair's "potential to both mirror and mould cultural meanings."[174]

CHAPTER FOUR

Production and Practice

JANET STEPHENS

Basic hairdressing skills are acquired from childhood through informal visual, kinesthetic, and oral learning traditions focused on the manipulation of hair and related technologies. All cultures develop preferences regarding the presence, absence, abundance, and conformity of hair upon the head and body. Once societies reach consensus on grooming standards, the daily rituals and techniques used to conform seem too obvious to record and, over time, can be forgotten.

Technical writing about hairdressing is scarce between 600 BCE and 800 CE. Some sources are lost[1] and surviving texts are overwhelmingly anecdotal, from Greek and Roman perspectives and tinted with cultural egotism, class, and patriarchal bias. Sources are neither chronological, systematic, nor exhaustive but, when pieced together, they form a rough outline of Greco-Roman grooming practices and provide sporadic glimpses into those of other cultures.[2] What *does* survive in abundance are figurative artworks and hairdressing artifacts. Depictions reveal much about how hairstyles were arranged and who wore them and artifacts help us avoid anachronistic speculation. Above all, we now understand hair biology—one must understand hair as a material[3] to fully appreciate ancient visual depiction, hairdressing implements, and literary references. Some hair characteristics are universal, others vary by individual. Variables are genetic and account for hair similarities among isolated population groups and immediate families—a fact noticed and commented upon in antiquity, but not understood.[4]

HAIR STRUCTURE

Hairs are thread-like appendages of the skin growing from small pocket-like depressions called follicles. They are composed of hard keratin protein and grow all over the body except the palms of the hands, soles of the feet, lips and eyelids. There are two types: vellus and terminal. Vellus hairs are fine, downy, short, and lightly pigmented; they help perspiration evaporate efficiently, thus regulating body temperature. Terminal hairs protect,[5] insulate, and adorn the body. They are coarser, longer, more densely pigmented and include scalp, beard, eyebrow, eyelash, body, underarm (axillary), and pubic hair. Terminal hairs have three structural layers: cuticle, cortex, and medulla. The cuticle is composed of five to fourteen layers of scaly, translucent, imbricated cells. It surrounds and protects the cortex of the hair shaft, much like the bark on a tree. Cuticle imbrications wick water, dirt, and impurities away from the skin. Light reflecting through the cuticle gives human hair its distinctive pearlescent shine. Cuticle damage makes hair easily tangle and matt.[6] The cortex supports the cuticle and is the most important structural layer. Cortex diameter indicates the hair's texture and behavior. Fine textured hair measures less than 60 microns and tends toward limpness. Medium texture ranges between 60 and 90 microns and is pleasingly malleable. Coarse hair measures between 90 and 120 microns and is stiff and unyielding. Cortex cells contain springy helical protein chains that make hair highly elastic and resilient and one hundred times stronger than steel wire of equal diameter. Because of these qualities, human hair was sometimes used for bow strings and catapult ropes.[7] The medulla is a channel of air pockets or soft keratin protein at the center of the cortex: it has no known function (Figure 4.1).

Tiny *arrector pili* muscles are attached to terminal hair follicles; they contract when the body becomes chilled, lifting hairs into "goose bumps" to better insulate the body. They also contract during heightened emotional states such as fear and horror.[8] Sebaceous and ecrine gland secretions blend on the skin, forming a protective acid mantle (pH 4.5–5.5) that is hostile to germs.

FLOW

Follicles project hairs away from the scalp in observable patterns. At the crown of the head, hairs appear to radiate from, while rotating around, one or two distinctive whorls called pivot points. Individuals with two pivot points often have pronounced ridges on top of the head where the contrasting flows meet. "Cowlicks" occur when small groups of hair project in the opposite direction from the general flow, usually at the forehead hairline and nape of the neck. Flow is easily observable on short hair (Figure 4.2).

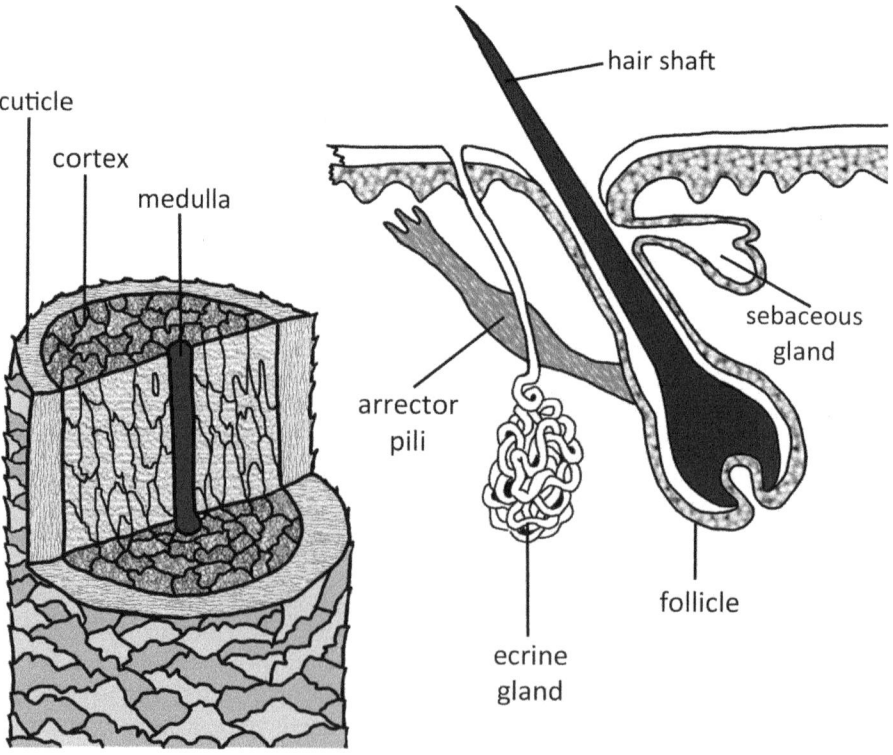

FIGURE 4.1 Hair structure and histology. © Janet Stephens.

FIGURE 4.2 A strong forehead cowlick. Portrait head of Pompey the Great, Roman, early imperial period (first half of the first century CE), marble. Ny Carlsberg Glyptotek, Copenhagen. IN 773.

GROWTH CYCLES

Follicles produce and shed hairs in repetitive, three-phase cycles. During anagen, scalp follicles produce 1/2 inch of hair fiber per month, for two to five years (although shorter and longer anagen phases are common). During catagen (3–4 days), follicles slow, then stop, producing hair fiber. During telogen, follicles are dormant for up to three months, shedding their hairs. After telogen, follicles begin new anagen phases. When anagenic hairs are cut, they do not stop growing.[9] Under normal conditions, growth cycles are randomized among all follicles, thus assuring a continuous coverage of protective hair on the head and body. For every follicle entering telogen, another follicle returns to anagen thus maintaining consistent hair density.

DENSITY

We are each born with all the follicles we will ever have—their number and distribution over the body determine hair density. Average scalp density varies by natural color: redheads: 95,000; brunettes: 110,000; and blondes: 140,000. All hairs are attached to the skin, but not all hairs are the same length, some are beginning anagen, some are entering catagen, and others somewhere in between. Therefore, proximal density (near the scalp) is always greater than distal density (away from the scalp). The difference between proximal and distal density is responsible for the gradual tapering of long braids, often depicted in Greek and Roman figurative art.

LENGTH

There is no biological difference in growth potential between women's and men's hair, but terminal length is limited by personal genetics. Provided the hair is never cut, a 2-year anagen phase yields about 12 inches of hair (24 months × 0.5 in. = 12 in.), a 6-year anagen yields 36 inches and a 16-year anagen, yields 96 inches of hair (although this is extremely rare). Cultural norms determine who wears what hair length. Mediterranean cultures assigned the longest hair to women and "effeminate" men. The culturally masculinized long hair of foreign, so-called "barbarian" cultures[10] left many commentators bemused.

TRANSITIONAL HAIR

Transitional hairs are located along the hairline. They are naturally finer and shorter than hair at the crown, and sometimes curlier or lighter in color. They live in front of the ears, at the recession corners at each side of the forehead, and at the nape of the neck. Both sexes have transitional hair, but it is more visible in long hair, since short haircuts and shaven beards camouflage its presence. Transitional hair is ubiquitous on ancient Roman female portrait statuary.

CURL PATTERN

The curvature of each follicle channel determines the hair's curl pattern. Straight channels produce straight hairs, slightly curved channels produce wavy hairs, and strongly curved channels produce curly hairs. Multiple curl patterns can coexist on a single head. All curl patterns are represented in ancient artworks (Figure 4.3).

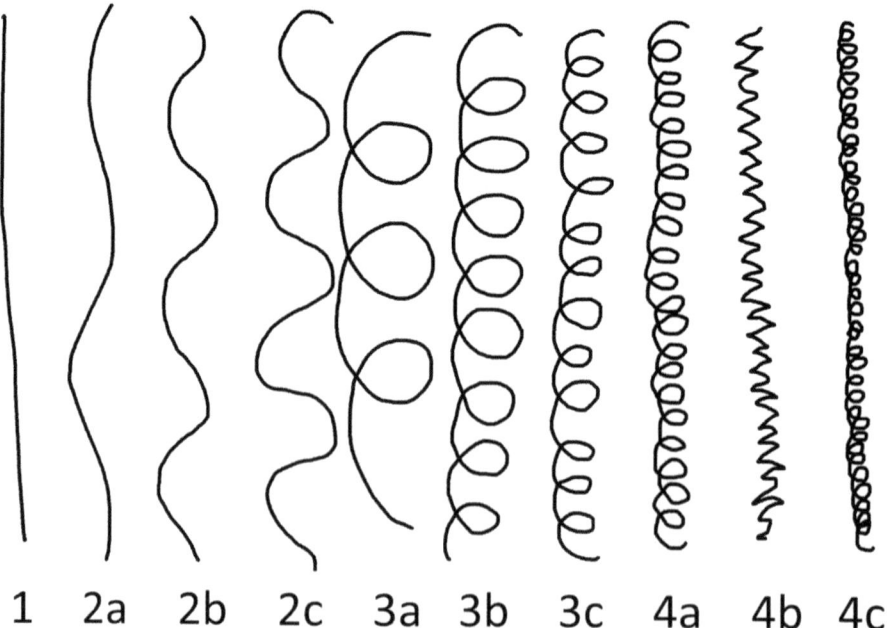

FIGURE 4.3 Standard curl patterns. © Janet Stephens

NATURAL COLOR

Two types of melanin pigment are deposited among the hair's cortex cells as they generate, blackish-brown *eumelanin* and reddish-orange *pheomelanin*.[11] Varying blends of the two produce the full range of human hair colors. Melanin density within the cortex determines the hair's darkness or blondeness: the darker the hair, the denser the pigment. In antiquity, populations had darker hair colors nearer the Mediterranean and lighter colors in the northern reaches of Europe and Britain. Among the Romans, light haired Gauls, Germans, Batavians, and Britons inspired wonderment, comment, and emulation.[12] Hairs turn gray or white as follicles cease producing melanin due to age or disorder. In antiquity, gray hair symbolized wisdom as well as advanced age.[13]

HAIR CHEMISTRY

Hair swells or contracts in response to temperature and pH (alkalinity swells, acidity contracts), making the cuticle scales lift or close, rather like venetian blinds. This property is important in artificial hair coloring (see below). Hair protein is composed of approximately 51 percent carbon, 19 percent oxygen, 18 percent hydrogen, and 5 percent sulphur. Keratin molecules are connected end-to-end with strong peptide links, forming springy chains. These chains are bundled together by chemical cross bonds of 55 percent sulphur, 40 percent hydrogen, and 5 percent salts. Sulphur bonds form the stable infrastructure of natural curl.

The hydrogen and salt bonds are hydrophilic and unstable: they can be broken and rearranged with exposure to humidity or intense dry heat; this property allows us to artificially curl hair. Hydrogen bonds break when hair is wetted, making it pliable and more elastic; if the hair is then bound in an unnatural shape until fully dry, the hair remembers the new shape. Even dry-dressed hair will do this because of atmospheric humidity; for example, after a few hours in braids, naturally straight hair displays rippling waves. It is unknown whether women in antiquity intentionally exploited this phenomenon, but it is impossible they were unaware of it. When dry hair is wrapped around a hot curling wand, numerous salt and hydrogen bonds break, then reposition as the hair cools. Heat produces weaker curl than water evaporation, but it is much faster. Artificial curls are temporary, however; atmospheric humidity and perspiration gradually disrupt the artificially positioned bonds, and the stable sulphur bonds revert the hair back to its natural curl pattern. In antiquity, it was more difficult and time consuming to artificially curl hair and keep it in curl than today.

HORMONES AND HAIR LOSS

At puberty, scalp and body hair coarsen, males grow beards and both sexes grow axillary and pubic hair. After puberty, individual genetic susceptibility may result in gradual, permanent scalp hair loss (androgenetic alopecia, AGA). Male-pattern AGA is concentrated, resulting in shiny zones of complete baldness. Female-pattern AGA is diffuse and mosaic. The hair on top of the head thins out, the partings appear wider and the ponytail wastes away. In advanced cases, a woman's scalp is visible through a veil of distantly spaced hairs. Genetic hair loss is often a serious blow to self-esteem, as the discussion of Synesius' baldness in the Introduction to this volume has shown.[14] Due to natural hormone fluctuations, many women experience sudden temporary hair loss after childbirth, and all menopausal women lose some scalp density[15] as they age.

Male castration, a common practice in antiquity, affects hair growth in different ways, according to developmental stage. When castrated before puberty, eunuchs do not develop pubic or coarse body hair, their voices remain high pitched and they do not suffer from androgenetic alopecia. If castrated after puberty, eunuchs lose their coarse body hair and their pubic hair diminishes. If balding at the time of castration, there is no additional hair loss.[16]

INCIDENTAL HAIR LOSS

Use of harsh colorants and overheated curling wands could result in catastrophic hair loss, including permanent baldness.[17] Hair loss from acute or chronic illness, fever, skin infections, parasites, and dietary deficiencies was commonplace in antiquity.[18] Communicable skin diseases such as sycosis and mentagra (folliculitis of the scalp and beard respectively) and fungal infections like ringworm (*tinea capitis*)[19] were transmitted by sharing contaminated razors and hairdressing implements. During some illnesses, the head was intentionally shaved in order to prevent hair loss and as therapy for headaches.[20] Plato claimed that lustfulness causes the eyelashes to fall out.[21]

HAIR ARRANGEMENT VERSUS HAIR MATERIAL

A hair arrangement is the product of a sequence of temporary physical actions performed with hair and appropriate technologies. Arrangement techniques include purely mechanical actions such as parting, twisting, braiding, combing, teasing, stitching, pinning, knotting, and physical alterations such as curling, cutting, shaving, plucking, and dyeing. Arrangement is imposed, material is genetic: arrangement cannot permanently change the hair's essential character, even when the effects are relatively long lasting, such as cutting and dyeing—regrowth reveals all. It is possible for two heads of hair to be arranged the same way and yet appear very unlike, because of dissimilar material (Figure 4.4).

FIGURE 4.4 Two identically dressed mid-second-century tower hairstyles. Model on left has waist length, high density, medium textured hair, model on right has shoulder-blade length, average density, fine textured hair. © Janet Stephens.

When hair fashion relies solely on arrangement techniques, anyone can conform, such as when Empress Faustina the Younger (120–175 CE) popularized simple buns.[22] But it often occurs that uncommon material attributes such as blondeness, a specific curl pattern, greater than average density, length, and so on are prerequisite for a fashionable appearance: deprived individuals must exert more effort and artifice to conform. Some are born fashionable, others must work at it.

HAIRDRESSING TECHNOLOGIES AND TECHNIQUES

By 600 BCE, the fundamental hairdressing technologies were already ancient. These can be divided into two classes: durable and consumable. Durable technologies, such as combs and mirrors, survive as artifacts. Consumables, such as hair oil, rarely survive, but can be traced through literary sources. Hairdressing tools were valuable, both symbolically and economically. They are routinely found among grave furniture of all ancient cultures, and Roman jurists opined that women were entitled to legal control over their costly beauty equipment.[23]

HAIR WASHING

Customs and frequency of hair washing varied.[24] On Greek ceramics, depictions of nudes bathing at lavers (pedestal basins) often show women, but seldom men, wearing their hair tied up—implying that female hair washing was separate from cleansing the body. Rarer depictions show Greek women or men wetting their hair while showering in fountain houses (see Figure 2.10).[25] Jewish women were required to thoroughly wet their hair during monthly ritual baths of purification.[26] Pliny writes that bathing the head with hot water followed by cold was healthful.[27] Supposing people of the ancient Mediterranean used additional cleansing aids when washing their hair, period appropriate consumables include natural surfactants such as ash water or *struthium* (juice extracted from the roots of the *saponaria officinalis* plant), egg yolk (a natural emulsifier), and natron (a naturally occurring salt mixture harvested from dry lake beds in Egypt). Urine (containing natural ammonia), was an effective degreaser used in ancient laundry facilities and *sapo*, a primitive cooked lye soap used to decolorize hair, was also an effective cleanser. All of the above would need to be rinsed from the hair after use. Alkaline cleansers (i.e. natron, urine, and *sapo*) would lift the cuticle, making it harder to comb (Figure 4.5).

Combs (item 1 in Figure 4.5) in a variety of designs were used by both sexes to detangle, smooth, arrange the hair in curls,[28] and to remove vermin. Many small single- and double-sided combs (with teeth cut on both sides of a central spine) made of bone and ivory survive. Metal and wooden combs were also common,[29] but fewer survive.

Before the first century CE, mirrors (item 8 in Figure. 4.5 and Figure 4.6) were made of polished metal—especially silver gilt bronze and solid silver. Square, round, or oblong, with or without handles or stands, artifact mirrors range from purely utilitarian to highly decorated luxury objects with elaborate engraved or relief decoration. Solid silver mirrors were prized dowry items and might constitute the bulk of a woman's personal wealth.[30] Pliny notes that when silver mirrors are polished on the concave side, the reflected image is greatly magnified.[31] Prone to tarnish, metal mirrors needed regular polishing—Pliny recommends using vinegar and chalk.[32]

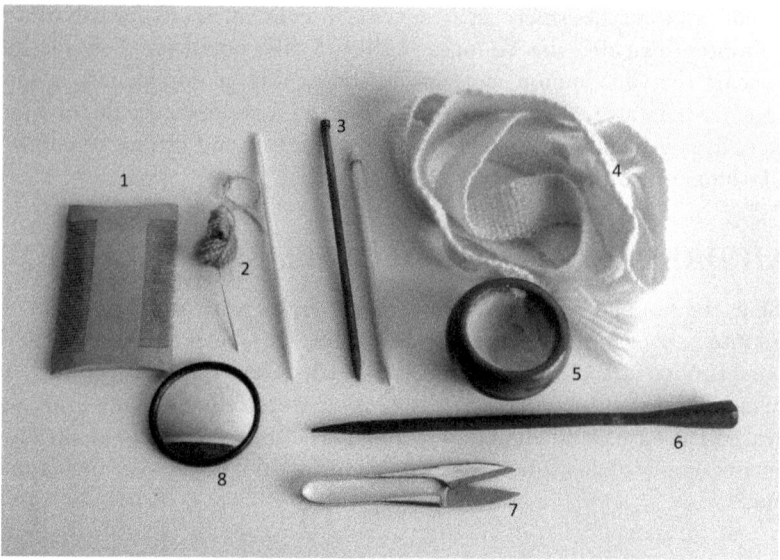

FIGURE 4.5 Modern reproduction ancient hairdressing tools: (1) comb; (2) gold needle and woolen thread, bone needle; (3) wooden hair bodkins; (4) woolen ribbon; (5) unguent; (6) *calamistrum* curling wand; (7) *forfex* shears; (8) convex glass mirror. © Janet Stephens.

FIGURE 4.6 Bronze mirror (early fourth century BCE), Etruscan. Metropolitan Museum of Art, New York, NY. Gift of Henry G. Marquand, 1897. Acc. No. 97.22.16.

During the first century CE, glass mirrors backed with gold leaf, silver foil, or coated with molten lead became available.[33] These were likely less expensive and more convenient than solid metal mirrors (since constant polishing was unnecessary), but performance may have suffered from imperfect glass production technology. Convex mirrors cut from blown glass bubbles reflected sharp images, but with a wide field in miniaturized form, making it harder to see fine detail. Spun disc and poured glass mirrors could be quite large, but planar and surface irregularities distorted the reflection.[34] Gold backings distorted colors and other metal backings were vulnerable to corrosion.

Mirrors are the only hairdressing implements widely discussed in primary sources. Perseus killed the Gorgon Medusa by reflecting back her own gaze in a polished shield.[35] Because of their mysterious properties, mirrors were used in divination.[36] Commentators speculated about how mirrors worked,[37] and were acutely aware that the ability to recognize and remember one's own appearance over the course of a lifetime has enormous psychosocial consequences. Mirrors allowed comparison of one's own appearance to that of others',[38] and to culturally defined standards—one's response to these comparisons revealed one's character. Excessive pride in one's fleeting, superficial beauty engendered conceit, arrogance, and meretricious behavior. Conversely, dissatisfaction in one's looks encouraged envy, falsification, self-obsession, and, with the ravages of aging or accident, emotions of regret, anger, and mortification.[39] For the philosophically minded, reflections, both literal and metaphorical, helped one to know and improve oneself, tame emotions, and practice moderation.[40]

CONSUMABLE STYLING AIDS

Both oil- and water-based styling aids were used. Oil smooths and controls hair, making it compact, shiny, and easier to comb. Olive oil, butter, animal fats, and costly perfumed unguents[41] (item 5 in Figure 4.5) were all utilized. Scent additives included saffron, cinnamon, cardamom, myrrh, honey, balsam, spikenard, and common herbs.[42] Water facilitates braiding by making the hair more pliable and it revives wilted natural curl. Acacia gum[43] dissolved in water stiffens and holds hair in place after drying. Some Celts applied "lime-water" to their hair, imparting a roughened, wild, and spiky appearance (see the Dying Gaul at Figure 2.7)[44] and lime-water or *sapo* may have helped keep in place the Germanic Suebian knot hairstyle.[45]

BRAIDING

Braids were worn during all periods of antiquity by both sexes but especially by women. Most common were three-strand braids in a variety of techniques (outside, inside, augmenting, and lace).[46] Four- to ten-strand plaits were common from the mid-third through the fifth centuries CE. Two-strand fishtail braids are visible on the Erechtheion caryatid hairstyles (see Figure 2.9)[47] and two-strand rope braids embellish the later portraits of Empress Julia Domna (d. 217 CE).[48]

FASTENERS

Many Greek, Etruscan, and pre-imperial Roman hairstyles were tied together with cords, fillets, and ribbons (item 4 in Figure 4.5) of natural fibers and leather. Men and women are depicted wearing single or multiple tied headbands, with the hair tucked up, under, or around the band. In sculptural depictions, tied styles are most commonly secured with square knots (aka *hercules knot* [Figure 4.7]).

Hair bodkins (item 3 in Figure 4.5) (single-prong hairpins) made of bone, ivory, metal, and wood[49] were used to part and section women's hair while arranging it, to fasten buns, to decorate finished hairstyles, and as head scratchers, makeup and perfume applicators, and weapons.[50] Most artifact bodkins have simple geometric heads, but some have elaborately carved figurative or jeweled-heads.[51] Sources claim that spear points were used like bodkins to part the hair of Roman brides when dressing their wedding hairstyles.[52] By 50 BCE, Roman women were sewing hairstyles together using needle and thread (item 2 in Figure 4.5).[53] Sewing creates more comfortable, durable, elaborate, and gravity-defying coiffures than are possible using bodkins and ribbons. Large, blunt sewing needles suitable for hairdressing are often found in Roman period female graves.[54]

FIGURE 4.7 Hercules knot. Head of a male votary (late sixth to early fifth centuries BCE), limestone, Cyprus. Metropolitan Museum of Art, New York, NY. The Cesnola Collection, purchased by subscription, 1874–76. Inv. No. 64.51.2632. Photo: OASC.

THERMAL CURLING

Both men and women had their hair thermally curled with metal wands (item 6 in Figure 4.5) heated over direct flame or in hot ashes.[55] As yet, no convincing artifact curling wands survive from antiquity, although one may be depicted on the funerary *stele* of the wife of P. Ferrarius Hermes,[56] located in the Uffizi Museum, Florence. If this depiction is correct, curling wands were long tapered rods, similar to ring mandrels. Overheated curling wands scorched and damaged the hair. Ovid complains that his girlfriend has ruined her fine, beautiful hair by overheating it, to the extent that she can only regain her beauty by buying the hair of German captives, and she only has herself to blame.[57] Commentators disapproved of men thermally curling their hair.[58]

HAIR REMOVAL

Epilation

Many ancients pulled out unwanted hair (*epilation*). Roman women allegedly removed all body hair, but not facial hair (a slight "monobrow" was considered beautiful among both Greeks and Romans).[59] Roman men epilated only beard and axillary hair (to remove any suspicion of effeminacy).[60] Depilatories were used for large areas of skin and tweezers for difficult to reach, or sensitive areas, and for detail work. Regrowth from epilation is slow and soft textured and, with repeated epilation, follicles can die—leaving the area permanently hairless. Depilatories may have contained pitch,[61] other plant resins, beeswax, and honey. They were probably solid when cold, with a low melting point. The warmed viscous depilatory would be spread thickly over the hairy skin, allowed to cool and harden, and then pried away in one quick rip taking the hairs with it. Depilatories are fast and efficient for denuding large or particularly hairy areas of skin, but the process is intensely painful, can irritate, bruise or burn the skin, cause follicles to bleed and scab, and can lead to infected ingrown hairs. Shared and recycled depilatories can transmit disease. Ancient tweezers were U-shaped metal tools[62] with which hairs were grasped and pulled out. The working tips were wide or narrow. Tweezering is perhaps less painful than depilatories, but can be more time consuming. Tweezers are suited to delicate areas such as ears, nose, and armpits. The skin rarely becomes irritated unless pinched, but follicles may bleed and scab, ingrown hairs may occur and hairs may break off rather than pull cleanly away, leaving bristly spots on the skin. Tweezering service was available at Roman baths. Seneca complains of the shrill voice of the hair-plucker at work in the baths below his lodgings, and of the even shriller screams of the customers.[63] Many women pulled out their gray hairs to appear younger—commentators encouraged them to dye their hair rather than go bald. The emperor Augustus once surprised his daughter while her maids were pulling out her gray hairs, and he was not impressed.[64]

Abrasion

Pumice stone was used to scrub off leg and arm hair and to exfoliate the skin.[65] Abrasion is not thorough and shared pumice stones can transmit disease.

Singeing

Some chose to have their hair and beards shaped and unwanted body hair removed by singeing with hot coals, burning walnuts, and, perhaps, overheated metal wands.[66] Singeing "melts" the hair, releasing acrid, choking smoke. The hair should be clean, dry, and unoiled to avoid combustion. Singeing leaves the tips of the hair damaged and frizzy. Skin burns are common.

Shaving

Ancient razors (Figure 4.8) made from bronze, copper, and iron have been identified in many sizes and shapes including lunate, chisel, axe, and knife. The sharpened, leading edge must glide over the body at the precise angle which will slice off the hairs without injuring the skin. It is unknown whether hair and beards were pre-softened with water or oil prior to shaving, or simply shaved dry, without lubrication. Ancient razors were sharpened on whetstones, and many have perforated handles suggesting they were hung when not in use. Some razors were stored in form-fitting sheaths or cases.[67] Shaving is quick and comparatively painless, but harsh, stubbly regrowth appears within hours, necessitating another shave.

Men grew or shaved their beards according to local custom. Celtic men wore mustaches.[68] Athenaeus claims that razors were forbidden in Constantinople for fear of assassins, and that the men of Rhodes were required to wear beards or pay a tax to go clean-shaven.[69] Alexander the Great is said to have made his soldiers shave so that they couldn't be seized by their beards in battle,[70] and from 454 BCE when Varro claims barbers first came to Italy from Sicily,[71] Roman men went clean-shaven until the emperor Hadrian (76–138 CE) popularized beards, a fashion enduring for some centuries afterward.

Head shaving was practiced by Egyptian men, male devotees of the goddess Isis, and inflicted upon slaves, convicts, and peoples conquered by the Scythians.[72] It is unknown

FIGURE 4.8 Bronze razor. Metropolitan Museum of Art, New York, NY. Acc. No. X21.131.

why the hair on the right hemisphere of the head of the bog body "Yde girl" (strangled in the Netherlands in the first century BCE) was shaved off and carefully placed next to her in the peat.[73] By the sixth century CE, Christian monks were partially shaving their heads (tonsure) to signify obedience to the teachings and hierarchy of the church. Some orders shaved the crown of the head, leaving only a narrow wreath of hair (known as the Roman, Saint Paul, or coronal tonsure), others shaved the entire head (Eastern, also Saint Paul tonsure), and still others shaved away a crescent of hair from the front of the head (Celtic or Saint John tonsure).[74]

HAIR CUTTING

Cutting is distinct from shaving, in that the hair is shaped to varying lengths that remain visible on the surface of the scalp. In most ancient cultures, men cut their hair and women didn't (although it is likely that many first-century CE Roman women cut their front hair to conform to the Flavian period fashion of high curly bangs).[75]

Cutting someone's hair without their consent was a grave personal violation;[76] it was routine to cut off the hair of female war captives both to demoralize them and to identify them as slaves. Greek slave women are frequently depicted with hair cut above the shoulders.[77]

Ancient haircuts could be created with either a razor or shears (item 7 in Figure 4.5), or both. In razor cutting, strands of hair are held taut with one hand, while the other hand moves the razor with fluid strokes to cut the hair. Razor cutting tapers the hair ends, resulting in a softer finish. Shears cut strands bluntly. Sheared haircuts have clean, sharp lines—such as those depicted on the colossal bronze head of Constantine I in the Capitoline Museum and in the mosaic portraits of Justinian's court in the church of San Vitale, Ravenna.[78] Before the ninth century CE, shears were constructed from two knife blades connected by a U-spring (*forfex*). As the U-spring is compressed, the blades slide against one another, cutting the material between them. As pressure is released, the blades automatically part. The forfex design is unstable: when overloaded, the blades separate and the material folds between them, warping the spring and potentially damaging the blades. Since the blades are parted when not in use, they are vulnerable to accidental damage.

We know the names of some ancient haircuts: the "bowl-cut"[79] the "Theseïs" (long back hair with a short cut fringe),[80] and "to be scythized" (*aposkuthisthai*) was a rough, poorly shaven head.[81] The "ganymede" style was imposed on slave boys serving at banquets:

> the hair of the head prettily [is] plaited and tightly bound. For they have long thick hair which is not cut at all or else the forelocks only are cut at the tips to make them level and take exactly the figure of a circular line.[82]

This circular line was likely achieved by compressing all the fringe hair to a single point along the nasal axis and cutting it at that position.

Some ancient hairstyles survive nearly intact on bog bodies: "Osterby Man" wore a "Suebian knot," and "Elling woman" a three-strand braided hairstyle.[83]

ORNAMENTS

Women wore hairnets (*sakkos, reticulum*) woven from linen, wool, silk, or gold thread (Figure 4.9), to contain and decorate their hair.[84] Roman girls wove a special yellow hairnet to wear the night before their weddings.[85] Construction techniques included

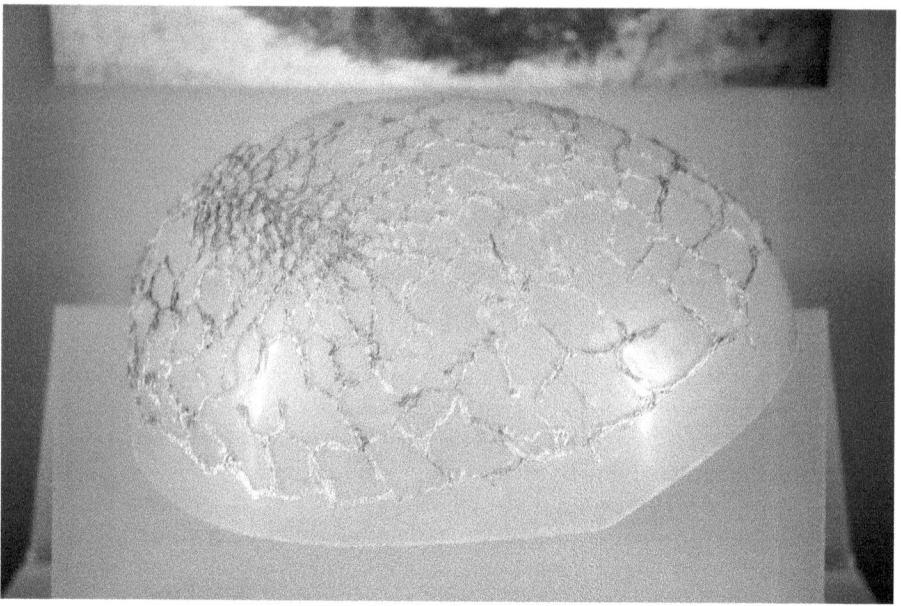

FIGURE 4.9 Gold hairnet, Roman period. Museo Nazionale, Rome. Photo: Heritage Image Partnership Ltd / Alamy Stock Photo.

fish-netting and sprang.[86] Hairnets are depicted in Pompeiian wall paintings and bronze statuary, and survive occasionally in the archaeological record.[87]

Symbolic and decorative hair ornaments are common in both ancient literature and visual arts, particularly garlands and wreaths of leaves, vines, grasses, and flowers, especially roses.[88] Rose garlands depicted on Egyptian cartonnage mummy portraits (Figure 4.10) resemble stacks of ruffled paper, with either the petals removed from their spiny receptacle before stringing, or whole flowers strung so that the receptacles nested in the stigmas of adjacent flowers. *Infulae* (rovings of unspun wool) are depicted wrapped around the heads of gods, such as the Juno Ludovisi[89] and the Vestal Virgin priestesses.[90] Roman brides wore wreaths of aromatic verbena and marjoram.[91] Precious diadems, circlets, and part decorations were also worn.

Turbans kept the head cool or warm, and the hair covered, contained, and clean. They were standard headgear among Bactrians, Persians, Parthians,[92] and eastern kings.[93] The god Dionysius is described wearing a purple turban.[94] In Roman culture, turbans were feminine accessories—men who wore them risked censure and ridicule.[95] Feminine turbans are depicted on Greek ceramics and Syrian funerary portraiture (Figure 4.11).

FALSE HAIR

Men and women wore false hair and wigs, including false eyebrows,[96] to enhance, augment, or cover their natural hair and scalp, thereby gaining temporary color, style, or length changes or to conceal hair loss. Hair for wig-making was taken from slaves and war captives[97] and imported from India.[98] In Rome, false hair vendors kept shop near

PRODUCTION AND PRACTICE

FIGURE 4.10 Roman mummy portrait of a woman with a jeweled garland (ca. 60–70 CE). Metropolitan Museum of Art, New York, NY. Inv. No. 19.2.6. Photo: OASC.

FIGURE 4.11 Syrian style turban in funerary relief of Aththaia, daughter of Malchos, Roman (Palmyra, Syria) (150–200 CE). Museum of Fine Arts, Boston, MA. Funds donated by Edward Perry Warren in memory of his sister. Inv. 22.659. Photo: © 2018 Museum of Fine Arts, Boston.

the temples of Hercules and the Muses.[99] Wigs need close-fitting caps (foundations) to support the false hair. Foundations were made from leather, such as goat skin[100] with primitive wefts[101] of human hair sewn over the surface, or possibly with the goat hair itself substituting for short human hair. Another type was a braided net-work foundation upon which tassels of hair were suspended.[102] Hair tassels and wefts could be permanently curled if wrapped around a terracotta form, then simmered in boiling water for several hours. Some wigs were coated with beeswax and resin, improving durability.[103] Ancient false hair was likely heavy, itchy, bulky, poorly color-matched,[104] and obviously false to sophisticated observers. Egypt, with its dry climate, yields more false hair artifacts than any other region. Of particular note is an early-second-century CE crescent-shaped diadem of human hair braided over a plant fiber core and studded with bronze sphere-headed pins.[105]

Social attitudes towards false hair varied. Although part of the social fabric of Egypt, and necessary to Greek and Roman stagecraft, the wearing of false hair by private individuals in daily life was criticized by Greek, Roman, and early Christian moralists as both deceptive and immoderately vain.[106] Second-century CE Talmud commentators found it necessary to clarify how and whether Jewish women might wear false hair on the Sabbath.[107]

HAIR COLORING

Ancient peoples relied on intuitive and practical knowledge of plants, minerals, and sunlight to cover gray hair, camouflage thinning hair, and to create novel color effects. Ancient hair colorants can be divided into five classes, decolorizers, temporary colors, vegetable stains, permanent metallic dyes, and wishful.

Decolorization is any process that disperses hair's natural melanin pigment. As melanin disperses, a predictable sequence of lightness and color changes occur. Hair colors are defined by two factors, their relative darkness or lightness on a grayscale (*level*) (Figure 4.12) and their color character (*tone*—redness, blueness, yellowness, etc.).

As it lightens, black hair (level 1) displays seven distinct changes in level and tone. Black hair first becomes brown (level 2), then red brown (level 3), red (level 4), red-orange (level 5), orange (level 6), yellow (level 7), and finally pale yellow (level 8). Black

FIGURE 4.12 Natural colors, levels, and corresponding tones of the stages of lightening. © Janet Stephens.

is the only hair color capable of displaying all seven stages of lightening. As lighter natural levels decolorize, they lighten first to the nearest stage above their original grayscale level (e.g. natural medium brown hair [level 3] lightens first to red [level 4] as it proceeds toward pale yellow, but natural dark blonde [level 5] lightens first to orange [level 6]). Decolorization permanently damages hair fiber: it becomes porous and less elastic. In the days before modern chemistry, decolorization was an unpredictable and sometimes dangerous process.[108] Sunlight, the most common decolorizor, imparts variegated warm highlights with the tips of the hair lightest overall.[109] Sunlight also tans the skin. Ancient standards of beauty required women to have pale complexions[110]—those who could, probably limited their sun exposure (for men, tanning was desirable).[111] Alkaline solutions decolorize hair. The cuticle lifts in response to the higher pH, allowing the alkali and free oxygen from water and air to disperse melanin pigment in the cortex. But too high alkalinity can burn the skin and irreparably damage the hair. *Sapo* (aka, *spuma Chattica, spuma Batava, pila Mattiaca*) was a primitive lye soap used by the Gauls, and later the Romans, as a decolorizor which "reddened" the hair.[112] Alkaline natron, ash water and orpiment (lye and toxic arsenic sulfide), Samian earth, and stale urine[113] could all decolorize hair. Inconsistent purity of these materials surely led to inconsistent results. Decolorization is permanent: once lightened, hair cannot re-darken itself. However, hair can be artificially toned by a variety of means.

Temporary colors were pigmented coatings. Romans used tinted opaque ointments to conceal baldness.[114] Gold dust and colored earths were sprinkled onto pomaded hair to make it glitter, change its color, and to conceal gray. Lamp black or antimony were used to darken eyebrows and lash area.[115] Temporary hair colors rubbed off and ran with perspiration or rain, and they removed completely with washing.

Vegetable stains were derived from walnut, elderberries, palm leaves, myrtle berries, and other plants.[116] These would first be boiled in water to release the dye, with or without a mordant such as alum.[117] False hair could be simmered in the dye pot, but not natural hair; desiccated dye material was likely ground to powder then mixed with boiling water to create a hot paste[118] that could be applied to the hair and later rinsed off. Heat opens the cuticle allowing the stain to penetrate deeper into the hair. They could also dab cold, vegetable dye liquid[119] onto the natural hair. Skin and clothing stains, uneven coverage, and unreliable color fastness were common nuisances.

Permanent metallic dyes contain lead, silver, or copper which bind to the sulphur in hair protein resulting in the gradual, permanent darkening of the hair. This could be done by grooming with metal combs, or by applying metal rich liquids to the hair. For example, the toxic, active ingredient lead acetate was the unconscious byproduct of Pliny's hair dye recipe of leeches and vinegar pickled for forty days in a leaden vessel.[120] Over time, metallic dyes make the hair dry, brittle, and dull looking. Poisoning is always a risk.

Wishful hair colorants involve rituals and ineffective materials meant to change or influence hair color, such as applying crushed flies so that light eyebrows will become permanently black[121] or applying raven's eggs to the head for blacker hair[122] or rubbing the ash of earthworms mixed in oil onto the scalp to prevent gray (actually a tinted pomade).[123]

PRACTITIONERS

Gender, class, religion, and patriarchal social mores influenced one's choice of hair care service providers. Some hairstyles could be dressed by the wearer himself, some had to be dressed by another person periodically (e.g. haircutting), or every time (e.g.

very young children). Depictions on pottery and tombs imply that most Greek women dressed their own hair; in the *Iliad*, even the goddess Hera dresses her own hair.[124] Greek men used barbers for hair cutting and shaving. An early-fifth-century Greek (Boiotia) terracotta figure (Figure 4.13) depicts a barber using both hands to guide large forfex shears. Greek sources do not specify whether barbers were freeborn, slaves, or both.

To the Romans, jobs involving the routine care of another's body, were low-status occupations performed by slaves and former slaves.[125] The dominance of slaves in Roman hair care can be inferred by the rule that only freeborn men were permitted to cut the hair of the high priest of Jupiter (*flamen dialis*).[126] Augustine scornfully describes pagan observance, wherein women pantomimed the movements of hairdressing during worship of cult images of Minerva and Juno.[127]

Barbers could be domestic servants, itinerant, or employed in shops catering to an exclusively male clientele.[128] Barbers cut hair, shaved beards, and trimmed nails.[129] Some specialized in thermal curling (*cinerarius*).[130] Apprentice barbers practiced shaving strokes with purposely dulled razors.[131] The skill levels of barbers varied, due to inconsistent oversight, training, personal will, talent, or care.[132] Barbering is a social interaction involving touch, trust, cooperation, and the risk of pain or injury, even

FIGURE 4.13 Barber cutting a man's hair (archaic period, ca. early fifth century BCE), terracotta, Greece (Boiotia, Tanagra). Museum of Fine Arts, Boston, MA. Inv. No. 01.7784. Photo: © 2018 Museum of Fine Arts, Boston.

death by a slit throat[133]—the ancients were keenly aware of this. Conspirators pressured King Herod's barber to assassinate him,[134] and the Greek king Dionysus made his daughters shave him for fear of barbers.[135] A tantalizing literary fragment from Roman mime is a props list for barbershop scenes: "scissors, mirror, bandages"[136]—one should assume these farces made the most of audiences' fears. As discussed above, diffident men opted for depilatories, tweezering, or singeing,[137] and some shaved themselves,[138] but others preferred to save time by having two barbers shave them at once (a feat of coordination).[139]

Only the largest Roman households retained full-time domestic barbers,[140] most men frequented barbershops or received house calls. There were many barbers of both sexes, enslaved and freed.[141] The ability to compare and choose among many service providers reduced the danger inherent in shaving by creating competition for customers. Barbers had an incentive to provide good service and ingratiate themselves, because they might receive tips (*peculium*):[142] with these, slaves could save to buy their freedom. All barbers, regardless of status or nation, were criticized for obsequiousness, garrulousness, and love of gossip.[143]

HAIRDRESSERS

Unlike ancient barbershops, there is no literary, epigraphical, or archaeological evidence of destination, fee-for-service women's hair salons.[144] During the Roman Empire, written sources state that both men and women served the hair care needs of men, and suggest that it was improper for men to dress women's hair.[145] This is prominent in tomb epigraphy: the Latin word "barber" has two genders (i.e. *tonsor*, *tonstrix*), but the Latin for a "woman's hairdresser" is exclusively feminine (*ornatrix*). Many women, especially slaves and the free poor, dressed their own and each other's hair, but "professional" hairdressers (see Figure 8.3) were trained female domestic slaves and freedwomen attendants of rich women. Epigraphic and legal evidence suggests that hairdressers started very young (the *ornatrix* Pieris died at age nine),[146] and that formal training took at least two months.[147] Hairdressers were expected to curl, color, remove, and style hair; apply makeup; and help their mistresses to dress. They also ran errands and acted as go-betweens in love affairs.[148] Physical abuse was inflicted upon all slaves. Literature describes *ornatrices* being whipped, stabbed, bitten, and even killed by their mistresses for trivial failures.[149]

Economic prospects appear to have been better for barbers than hairdressers. Sources imply that barbers enjoyed more frequent manumission, and that some were successful entrepreneurs or received generous testamentary bequests from their patrons. Funerary dedications imply that some barbers had the means to pay for tombs[150] while *ornatrix* tombs were provided by others, suggesting lifelong economic dependency.

CONCLUSION

Ancient peoples took advantage of a wide variety of simple technologies and service providers to fulfill their hair care needs. Ancient sources accurately describe hair phenomena and behavior. The perceived differences between ancient and modern hair care are aesthetic, cultural, political, and technological, *not* biological—hair as a material is unchanged.

CHAPTER FIVE

Health and Hygiene

LYDIA MATTHEWS

Hair played a small, but important role in thinking about health and disease in the ancient world. Medical writers, from the authors of the Hippocratic corpus (collectively our earliest body of Greek prose texts, with some works dating from the fifth century BCE) to Caelius Aurelianus (in the fifth century CE), understood hair as something that could provide clues about a patient's constitution and state of general health. This chapter will first look at the various ways that the physiology of hair and its relationship with the rest of the body was imagined, before examining the medical descriptions of diseases of the hair and of treatments that involve the hair.

THE PHYSIOLOGY OF HAIR

According to Hippocratic author of *On the Nature of the Child*, moisture plays the key role in producing hair.[1] Hair grows where there is moisture and where the epidermis is most porous.[2] The porosity of the flesh is crucial in that it allows for the passage of moisture that is needed for the growth of hair. The author finds proof of this in the fact that hair will not grow on flesh that has been scarred by burns; this flesh is too dense to allow for the growth of hair.[3] The passage of moisture through rarefied flesh is used to explain the new hair that grows at puberty. As the flesh becomes more porous and the small vessels of the body become more open so that seed and menstrual blood can pass through, so too does the epidermis become more rarefied and more moisture passes through, allowing for the growth of hair on the pubes. The growth of the beard is also accounted for by the movement of moisture, this time from the head. Moisture flows down from the head to the chin, increasing the porosity of the flesh there. This happens especially during intercourse, when the bodily fluids are agitated. According to the author, it is for this reason that women are relatively hairless: their fluids are not agitated during intercourse. People who become eunuchs before puberty do not have beards or pubic hair because no passage is formed for the flow of their seed and so their skin remains relatively dense.

The role given to moisture in *On the Nature of the Child* is very similar to that found in the Hippocratic treatise *On Glands*, and in fact the similarities between these two texts are so great that Craik has hypothesized the same author for both works.[4] In *On Glands* the author explains that both glands and hair are closely associated with moisture.[5] He proves that glands are present wherever the flesh is "boggy" (*telmatōdea*) by way of comparison with hair: both glands and hair profit from the body's surplus moisture and so they are both found wherever there is moisture, whereas, neither glands nor hair are to be found in the dry places of the body. While glands channel this excess moisture, the hair uses moisture that is provided from the glands to grow. Therefore hair and glands are to be found in the same areas of the body: near the ears on the upper parts of the neck, in the armpits, and in the groin. These parts form the hollows of the body and therefore moisture is especially liable to collect in them. To explain the absence of hair over the belly despite the profusion of glands in this region, the author of *Glands* 5 expands on the botanical metaphor introduced when he described moist areas as boggy. Hair, it is explained, does not grow in the very moistest areas, like over the intestines, for the same reason that seeds do not geminate in marshes: in marshes moisture overpowers and suffocates seeds just as the excessive moisture of the intestines overpowers hair.

The use of plant growth as a metaphor for the growth of hair in particular is found in later authors, from Aristotle to Galen. The idea that plants take on the quality of their moisture from quality of the moisture in the ground in which they grow can be seen in *On the Nature of the Child* 9 where the author describes the factors that determine hair color: the hair takes on the color of whatever kind of moisture is closest to the skin, white, red, or dark. Hair become gray in old age because when moisture has been in motion for a long time, "the white part separates off and moves towards the skin." The hair, drawing on this white moisture, in turn becomes white.

Moisture also plays a key role in *On Fleshes*.[6] But here, alongside moisture, heat is given a central role.[7] Heat acts on the body to produce its various parts. The "fatty" parts, being also the driest parts, are the most susceptible to the processes of heat—e.g. bones are formed when heat burns up fat.[8] The "gluey" parts are the wettest and coldest and are therefore the least susceptible to heat. Hair is formed in a similar way to joints and nails: when the bones are being formed from fat, that which was gluey could not be burnt up, but instead was thickened into joints and joint fluid, the latter being comprised of the most fluid part of that which was gluey.[9] Nails are formed from the liquid parts of the gluey material that is discharged from the bones and the joints, and this, when heated, dries up to become nails.[10] When it comes to the formation of hair, the author starts first with the hair of the head. The brain, he has already explained, is "the metropolis of the cold and gluey."[11] It is from the brain and the bones (of the skull) that the growth of hair occurs. The exterior of these is gluey and so produces hair.[12] The process by which it does this seems to be imagined as similar to that by which nails are produced: the liquid part of the gluey exterior is dried by heat to become hair. Body hair, especially pubic and armpit hair, is created by the same process: wherever any gluey substance is present it is acted on by heat and becomes hair.[13]

Heat had a very different relationship to hair in *On the Nature of the Child*. In *Diseases* 4, another text by the same author, it has been explained that the head is the "spring" of phlegm in the body.[14] In *On the Nature of the Child* 9 the heating of this phlegm in those that have a tendency towards this type of moisture destroys hair. During intercourse phlegm is agitated and warmed and burns the roots of the hair, leading it to fall out. The immunity of eunuchs to baldness is explained by the fact that they do not experience the violent movement that occurs during intercourse and so their phlegm does not become heated and does not attack the roots of their hair.

For the authors of *On the Nature of the Child* and *Glands* moisture played the key role in hair growth. Moisture was also important in *Fleshes*, but heat was introduced as the force acting on this moisture to produce hair from the gluey substances of the body. Our next two authors to provide physiological theories of hair are not strictly medical, but fit more comfortably into the category of natural philosophy. Plato and Aristotle, the latter especially, present theories of how and why hair is generated. Their explanations have much in common with those of the Hippocratic authors, with the exception that they are less interested in pathological hair growth and its treatment.

For Plato hair was a product of the natural moistness of the head. In the *Timaeus*, Plato explains that it was necessary for the brain to be protected from extreme heat and extreme cold.[15] However, were it to be covered by a large quantity of flesh, then our senses would be dulled. Some other sort of covering was therefore necessary. While protection is the real or final cause of hair, it does not create the necessary physical condition for hair to grow. Therefore Plato's Demiurge, a kind of divine craftsman who imposes order on the kosmos, intervened to create the auxiliary causes for hair, its physiological preconditions. The skin of the head traps the moisture that rises up from the brain, passing through the sutures of the skull. The Demiurge punctured the skin of the head and moisture escaped through these holes. The part of this moisture that was not pure, and which therefore did not simply evaporate, rooted itself in skin, and, having been cooled and constricted by the air, became hair. The thinness of the hair matched the fineness of the holes that the Demiurge had made in the skin of the head.

Like Plato, Aristotle thinks that the final cause of hair is protection. We find this explanation in the section of *Parts of Animals* dealing with eyelashes as an answer to why man is the only animal with eyelashes on both his upper and lower eyelids.[16] Eyelashes and eyebrows protect the eyes: eyebrows are likened to the eaves of a house, protecting the eyes from the fluids that run down from the head; eyelashes are like palisades, keeping things out of the eye.[17] Four-legged animals do not have two sets of eyelashes because, unlike man who goes around upright, they need less protection on the front of their bodies. This is also the reason that animals do not have armpit hair or pubic hair, and instead have thick hair on their backs or manes. Man has the hairiest head of all animals because his brain, being the largest and most fluid of all animals' and therefore the most susceptible to violent changes in temperature, needs more protection from heat and cold.

Aristotle's most detailed description of the growth of hair and the factors affecting it comes in *Generation of Animals*.[18] Here he explains that hair, along with bones and sinews, is created out of the "residues," the surplus nourishment.[19] In particular hair is formed out of the residues of "growth-promoting" nourishment.[20] Nourishment comes in two grades, the first, superior type is called "nutritive" or "seminal"; out of this the sense organs are constructed and this maintains the animal's being.[21] The second "growth-promoting" nourishment is inferior, and is used to add bulk. This nourishment is taken from the mother or from food, and therefore lacks the "soul" that is present in what comes from the father; instead it is earthy in quality.[22] Hair will continue to grow as long as there is residual nourishment, an idea that is used to explain the growth of hair in old age and even after death—the rest of the body does not need to make use of nourishment and so there is more for the hair to use.[23] This brief outline of how hair is formed is followed by a long discussion in book 5 of the factors affecting hair's density, length, degree of curl, hardness, and color as well as the question of baldness.[24] Here, as in the Hippocratic treatise *On Glands*, the forces of heat and cold, dryness and moisture play important roles in the growth of hair and in determining its characteristics.

The thickness of hair is determined by the qualities of the skin: if the skin is loose-knit and thick then the hair growing from it will be thick.[25] This is on account of the size of the passages in the skin, fine passages only permitting fine hair. A further factor contributing to the thickness of the hair is the quality of the fluid present in the skin. If the fluid is greasy then it will not evaporate easily, but if it is watery then it dries very quickly and the hair is unable to become thick. Aristotle explains that this is the reason that the hair is thickest on the head: the skin there is thick loosely knit and it is situated over the very fluid brain.[26] Moisture also has a great effect on the length of the hair: hair becomes long when the moisture is not easily dried off, either because there is a lot of it, or because it is greasy in quality. Again, this accounts for the long hair of the human head—the brain provides fluid in abundance. The same argument is seen in *Parts of Animals*, while the final cause for man's eyelashes, eyebrows, and hairy head in this work was protection, another cause was also offered, that of necessity.[27] A large amount of hair grows on the head because of the fluid nature of the brain, which also has the heat needed to transform this fluid into hair.[28] The sutures of the skull allow this fluid to escape and the eyebrows grow thick in old age because they are placed over one of these joins in the bone.[29]

Two theories are put forward for what determines hair's curliness. The first is that curl is a product of the exhalations of the hair. According to Aristotle, there are two sorts of exhalation: a smoky one that is made up of air and earth, and which is hot and dry; and a watery one, which is cold and moist.[30] Curly hair has a smoky exhalation that causes the hair to bend in different direction: the earthy part of the exhalation forces it downwards, while the hot part pushes it upwards. The second theory that he puts forward is that curly hair does not contain as much moisture as straight hair. This causes the hair to become dry and to contract. He points out that straight things bend if their moisture is drawn off. He offers the differences in the hair of people living in different regions as proof of this theory: the Scythians and Thracians have straight hair because both their constitutions and climates are moist; Ethiopians have curly hair, because both their brains and the air of the region in which they live is dry.

The evaporation of fluid also has an effect on whether hair is soft or hard. Dry things, including hair, are hard. Both cold and heat can have a drying effect. In the case of heat the fluid is evaporated, while in the case of cold the fluid is expelled at the same time as the heat, making both hair and skin become earthy and hard. In particular cold causes compression alongside hardness, whereas heat causes hardness and lightness. Although the fluid of the brain is relatively cool, it still contains some warmth, but as man ages he loses this heat, which is why hair becomes drier and harder in old age. In *History of Animals* temperature was also used to explain why hair in different parts of the body was hard or soft. Hair is hardest in the warm parts, and softest in the cool ones, added to this is the idea that straight hair is soft, while curly hair is hard.[31] Evaporation rather than cooling is the process that hardens the hair of the body. The head, being cooler than the rest of the body therefore has the softest straightest hair, while the drying effects of heat give rise to curly hardness of the body hair.

Some of these theories are picked up by the pseudo-Aristotelian author of the *Problems*, who compares the hard hair of people from the south with the soft hair of those from the north.[32] In the south external heat penetrates deep into the body and evaporates off the concocted nourishment. This is also used to explain why some groups of people have curly hair. The author of *Problems* (909a.28–32) poses the question "why are Ethiopians and Egyptians bowlegged?" His answer is that their bones have been bent by being dried, just as planks warp when they dry. Proof of this theory is to be found in the curliness of their hair—this part has also been bent by being dried.

Cooling is also the main factor that causes baldness, a condition that Aristotle notes is uniquely pronounced in humans. Animals and plants shed their growth seasonally, but in humans it is "the seasons of life which play the part of summer and winter."[33] Cooling is itself a product of sexual intercourse—men expel their "pure natural" heat in their semen. This is the reason that men don't go bald before the time of sexual maturity. The cooling effects of intercourse are felt first around the brain, the coldest part of the body where the most fluid is to be found. This is the reason that men go bald at the front of their heads (Aristotle believes that the back part of the head does not contain any brain). The brains of humans, being by far the largest of any animals, produces the greatest cold. Women, children, and eunuchs are immune from baldness because they do not produce semen and are therefore not cooled when they expel it. As for the hair that grows during puberty, he claims that eunuchs either do not grow it, or if they already have it, it falls out. The only androgenic hair that eunuchs keep and that women grow is pubic hair, although in *History of Animals* (518b.1–2) he does admit that women have these later growths of hair, but just on a lesser scale to men. Aristotle calls this absence of hair a "maiming" because it is a change from the masculine to the feminine.[34]

The connection between hair and semen is explained more clearly when Aristotle discusses the hairiness of the hare, the only animal to have hair under the feet and inside the mouth. For Aristotle this characteristic is linked to the fact that the hare is abundant in semen (*spermatikos*).[35] The same is true in humans; hairy men are more abundant in semen and more inclined to sexual intercourse. Both hairiness and seminality is a product of abundant residue. Residues, concocted by bodily heat, become a variety of useful things, including semen and hair. How then are we to understand the reference in *Generation of Animals* (783b.37) to the idea that men who are *spermatikos* are also very prone to going bald? The reason seems to be that hairy *spermatikoi* loose more heat than other men because they expel more semen. This leads them to become cooler than the norm, and so produces baldness.[36]

The final characteristic of hair that Aristotle discusses in *Generation of Animals* (784a.24ff) is color.[37] In animals, hair color is determined by skin color. However, this is not the case in humans: very fair skinned people can have very dark hair. The reason for this difference is that, proportional to his size, man has the thinnest skin of any animal, and the skin therefore does not have the power to affect the color of the hair, which can be any shade between black and white.[38] Most of the discussion in this section is dedicated to discussing the causes of graying: like baldness, grayness is associated with the cooling that occurs in old age. Aristotle argues against unnamed authorities who claim that grayness is caused by the withering of the hair, and notes that gray hair grows out gray, rather than going gray from the tip, as proof against this theory. Instead, he contends, graying is caused by putrefaction (*sepsis*).[39] When nourishment reaches each part of the body it is concocted by heat, but as the body cools, it loses the ability to do this.[40] Hair, because of its nature and situation, already contains very little heat, while the amount of fluid that surrounds it is very abundant. When this fluid cannot be concocted it putrefies. White is the color of putrefaction, as seen by the fact that mold is white. Graying first takes place at the temples because it has neither too little nor too much fluid: beneath the front and top of the head is a large volume of fluid and large amounts of fluid are more slower to putrefy; there is no fluid at the back of the head because there is no brain there.

We find a different account of hair color in the pseudo-Aristotelian treatise *On Colours*. The author of this text attributes hair color to three main causes: skin color, men who have a ruddy complexion have pale red hair; nourishment, hair grows darker as a child becomes older because more nourishment flows into it and it is colored by this; and moisture, when moisture dries off hair becomes paler.[41] These three factors are closely related to each other, as well as to heat. Hair and skin are dyed by the nourishment-rich moisture of the body. As in genuine Aristotelian writings, heat also plays an important role in this process because it concocts the nourishment.[42] However, in this text white hair is not associated with putrefaction, but rather with a lack of moisture and nourishment.[43] Hair is palest furthest from its root because less nourishment reaches it and so it dries out more quickly. Likewise, people go gray in old age when nourishment fails to reach the hair and it dries up.[44] The explanations for the whitening of the hair with age that the author of *On Colours* offers are very much of the sort that Aristotle argues against in *Generation of Animals* (785a.28), when he criticizes those who think that grayness is a form of withering. Despite this difference, we can still see clear similarities with Aristotle, most notably the role of heat and nourishment, as well as the importance of moisture. Moreover, the idea that the color of the skin is related to hair color has already been seen in *Generation of Animals*;[45] for Aristotle this is only true of animals, while the author of *On Colours* also extends this to humans.

Our next source to discuss the growth of hair in detail comes half a millennium after Aristotle. Galen's *The Art of Medicine* and *On the Usefulness of the Parts* show the influence of both Hippocratic and Aristotelian theories of hair growth. Galen follows the Aristotelian idea that hair serves two purposes. On the one hand hair is created out of residues and the body uses hair as a way of getting rid of these.[46] This idea is similar to that seen in Aristotle's *Parts of Animals* (658b.4) where the necessary cause of hair was the moisture of the brain and the heat of the body. For Aristotle the final cause of the hair was protection; Galen also emphasizes this, but he adds ornamentation alongside this.

In *On the Usefulness of the Parts* Galen works his way through a teleological explanation of the protective and decorative functions of various types of hair, explaining the technical ways that the creator, akin to the Demiurge of the *Timaeus*, ensured that it would perform these roles properly.[47] Galen's main example of the protective function of hair is the eyelashes, and he follows Aristotle in comparing them to palisades that keep things out of the eyes.[48] However, he is more interested than Aristotle was in explaining how they are designed to do this, and in so doing displays his anatomical knowledge. For the eyelashes to keep things out they need to stand erect and stiff, they shouldn't turn up (or else they would lose their usefulness) or down (as they would hurt the eyes). Even the spaces in between them is useful—if further apart they wouldn't keep small objects out of the eye, if closer together they would shade the eyes too much.[49] Galen's Creator does not simply command the eyelashes to grow in a certain way; rather he ensures that they do through careful design. For this reason the tarsus, a hard membranous body, lies underneath the eyelashes that keeps them upright. The tarsus also helps to limit the growth of the eyelashes, keeping them at their constant, useful, length.[50]

Galen uses the Hippocratic analogy of hair and plant growth to prove the Creator's role in determining how and where hair grows: flesh is like earth; hair is like the plants growing in it.[51] Just as plants growing in dry rocky soil do not grow very tall, so the hair of eyebrows and eyelashes is kept short because of the hard tarsus and bone underneath that limits the growth. Hair growing on the soft moist parts of the body (the hair of the head, armpits, and pubic region) is like plants growing in rich damp soil; it has good thick growth. However, not all hair growth is specifically ordained by the Creator and some hair, in particular armpit hair, simply arises because of the warmth and moisture present in some parts of the body. He proves this with another horticultural analogy: some hair grows like plants in a field laid down by a farmer, in straight lines, with well-defined borders. Other hair grows thick and irregular, with no defined border. Armpit hair is like spontaneous plant growth in warm moist soil—no farmer sowed it, but the nature of the place allowed for its growth. On the other hand, the hair of the eyebrows, eyelashes, and head shows the hand of the Creator because it grows within well-defined boundaries.

Aside from the utility of the eyelashes, Galen also explains the causes and usefulness of head hair, eyebrows, beards, and pubic hair. Like eyelashes, the eyebrows protect the eyes, catching anything that flows down from the head. Both men and women require the protection and ornamentation that head hair provides. Beards, on the other hand, are particular to men; they protect a man's face from cold and ornament him, making him look stately. Women lack beards because they are not as dignified as men therefore do not need as stately a form. Likewise, they do not need protection from cold because they spend their time indoors. The pubic hair provides an ornament and covering for the genitals. Aside from the causes of protection and ornamentation there are also causes from necessity for beards, head hair, and pubic hair. In the case of the beard, exhalations of the humors rise to the head and the body eliminates these residues by using them to nurture hair; men, being hotter than women, have more residues and therefore more hair. In the case of head hair, it absorbs the excess moisture of the head, so preventing it from harming the underlying parts of the head. Pubic hair arises from the warm moisture of the pubic region. Galen notes that in each of these cases the Creator ensured that the sorts of causes (necessity and protection and ornamentation) worked together: useful hair is created where hair would also grow by necessity.

In *On the Usefulness of the Parts* warmth and moisture play a role in promoting hair growth: warm moist constitutions and parts of the body produce more hair than cold dry ones. The role of these three forces is laid out in more detail in *The Art of Medicine*. For Galen health and disease are defined in terms of balance and imbalance (*eukrasia* and *dyskrasia*) of four qualities.[52] In a healthy body the qualities of heat, cold, moisture, and dryness must be combined in balance.[53] These qualities are in turn related to the four humors: blood, phlegm, yellow bile, and black bile. The organs of the body are divided into four main types: the principal parts (brain, heart, liver, and testicles), whose actions determine the character of the regions around them; those growing out of the governing principal parts and serving them; those parts that are entirely self-governing; and those that govern themselves but need nerves, arteries, and veins. In addition to these four types of part there is a fifth type, made up of hair and nails. These are unlike the other parts in that they neither govern themselves nor are governed by any other part: the genesis of hair and nails is determined by the parts of the body from which they grow, but that is all.[54]

The hair of the head is therefore very useful in diagnosing *dyskrasiai* of the brain, the principal part lying closest to it, and determining its genesis. In *The Art of Medicine* (323K–329K) Galen explains the signs or balance or imbalance relating to the head. He begins with signs of *eukrasia*, then moves on to simple *dyskrasiai* (too hot, too cold, too dry, too moist), before explaining the more complex *dyskrasiai* (combinations of hot and dry, hot and moist, cold and dry, and cold and moist). Each *dyskrasia* is characterized by a type of hair growth that differs from that seen in eukratic constitutions: in such people "the hair is reddish in infants, light blonde in children, and becomes fair in those reaching maturity. It is somewhere between curly and completely straight, and people do not readily become bald."[55]

Signs of the simple *dyskrasiai* are detectable from a variety of symptoms: the color and quality of their hair, the quality and quantity of the patient's sleep, the acuity of their senses, the sorts of illnesses they are prone to, and the amount and quality of the residues produced by the eyes, nose, ears, and mouth. In the case of patients who are hotter than the norm, the hair on their head grows quickly and is black.[56] The hotter they are the more quickly their hair becomes black. The hot are also more liable to become bald, and the hotter they are the quicker this happens. Those that are colder than the norm have straight, red hair that does not fall out. Their hair only begins growing a long time after birth and even then it is thin and weak.[57] Signs of a drier than usual head are strong curly hair that grows very quickly after birth. Like the hot, the dry become bald quickly.[58] Moist constitutions have hair that is straight and permanent.[59] Complex *dyskrasiai* also produce signs of themselves in the hair and in other parts of the head. Hot dry constitutions go bald very quickly, although at first they produced black curly hair quickly and vigorously.[60] Those that are a little moister and hotter than the ideal have straight brown hair, and don't go bald easily.[61] The cold and dry go gray quickly and their perceptive abilities are generally weak as are the other qualities of their heads.[62] They do not produce hair easily, and the hair that they do produce is thin and red. They are protected against baldness by the cold, but if they are drier than they are cold then they do go bald. Those who are moist and cold do not go bald.[63]

The effects of the four elemental qualities of heat, cold, dryness, and moisture also pertain to the rest of the body, especially the principal parts. So, for example, a hot liver produces lots of hair over the hypochondrium and abdomen, and hot testes encourage the rapid growth of pubic hair.[64] A cold liver produces a hypochondrium and abdomen that are free of hair, and cold testes likewise discourage hair growth. Galen eulogizes the well-balanced constitution, which is neither too hot nor too cold, not too dry or too moist. Such constitutions produce hair that is moderately fair and somewhat curly. It is neither too bare nor too hairy, but perfectly balanced between the extremes.[65]

In *The Art of Medicine* Galen had focused on the effect that the elemental qualities had on hair growth, leaving the precise role of the different humors somewhat obscure. But in *Method of Medicine*, where he treats baldness and varieties of pathological hair loss, the humors come to the fore.[66] He starts off by cross-referencing the explanation of the genesis of hair that he had provided "in the physiological books." This would seem to be a reference to the explanation found in *On the Usefulness of the Parts* of how hair is produced from bodily residues.[67] In *Method of Medicine* hair is produced out of the "transpired humors." This moisture nourishes the hair, and when its supply is disrupted or when its quality is affected then hair does not grow. The sort of baldness that is caused by old age is due to a lack of the moisture that nourishes the hair; alopecias and conditions such as the loss of the eyelashes occur when the moisture has become bad in some way. Alopecias and other pathological hair loss seem to be caused by an imbalance in the humors, and it is possible to diagnose this by looking at the skin in the affected area. The skin takes on qualities of the underlying humors: for example, if the skin looks yellow then you need to purge yellow bile; if it is whiter than normal then you need to purge the phlegmatic humors.

It is worth comparing Galen's model with Aristotle. According to both Galen and Aristotle, heat produces hair. For Galen, people who are hotter than the norm grow thick dark hair quickly and the same is true for those who are drier than the norm. The cool and the moist grow hair more slowly and their hair is straighter and fairer than that of the hot and dry. However, those with hot and dry constitutions are paradoxically more prone to baldness. This recalls the Aristotelian idea, discussed above, that those who are hotter, who have more abundant semen, and who concoct more residues through their heat are at once hairier and yet more prone to baldness. For Aristotle this is because such individuals expel more heat through their semen and so end up cooler than they would otherwise be. Galen's reasoning is more difficult to discern, but it seems to be the case that in hot dry constitutions the moisture needed to nourish the hair is lacking because it is burnt off or dried up.

In Macrobius we see how these theories about hair percolated beyond strictly medical and philosophical texts. Macrobius' *Saturnalia*, written in the fifth century CE and taking the form of dialogue, is an encyclopedic compilation, drawing on the works of mostly unnamed authors from a variety of disciplines.[68] In book 6, two of his more elderly characters, Eusebius and Dysarius, discuss hair after Eusebius asks why it is that Homer talks specifically of old men who are "gray at the temples."[69] Dysarius, we are told, was the foremost doctor of his day in Rome, and is probably to be identified with a doctor of the same name mentioned in a letter of Symmachus from around the last decade of fourth century CE.[70] In response to Eusebius' questions, Dysarius sets out a theory of hair growth that has a good deal in common with the other sources discussed in this chapter. Like the Hippocratic author of *On the Nature of the Child*, he believes that hair grows more easily where the body is porous, and like Aristotle in *Parts of Animals*, he sees the sutures of the skull as one of the passages that moisture takes from the brain to the hair.[71] Aristotle explains in *Generation of Animals* that the front of the head is naturally moister than the back and that this is the reason men first go gray at the temples and Dysarius echoes this opinion.[72] Dysarius also agrees with Aristotle in thinking that the coolness of this fluid is key to graying.[73] However, he does not attribute the color to putrefaction as Aristotle did, but rather to the color of the cool moisture that the hair takes on. Dysarius explains people who have thin hair, nourished by an abundance of cool white phlegm, do not go bald easily, but their hair does take the color of this humor and so they go gray easily. Conversely, people who have dark curly hair have a drier constitution and do not go gray quickly as the phlegm does not discolor their hair. Phlegm is particularly abundant in old age. These ideas are reminiscent of Galen's in *Method of Medicine* where people with dry constitutions also had curly hair, where an unnatural abundance of the humors discolored the skin, with phlegm making it white.[74] Dysarius explains baldness as a product of dryness, and like Galen he thinks that those who are dry and curly-haired go bald more quickly.[75] Old age is particularly associated with baldness because in old age the life-giving humors dry up and so there is nothing to nourish the hair. It is also associated with coldness as the vital heat is extinguished. However, while the good humors dry up in old age, there is a superabundance of other, chillier sorts of humors: old age is only dry in regard to the good humors, not to the bad ones, and these humors have a detrimental effect on the growth of hair.

DISEASES AND TREATMENTS

Outside these physiological discussions, medical authors tend to view hair as a tool for prognosis or as something to be cut or shaved off before other treatments can be applied to the head. Because the various medical traditions tended to view the characteristics of the hair as reflecting the constitution of the patient more generally, very few medical interventions are focused on the hair itself. Instead, hair is understood as one of the things that informs the physician about the state of the patient's health. So the Hippocratic author of *Epidemics* 4 tells us that hair is one of the sources of knowledge for a physician, and in *Epidemics* 6 the reader is told to observe whether hair growth occurs earlier or later than appropriate, or whether the hair is defective in some way.[76]

We are presented with just such case of pathological hair growth later in *Epidemics* 6, when Phaethousa, the wife of Pytheas, stops menstruating after her husband has been exiled.[77] After her menses stopped she developed pain and reddening in her joints, her body became masculinized and grew hairy all over, she also grew a beard, and her voice grew harsh. The doctors try to cure her by attempting to bring on her menses, but they are unable to do so and she dies. Phaethousa's unusual hair growth is one of the symptoms of her illness, but its cause is her failure to menstruate.[78] The author does not explain why it is that suppressed menses should give rise to excess body hair, but there is some suggestion that temperature plays a role: Phaethousa's joints grow red and this may suggest increased heat.[79] Whatever the exact mechanism that is imagined here, it is clear that Phaethousa's hair growth is seen as a symptom of her disease and it reflects the central problem of her illness. For a woman to be healthy in the Hippocratic tradition she must regularly expel excess moisture through menstruation; Phaethousa's inability to do this has repercussions for her body as healthily feminine.[80] Her symptoms therefore all display her ailing femininity and as she becomes sicker so she becomes more masculine, with a deeper voice, possibly a hotter constitution, and a hairy body and face.

Likewise, the discussion of the qualities of hair that we found in Galen's *Art of Medicine* is primarily intended as a tool for diagnosing *dyskrasiai*. Hair growing in the region of any of the principal parts tells you about the balance of qualities in that part, while the hair of the body as a whole provides information about the overall balance.[81] For Galen, hair is not important for its own sake but rather acts as a tool for knowing what sorts of illness a patient is susceptible to because of their constitution. So, for example, it is worth knowing that straight reddish hair, which doesn't fall out, is characteristic of a cold *dyskrasia* of the head because it tells you that such patients are particularly liable to being harmed by cold and are prone to catarrh and coryza.[82]

When it comes to treating illness, hair is often seen as an obstacle to treatment that needs to be got rid of. Galen tells us in *Method of Medicine* that when applying medicine to the head it needs to penetrate deeply into this part if the drug is to achieve its greatest potency. For this reason he recommends cutting or shaving the hair, before rubbing the surface of the scalp.[83] Cupping and bloodletting performed on the head, or any especially hairy part of the body, also necessitated shaving as a precursor. Galen, when prescribing arteriotomy as a way of getting rid of blood that is hot and full of air and which has traveled to the head, recommends carefully shaving the head as the first step.[84]

Hair plays a larger role in Methodist therapies than in Galen or Hippocratic treatments. Doctors from the Methodist school of medicine, which flourished in the first century CE, believed that diseases could be classified and treated according to sets of common features (*communia, koinotētes*): looseness (*status laxus*), constriction (*status strictus*), and mixed (*status mixtus*).[85] The pores, small openings between the atoms of the body, could become too loose and open or too constricted, or they could be subject to a mixture of stricture and looseness. Treatment consisted of making looser that which was too constricted and vice versa.[86] In order to achieve this two main cycles of therapy are prescribed by Methodist physicians: the first aimed at building up the patient's strength in preparation for the metasyncritic cycle which alters the make-up of the patient's body.[87]

According to the therapies described by Caelius Aurelianus, a Latin translator of Soranus, our main sources for Methodist medicine, cutting the hair or shaving the head could play a role in both recuperative and metasyncritic treatment. Caelius describes how it is necessary to shave the hair to apply the astringent, constricting remedies necessary to treat flux (a disease of looseness), but notes that in general hair cutting has a relaxing, loosening effect.[88] In his description of the treatment for chronic headache, Caelius also describes how hair cutting causes "emptiness of the pores" and facilitates "a kind of evaporation from the deeper parts."[89]

This idea seems to go back to Asclepiades of Bithynia, a medical writer of the early first century BCE whose general principle of disease as caused by blockages and congestion of the pores of the body was very influential on later Methodist theory.[90] In fact, the longest passage of Caelius Aurelianus' to treat the role of hair cutting is given in response to Asclepiades. The disease in question is phrenitis. Caelius reports that in book 1 of his *Acute Diseases* Asclepiades defines phrenitis as "a stoppage or obstruction of the corpuscles in the membranes of the brain."[91] Asclepiades, he says, thinks that cutting the hair is very dangerous in cases of phrenitis because it stimulates bodily fluids. This causes fluids to rise to the head producing constriction in the head. When the hair is cut, matter is attracted upwards and the pores and hair grow thicker and stronger. It is for this reason, according to Asclepiades, that even healthy people sometimes get a cough, catarrh, or inflamed eyes if they cut their hair just after eating—this presumably being the time when there is most matter that can rise to the head and cause congestion.[92]

Caelius, however, disagrees with Asclepiades' complete ban on hair cutting, as he does with the idea that phrenitis is caused by a stoppage.[93] It is not hair cutting per se that is the problem, but hair cutting at the wrong time. Caelius agrees that even the healthy get sick when their hair is cut after eating, but he says it is fine to do this before eating. Although in most cases the benefit of cutting the phrenitic patient's hair is only so that you can apply remedies directly to the head, in cases where the phrenitis is caused by stricture Caelius recommends shaving their head. This, he says, allows "the parts [to] breathe freely again."[94]

It is not immediately clear what the precise physiological theory is that underlies these treatments, however it may help to summarize what we have learned about Methodist theories of hair: hair cutting has a loosening effect; it allows the head to breathe freely; it empties the pores and allows for evaporation; to ensure that it doesn't cause blockage it is best done before eating. We can add to this the idea that a haircut at the wrong point in treatment for epilepsy robs the patient of their strength.[95] We can therefore hypothesize that at least for Soranus and Caelius Aurelianus hair is imagined as being produced out of the nutrition of the body when it is drawn up towards the head. When the hair is removed matter can evaporate out of the pores, emptying them. But it can cause the patient to lose strength, especially if they are ill, but even if they are well, as we see when Caelius recommends that even those who are healthy should cover their heads with wool after a haircut.[96]

Caelius Aurelianus' translation of Soranus' *On Chronic Diseases* also preserves our most detailed account of a disease called phthiriasis, characterized by infestation of lice.[97] A modern reader might justifiably expect that medical descriptions of lice and treatments for infestations of this parasite would focus on hair. It seems safe to assume that lice was a widespread problem in antiquity: ancient encyclopedists, like Pliny the Elder and Celsus record various treatments for lice, and pubic lice have even been found preserved in sediments from Roman Britain.[98] However, by and large ancient medical writers do not see lice as a problem of the hair specifically, but of the whole body.

According to Aristotle lice are born out of flesh, just as fleas are produced from rotting matter, and bugs (κόρεις) from "the moisture from living animals as it congeals outside them."[99] The lice emerge from small eruptions on the skin, and can be deadly. Aristotle recounts the rumors that the poet Alkman was killed by this disease. Lice then are not a parasite, but a product of a person's own body. For this reason infestations of lice are closely tied to one's state of health: those who are very moist are prone to it, and women and children have lousier heads than men.[100] This theory of how lice are generated is ubiquitous in Greek and Roman texts from Aristotle onwards, and the disease they cause is commonly called phthiriasis.[101] Pliny the Elder, recounting how Sulla the dictator was killed by phthiriasis, explains that the lice are born from the blood of the patient and consume his flesh.[102] Celsus seems to associate the beginnings of phthiriasis with the eyelashes, and lice are born from between the eyelashes. Like Aristotle, he thinks that this disease is caused by a more general state of ill-health.[103]

Caelius, devoting an entire chapter to phthiriasis, explains that this name does not refer to any specific sort of lice, but rather to the number of lice present; both lice of the normal sort and a broader, harder, and fiercer biting sort may be involved.[104] It develops when a patient is in a generally run-down state (*cachexia* in Greek and *mala habitudo* in Latin). In some cases the lice may cover the whole body, sometimes they are found just in the parts covered by hair. The symptoms that he lists (apart from the lice themselves one presumes) are itching, sleeplessness, loss of appetite, weakness of the esophagus, and loss of hair. Phthiriasis, he explains, is characterized by a state of looseness. Reddish bile is emitted from the pores of the body and it is out of this that lice are born. Treatment involves shaving off all hair, using pitch plasters, and various astringent remedies to counteract the looseness of the disease.

The way infestations of lice are understood in these texts seem so strange to a modern reader mostly because of the difference between ancient and modern conceptions of disease and illness. While modern ideas of disease tend to focus on contagion, ancient medical authors are more interested in the balance of each patient's constitution, how this interacts with their environment, and how it is affected by their diet and behavior. Therefore, when treating phthiriasis, it is not simply enough to eliminate the parasites, but to remedy what made the patient susceptible to the disease in the first place. For the same reason Caelius is not particularly interested in distinguishing between different species of lice: it is not the type of lice that matters, but the constitution of the patient.

CONCLUSION

The way hair grows and its characteristics, as well as diseases affecting it, all provide knowledge about the hidden depths of the patient. In medical texts this information tends to be about the balance of different forces within the body, heat and cold, dryness and moisture, or looseness and constriction. Depending on the source, these forces also determine the character of a person. For example we can think back to the Aristotelian idea that hairy men have more abundant semen and are more inclined to sexual intercourse.[105] Galen is very explicit in *Art of Medicine* about the link between different dispositions and hair growth and the simple and complex *dyskrasiai* are linked to specific traits: for example, people who have thick, curly, black hair which grows quickly are hotter than the norm and do not require much sleep, and when they do sleep they do so only lightly.[106] For Galen the balance of forces in the heart was particularly important in determining character and chest hair was therefore particularly informative. For example, he explains that if the heart is colder and moister than normal then the pulse is soft and the character of the patient is cowardly, timorous, hesitant, and they are not easily angered. Such people also lack hair on their sternum.[107] For medical authors, just as hair can tell you about a patient's physical constitution, it can also tell you about their moral constitution.

CHAPTER SIX

Gender and Sexuality

MARY HARLOW

THE PERFORMANCE OF GENDER—ARTICULATION AND AMBIGUITIES

As the reader of this volume will have gathered, the political and social world of antiquity was highly gendered in the sense that particular roles were marked out for each sex, and gendered behavior was fenced by tradition, social and cultural practice, and law. In both Greece and Rome the dominant role of the male was taken for granted and deemed one of the natural laws of society. Thus, one of the problems with examining the world of antiquity is the complete dominance of the male point of view and the privileging of that view in almost all of the available sources: it was men who did most of the writing and most of the commissioning of artworks. This is not to say that women were not educated or articulate, evidence suggests they could be and were both, it is rather that their opinions are muted or come down to us through the prism of a male-centered context.

In terms of understanding the body and its functions, ancient writers started with the presumption of male dominance and superiority. Although they gave an important role to the female, focused on the necessity of reproduction, it was a secondary and subordinate role. The inability of women to take ruling positions in society was explained by their deficient biology. The very nature of male and female bodies was thought to be intrinsically different, the one with the power to generate another human being, the other to gestate and nurture it. One of the earliest articulations of the workings of the human body is found in the collective of works known as the Hippocratic corpus. In the Hippocratics, the female body is differentiated from the male by its more spongy, porous, and fluid consistency. Women regulate their moisture levels partly through regular menstruation and/or pregnancy. Men were generally considered hotter and drier than women. Hair was the product of moisture and semen and it grew on the head because semen was stored in the brain, and the skin of the scalp is most "rarified."[1] In this explanation, both men and women produce seed, but the female seed is weaker. This weakness also explains the lack of body hair for women. Secondary hair grows at puberty as other parts of the body become more porous. Male body hair is the result of moisture passing from the head, down through the chin and the chest, particularly at times of sexual intercourse. The agitation of sperm and increased heat that accompanies the male during intercourse is also why men, and not women, become bald. The heat generated in the scalp was thought to burn off the roots of the hair. Women, generally thought to be less active and their semen less agitated, particularly during sex, do not develop chest hair, but the pubic region is more moist to encourage pregnancy, thus also encouraging hair growth.

In the fourth century BCE, Aristotle, operating within a similar cultural field, developed a rather different idea about the body. He was convinced that male and female were similar in form, but that the deficient heat of the female resulted in her not being able to generate—the primary male activity. Aristotle accounted for the difference in the male and female body in terms of this deficiency: a female was the product of insufficient concoction in the womb; women were thus "failed men."[2] His theory of generation hinged on the principle that only the male had the power of creation, and this position justified and legitimated many other sorts of relationships wherein the standard by which all activity was measured was that of the adult citizen male. Females, and also young males, and by implication all noncitizen or unfree males, were judged by their failure to meet this standard. For Aristotle, hair growth was also linked to moisture and heat. Hair grows on the head because that is the most moist part of the body, and pubic hair begins to grow at the time of life when the production of seminal fluid made the genital area more moist and the flesh in that part of the body less firm.[3] Aristotle explains that hair growth is closely associated with the ability to produce heat and moisture through blood and semen and various stages in the life course at which the male heats up or cools down affect hair growth.[4] The arrival of facial, body, and pubic hair signals the heating of the body during puberty, and explains why "no one goes bald before the time of sexual intercourse."[5] For him baldness is caused by the loss of heat caused by sexual intercourse and as the head and brain are by nature the coldest parts of the body, they are the first to feel the effect of heat loss. Women, on the other hand, do not go bald "because their nature is similar to that of children: both are incapable of producing seminal secretion" he goes on to explain that:

> Eunuchs too, do not go bald, because of their transition into the female state, and that hair that comes at a later stage they fail to grow at all, of if they already have it, they lose it, except for pubic hair: similarly women do not have the later hair, though they do grow the pubic hair. This deformity constitutes a change from the male state to the female.[6]

Women, like other "failed" men, do not have the requisite heat to produce secondary hair, particularly facial and body hair. Gray hair is explained in a similar way, as a result of the loss of heat which comes with age.[7]

Although the social and political climate was much altered between fourth-century BCE Athens and second-century CE Rome, medical assumptions about how the body worked were still subject to social and cultural coding. Galen, one of the most influential "doctors" operating in the imperial period, was also Greek. He offered a critique of both the Hippocratic and Aristotelian treatises of the body, demonstrating their continued influence into the Roman period.[8] He refined Aristotle's view of the male and female body and reinforced what Thomas Laqueur has called "the one-sex body": the idea that male and female essentially possessed the same physiology, and that female genitalia were an internal version of male genitalia. The internal version being inferior to the ideal, external male version.[9] This inferiority was again the result of the female being inferior in terms of heat, and like Aristotle, Galen viewed women as "mutilated."[10] There was a positive side to this mutilation, however, in the essential role of women in procreation. The Hippocratics, Aristotle and Galen, might differ in their assessment of the reasons for female inferiority but their ideas reinforced and, indeed, informed notions of gender roles and behavior at a very fundamental, physical and physiological level. The reason I have elucidated this position at some length is twofold: the ancients' understanding of the biological and physiological nature of hair is predicated on their understanding of the body and the role of heat or lack of it; and, significantly, these theories revolve around a series of conceptual oppositions that were held to be logically and naturally correct: male/female; hot/cold; strong/weak; powerful/powerless. The astute reader of this volume will have noted that male and female hair and hair behavior often stand in opposition to each other in antiquity, and this opposition forms part of the wider gender play of the period.

Such notions of male power in terms of the ability to generate, and the idea that women are in some way biologically disabled or inferior fed into and informed attitudes about normative social roles and behavior. Women were thought to have a natural affinity with matters domestic and with childcare, where men were creatures of the public, political, and military realms. Men were active initiators of events, both large and small, while women were ideally passive in their responses.[11] Ideals, however, are often countered and contradicted by realities, and the realities of the lived world are never quite so clear-cut as male source material might imply. In both classical and postclassical Greece, and Rome, for instance, some women wielded a great deal more social and economic power, and in certain moments, also political power, than male-centered sources might lead us to believe.[12]

Hair undoubtedly worked as a marker of gender throughout the period, but the way it played was neither constant nor static. One rule of thumb, might be, however, that whatever the ideal or normative type of hairstyle for men, women wore the opposite.[13] Even this, however, is not a rule without exceptions. As this volume repeatedly demonstrates, hair length and style were also markers of age in the ancient world, and changes in the way hair was worn, as well as the growth of secondary hair, often marked changes in the life course. In archaic and classical Athens and in Rome, children, both boys and girls, usually wore their hair long and as they grew it was progressively controlled, either by cutting it short or by binding, braiding, or covering.[14]

Ancient Greek culture made a link between hair, age, and emerging sexuality for both boys and girls. In archaic and classical Athens and Sparta it was common and accepted practice among citizens for older men to engage in sexual relations with adolescent boys. These relationships were intended to train the young men and could encompass a series of "courtship rituals" such as gift-giving, education, and guidance, including instruction on how to behave in the adult world. The relationship was asymmetrical, with the older lover (*erastês*) taking the active part in any sexual activity with the younger partner (*erômenos*).[15] The age and suitability of the youth was defined partly by his stage of physiological and biological development, identified by the presence, or lack of, secondary hair. The beginnings of the growth of facial hair is seen as particularly attractive and is associated with the commencement of adult intellect. In Plato's *Symposium*, Pausanias comments that "they love boys only when they begin to acquire some mind—a growth associated with that of down on their chins."[16] The youth on the cusp of manhood becomes eroticized, but the period of playing the *erômenos* is relatively short. It might start with the appearance of the first fuzz of facial hair, but it must end when the young man is socially considered an adult, and certainly by the time he has a full beard (Figure 6.1).

A series of epigrams which survive from the Hellenistic period and later are evidence that this practice continued into Roman times, and that the arrival of facial and bodily hair defined the status of the youth, and eventually put him outside the acceptable group for lovers. Many of these short epigrams express regret over the passing of time or missing the moment when a youth would be available to become *erômenos*.

FIGURE 6.1 Older man titillating younger man. Brygos painter (500–475 BCE). © Ashmolean Museum, Oxford, 1967. 304.

> When you were pretty, Archestratus, and the hearts of the young men were burnt for your wine-red cheeks, there was no talk of friendship with me, but in sporting with others you spoilt your prime like a rose. Now, however, when you begin to blacken with horrid hair, you would force me to be your friend, offering me the straw after giving the harvest to others.[17]

> Your leg, Nicander, is getting hairy, but take care lest your back-side also gets the same unnoticed. Then shall you know how rare lovers are. But even now reflect that youth is irrevocable.[18]

Young men were encouraged to make the most of themselves and the friendships they could cultivate before the growth of hair and the loss of youth made them less attractive. Youthful beauty was encapsulated in the adolescent body in the moment before early secondary hair growth was fully established, and the young man should take advantage of this short period of time. In Plato's *Symposium*, Alcibiades tells the story of his attempts to seduce the older Socrates. The younger man, convinced of his own attractiveness, believed that Socrates "has a serious affection for my youthful bloom" and imagined the advantages he might gain by having such a revered adult as Socrates as his *erastês*.[19] He sets out to seduce him, by engaging in athletic activities with him, inviting him to dinner, sending away his slaves and sleeping in the same room, eventually climbing into Socrates' bed. Socrates remains unaroused.[20] Alcibiades is affronted at this perceived insult to his beauty, but impressed by the integrity of the older man. Interestingly, another of Plato's works, *Protagoras*, opens with a friend criticizing Socrates for chasing after Alcibiades and his "youthful beauty" as now "as I looked at him, I thought him still handsome as a man—for a man he is, Socrates, between you and me, and with quite a growth of beard."[21]

In the world of classical and, to a certain extent, Hellenistic Athens, the eroticization of the youthful male body was expressed in the first appearance of secondary hair, particularly on the face. The youth was not yet a full male and could take the passive role in sexual activity. However, as the example of Alcibiades demonstrates, youths could take advantage of this short period of their growing up to create relationships that might work in their favor. This practice lasted well into Roman times. In the second century CE, Strato exploited a similar literary motif, but in some of his epigrams the friendship has continued past puberty:

> Even though the invading down and the delicate auburn curls of your temples have leapt upon you, that does not make me shun my beloved, but his beauty is mine, even if there be a beard and hairs.[22]

These epigrams exist in a very literary world, they draw on earlier models of classical and Hellenistic epigrams and manners. While some adult Roman males shared this view of boys, the discourse tended to be more critical.

In both Greece and Rome transitions in the female life course were also marked by changes in hairstyle. Young girls generally wore their hair long until either puberty or marriage and then wore it in some form of binding or covering. Control of the hair became a visual sign of the control of their nature, now bound by the social laws of marriage and conformity to the wider gendered roles demanded of them. The various ways in which women bound their hair are discussed in several other chapters in this book; here we are concerned particularly with the ways in which gender dictated certain hair behavior.

Sparta is often seen as a society that behaved very differently from the rest of classical Greece and its hair culture is one element of this. Spartan males, growing up in an all-male world from the age of seven were trained to be warriors, and the custom was first to be shaven as a youth, perhaps at the age of twelve, but then to wear their hair long as adults, and particularly to groom it before a battle. Plutarch, writing many centuries after the events, describes the traditional understanding of Spartan behavior in his own time thus:

> In time of war, too, they relaxed the severity of the young men's discipline, and permitted them to beautify their hair and ornament their arms and clothing, rejoicing to see them, like horses, prance and neigh for the contest. Therefore they wore their hair long as soon as they ceased to be youths, and particularly in times of danger they took pains to have it glossy and well-combed, remembering a certain saying of Lycurgus, that a fine head of hair made the handsome more comely still, and the ugly more terrible.[23]

Hair played a key role in the expression of Spartan masculinity, particularly at times of crisis. At the Battle of Thermopylae, where three hundred Spartans held the entire Persian army at a narrow pass, the Persian general, Xerxes, assumed that his opponents were naturally weak as they prepared for battle against inordinate odds by grooming their hair. The Spartans held their ground for three days until betrayed, but bought essential time for the rest of the Greek forces. The Persians revised their view of Spartan hair care![24]

While Spartan boys had shaven or short hair and grew long, luxurious locks as indicators of their adult masculinity, the inverse applied to girls and women. They had long hair in their youth, but had it shaved for the wedding and wore it short and covered during their married lives. Sparta was unusual in ancient states in that while it remained intensely conservative over all, it did advocate some form of education and physical training for its girls, who also married later than their Athenian counterparts, at around the age of eighteen. Spartan maidens often took part in choirs as part of ritual performances, in which they would learn recitation, singing, music, and dance. Some of the poems sung at these occasions survive. Those by Alcman (seventh century BCE) often mention hair as part of the description of the young maidens: "the hair of my cousin Hagesichora blooms like gold" ... "And she with her thick blond hair."[25] Blonde hair also features in another of Alcman's works where he also mentions "the moist grace of Cinyras [perfume] sits on the maiden's hair."[26]

Young Spartan women were readied for their weddings by having their hair shaven or cut short, and dressed in a man's cloak and sandals, and left to lie in the dark to await the arrival of their bridegroom who had spent the evening sober and eating at the all-male mess as usual.[27] This inverse of the usual rules of hair behavior in other Greek states is explained by modern commentators in a number of ways. Jean-Paul Vernant read the shaving of the head as the final removal of any elements of masculinity or wildness, thus ensuring the bride's secure move into the world of the adult female; Sarah Pomeroy also sees it as part of a transition rite from the stage of maidenhood to married life. The transvestite nature of the event allowed the symbolic pretence that the woman (as a male youth) had participated in the Spartan system of education (*agoge*) and could thus, like her husband, now be considered a full citizen. It is also suggested that the bride's appearance as a male may have helped her husband make his own rite of passage from homosexual to heterosexual sex.[28]

As bound, contained, or covered hair marked conformity to society, so unbound hair came to convey a series of very different meanings. Loose, unconfined, or untied hair had socially acceptable associations in ritual contexts of cult and funerary activity, as discussed in Chapter One. These ritual and/or religious contexts stood outside the normal rules of society, temporarily suspended for the occasion, and thus were socially acceptable and, indeed, socially required activities. Unbound hair in other contexts brought with it a range of very different meanings. The act of unwrapping or letting down the hair had strong erotic connotations as a prelude to sex, and often the prelude to illicit sex, outside the control of a husband. In Euripides' *Hippolytus*, Phaedra, the stepmother of the hero, talks of her unacceptable passion for her stepson as the nurse unbinds her hair.[29]

In his tale of Lucius who is transformed into an ass, Apuleius tells the story of the hero's affair (before his transformation) with the slave girl, Photis. Part of his adoration for her included an encomium on female hair, a bald Venus he says, would never be attractive:

> But think what it is like when hair shines with its own lovely colour and brilliant light, and when it flashes lively against the sunbeams or gently reflects them; or when it shifts its appearance to produce opposite charms, now glistening gold compressed into the smooth shadows of honey, now with raven-blackness imitating the dark blue flowerets on pigeons' necks; or when it is anointed with Arabian oils and parted with a sharp comb's fine tooth and gathered at the back so as to meet the lover's eyes and, like a mirror, reflects an image more pleasing than reality; or when, compact with all its tresses, it crowns the top of her head or, let out in a long train, it flows down over her back. In short, the significance of a woman's coiffure is so great that, no matter

how finely attired she may be when she steps out in her gold, robes, jewels, and all her other finery, unless she has embellished her hair she cannot be called well-dressed.[30]

Lucius is contemplating the role of female hair while observing Photis working in the kitchen, where her hairdo was not elaborate but held in a loose bun. Later when they are finally in bed together, she stripped off her clothes and let down her hair and with "joyous wantonness" transformed herself into Venus rising from the waves.[31]

Free-flowing hair is often associated with the virginal state, and with closeness to nature. Unmarried girls were not yet fully "tamed" by marriage and their hair, as in Apuleius' view above, was a mark of their beauty and could presumably be used to attract potential husbands.[32] Children and adolescent girls have long, loose hair, topknots, or ponytails, adult women, on the other hand, have braided hair, or hair bound up in some way, or are veiled.[33]

While Apuleius sees loose hair as playfully erotic, it was also seen to have a dangerous side in its potential to seduce men. This is most clearly expressed in Ovid's version of the Medusa myth where Medusa's beautiful hair attracted the attention of Poseidon, who raped her in the shrine of Athena. In response, Athena turned her hair into a mass of writhing snakes. Later, she will also lose her head to the hero Perseus.[34] The Jewish world shared the Greco-Roman attitude to female adornment and its relationship to female sexuality, and the ability to attract men other than a woman's husband. In the Bible, in order to shame a woman accused of adultery, the priest unbinds her hair[35] and in later commentaries, the detail of a woman's behavior is described and reversed, so that actions that were done to seduce a man are now turned against her: "She spread out a sheet for [her lover]; therefore the priest removes her head-covering from her head and places it beneath her feet. She braided her hair [for her lover]; therefore the priest undoes [her hair]."

Across ancient cultures, adult women with untamed or unbound hair, unless in a particular ritual context, are markers of a wildness or madness, and often presented as dangerous, especially for men. The Bacchantes, women driven to frenzy by the god Dionysus and who destroy Pentheus, the king of Thebes, have free-flowing hair (see Figure 2.4); the wildness of Ariadne's emotions, when abandoned by Theseus, after helping his escape from the Minotaur, are expressed in her loosened clothes and hair. Other women feared by men and often perceived as being outside social control were witches and sorceresses and these too were often identified by their untied and disheveled hair, which presumably added to their fearful appearance.[36] Horace's witch, Canidia, is described as having short vipers intertwined with her disheveled locks, clearly recalling the horror Medusa inspired (see Figure 9.12).[37] Ideas of emotional excess, frenzy, and subverting of social norms could all be expressed through hair. While ideas of social conformity and sexual containment could be marked by controlling the hair.

DISCOURSES OF DEPILATION

Unsurprisingly, discourses of depilation work differently for men and women, although the evidence for both sexes is ambiguous at best. For ancient Greece, most of the evidence comes from Athens and from old comedy, so works in a particular comic context, and requires modern interpreters to consider how far such practices, expressed by men about women, reflect actual and common practice or perform a role in the "semiotics of gender and the body." David Lavergne argues that in classical Attica at least, women made their whole bodies hairless in order to be more attractive while Martin Kilmer begins from an assumption that the Athenian man possessed a phobia of female genitalia, and that partial hair removal or shaping of hair on the *mons veneris* exposed the vulva and it was this that was considered erotic.[38]

Aristophanes uses the trope of depilation to comic effect when expressing the difference between the sexes. Removing body hair appears to make women both more attractive and visibly and tactilely different from (hairy) adult men.[39] In the *Women of the Assembly*, a female character grows her armpit hair in order to pass for a man and attend the all-male political gathering, while another throws her razor away so that she will "get bushy all over and no longer resemble a woman at all."[40]

Removal of hair could presumably be achieved by shaving, a razor is mentioned in the citation above, but more common practices appear to be singeing and plucking. Praxagora, one of the key characters of *Women of the Assembly*, sings the praises of her lamp: "You alone light the forbidden nooks of our thighs, when you singe off the hair that blooms there."[41] This may refer to the pubic area and to the tops of the thighs. In the *Lysistrata*, another play which involves the topsy-turvy notion (to an Athenian audience) of women going on a sex strike to stop the war between Athens and Sparta, a description of pubic grooming and shaping forms part of the seductive preparation of wives, who are then going to refuse sex to their husbands.[42]

The visual evidence for depilation is similarly ambiguous. When naked or semi-naked women appear in vase paintings they are often in profile or in such a position as to obscure the genital area. Kilmer, Lavergne, and Lee between them have collected a catalogue of images which show either shaped or very minimal pubic hair, and images which demonstrate singeing and plucking, two of which are shown here.[43] The first image (Figure 6.2) shows a frontal view of a naked woman, holding the flame of a lamp to her pubic area while squatting over a bowl. Both Lee and Lavergne understand the woman to be holding a sponge in her right hand, presumably to control the heat and avoid burns. The artist has depicted the pubic area as completely hairless. The open, directly frontal nudity and position of the woman, and the ornament on her thigh, suggest she is a *hetaira*, a courtesan, not a respectable wife. The second image (Figure 6.3) shows two women, one standing and being tended to by the Eros figure, who holds a burning lamp in one hand and is examining the woman's pubic area with the other. To the left a seated woman examines her own body with one hand, while holding a lamp in the other; it is unclear if she is awaiting her turn or checking the finished grooming.[44]

There is little actual evidence to show that women removed hair from other parts of their bodies, including facial and leg hair. These practices are rarely mentioned in texts nor are they depicted in iconography, where body hair, even in men, is rarely shown. It may be that male authors simply took such practices for granted in sophisticated women, be they respectable matrons or courtesans. Only female slaves are referred to as having body hair.[45]

In the Greek world, as we have seen, adult men were hairy but groomed. Beards were trimmed and not shaggy. Apart from facial hair, male body hair is also rarely depicted in Greek iconography, although it may have been added to sculptures with paint, and is sometimes shown in a very stylized manner which may reflect actual grooming practices.[46] Male depilation was often presented in a humorous or satirical context, and perhaps suggests more about male ideas about women than any actual practice; it often also has connotations of effeminacy or of prolonging the *eromenos* stage. Agathon, a tragedian, contemporary with Aristophanes, is ridiculed for his effeminacy in the *Thesmophoriazusae*, in terms of his dress and general appearance, but importantly because he could be dressed

GENDER AND SEXUALITY   105

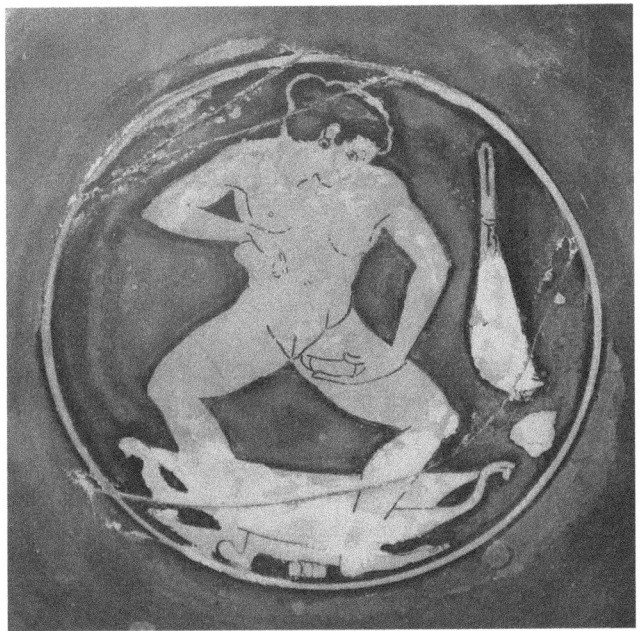

FIGURE 6.2 Tondo of red-figure kylix in the manner of Onesimos (ca. 500 BCE). David M. Robinson Memorial Collection, University of Mississippi and Historic Houses.

FIGURE 6.3 Attributed to the Dinos painter, bell-krater (mixing bowl for wine and water): Eros with two women; three cloaked men (not visible) (ca. 430–420 BCE), red-figure, terracotta, 30.3 × 30.8 cm. Harvard Art Museum / Arthur M. Sackler Museum at Harvard University, Cambridge, MA. Anonymous loan, 9.1988. Photo: Imaging Department © President and Fellows of Harvard College.

up to appear female, and attend the women-only festival as he is "good-looking, pale, clean shaven, soft, presentable," and sounds like a woman. Comments in Plato suggest that Agathon might have chosen to shave off his beard in order to remain the lover of Pausanias for longer than was socially acceptable. Aristophanes certainly makes the most of this notion in the opening of his play, referring several times to Agathon as "fucked," implying he was still playing the passive partner in a relationship.[47]

In the Roman world, the system of attention to the body was more carefully articulated, although bounded by similar gender lines. Romans, both male and female, walked a fine line between looking correctly groomed and dressed and expending excessive care on the body and its appearance. The discourse of *cultus* stereotypically allowed women more leeway than men, and men who spent too much time cultivating their looks were in danger of being ridiculed as effeminate. In the Roman world, the removal of facial hair was the preferred look for men for long periods of time but the removal of body hair raised questions about the status of an individual's masculinity. Such character assassination is common in Latin rhetoric. Scipio Aemilianus attacked P. Sulpicius Gallus for, among other apparently disreputable attributes, his shaven eyebrows, his plucked beard, and his smooth thighs.[48] Latin authors, and their audiences, were sophisticated enough to play with notions of hairiness and hairlessness, and to recognize that stereotypes are not necessarily reflections of reality. The poet Martial insults a certain Labienus:

> You pluck your chest, your legs and your arms, and your shaven cock is ringed with short hairs. This, Labienus, you do for your mistress's sake, as everybody knows. For whose sake, Labienus, do you depilate your arse?[49]

Some Romans, despite the risk of censure, sought smoothness, and sometimes this might also be attractive to women. For Martial, the topos of depilation allowed him to doubly insult Labienus, for looking effeminate, even though his mistress liked it, and for taking the passive role in sex. For Romans, it was always important to find the middle way. Seneca, in a letter about style, can use the analogy of depilation to make his point: "One is, I believe, as faulty as the other: the one class are unreasonably elaborate, the other are unreasonably negligent; the former depilate the leg, the latter not even the armpit."[50] While advising on the ideals of masculine appearance, Seneca could also complain about the screams of customers emanating from the armpit-hair plucker's stall at the baths.[51] Having hairs plucked out was presumably a painful and irritating process. Pumice stone is also noted for its depilatory effects, and gossip held that as a young man the emperor Augustus singed his leg hair with red-hot nutshells to make the hairs softer, and Seneca, again, complained that in his time resin was used as a depilatory for men.[52] However, it is clear that a sophisticated Roman needed to spend enough time on his appearance as to not look unkempt, and thus like a rustic or a barbarian, or too smooth, and risk looking like a woman.

In the early Christian period, writers continued to be anxious about male grooming habits. They still held to the underlying belief in the role of heat, and gender conventions of the classical world, but added the divine and biblical dimension to their reasoning. For Clement of Alexandria (150–215 CE) hairiness, and particularly the beard, were both symbols of masculinity and signs of Adam's superiority over Eve. In removing body hair a man was undermining his essential nature and risking damage to his spiritual health.[53] Men also offer themselves up to public ridicule when they express their shameless immodesty in contorting their bodies for the hair-plucker at the gymnasium, a place associated with the physical expression of masculinity, and the training of younger men. Such men offer a poor example and deny their own manhood.[54]

Roman women, like their Greek counterparts, practiced depilation and a smooth body was thought to be desirable, and natural. In his handbook on how to attract men, Ovid addresses his supposed female audience that "no rude goat should find his way beneath your arms and that your legs not be rough with bristling hairs."[55] It was not just courtesans who should ensure their smoothness, a funerary epitaph to Allia Potestas dated to between the first and fourth centuries CE, praised, among other virtues, her "smooth limbs" in which "she sought out every hair."[56] In the Roman period we see the first appearance of methods of hair removal that might equate with waxing, that is the smearing on of a substance which either brings the hair with it as it is removed or killed the hair by its very toxicity. In the first century CE, Pliny the Elder recorded several of these "remedies" in his encyclopedic *Natural History*;[57] but the efficaciousness of his recipes is uncertain to say the least. He collected a myriad of plant, animal, and mineral properties in his remedies. One example rather makes the point that it is often the exotic nature of the ingredients that might suggest arcane knowledge and power if not effectiveness:

> Others in three *heminae* of oil thoroughly boil a viper after taking out the bones, using the decoction as a depilatory after first plucking out the hairs they do not wish to grow again. The gall of a hedgehog is a depilatory, especially when mixed with a bat's brain and goat's milk, as is also the ash by itself. Parts rubbed with the milk of a bitch with her first litter, when the hairs have been plucked out or not yet grown, do not grow hair again. The same result is said to be produced by the blood of a tick plucked from a dog, by the blood or gall of a swallow, or by the eggs of ants. They say that eyebrows are made black by crushed flies; if however it is desired that the eyes of babies should be black, the expectant mother must eat a shrewmouse; hair is prevented from turning grey by the ash of earth-worms mixed with oil.[58]

We need not be overconcerned by the efficaciousness or otherwise of such recipes and remedies but rather note that there was clearly a demand for depilatories, and hair dyes, which suggests a cosmetic/beauty industry which catered to the demands of an ideal. It may be that the supplier of the more exotic potions might charge more, and project a sense of their own expertise and craftsmanship, but also presumably suggests there was a market for such things. It perhaps should not surprise us that women sought less painful ways of removing unwanted hair. This ideal required women, in particular, to remove facial and body hair that was deemed unsightly. The evidence for the removal of pubic hair is more contentious as it come from sources such as Martial, whose satiric, bawdy approach makes it difficult to ascertain how widespread that practice might have been, and among which groups of women. The epigrams which address plucking the pubic area or using "foul resin" are aimed at aging prostitutes.[59] We are not privy to the intimate practices of the smooth-limbed matron, Allia Potestas, but the eroticism of Apuleius' slave-girl lover, Photis, is heightened by her holding "one rosy hand in front of her smooth-shaven pubes, purposely shadowing it rather than modestly hiding it."[60]

NATURE VERSUS CULTURE

In antiquity male and female hair was seen as a natural part of human existence, as part of an earlier world, before man was civilized and was closer in nature to the animal world. Writing in the first century CE, the philosopher Seneca, thinking of a world before the invention of mirrors in which a man might see himself reflected, thought that life was better and virtue safer when:

> [Men] took care to arrange their hair and to comb their flowing beards, and in this task each man attended to himself, not to another in turn. That hair, which it was the custom of men formerly to let stream down, was not touched by the hand even of a wife; but men shook it out for themselves, handsome without any artifice, just as noble animals shake out a mane.[61]

Ancient classical, biblical, and early Christian narratives all use hair to elucidate the relationship between nature and culture which is often articulated in terms of man versus animal; male versus female; civilization versus barbarity. Ancient writers were, however, also aware of the golden mean—too much hair might be as bad as too little in certain contexts. Molly Myerowitz Levine gives the example of the conflict between hairy Esau and smooth-skinned Jacob told in Genesis, where the eventual victory of Jacob over his hairier, and thus more animal, brother, proves the wider rule, and divine plan, that man should rule over nature.[62] In Ovid's *Metamorphoses*, the angry Juno pulls lesser women by the hair and turns them into animals: Galanthis, a redhead who is turned into a weasel, for tricking her into letting the birth of Hercules take place, and Callisto who has been seduced by Jupiter and borne a child, is caught by the hair and flung on the ground, where her arms began to grow rough with black shaggy hair; her hands changed into feet tipped with sharp claws; and her lips, which but now Jove had praised, were changed into broad ugly jaws; and, that she might not move him with entreating prayers, her power of speech was taken from her, and only a harsh, terrifying growl came hoarsely from her throat. Still her human feelings remained, though she was now a bear.[63] Callisto has the worst of both worlds, an animal who thinks like a human, and while she is condemned to live in the wild is as afraid of other beasts as she is of man.

For the most part, Jewish and early Christian writers followed the accepted Greco-Roman moralizing tropes in articulating a version of cephalic, facial, and body hair which held male appearance as notably different to female, and while men should do some grooming, overattention to the hair was to cross the line into effeminacy. Some Christian authors, and if they are to be believed, ascetic devotees, however, shifted the goal posts a little further. In their attempts to deny the physical world and all its attributes, those who lived as hermits or in ascetic communities were often identified as closer to god. Their removal from normal society and social behavior was often expressed by their excessive hairiness. Macarius of Rome, for instance, lived in a place so outlandish that it was described as a land peopled with "serpents, dragons, asps, basilisks, vipers, unicorns and other horned animals," and here he lived, his whole body covered with white hair which floated in the wind, and "his toenails and fingernails were exceedingly long, and his beard and hair covered his whole body."[64] At the same time, Macarius' face was "like that of an angel." His holy, ascetic life has taken him away from society towards the divine; his placing at the edge of the known world and his angelic qualities, and his hairiness, are physical expressions of his holiness. Such a description denies the cultural expression of moderately groomed masculinity and creates a version that realigns closeness to nature with closeness to the divine. The hairy man is now beyond *cultus* and decidedly holy.

As with other aspects of gender and hair, the hair of early Christian female ascetics moved in the opposite direction to male hair. Where male ascetics might assert their "other-worldliness" by excessive hair, female ascetics who did not follow the traditional prescription to simply cover their hair, cut their hair or shaved it off. While this was not a practice approved of by most church fathers, it was, like male hairiness, a rejection of associations which tied women to the earthly realm. The holy woman Syncletica, for instance, cut off her hair as part of a regime to reject the trappings of the feminine role. At the same time she also cut off attention to beauty (*cultus*), and stopped wearing attractive clothes, attending the baths and generally being part of society.[65]

CONCLUSION

The malleability of hair means it works well as a "locus for the signification of this dialectic between nature and culture,"[66] as while its physical qualities are self-evidently part of the natural body, it can also be manipulated and controlled to suit the demands of culture, and of a gendered culture in particular. Given what was said at the outset of this chapter about the gendered understanding of the differences between men and women, it is clear that the cultural language and symbolism of hair would be coded differently for each sex. As the extract from Seneca cited above states, shaggy men, while lauded, are a thing of the past in a world where a moderate amount of male grooming is expected, but where smooth-skinned males might overstep too far and enter the female realm. Women, who by their very (nonmale) nature and by their closeness to reproduction, were imagined as closer to the natural world and in need of taming. This perceived position of women could be culturally expressed by the control of the hair, which could be covered and bound up. As we have seen unbound hair could imply a breaking of social boundaries, or standing outside normal society.[67] At the same time, the vast amount of anxiety about women's hair expressed in texts, coupled with the extensive finds of hair accoutrements found in the archaeological record and the visual images of both highly coiffed and natural-looking hairstyles, suggest that women could use their hair to articulate their own identities, and while we may not hear their words we can see their hair.

CHAPTER SEVEN

Race and Ethnicity

MARGUERITE JOHNSON

In the third century BCE, the Romans sent ambassadors to Tarentum to negotiate peace. In the account of Cassius Dio, negotiations disintegrated due to a fashion faux pas:

> the men of Tarentum laughed scornfully at the Roman toga and the general appearance [of the envoys]. It was the city attire that was worn in the Forum. They had donned it, either to present an appropriately dignified manner, or believing it would inspire fear-borne respect in the Tarentines. A group of revelers jeered at them.[1]

The situation worsened when one of the Tarentines defecated on an envoy's toga, which incited yet more hysteria and jeering.

The story is as powerful as it is funny. It is a salient reminder that ideas of alterity, absurdity, and barbarism are in the eyes of the beholder. Ancient source material on race and ethnicity is dominated by the Greeks and Romans. It is easy to forget, therefore, that those placed under their ethnographical gaze would have found them equally as strange, barbaric, and risible. Who or what appears to be the Other is a matter of geography. This is not to dismiss the moral corruption of imperialism or the widespread cultural damage enacted by the two leading colonizers of western antiquity, but to stress that alterity is a symbiotic interpretive process. To acknowledge this is to better manage a postcolonial reading of invasion narratives to privilege the agency of the colonized and emphasize the ambivalent, contested nature of ethnography.

Hair is important here. It has roots in the individual, in ethnicity, and in race. But its long, intertwining locks need to be untangled.

From a Greek and Roman perspective, ethnographic interpretations assigned to the hair and hairstyles of other peoples reinforced their own sense of cultural hegemony and superiority. They were better, in part, because of their perfectly coiffed hair. But their accounts of Libyan, Ethiopian, Celtic, and Gallic hair—the focus of the examples employed herein—reveal ignorance and anxiety. The following, therefore, examines artistic and written representations of foreign hair within the confines of race and ethnicity while combing the accounts for the meanings matted within them. The metanarrative of the Other is still recognized and discussed because, at times, it is impossible to avoid. It is not, however, the only means by which the knotty problems of other people's hair can be straightened out.

THE HEGEMONY OF BEAUTY—ORDERED HAIR IN THE ANCIENT MEDITERRANEAN

In the ancient Mediterranean there was a distinct hegemony of physical beauty that was idealized and aspirational. In Greece, the standard for beauty reached its fetishized pinnacle in the classical and Hellenistic ages in both literary descriptions and artistic representations of divinities, heroes, and athletes. From the rigid, austere bodies of archaic Greek sculpture came the more gracious, lithe physiques of Myron, Polycleitus, and Praxiteles, which were followed by masterpieces such as "Aphrodite of Rhodes" and "Nike of Samothrace."

Sculpture emphasized height, and symmetry of face and body. But it also included markers of a collectively defined "high culture"—particularly styled hair. Myron's "Discobulus," a precursor to the fluidity sought by the sculptors of the fourth century and beyond, has carefully arranged hair.[2] Other athletes captured in marble or bronze, on the brink of, or engaged in, "action," were always coiffured, as evidenced by "The Victorious Youth" and "The Wrestlers" respectively. Bodies "moved." Hair did not.

Hair proved to be difficult to depict realistically in sculpture. Nevertheless, the highly stylized hair of Greek sculpture was a cultural necessity: it communicated elegance, refinement, and other hallmarks of their civilization. Works such as the "Kouroi of Argos," and later masterpieces such as "The Artemision Bronze" (Figure 7.1), privileged elegant hairstyles that symbolized the values of the sophisticated Greek. The Kouroi, Cleobis, and Biton, for example, promoted masculinity as a self-controlled and severe ideal. This awe-inspiring power was partly achieved by the detailed representation of their hair: the forehead was crowned with disc-shaped curls, the jawline was framed by three thick coils on each side, and at the back were more subdivided braids, held in place by a cord.

FIGURE 7.1 Artemision bronze. Statue depicting God Zeus or Poseidon, severe style, detail (460 BCE). National Archaeological Museum, Athens. Photo: PRISMA ARCHIVO / Alamy Stock Photo.

Similarly, "The Artemision Bronze" captured a hypermasculinity of controlled power: the precision of the execution of the hair and beard emphasized the bodily perfection of the statue and its overwhelming sense of authority.

Roman sculpture attempted to replicate the Greek masterpieces and the messages they conveyed. Like the Greeks, the Romans placed artistic emphasis on simple elegance (*munditia*) and proper grooming (*cultus*),[3] which included attention to the representation of hair. Ideals of masculinity were communicated by modest hairstyles such as the one adorning the head of the emperor in the "Portrait Head of Augustus." This statue has the typical idealizing style employed for portraits of Augustus, which included hair characterized by forked locks arranged in a crescent shape along the forehead (see Figures 1.6, 2.3, 3.8). The preference for simple, unadorned hairstyles was replicated in numerous busts of powerful Roman men during the republic and early imperial ages, including those depicting Julius Caesar. Awe-inspiring yet balding, Caesar was regularly cast with short hair and a cropped vertical fringe that was styled forward to conceal the scalp.[4]

Women in both Greece and Rome were depicted wearing their hair in styles that drew attention to the idealized feminine qualities of purity, circumspection, and modesty. Markers of civilized women included simple as well as ornate hairstyles such as those depicted on the Caryatids adorning the Porch of the Erechtheum on the Acropolis (see Figure 2.9), and the marble busts of Augustus' wife, Livia. Hair was also veiled in portraits depicting both men and women, principally as a sign of decorum and restraint. As a woman's hair was innately connected with sensuality and desirability, a veiled head marked her as unavailable to the erotic gaze. Similarly, though rarer, a man's piety was communicated by the addition of a head covering, such as that of Augustus as Pontifex Maximus (see Figure 1.6).

CROSS-CULTURAL INTERACTIONS—OTHER PEOPLE'S HAIR

Greek and Roman belief in their own cultural superiority over the vast number of encountered and colonized ethnic groups is expressed in ethnographical analyses and observations.[5] Herodotus, the first major ethnographic source in western antiquity, chronicled historical interactions between Greek and non-Greek peoples. He employed several discrete techniques that were regularly predicated on defining foreigners as, essentially, the antithesis of Hellenes.[6] His ethnography, comprising lists of foreign customs and traditions, was formulaic in structure and content,[7] which contributed to characteristically impersonal or, at most, ambivalent descriptions.[8] Nevertheless, Herodotus had a racial gaze that permeated *The History* and an approach to ethnography that privileged odd or unusual details, which a Greek audience would have received with interest and, at times, unease.[9]

One result of Herodotus' process of cultural delineation was a reiteration of the motif of hair as a signifier of a particular people's closeness to, or distance from, nature.[10] In the section on Libya (4.168–99),[11] Herodotus recorded various physical features of the indigenous peoples, including hair. On the Adurmachidae, the first of the Libyan peoples on Herodotus' list, he wrote:

> Their women wear twisted bronze anklets around both shins and let the hair on their heads grow long, and when a woman catches a louse on herself she bites it and throws it away. These are the only Libyans to do this, and they are the only ones who present

their young women, about to be married, to the king. Whoever pleases the king loses her virginity to him. The Adurmachidae dwell in a region that extends from Egypt to a bay named Plynus. (4.168)[12]

Without elaboration or overt cultural censure, Herodotus evoked an exotic and unkempt group of women whose proximity to nature was denoted by their hair. For the Adurmachidae women, as distinct from something that required treatment (culture), hair was merely part of the body (nature).[13] The distinction between nature and culture, designated by the women's hair, further emphasized their distance from civilized females who paid attention to the symbolic capital of their hair. The context in which the women's culturally inscribed appearance was embedded was also important to Herodotus. Descriptions of broader ethnographic contexts, including details of customs and lifestyle, were often negatively charged in ancient ethnographies. In the case of the Adurmachidae women, Herodotus referred to the practice of sending brides-to-be to the king who had the first right to deflower them, if he so desired. Details such as these, emphasizing difference, ensured that the information was interpreted within a Greek moral framework.

When Herodotus addressed hair ethnography in terms of human intervention, it was not to allude to culture as the Greeks would define it, but to emphasize ethnic alterity. This was evidenced by the passages on other indigenous peoples of the Libyan coast, the Macae and Maxyes, respectively:

> These are the ones who live inland of the Nasamones; the neighboring seaboard to the west is the country of the Macae, who cut the hair upon the crown, leaving the middle of the hair to spring up, and shaving clean off what is on each side; into war they always carry shields made of ostrich skins. (4.175)

> To the west of the river Trito and next to the Auseans begins the country of the Libyans who already practice farming and have acquired houses; they are called the Maxyes. They let the hair grow long on the right side of the head and shave the left, and they paint their bodies with red dyes. (4.191)

Herodotus' references to hair, particularly long hair, were almost exclusively associated with foreigners and difference, only occasionally denoting long hair as a feature of the Greek peoples. On the conflict between the Argives and the Lacedaemonians over Thyrea in ca. 547 BCE, he described the Argives vowing to keep their hair short after their defeat, and the Lacedaemonians legislating to keep their hair long after their victory (1.82). Here, hair commemorated a significant event and ensured remembrance.[14] Elsewhere, Herodotus described Xerxes' amused response at the Spartiates preparing for the Battle of Thermopylae by combing their hair:[15]

> When Xerxes heard the report, he could not comprehend the fact that the Lacedaemonians were in fact, to the best of their ability, preparing to kill or be killed. What they did appeared laughable to him, so he sent for Demaratus the son of Ariston, who was in his camp. When Demaratus arrived, Xerxes asked him about each of these matters, wanting to understand what it was that the Lacedaemonians were doing. Demaratus answered: "You have already heard about these men from me, when we were setting out for Hellas, but when you heard, you mocked me, although I told you how I expected things to turn out. It is my greatest aim, O King, to be truthful in your presence. So hear me now. These men have come to fight us for the pass, and it is for

this that they are preparing. This is their custom: when they are about to risk their lives, they arrange their hair."[16]

Xerxes' arrogance is detectable in his underestimation of the Spartiates because of their tonsorial preoccupation, but so too is his humanity. Like the Tarentines who laughed at the Romans in their togas, Xerxes' bemusement exemplified the mundane reactions that were also part of cross-cultural contact. Xerxes becomes, for a brief moment in time, a confused traveler, a befuddled would-be colonizer, liberated from his role as wicked tyrant, and cast as a down-to-earth gentleman, who simply did not understand those strange Greek ways.

Hair as natural feature, and as cultural artifact, also characterized the ethnographic writings of the Romans. Tacitus, like Herodotus, described the hairstyles of northern Europeans as a marker of their alterity.[17] In his descriptions of the Gauls and the Celts, Tacitus regularly specified hair in both its natural and its altered states, not only as a means of signifying difference but also to inject narratives with drama and, at times, heightened emotion. Like Herodotus, Tacitus was more interested in describing the hairstyles of men. This may have been the result of the specificities of traditional practice in cultures where men styled but women did not, and where men styled with the goal of a more martial appearance. Whatever the reason, Tacitus' northern women were regularly depicted with natural, uncultivated hair. In his description of the women of Mona (Anglesey), the bastion of British resistance to Rome in 61 CE, Tacitus focused on hair as a symbol of wildness that, as noted above, injected the narrative with dynamism:

> Standing on the shore was the opposition: a mass of arms and men, with women moving in-between as would the Furies in funereal robes, with streaming hair, carrying torches; while a circle of Druids poured out ill-omened curses and raised their hands to the sky. The strangeness of the sight struck the troops as though their limbs were bound, and they offered their immoveable bodies to wounds. Then with the encouragements of their leader and inciting each other lest they fear a womanly and fanatic band, they brought to bear the standards against the enemy so as to meet and cut them down, enveloping them in their own flames.[18]

Tacitus' use of the participle from the verb *deicere* to describe the hair of the women (*crinibus deiectis*/"with streaming hair") was a powerful choice. *deicere* not only depicted hair that was tumbling down, but denoted the act of cutting down, driving out, or dislodging an enemy. In essence, the women's hair was their weapon. Untamed, like the women themselves, and in combination with the rest of the spectacle, female hair rendered Paulinus and his men surprised and frightened (*haerere*), with bodies immobile (*immobile corpus*).[19] The comparison of the women of Mona to the Furies,[20] the terror-inducing, chthonic goddesses of Greek and Roman mythology, made them hybrid beings, part-human and part-monster. The ethnographic tendency to align enemy peoples with animals, as suggested in Herodotus' image of the Libyans who picked lice from their hair, has thus been developed by Tacitus' emphasis on women as semi-monstrous.

Tacitus' wild women of Mona were matched by Cassius Dio's account of the ultimate female warrior of the Britons, Boudicca. While, from a Celtic perspective, Boudicca and other noble women "would have grown their hair to show status, as well as being attractive for its length and colour,"[21] Dio made no such interpretation:

> Her body was exceedingly large, and most ferocious her appearance, and most terrifying her gaze, possessing a rough voice, with voluminous intensely yellow hair

down to her hips, she wore a huge golden twined-collar, a multi-colored tunic with a thick mantle fastened over the same with a brooch. Thus, in truth, she presented herself, as always. But at this time she had also taken a spear so that she could use it too, to strike universal awe.[22]

Boudicca was presented in an essentially natural state. Besides her torc, mantle, and brooch, the focus was on her physique, gaze, voice, and hair. Much has been written on the color of Boudicca's hair, with most commentators suggesting that it was red. The word used by Dio, however, specified that it was ξανθός, which denoted a yellow color of various shades, including rust red to light brown.

Arguably, the most memorable ethnographic account of wild-haired women was recorded in the "Periplus of Hanno" (ca. fifth century BCE), a Greek translation of a Punic inscription that had supposedly been established in the temple of the Carthaginian god, Ba'al Hammon (ca. sixth century BCE). The inscription was believed to have commemorated the voyage of Hanno beyond the Pillars of Heracles (the Straits of Gibraltar), quite possibly into the realms of Britain.[23] Amid the miraculous encounters was Hanno's description of the hairy women of the Southern Horn who were sighted on the last leg of the journey:[24]

> In the recess of this bay [i.e. the Southern Horn] there was an island, like the former one, having a lake, in which there was another island, full of savage men. There were women, too, in even greater number. They had hairy bodies, and the interpreters called them *Gorillae*. When we pursued them we were unable to take any of the men; for they had all escaped, by climbing the steep places and defending themselves with stones; but we took three of the women, who bit and scratched their leaders, and would not follow us. So we killed them and flayed them, and brought their skins to Carthage. For we did not voyage further, provisions failing us.

Pliny and Pomponius Mela also described the *Gorillae*[25] and, unsurprisingly, all three accounts reflected the anxieties surrounding hirsute women as the antithesis of the smooth-skinned, coiffured beauties of the ancient Mediterranean. Indeed, the hirsute woman went well beyond traversing the feminine ideal, blurring not only the boundaries between female and male, but those between species. Hair became fur. "Barbarian" women became subhuman. Accordingly, Hanno had no qualms about revealing that three of the *Gorillae* were slain, flayed, and their skins taken to Carthage. Likewise, Pliny, who recorded the same acts, did so without comment.[26]

While nothing surpassed the furry women beyond the Pillars of Heracles, other accounts of foreign hair were used as code language to establish a hierarchy of civilization. In Caesar's *De Bello Gallico*, the eye of the ethnographer was cast on the Cantii:

> Of all these [Britons], the most civilized by far are those who live in Cantium [Kent], an entirely maritime region, differing only slightly in Gallic customs. Most of the interior peoples do not sow grains, but live on milk and meat and dress in skins. All of the Britons, in fact, dye themselves with woad, which produces an azure color, and thus they have a more frightening appearance in battle; with long hair and with every part of their bodies shaved except for the head and upper lip. Ten and even twelve have wives shared among them and particularly brothers with brothers and parents with offspring; but if one of the wives produces a problem, they are immediately regarded to be the property of the one by whom each was first taken when a virgin.[27]

Like the Maxyes who grew their hair on the right side of the head and shaved the left, and painted their bodies with red dyes (4.191), the Cantii modified their hair as well as their bodies, which they shaved except for the head and upper lip. While removing body hair was regarded as unbefitting for Roman men, the clean-shaven Cantii were depicted as awe-inspiring opponents. Hair and hairlessness mattered in the schema that constituted this stereotype as it was intrinsically part of their identities as warriors. As hair symbolized strength and thus bellicose prowess for the Spartiates, it was also a marker of the power of the Celtic warriors on the battlefield, which in turn explained the difficulties Caesar experienced in his attempts to overcome them.[28] In this context, hair is an ambivalent physiognomic and cultural signifier. The Romans, like the Greeks, interpreted themselves as being at the epicenter of civilization and the distant lands and people they encountered were described in a way as to provide evidence of this. The Cantii located in remote Britain, were depicted by Caesar as both worthy and ferocious, possessing imposing physiques and proving to be formidable opponents, yet morally and socially inferior. Their hair was unfamiliar and therefore anxiety-inducing, like their painted bodies, yet it also implied that the Cantii, in their unspoiled state, were a remnant people untouched by the decadent influences of "civilization."[29]

Such dichotomies of "hard primitivism"[30] were also present in Diodorus Siculus' *Bibliotheca Historica*, in the description of the Gauls:

> The Gauls are tall in body, with pale flesh and rippling muscles. Their hair is not only naturally blond but they undertake preparations to augment the natural, characteristic color. The regularly wash their hair in limewater and pull it back from the forehead to the top of the crown, drawing it along the nape of the neck, so as to have the appearance of a Satyr or Pan. So thorough is the teasing up of their hair that it resembles the manes of their horses. Some shave their beards but others grow them a little. The nobles, though, shave their cheeks but let the moustache grow until it covers the mouth. As a result, when they eat, food becomes trapped, and when they drink, the liquid passes through as though something like a sieve.[31]

Once again, hybridity is implied as the Gauls were presented as between species,[32] a metaphor for alterity embedded in their hair, including the description of the unfortunate union of hair and food (or hair *in* food).[33] Diodorus, warming to his theme, went on to describe a Gallic meal, depicting the Gauls sitting on animal skins, not chairs, and being served by their younger children, not slaves. Further, the Gauls were described as mistreating guests who were unfortunate enough to have partaken in a feast with them (declining to ask their names or what it was they required until after the meal, and seizing upon spurious reasons for offense to initiate combat).[34] Yet, as with other accounts of the Gauls, Diodorus' description also suggested an admiration for them. Gallic bodies were impressive and therefore worthy of appreciation, which must have prompted a comparison between their physiques and those of their Roman adversaries. Additionally, the Gauls were likened to the Homeric heroes in their custom of rewarding admirable men the best cuts of meat (5.28).

As with Boudicca's cascading locks, the long hair and distinctive mustache of both Gallic and Celtic warriors, were clear markers of distinction in their own cultures.

In Figure 7.2, a terracotta Celtic warrior with characteristic long hair and curving mustache, the emphasis has been placed on military prowess and preparedness as well as a sense of dignity, which was augmented by the very feature—hair—that Diodorus used to mark their alterity.[35] As the Romans failed to recognize the "barbarian" body as

FIGURE 7.2 Figure of a Celtic warrior, early Roman period, terracotta. © Ashmolean Museum, University of Oxford.

a collective and individual weapon, they failed to identify the martial advantage of lime-washed hair, which had "a practical benefit … since the process coarsened and stiffened the hair, providing a degree of protection from blows to the head."[36] Likewise, comments about shaved bodies painted with woad revealed that ethnographers and historians did not understand that body paint, like tattoos, were more easily applied to smooth skin.[37]

HAIR AS A RACIAL SIGNIFIER—AFROED ETHIOPIANS AND REDHEADED GAULS

Hair was, and remains still, an effective means of categorization. As Synnott summarized: "opposite sexes have opposite hair, head hair and body hair are opposite, opposite ideologies have opposite hair."[38] In the obsessive pursuit of categorization, ancient authors also turned to hair not only as a marker of cultural evolution, or lack thereof, but also as a characteristic of racial identity. Hair as a marker of race was regularly explained in relation to natural environment, predicated upon the assumption that location influenced physical features. This theory surfaced in the writings of Herodotus as seen in his explication of the pleasing temperaments and physiques of the peoples of Asia Minor, which he attributed to the temperate climate (1.142). Geography and climate were also used to explain less appealing characteristics of the same peoples, such as their lack of energy, willpower, courage, and fortitude, which ultimately rendered them servile to the yoke of monarchy (1.143). The effects of environment were emphasized in the Hippocratic text, *Airs, Waters, Places*,[39] which became the most important and influential text in antiquity on the topic of humanity and indeed race and environment.

Representations of the Ethiopians[40] in both Greek and Roman literature placed emphasis on the influence of environment and climate on both physical characteristics, interpreted by the ancients as racial features, as well as temperament.[41] The racial classification of the Ethiopians was partly based on the fixation ancient Mediterranean authors had with the ethnography of hair, which was part of their racial taxonomy. Herodotus (7.70), for example, described the hair of the African Ethiopians with the superlative οὐλότατον (woolliest) as distinct from the Asiatic Ethiopians, described as ἰθύθριξ (straight-haired).[42] While Herodotus did not attribute location and climate to the hair or other physical features of the Ethiopian peoples, the connection came in later writings, such as the works of Aristotle where there was a direct connection made between woolly hair and a dry environment.[43]

In Ptolemy's *Tetrabiblos*, the theory was extended to incorporate the role of astronomical and, expressly, astrological cycles. On the Ethiopians, for example, Ptolemy wrote:

> The features of all national characteristics are established in part by entire parallels [north or south] and angles [east or west], through their position relative to the Elliptic and the Sun. The region we inhabit is in one of the Northern Quarters, but the peoples who live under the more southern parallels, that is, those from the equator to the summer tropic, since they have the Sun in their zenith are constantly burned by it. Thus they have black skins and thick, woolly hair, are contracted in form and shrunken in stature. They are sanguine of nature, and in habits they, for the most, are part savage because their homes are continually oppressed by the heat; we call them by the general name Ethiopians. Not only do we see them in this condition, but we likewise observe that their climate and the animals of their region plainly give evidence of this baking by the sun.[44]

In Figure 7.3, the black-figure vase, "The departure of Memnon for Troy" (550–525 BCE),[45] the legendary Ethiopian king stands between two Amazons, his dark, curly hair represented by painted dots and restrained with a red headband. The Amazons accentuate the bellicose alterity of Memnon, appropriate to his role at Troy as an enemy leader against the Greeks. The painting therefore encapsulates the, at times, mixed attitude the Greeks had towards the Ethiopians. Like Caesar's Cantii, acknowledged as essentially worthy, albeit savage opponents, Memnon embodied the notion of the "barbaric," yet heroic opponent.[46]

The connection between the Ethiopians and the Amazons was also portrayed in a series of alabastra from the fifth century BCE, which regularly featured individual examples of each stereotype on the one artifact, or incorporated one of each figure on the same piece.

FIGURE 7.3 *The departure of Memnon for Troy* (550–525 BCE), black-figure vase. Royal Museums of Art and History, Brussels.

The face, hands, and feet of the Ethiopian in Figure 7.4 (ca. fifth century BCE)[47] have been rendered black—the head, white—in order for a tonal distinction to differentiate face and head. Nevertheless, despite the "loss" of the typical black hair, the artist has managed to capture the suggestion of tight, curly hair by the decoration of the head with the typical dotted design evident in other visual representations of Ethiopian hair.

The challenge of rendering both face and hair black was also evident in numerous vases and cups cast and decorated in the shape of Ethiopian heads from locations such as Attica, Etruria, and Apulia. With these artifacts, the face was usually rendered black and the hair was rendered white (with black embossed dots to denote its thick, woolly texture). In Figure 7.5 (fourth century BCE), the Etruscan vase (mug) of an Ethiopian

 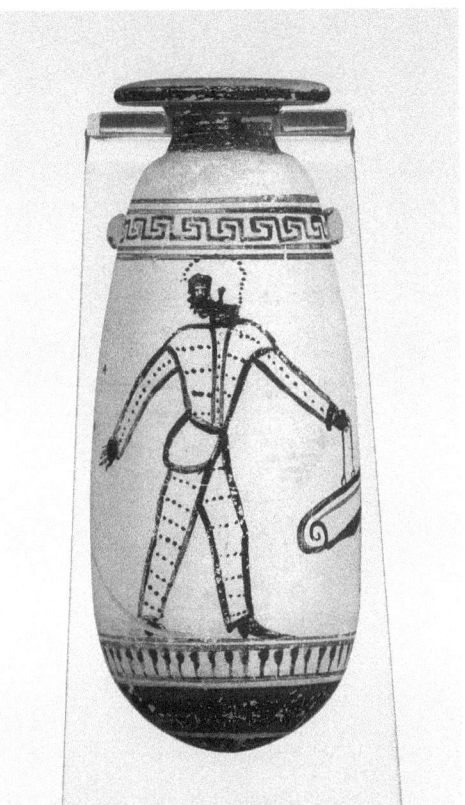

FIGURES 7.4 Alabastron, showing "Ethiopian and Amazon" (ca. fifth century BCE). Staatliche Museum, Berlin. Inv. No. 3382. © bpk Antikensammlung, SMB / Johannes Laurentius

head exhibits an exquisitely executed whitened hair that consists of stylized pin-curls to create the required effect.[48]

The theory of environmental adaptation was preceded by the pseudoscience of physiognomy,[49] which was already developed by the classical age, "dating at least as far back as Pythagoras."[50] The most informative text was Pseudo-Aristotle's *Physiognomonics* (ca. 300 BCE), which explicitly presented the theory as a well-established one and, at times, also acknowledged the theory of environment and its influence on race.[51] The *Physiognomonics* included interpretations based on hair: men with stiff hair were described as cowards as were those with woolly, thick hair (οὖλος) such as the Ethiopians (812b), while men from the south (the Egyptians) with soft (μαλακόν)[52] hair were also cowards (806b).

The theories of environmental shaping and physiognomy were adopted by Roman scholars and along with skin color, hair was listed as the main physical marker of race.[53] In addition to the texture of hair, the Romans were particularly interested in the color of hair as a characteristic of race and/or peoples. In the earlier passage from Dio on Boudicca (*Epitome* 62.2), the color of her hair was incorporated to bring her historical

FIGURE 7.5 Etruscan pottery mug in the form of the head of a black slave, Etruria (fourth century BCE). Photo: © Ashmolean Museum, University of Oxford.

portrait to life. The Roman anxiety over northerners, expressly the Gauls,[54] regularly communicated via physiognomic and climate taxonomies, was often revealed in the references to their red hair. In a passage from Vitruvius (*On Architecture* 6.1), northern Europeans were depicted as possessing powerful physiques, fair complexions, and red hair. Tacitus (*Agricola* 11) also made similar remarks, specifically about the Caledonians, including their red hair. In various ancient references to red hair, the northerners were also described as bellicose, which indicated an association between redheads and hot temperedness. The tendency of ancient writers to classify northerners as characteristically red-haired exemplified the habit of racial stereotyping. As the passage from Dio on Boudicca revealed, not all northerners were red-haired but peoples with hair of various hues, albeit there would have been a predominance of what the ancient Mediterranean commentators interpreted as "light" hair.

The association between red hair and trickery, as well as a sense of distaste towards redheads as unattractive, were the most likely explanations for the red-haired masks of male slave characters in ancient comedy. Wariness towards redheads was something the Romans shared with the Greeks, as illustrated in *Physiognomonics* (812a) in which Pseudo-Aristotle stated that flaming red hair (πυρρός) denoted a wicked character and compared redheads with the fox. This unease continued into the Christian era, with writers such as Tertullian (*De Cultu Feminarum* 2.6), who castigated women for dyeing their hair fiery red (*flammeus*):

> I see women who dye their hair golden. They are so ashamed that their birth was not of Germany or Gaul. So they forge a lineage with their hair. And worse yet, they augur ill for themselves with a fiery red head. Though they think it graceful, really it is an act of sin.

As Tertullian chastised women—and men—for many alleged sins against an ascetic lifestyle, this brief tirade on fiery red hair dye should be kept in perspective. Nevertheless, it highlighted the dislike of redheads in antiquity that focused on "barbarians" with warlike demeanors such as the Celts, Gauls, and—another group generally disliked by both the Greeks and the Romans—the Thracians.[55] The passage from Tertullian further added the element of sexuality to the ancient interpretation of hair, particularly to red hair, and to the practice of dyeing hair. To color one's hair in the ancient Mediterranean, particularly to dye it blonde or red or hues thereof, was interpreted as not only mimicking "barbarians" but also as emphasizing one's sexuality or sexual availability. Both interpretations of this practice informed Tertullian's diatribe and, even before the patristic age, such responses were evident in Roman writings, particularly in the work of Roman elegiac poets. Propertius (2.18.23–28), for example, railed against his mistress for dyeing her hair in the style of the northern peoples:

> Oh mad one, do you now even imitate the dyed Britons,
> and play the coquette with a foreign tint on a dyed head?
> Looks as nature bestowed them are always most becoming;
> Belgian color on a Roman head is ugly.
> Let many evils come to that girl in the underworld,
> who in her stupidity cheated and altered her tresses.

Likewise, Ovid, who usually adopted a milder stance on women's artificial adornment, dedicated an entire poem, *Amores* 1.14, to the disastrous effects of his mistress' overuse of hair dye. While both the Greeks and the Romans were alert to different peoples and emphasized the physical markers of such, Stewart has pointed to this ambivalence in beauty aesthetics, noting that paleness of both skin and hair was regarded as pleasing to the Romans.[56] As a result, and as the Italic people did not tend to be naturally blonde, there were various formulae for lightening and bleaching hair.[57] Additionally, as the empire expanded, the Romans imported hair and hairpieces from the north, particularly Germany, as the hair tended to be light in color as well as thick in texture.[58]

HAIR AS A MARKER OF RESISTANCE, SUBMISSION, AND ALLEGIANCE—BRITISH HAIR

Such incongruities or contradictions inherent in cultural interpretations of hair, as evidenced by the Roman sources, illustrate the reality and dynamics of the theme of hair styling as resistance in antiquity. This was evident not only in the propensity of Roman women of the early imperial age to dye their hair the colors of so-called barbarian peoples, but also in instances where the peoples themselves adhered to their own cultural markers as a symbol of defiance. In Tacitus' *Histories* (4.61), the account of the Batavian ruler, Gaius Julius Civilis and his revolt against the Romans in 69 CE, was described in terms of hair:

> Civilis, in accordance with a vow, much like those the barbarians take, dyed his hair red, and grew it out from the time he turned on the Romans. But now that the legions had been hewn down, he once again cut his hair short.

Civilis wanted independence from Rome and envisaged himself as the future leader of a Gallo-German empire, which he expressed in part through the symbolic power of Batavian customs of group identity. Here, hair was political, rebellious, bellicose, and antagonistic. In Rembrandt's (1601–69) *The Conspiracy of Claudius Civilis* (Figure 7.6),[59] Civilis has been placed, almost Christ-like, amid his supporters, his typical Batavian hair color rendered tawny-gold, and its length emphasized by a portion of it that falls over his shoulders.

In contrast, there were several written and pictorial representations of the oppression of enemy peoples via their hair. As Aldhouse-Green wrote:[60]

FIGURE 7.6 Rembrandt, *The Conspiracy of Claudius Civilis* (1601–69). Nationalmuseum, Stockholm. Photo: PAINTING / Alamy Stock Photo.

RACE AND ETHNICITY   125

Grabbing someone's hair is a complex and loaded action that includes abuse, restraint and shame. It also conveys messages associated with alien ownership: the person holding the hair "owns" both it and the head to which it is attached. Indeed, grabbing the hair may be associated with pulling back the head either to cut the throat … or to behead the victim.

In the relief on the Sebasteion of Aphrodisias (Figure 7.7), Claudius has been depicted in the act of subjugating Britannia. Here Britannia, the symbol of Britain, was represented in a completely suppressed, violated pose: she is shown sprawled at the feet of the

FIGURE 7.7 Relief from the Sebasteion of Aphrodisias showing Claudius victorious over Britannia. © New York University Excavations at Aphrodisias (G. Petruccioli).

conquering Claudius, the symbol of Rome; her body kept immobile by the muscular knee pressed to her flank; semi-clothed, with one breast displayed, she communicates her vulnerability; held up by her hair to endure subjugation and inevitable decapitation. To augment the "Otherness" of Britannia, the artist has rendered her Amazon-like, with imagery recalling earlier iconic representations of fallen or falling Amazons, such as the one from the Amazon Frieze on the Mausoleum of Halicarnassus (ca. 357–350 BCE) (Figure 7.8).

While Britannia's hair remained relatively Celtic in order for the principal action of repression to be depicted (being dragged by the hair), her Amazonian persona also emphasized the artistic dominance of the colonizers on the colonized. Like the Amazons of Greek art, Britannia wore a *peplos*.

In a well-known passage from the *Agricola* (21), Tacitus described the Romanization of the Britons. The Britons began to speak Latin, adopted Roman dress, and coveted the less admirable and morally upright markers of Roman culture, such as lounges, baths, and luxurious banquets. Agricola trained young noblemen in the liberal arts and encouraged architecture and town planning along Roman lines. This cultural contamination was arguably the most powerful means of ultimate conquest, as Tacitus commented: "This was called civilization by those to whom it was a novelty, when it was in fact a sign of their enslavement." Of course, the complex nature of Romanization and the inherently protracted process of cultural colonization must be acknowledged in order to avoid simplifying the course of what ultimately led to the creation of Roman Britain.[61]

FIGURE 7.8 Mausoleum of Halicarnassus, detail of Amazon warrior in defeat. Photo: Ali Kabas / Alamy Stock Photo.

Hair changed. As the process of civilizing the barbarians progressed and, in turn, the instances of open reception of the material markers of "civilization," hair began to morph into the styles of the Mediterranean peoples. As mentioned above, such fraught transitions happened gradually and did not operate homogeneously. Some hair changed early on but other hair did not. Verica, a leader of the Atrebates in the first century CE, certainly changed his hair relatively early in the Roman invasion of Britain. As shown on coins minted in Verica's honor, he was not depicted with the typical hair of his people. Instead, Verica had a distinctly Roman hairstyle: cropped, wreathed with laurel, and copied from coins issued during the reigns of Tiberius (14–37 CE) or Caligula (37–41 CE).

CONCLUSION

Verica's transformation, denoted by his hairstyle, revealed the complexities of hair in antiquity. Hair was an intimate and individual symbol. Hair was also a cultural, colonial, and collective symbol. In the case studies provided above, hair was clearly depicted as a marker of group distinctiveness and, as such, it symbolized self- and cultural-identification. Hair functioned in fostering group cohesion, as well as furnishing a pretext for exclusion from hegemonic taxonomies of beauty and "civilization." It should be noted, however, that the uneasy fascination with, and homogenization of "outsiders" by "insiders," was dependent on the dynamics of Object and Subject. The identity of the author of the ethnography contributes to this in no small way.

Ambivalence and antagonism towards foreigners set in motion a form of protoracism.[62] This was based in part on physicality and physiognomy, and associated with a hyperawareness of markers of ethnicity. As a sign of both race and ethnicity, hair, like skin, was useful in antiquity to categorize, interrogate, limit, and interpret a particular race of people as well as their cultural practices. That these assessments were often derogatory is testament to the powerful and dangerous properties of hair as a marker of alterity in the ancient world.

ACKNOWLEDGMENTS

Thanks to Thomas Sharkie for research assistance on this project.

CHAPTER EIGHT

Class and Social Status

SUSAN STEWART

INTRODUCTION

In societies where class divisions are important, visual signals that could give clues to a person's class or status could be crucial. As several chapters in this volume have stressed, in antiquity appearance was loaded with significance and a means by which an individual could help define his or her place in society. At the same time, these messages could be, and were, manipulated. Hair formed an integral part of overall image. Because it could be arranged in a number of different ways—cut, colored, curled or straightened, worn loose or bound up—hair proved an ideal medium for conveying a sense of social identity: that is to say, whether an individual was an aristocrat or slave, freedman or freedwoman, prostitute or respectable woman, citizen or foreigner. However, worryingly for many ancient authors, a person's coiffure was as likely to be part of a disguise or an attempt at misrepresenting their character and place in society perhaps even to suit a nefarious purpose as it was to represent them in their true colors. While class and status were important categories in defining ancient identity, they are inextricably embedded in notions of gender and of age. A change in an individual's status was often marked by a change in hair behavior. As an individual matured and moved through a series of life stages, rites of passage were made visible in temporary or permanent changes of hair and headgear.[1] Social mobility, particularly from slave to freed status could also be marked in physical appearance, as could a move in the other direction, down the social scale.

Undeniably hair, in terms of both style and color, is given prominence as a point of beauty in both the written sources and works of art throughout antiquity. In sculpture, painting, mosaic, and funerary reliefs, both women and men were depicted wearing their hair in a variety of different styles. Paintings and mosaics may reference hair color. Sculptures and reliefs, which were once painted but have largely lost their color, nonetheless remain a useful source of information about hairstyles. The style and sometimes the color are factors that help identify the individual's rank on the social scale: the more elaborate the hairdo, the higher the social class, given the time and assistance required to create some of the complex arrangements seen on sculptures.[2] However, this rule was far from being hard and fast. We need to take account of the rest of the signals in any given image: for example, the setting, dress, and overall iconographic theme also dictate how an image might be read. It is not simply the nature of the imagery which controls how we read ancient art but also the context of the artifact itself. Greek vase painting, for instance, is one of our main sources for the physical appearance of hair, but images have to be carefully decoded: are they really images of the everyday or are they portraying mythological events, divine persons, or indeed a courtesan's toilette? Every image needs careful contextualization.³ Similarly, public monuments may reflect cultural norms and tend to idealizations, while private commissions may have assumed a smaller audience and allow for some more personal agendas.

Men wrote about the appearance of other men, and were also the main recorders of intimate details about women, including the many ways in which they dressed their hair. Men, in both Greece and Rome, set a high benchmark for women to achieve with regard to their outward appearance. Regrettably, the few texts written by women that survive from this period add little to our understanding of female *cultus*. As a result, we know little or nothing about how women thought about their own physical presentation, or indeed their attitudes to each other's appearance as individuals, although it is probably safe to assume that women too bought into ideals of physical beauty. Indeed, it seems that as hair behavior was a clear marker of class and status, it was in their interests to conform to social convention about appearance.

Hair is mentioned frequently in comedy, in poetry, in historical narratives and even in medical texts and religious treatises. For instance, the comedic plays of the Greek dramatist Aristophanes and his Roman counterparts, Plautus and Terence, used visual stereotypes of physical appearance that their audiences would understand. Their plots were repetitive and easy to follow with a strong element of slapstick but at the same time could, particularly in the case of Aristophanes, contain insightful political comment. The physical appearance of the actors on the stage was a key means of telling the story. Theatrical masks were designed to make the actor's character and status clear to the audience (Figure 8.1).

These masks had hair attached and represented stock character types: the well-to-do young girl had long hair while the prostitute might have crimped and colored hair upon which she had spent much time in order to attract a client; the young man had a full

FIGURE 8.1 Mosaic of theater masks. Capitoline Museums. Photo: B.O'Kane / Alamy Stock Photo.

head of hair where the old man had not. Hair is often the butt of a joke. Bald-headed old men, like Dorio in Terence's *Phormio* are immediately judged to be buffoons (often miserly ones), while slaves, are easily identified by, among other attributes, their red hair.[4] Pollux's catalogue of the masks of Greek new comedy compiled in the second century CE describes the coiffure of the soldier characters as "wavy-haired."[5] In the opening scene of *Miles Gloriosus* (*The Swaggering Soldier*) Pyrgopolynicos (the soldier himself) has had his hair curled and perfumed, immediately signaling to the audience that he is not behaving with the exaggerated masculinity expected of a soldier but is a bit of a dandy.[6] These stereotypical characters of drama offer an insight into both hair behavior and the ways in which it could be viewed, and ridiculed, in society. In a historical text the description of hairstyles can also be used as a means of character description, and defamation— Suetonius describes Julius Caesar as trying to hide his baldness with an early version of the comb-over or by wearing a laurel wreath[7]—or as an expression of difference, of being an outsider or on the fringes of society as opposed to someone who belonged. In the words of the historian Tacitus: "The red hair and large limbs of those who inhabit Caledonia affirm their German origin."[8] Different literary genres will always stress different aspects of character and appearance but still, used with circumspection, they provide an interesting range of attitudes to class and status, and relative hair culture, across the ancient world.

The physical evidence for hair culture is of a more random order, given the accident of survival, but it is also evidence of different classes taking care of the self to varying degrees. Tools and ornaments including curling tongs (*calamistrum*), hairpins (*acus*), and combs (*pecten*) were used to style the hair and to hold it in place (see Figure 4.5). These are mentioned in literary texts and depicted in works of art. Actual examples of the objects themselves have been uncovered and add another dimension to our research. Hairpins, largely a female ornament, could be easily dropped and lost and, as a result, are frequently discovered lodged in the drains at public bath complexes as well as being excavated from burial sites and domestic and commercial premises.[9] This material evidence provides the scholar with a physical context within which to understand the presence, meaning, and significance of hair. More especially, because some of these items are found in public places such as baths or religious sites, we gain a sense of the presence of women on the municipal stage, so to speak, as well as in the private domestic environment with which they are more often associated. Men used implements to care for their hair too. Both sexes used curling tongs: these were composed of a simple metal tube heated in the fire before use.[10] Double-sided combs made of boxwood or bone were used not only to comb but also to delouse hair. These are common finds in urban and in military contexts and probably used not only by the camp followers but by the serving soldiers as part of their hygiene routine.[11] Both men and women across the social spectrum groomed themselves as part of a basic hygiene routine. The better quality and likely more expensive artifacts (elaborate combs, mirrors of polished metal, or pins with ornate designs) would have been owned by the wealthy. They are more durable and survived due to being placed in lavish tombs which have preserved them for our examination. Lower classes would have had at least some of these same items but theirs would have been less ornate and made of cheaper (and less durable) materials such as wood or cloth.

Class and status in the ancient Greek city states was entirely bound up with citizenship. Among citizens, physical appearance added to a sense of belonging. As we have seen in other chapters, ideas about how to wear one's hair differed between the important city states of Athens and Sparta but in both societies was influenced by their perception of class and status. As several authors in this volume have noted, Spartan men wore their hair long. According to the historian Herodotus, the elite male citizens of Sparta who belonged to established families (Spartiates) took great care of and great pride in their locks: he remarks upon "men exercising naked and others combing their hair."[12] For the Spartans, long hair represented virility and masculine strength and identified the small ruling, warrior class of Spartiates from all other men in the *polis*. Combing one's hair in the exercise yard would seem entirely appropriate masculine behavior. According to the geographer Strabo the free citizens of the *demos* recognized each other by their hair.[13] Slaves or helots did not have long hair. The helots wore a head covering while free citizens of Sparta had their heads uncovered, proud of their hair as a symbol of power both socially and physically.[14]

In contrast, free adult, Athenian males in the classical period tended to wear their hair long when young and shorter as they matured.[15] Adult citizens were expected to control their hair, as they controlled other aspects of their lives. Moving away from controlled hair suggested moving away from social norms and was only acceptable for certain identifiable groups such as philosophers, the elderly, and those in mourning. In Athens young men who chose to have long hair were often characterized as "Laconian" (Spartan) and the style carried connotations of effeminacy, excess, and a general flaunting of the usual social rules.[16]

In Greek culture young girls and unmarried women wore their hair long or perhaps loosely bound up, but as they matured into brides and married women hair became progressively controlled and covered. A young woman on the verge of marriage might wear her hair bound up by a band, while a respectable wife would be expected to cover her hair with a veil of some description.[17] Hair behavior clearly marked the status of women in classical Athens. In Sparta brides went through a ritual which required their hair to be cropped or shaven, a physical act which clearly marked their new status.[18] In antiquity Athenian authors criticize the excessive freedom given to Spartan women. This is partly due to the fact that they were seen out in public unveiled, with their hair in simple styles. Roman poets found the traditional image of Spartan women particularly erotic. Propertius thinks of them as exercising naked with young men, while Horace imagines a prostitute "with uncombed hair in a knot, Spartan style."[19]

Little evidence survives of the lower classes in classical Athens and we assume they adhered to similar hair behavior. One class of whom we have more information are courtesans, and evidence from vase painting would suggest they followed similar patterns to more respectable women in terms of how they dressed their hair (see below). Slaves, on the other hand, were likely to be represented with shorter or cropped hair, identifying their lack of power and status. Mireille Lee makes the point that in Athens, for women at least, gender was a much stronger identifier of hair than social status.[20]

While in ancient Greece loose locks had their place for both sexes, both adult men and women in Roman times wore their hair under greater control; neatly cut for men, bound up and styled for women. As a general rule, care of the self, including keeping hair clean and tidy, was essential for men, in order to avoid what Cicero referred to as "boorish slovenliness."[21] However, the poet Ovid, who has a good deal to say about hair and, indeed, adornment in general, warned men against paying too much attention to their person with the following instruction:

> Let it not please you to curl your hair with irons and rub not your legs with rough pumice ... a neglect of beauty becomes men.[22]

Women were allowed more leeway, and expected to maintain at least some standards of beauty in order to reflect the class and status of their menfolk, but they too, had to walk a fine line between excess and modesty.[23]

Hairstyles of upper-class women set trends in hair styling. The images of the wives and daughters of Roman emperors depicted in stone, paint, and mosaic are the equivalent of images of celebrities and glamorous models airbrushed to perfection in modern-day media: a false representation of reality that was, and is, not only false but largely unachievable.[24] The general populace might never see these elite women in person. For the lower classes any idea as to what the members of the ruling family looked like was probably based on the images displayed in public places and on coinage. The "architectural" hairstyles such as that displayed on the *Fonseca Bust*, sometimes identified as Vibia Matidia, niece of the emperor Trajan, indicate the time and care that must have employed used to achieve this particular look (Figure 8.2; see also the side and back view of this hairstyles at Figures 3.12a and b).

Juvenal makes reference to a woman wearing a similar style:

> See the tall edifice rise up on her head in serried tiers and storeys! See her heroic stature—at least that is from the front; her back view is less impressive.[25]

Meeting a woman wearing such a tall hairstyle face-to-face conveyed the unspoken message that this woman was a person both literally and metaphorically of some stature

FIGURE 8.2 *Fonseca Bust*. Photo: B. Malter DAI Mal615-10_16304.

in society. Even the inches added to a woman's physical height by a wig or an elaborate hairstyle brought her closer to an ideal, and imposed a certain posture and body language in order to maintain it. We might question whether women realistically could have worn some of these very ornate hairstyles on a day-to-day basis but as Janet Stephens has shown in this volume and elsewhere, many such styles were certainly possible, with some help. It is not hard to imagine some practical problems with these styles in terms of movement and posture. Janet Stephens has in fact recreated the Fonseca hairstyles using a manikin with wavy hair, bodkins, curling tongs, and a bone needle for sewing.[26] It seems reasonable to conclude that such styles would have restricted movement and indeed the ability to perform even simple tasks. However, the female elite would not have been expected to do much for themselves as they had a retinue of slaves to cater for their needs. Concentrating on holding the head correctly also aided deportment and added to the sense of self-control a woman was meant to show in life. Statues of the Severan empresses, Julia Domna for example, have detachable marble coiffures which could indicate that these elite women wished their hair shown styled in up-to-the-minute fashion in keeping with their elevated social status; after all they set the trends for others to follow.[27] Items used to keep hair in place could also serve as hair decoration and means of displaying wealth and social status. Diadems such as that shown in the Fayum portraits from first-century Roman Egypt made of gold and other precious metals would have been owned by wealthy. Plain bone pins are common site finds suggesting these were used by the many rather than the few. Some are more elaborately carved such as the one shown in Figure 8.3. However, other more lavish hairpins made of precious metals have been found.

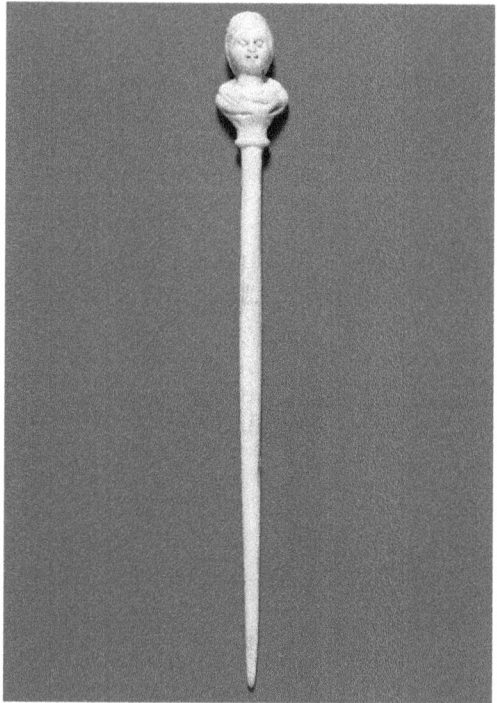

FIGURE 8.3 Bone pin. Roman Cypriot (first to fourth centuries CE), 10.6 cm in length. Metropolitan Museum of Art, New York, NY, The Cesnola Collection. Purchased by subscription, 1874–75. Acc. No. 74.515206.

To maintain one's make-up and hair over the day into the evening would have required much attention. Time and money were something that women belonging to the upper echelons of society possessed. The toilette included washing, arranging the hair, caring for the complexion, and applying cosmetics. Funerary reliefs often show a woman at her toilette.[28] A panel on a funerary monument from Neumagen dating from the third century CE is a good example of this type of image (Figure 8.4). Its sheer physical size, together with the number of servants shown attending the mistress in front of a mirror, is intended to convey wealth, respectability, and comfortable domesticity. The high social status of the mistress, seated in the wickerwork chair in the center of the image, and the subject matter of the relief, would have been immediately obvious to the contemporary onlooker. The inclusion of female servants who styled the hair and applied make-up as well as the allusion to the products themselves in the form of containers and other dressing-table accessories convey the message of personal wealth and status. While one servant girl is acting as hairdresser, another holds a bottle, perhaps of hair oil, another the mirror for the mistress to watch the progress of her toilette, and the last a jug. The servant girls all have uniform hair, pulled away from the face and held in a bun on the top of the head. The mistress, on the other hand, is in the process of having her hair arranged. Showing the act of hairdressing is a relatively rare motif in Roman art and it is interesting to note that it occurs in a provincial context. The mistress' hair would presumably have been braided and arranged on top of her head, and perhaps covered with a veil of some description, but this is left to the viewer's imagination. The presence of such an iconographic program in the provinces suggests the spread of Roman values about *cultus* and its place in the

FIGURE 8.4 Toilette scene from Neumagen. Image © GDKE / Rheinisches Landesmuseum Trier. Photo: Th. Zühmer.

creation of the respectability of the upper-class Roman in the provinces, or the provincial who wished to align themselves with Roman cultural values.

The monument to Hegeso, dating to ca. 400 BCE, and discussed in Chapters Two and Three (Figure 2.5), portrays a similar scene of the deceased mistress being attended by her slave girl. As in the Neumagen relief, the status of the mistress and slave is shown not only by contraposing the seated mistress with the standing slave but also by hairstyle and dress. The maid's hair is bound up and covered while Hegeso's is also bound up, but in a far more elaborate style in a *kredemnon*—a style of head covering that was associated with marital chastity. The hairstyles and the dress of the two figures here, as in the Neumagen relief (and those mentioned in the Introduction), illustrates the world of class and status difference between mistress and maid.[29]

The visual portrayal of the woman before her mirror legitimized the time spent on making-up and adornment; hairdressing was an important part of the process. Dyeing and arranging the hair or fitting a wig took time and sometimes a good deal of money to purchase the hair or hair products, and a specialist slave with the skills to carry out the task. Images such as the Neumagen relief speak to us in much the same way as the epithet, *lanam fecit* (she worked with wool), and its derivatives work in epitaphs; they imply idealized female behavior and virtue.[30] It also stresses the unequal relationship between mistress and slave. A mistress could be very dependent on her slaves and their expertise in hairdressing and applying cosmetics. She would also have to rely on their judgment of the finished appearance as polished metal mirrors offer a very limited reflection. In the literature of the day, the lady of the house often reinforces her own superior position by acting in a cruel manner towards her servants:

> A single ringlet out of the whole circle of hair had gone amiss fixed insecurely with an unsteady pin. Lalage punished the misdeed with the mirror in which she had seen it, and Plecusa fell smitten, victim of cruel tresses.[31]

The toilette is one setting where the superiority of the mistress (or master) could be reinforced through cruelty. Such behavior would, however, be out of place in the context of the funerary relief that is intended to honor its subject. While men are never the subject of the toilette scene in art, the images of their female relatives (whether wives, mothers, or sisters) infer the wealth and importance of male members of the family to which the woman belonged.

The elite male kept his hair short though some of the more flamboyant Roman emperors adopted more elaborate styles. Trends in facial hair came and went.[32] If a man paid too much attention to his hair he could be judged effeminate and not suited to holding public office. Even if he held a public office, a man could be demeaned by those opposed to him making references to his appearance. Cicero mocks his adversary, Gabinius, consul in 58 BCE, describing him as "dripping with unguents, with waved hair."[33] Lack of hair was another common complaint among men. There are statues of bald men revered as elder statesmen, following the veristic style common in the late republic (Figure 8.5)[34] even though the bald man is a stock character intended to raise a laugh in Greek and Roman comedy.[35]

Baldness might change individual male status from young and virile to old, superfluous, and an object of ridicule. Suetonius' description of Julius Caesar (which includes a reference to his sparse locks) is one which is intended to cast doubt on his character and give just such an impression. The biographer remarks:

FIGURE 8.5 Late Roman republican statue, holding ancestor busts. Photo: D-DAI-ROM-2001.2076.

> [Julius Caesar] was somewhat overnice in the care of his person being not only carefully trimmed and shaved but even having superfluous hair plucked out as some have charged; while his baldness was a disfigurement which troubled him greatly since he found it was often the subject of gibes of his detractors. Because of it he used to comb forward his scanty locks from the crown of his head.[36]

This is perhaps an early example of the comb-over often resorted to today by men who are self-conscious about their lack of hair. Men did wear wigs. However, unlike women they hoped, on account of the negative impact this might have on their status as a man, that no one would notice if they were wearing one. The historian Suetonius says that the

Roman emperor Otho wore a wig (see Figure 9.9).[37] He points this out to cast aspersions on the emperor's character and to belittle his status.

COURTESANS, MISTRESSES, AND PROSTITUTES

For women engaged in the sex trade, appearance really mattered. Among this group of women there were, in effect, those of high and low social status. In literature and art, Greek *hetaerae* often sport the same hair arrangements as respectable citizen women. In Athenian culture, it is often courtesans who are the only women whose names we know as it was not thought honorable for respectable wives to have their names mentioned in public. Demosthenes defines the difference between varying classes of women: *hetaerae* are for pleasure, concubines for the day-to-day care of our body, and wives in order to procreate lawfully and have a trusted guardian of the household.[38] This comment came in a law court speech *Against Neaera*, a Corinthian prostitute who lived with an Athenian citizen as his wife, an arrangement which was illegal in Athens, because both her class and her Corinthian birth disqualified her from legitimate marriage. We know little of Neaera's appearance but given that she had passed as an Athenian wife to the extent that her daughter from a previous relationship had been married off to an Athenian citizen, another illegal act, we can assume that nothing in her physical appearance exposed her false status.

The girlfriends of the Latin elegiac poets writing in the late first century BCE and early first century CE, Lesbia (Catullus), Corinna (Ovid), Cynthia (Propertius), and others are based on a contemporary type, perhaps stand-ins for specific individuals. These women were courtesans (*hetaerae*) rather than street prostitutes (*pornē*) bestowing their favors on one or perhaps two wealthy men from whom in turn they expected payment both in money and in expensive gifts (including beauty products). In Propertius' description of his girlfriend, the association of the color of her hair and her build is important; Cynthia has "red-gold hair, long hands, big build—she moves like Juno."[39] She is presented as a goddess. Her "well-groomed hair" is indicative of her well-controlled character, although there clearly is some poetic imagination at work here, since her sexuality is obviously less controlled.[40] The first-century CE poet Ovid uses references to hair as evidence of his girlfriend's erotic beauty. He reinforces her singular superior status by comparing her to a past female regent of the Assyrian Empire:

> Behold, my Corinna comes, dressed in a tunic wrapped around her, with her divided hair falling over her white neck, just as the notorious Semiramis is said to have gone into her bedchamber.[41]

However, Ovid devotes one whole poem to chastising his girlfriend for using hair coloring, combs, and curling irons against his advice.[42] As a result of her overattention to her hair, and transforming it from its natural state, it has fallen out. The poem is mock heroic and concludes by comparing the status of the Romans as a conquering nation over the Germans; the hair of the conquered German tribes is cut off to make fashionable wigs for women like Corinna.[43] In other works Ovid advocates moderation in hair behavior and the wearing of clothes in colors which suit the wearer's complexion and hair coloring.[44]

Women working in the sex trade in particular relied on their looks to earn a living and no doubt many, if they could afford it, resorted to dyes to or to wearing a wig to cover gray hair in the hope of securing their continued earnings. Poorer prostitutes touted for business in public places including the streets and even the graveyards. Their lowly social status is often implicit in their physical description—for example, Vetustilla, an aged prostitute described by Martial has having "three hairs and four teeth."[45] Lower-class women could also be defined by the products they used on their hair just as the wealth and status of upper-class women could be flagged up by their possessions. Some of the cheaper and more readily available hair products such as gum resin (*resina*), a harsh treatment for the removal of unwanted body hair was, according to Martial, used by the lowest of prostitutes.[46]

FREEDMEN AND WOMEN

Freedmen and women had clearly undergone a change in their social class and status by becoming freed citizens where previously they had been slaves. In commemorative monuments it is common to find freed persons expressing their status through dress. They wear the garments now permitted to them as freed citizens, the toga for men and often the *stola* and *palla* for women.[47] Their images are often completed with hairstyles which emulate those popular in sculpture of the upper classes of their time (Figure 8.6).[48]

In Figure 8.6, which is typical of many, three figures are depicted in a rectangular frame. To the left an older man and woman are shown with joined right hands, the traditional symbol of legitimate Roman marriage. Their names reveal their status as freedmen and freedwoman. Sextus Maelius, the *praenomen* and *nomen* shared by the older and younger man, and the presence of the letter L, indicate they were freed by the same patron. The woman in the center, their wife and mother respectively was freed by a different patron, a woman. Her name Vesinia, followed by the backwards C, indicates her freed status. As slaves they would not have been allowed to marry legally, and any children born to them would be illegitimate and have taken the slave status of their mother. Their upward social mobility is reflected in the monument itself but also in the ways they choose to be

FIGURE 8.6 Funerary relief of Sextus Maelius Stabilio, Vesinia Iuncunda, and Sextus Maelius Faustus. North Carolina Museum of Art, Raleigh. Purchased with funds from the State of North Carolina, 79.1.2.

represented. They wear clothing which reflects their newly acquired freed status, as does their hair. Their images are a mirror of the upper-class free citizens they aim to emulate in their monument. Their posture, the *dextrarum iunctio* and the *pudicitia* (modesty) pose similarly display their desire to align themselves with upper-class values.[49]

Another epitaph to a freedwoman named Allia Potestas is notable for its rather gushing wording. It was paid for by two men with whom she had relationships, and is surprising in its comments about her body and suggests that she was a *matrona*, when she was in fact a freedwoman, but again, it stresses the assimilation of upper-class values by those who were socially mobile:

> To a unique degree, so that she could cope with all tasks. She was uncensured because she attracted little gossip, She was the first to slip from her bed; she was likewise the last there. To return to rest when affairs had been set in order. The wool never left her hands without a cause; No-one was before her in deference or in salubriousness of morals. She never had a high opinion of herself, she never fancied herself a free woman. She was beautiful with lovely eyes, was golden-haired. There was an ivory gleam in her face Such as they say no mortal had. And on her snow-white breasts the shape of her (?) nipples was small. What about her legs? She had quite the pose of Atalanta on the comic stage. She was not sparing, but generous with her lovely body. She kept her limbs smooth and the hair was sought out everywhere.[50]

The description includes references to her hair being blonde and to her removal of body hair in the final lines.[51] The lengthy physical description in fact blurs features associated with women of low and high status. Her lack of body hair helps to raise her social standing from lower class to a position of respectability. Her blonde hair would have been by the time she was living (sometime between the third and the fourth centuries CE) a feature of fashionable women of all classes even though in some contexts blonde retained the stigma of the lower-class woman (perhaps slave woman) who was sexually available.[52]

In literature written by the elite, the freedman image is not quite as respectable and conservative as it is in much of the self- or patron-commissioned iconography. Petronius' description of the nouveau-riche ex-slave Trimalchio betrays all the upper-class prejudices surrounding former slaves and their assumption of status. In commenting on Trimalchio's entrance to his own dinner party, one of his guests cannot prevent himself from impolitely smiling at the incongruity of his host's appearance. Trimalchio is carried in, wearing a cloak of blazing scarlet, with a napkin with broad purple stripes and tassels wrapped around this neck—and from this display of clothing and its pretensions to upper-class and even senatorial values, protrudes a head close-cropped in a haircut reminiscent of slavery.[53] His haircut is clearly used to comic effect. Everything about Petronius' characterization of Trimalchio is hyperbole and plays into the prejudices of his own class. In reality freedmen and women made up much of the population of Roman towns and presumably mixed as social equals with those outside the elite. It was in their interests to present an image which reflected their new status, rather than their former one, and both dress and hair could be used to that end.

SLAVES

Both Greeks and Romans had uneasy relationships with slaves and express anxiety about the lack of difference in appearance between free and slave. In fifth-century BCE Athens, the so-called "Old Oligarch" complained that slaves were treated with as much respect as free citizens.⁵⁴ Writing in the second century CE about the situation in Rome after the death of Julius Caesar (44 BCE), the historian Appian worried in a similar vein about the apparent degeneration of the populous:

> The Roman plebs [free citizens] is very mixed up with immigrants. A freedman has the same civic rights as they have, and a man who is still a slave wears the same clothes as his masters; for the dress of the rest of the population, excepting that of senators, is that same as that of slaves.⁵⁵

For the most part, it appears that the distinction between free and slave was not expressed by dress or hairstyle, but rather by body language and a shared cultural understanding, informed by other visual symbols which could be ambiguous even to the Greeks and Romans. The upper classes in any ancient society would be identifiable by dress, hairstyles, and demeanor, and by being surrounded by groups of slaves and retainers when out and about. The mass of the people, on the other hand, as Appian complains, could look very similar to the aristocratic eye. On occasion a slave might be more visible by having a shaved head but this commonly marked a punishment, rather than the norm. Punishment which marked the head, signaled the status of the slave: a female slave might have her hair cropped to the scalp while slaves who ran away and were subsequently recaptured might have half of their head shaved as a mark of their misdeeds.⁵⁶ In the *Satyricon* two of the characters adopt a slave disguise by shaving their hair and eyebrows. This disguise is eventually detected but not before the shame of having a bald head is noted several times. The miscreants are even given wigs and fake eyebrows to redress literally their situation. The humor of this text is of course fundamental but in order to understand that comedy the reader must first understand the social conventions of appearance.⁵⁷

In iconography slaves are often identified by being of shorter stature than the main characters of a scene. The Greek lower classes including slaves (both male and female) wore their hair cropped in a short style. If they wore a head covering then they might have slightly more of their hair exposed or they might be noticeably different from the central important figure—as in the image of Hegeso and the Neumagen relief.⁵⁸ A similar funerary relief from Arezzo, dating from around the third or fourth century CE, depicts another version of a toilette scene where the *matrona* in the center is attended by a large number of servants.⁵⁹ Our eyes seem irrevocably drawn not only to the seated mistress but also to one servant in particular, that is, the slave who is styling her hair. This is the *ornatrix* or hairdresser, a trained slave or, sometimes following manumission, a freedwoman. By virtue of her knowledge and training the *ornatrix* is a servant of some importance within the hierarchy of slave women attending their mistress. Her job may have included fitting wigs and pulling out gray hairs as required.⁶⁰ She may also have overseen the make-up as well as the dressing of her mistress' hair. In this scene, as in the Neumagen relief, this particular servant is given a prominent position. In literary texts too, the hairdresser may take on a superior status when compared with the rest of the servants involved in the mistress' toilette: "besides she is your coiffeuse—her skill makes her favourite of yours."⁶¹ Juvenal remarks upon one Psecas who is employed simply to perfume her mistress' hair and is in charge of the hair oil as her name indicates.⁶² He also notes that "another maid combs out the left side of her mistresses hair and rolls it into a curl."⁶³ The status of these women as individuals would depend on their relationship with their mistress and no doubt their specific roles in dressing her hair, putting on her clothes, and applying her make-up helped to define their standing within the servant class itself.⁶⁴

Literary texts also allude to the ill treatment of the hairdresser and other maid servants. According to both Martial and Ovid they could on occasion be stabbed with hairpins or have the mirror thrown at them if their mistress was displeased. Allegedly, the *acus*—an ornamental pin used in the construction of often elaborate hairstyles, made of metal, wood, or bone with a sharp point at one end—was used to punish the maidservant who did not do her job effectively.[65] No doubt, some mistresses did treat their slaves badly but a slave's circumstances varied from household to household.

GLAMOROUS HAIR: GODS, GODDESSES, AND BLONDNESS

Real people, women in particular, were under some pressure to achieve the high standard of beauty represented by the unrealistic images of gods and goddesses. The gods represented glamor and the ideal. A full head of hair indicated strength and sexual prowess in the case of a male deity, and great beauty and erotic appeal in respect of the goddess. Traditionally the goddesses Venus and Ceres, had blonde hair as did Mercury the messenger of the gods, among others. Blonde hair possessed a certain cachet in antiquity, and at certain periods was much sought after. It is also important to note that the ancient notion and description of color was somewhat different to our own. Blonde, often referred to as *flavus* in Latin, might in fact be red, for example.[66] Blonde hair certainly carried erotic connotations, and often these are part of the characterization of lower-class women: the poet Menander (342–291 BCE) stated that "no chaste woman ought to make her hair yellow."[67] Horace's young prostitute, Pyrhha, had flaxen hair (*flavam comam*), tied up for an unknown lover, and when the empress Messalina went out in Rome to act the prostitute, she wore a blonde wig.[68] In Pompeii a more pertinent piece of graffiti complained: "Blondie has taught me to hate dark girls. I shall hate them if I can but I would mind loving them. Pompeian Venus Fisca wrote this."[69] In more epic literature, Virgil's queen Dido has golden hair, as does the Latin princess Lavinia.[70] Blondness is also a color of seduction and glamor for men. Plutarch notes that Sulla, the Roman general and statesman (139 BCE–78 BCE), considered that "his golden head of hair gave him a singular appearance."[71] Not only was the amount of hair Sulla possessed worth mentioning but the color was also important. Blond singled him out, as Plutarch acknowledges, giving a godlike appearance while his thick locks indicate youth and virility even perhaps his military prowess. According to the *Historia Augusta*, the emperor Lucius Verus took such pride in his yellow hair that he used to sift gold dust in it in order to make it shine and look more yellow.[72]

Not all mythical gods or demigods were portrayed as fair. Many in the Roman pantheon had dark hair, for example. Leda, the mother of Helen, was also described as a raven-haired beauty. Note Ovid's poetic appreciation of the beauty of fair and dark haired women:

> Black hair on snow white shoulders reminds one of Leda's raven locks. A platinum blonde of flax-haired Aurora.[73]

HAIR, STATUS, AND DISGUISE

Women might also change their hair, or be said to change their hair in order to assume a completely different persona. Famously as mentioned above, in Juvenal's Sixth Satire, the empress Messalina sports a blonde wig as she conducts herself wantonly in a public brothel: "Hiding her black hair in a yellow wig she entered the brothel."[74] This anecdote is clearly an attempt to present the empress on a much lower social scale and lower morals in the guise of a prostitute. The use of hair or head covering as a disguise was not confined to women. According to his biographer Suetonius, the emperor Nero too prowled around the city of Rome at night committing heinous crimes while wearing some sort of head covering which may be a wig or a hat.[75] Hair could be a useful disguise. Just as a slave once freed might try to disguise a slave mark by covering it with a patch or *splenium* he or she might also try to hide the mark of his previous status by covering this with a lock of his or her hair. Martial pokes fun at a slave who tried to conceal his branding with a fringe.[76]

Hair could be used to switch genders, usually for comic effect. At the behest of their master or mistresses male domestic slaves were made to look like women not only by dressing them as such but also by keeping them beardless and free from body hair. Nero was said to have castrated the boy Sporus and tried to make a woman of him.[77] In Aristophanes' play *Women at the Thesmophoria*, the kinsman of Euripides assumes the guise of a woman by shaving his beard and singeing his pubic hair. In the *Assembly Women*, another play by Aristophanes, women pretend to be men by wearing false beards.[78]

LATE ANTIQUITY

The increasing influence of Christianity reinforced this condemnation of the toilette and attention to one's appearance. Ascetics or religious fanatics went to the opposite extreme of sporting shaved heads or unwashed tangled locks. However, the Christian religion was nowhere near as influential in this period as it would become in later times and did not deter many women from spending time on their hair and make-up. There may have been some danger for Christian women in appearing too different to their pagan friends and neighbors. Saint Perpetua, martyred in 203 BCE, at the point of death "pinned up her dishevelled hair for it was not fitting to suffer martyrdom with her hair loose since she might seem to be mourning in her hour of glory." Here a Christian who is also a married woman of high status bows to society's long-standing conventions and makes the symbolic statement that death by martyrdom is not death at all.[79] Many early Christian writers picked up on traditional classical tropes of idealized masculinity and femininity expressed through appearance. In the early third century Clement of Alexandria wrote a long treatise of instructions on how to be a good Christian, much of which focused on manners and appearance. His attitude to hair care and hairdressing was very much in the vein of classical moralists. On women:

> So those women who wear gold, occupying themselves in curling at their locks, and engaged in anointing their cheeks, painting their eyes, and dyeing their hair, and practising the other pernicious arts of luxury, decking the covering of flesh—in truth, imitate the Egyptians, in order to attract their infatuated lovers.

> … Head-dresses and varieties of head-dresses, and elaborate braidings and infinite modes of dressing the hair, and costly specimens of mirrors, in which they arrange their costume,— hunting after those that, like silly children, are crazy about their figures—are characteristic of women who have lost all sense of shame. If any one were to call these courtesans, he would make no mistake, for they turn their faces into masks.[80]

And on men:

> But for one who is a man to comb himself and shave himself with a razor, for the sake of fine effect, to arrange his hair at the looking-glass, to shave his cheeks, pluck hairs out of them, and smooth them, how womanly! And, in truth, unless you saw them naked, you would suppose them to be women.[81]

Clement goes on to describe the effeminate male who has his body hair removed and the number of shops that have sprung up to supply such a service, so that men are not even ashamed to be witnessed undergoing such a procedure in public. While such diatribes are not aimed at particularly classes per se, they do speak to general attitudes prevalent in both Greek and Roman culture towards notions of gendered behavior for men and women of status, and the ways in which Christianity absorbed current social mores.

CONCLUSION

While the Greeks and Romans might want to use hair as a visual means of defining social class, there was a good deal of inconsistency and blurring of boundaries. While the majority of the population may have observed social norms in terms of their hair, there were always exceptions, and hair could be arranged to ensure an individual was not what he or she might seem at first. Social mobility in the classical world was not straightforward and the social structures of both Greek and Roman societies were very complex. The messages of hairstyles are not always clear and need to be taken together with other clues such as dress, context, and genre to avoid confusion, or at least understand the nuances.

CHAPTER NINE

Cultural Representations

GLENYS DAVIES

We are highly dependent on the visual arts of Greece and Rome for our knowledge of what hair looked like in the ancient world. But how far can such representations be taken at face value, as illustrations of what people really wore? Hair carried a lot of cultural baggage, and it rapidly becomes clear that artistic representations of hair are seldom straightforward. Hair on the scalp is only part of the story: beards (and their absence) also play an important part, as does the presence, or, more often, absence of other body hair in representations of nude and partially clothed figures. Hair as presented in art played an important role in creating character and expressing individual identity: the choice of a particular hair or beard style not only reflected but also constructed the status and social role of the person depicted. As this volume has demonstrated, hair could be used to indicate the age, gender, race, status, and moral standing of the figures shown, whether these were portraits of real individuals or characters in a narrative or myth. Social attitudes to a variety of aspects of hair (such as baldness, being clean-shaven as opposed to wearing a beard, depilation and grooming, and elaborate female coiffures) are only partially revealed in the written sources, which need to be supplemented by careful reading of the visual images. But fashions and attitudes did not remain static: they changed over time and differed from one social group to another.

AESTHETIC CODES AND CONSTRUCTIONS

Artists of the ancient world producing sculpture in marble or bronze, vase and wall painting, mosaics, carved gems and coins were fascinated by hair: hair could be as, or more, challenging to represent than drapery. Recreating the texture and color of hair and representing the hairstyles worn exercised artists of all periods, who attempted both to show hair realistically and to exploit its decorative properties.

Representing texture, color, and hairstyles

Although hair could simply be indicated by a solid mass (of color or stone) without added shading or carving to indicate the strands of hair, many artists were fascinated by the various methods that could be used to indicate the texture of hair. Most impressive are the marble portrait sculptures of Antonine men (mid-Roman imperial period: e.g. Marcus Aurelius—Figure 9.1; see also Figure 3.9)[1] with curls (both on the head and in the beard) recreated using the drill and the chisel, the hair texture contrasted with the smooth polished skin; or the highly structured hairstyles of elite women earlier in the second century (Figures 9.2a and b; also Figures 3.12 and 8.2).[2] Later, however, the mid-third-century male fashion for close-cropped hair and a beard closer to designer stubble was represented using "negative modelling," in which the surface of the head is cut into by short chisel strokes (Figure 9.3).[3]

FIGURE 9.1 Marble portrait bust of Marcus Aurelius. Vatican Museum, Rome. Photo: DAI-ROM-96Vat2081.

FIGURE 9.2a Marble portrait of Matidia. Capitoline Museum, Rome. Photo: B. Malter DAI-ROM Mal2005-04_16577,01.

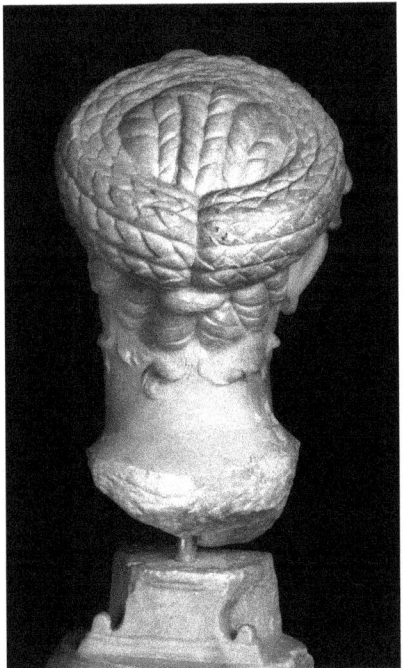

FIGURE 9.2b Back view of Matidia. Capitoline Museum, Rome. Photo: B. Malter DAI-ROM Mal2005-06–16577,03.

FIGURE 9.3 Detail of a bronze statue of Trebonianus Gallus (emperor 251–253 CE). Metropolitan Museum of Art, New York, NY. Rogers Fund, 1905. Acc. No. 05.30.

On statues made of bronze, curls and short ringlets might be modeled separately and attached while the texture of hair lying closer to the skull was indicated by lines or indentations created either by modeling or by chasing the cold metal.[4] Indicating texture in painted media was achieved mainly by painting strands of hair, waves, and curls using brush strokes of contrasting shades or colors: this was easily achieved in painted media such as mummy portraits (Figures 9.4 and 9.6),[5] but more difficult in mosaic where *opus vermiculatum*—worm-like lines of small tesserae—were used to indicate strands of hair.[6]

Texture was not so easily indicated in Attic black-figure vase painting but red-figure allowed for more gradations of tone and curvaceous lines, and the thickness of the slip or paint could be exploited to create textured effects (Figure 9.10).[7]

Artistic experimentation with representing different textures and types of hair can be seen in the pediments of the Temple of Zeus at Olympia (ca. 460 BCE) where one young Lapith has short curls in a cap all over his head, with a hole drilled in the center of each curl, Apollo has straight strands of hair ending in curls (see Figures 1.1 and 3.3), and the old seer is bald on top with similar strands to Apollo below (Figure 9.5).[8] The women have straighter strands of hair, or their hair is bound up in a scarf. Later sculptors attempted to express the textures of tousled hair,[9] and to distinguish between the hair textures of different ethnic groups (such as the "Dying Gaul" (see Figure 2.7) or the tight corkscrew curls of images of Africans, see Figure 7.5).[10]

The usual color for hair, where it survives, is black or dark brown: this is used for most mummy portraits. The hair on marble statues and figures sculpted in relief was

FIGURE 9.4 Mummy Portrait of a Young Woman (ca. 170–200 CE), tempera on wood, 34.9 × 21.3 cm. The J. Paul Getty Museum, Los Angeles, CA.

FIGURE 9.5 Detail of the marble figure of an old seer from the East pediment of the Temple of Zeus at Olympia (c. 460 BCE). Photo: D-DAI-ATH Hege - 0321. Arachne 34462.

usually painted, but it is rare for traces of paint to survive, and when it does it may be the undercoat that we see, not the final color.[11] It was possible in both Greece and Rome for hair to be represented as a light brown, auburn, or blond color. In red-figure vase painting figures shown with lighter colored hair are often characterized as slaves/servants, who may have come from outside Athens, their hair color serving to underline their foreignness.[12] The women reclining in the banquet scene in the Etruscan Tomb of the Leopards, Tarquinia, Italy, appear to have blonde hair, although it is not obvious what significance this has.[13] It is impossible to know whether portraits attempted to represent the actual color of the subject's hair, but achieving realistic hair color was not always the aim of the artist: color could also have symbolic meaning. The hair of some statues of the Roman imperial period (especially those depicting emperors) was gilded, giving a godlike rather than a realistic appearance.[14] Also "unrealistic" is the bright blue occasionally used for beards, possibly intended to emphasize the supernatural character of the figure.[15]

Older figures might also be represented with white or gray hair, where the medium made this possible (white was easily achieved by vase painters, but not gray). Men with white hair and beards can be found in Attic and south Italian red-figure vase painting, and some mummy portraits show both elderly men and women with dark hair streaked with gray (Figure 9.6).[16] The painted tondo of Septimius Severus and his family (from Egypt, now in Berlin)[17] shows him with gray hair and beard, painted with brushstrokes of white, gray, and a darker shade, recreating a pepper-and-salt effect (his wife, Julia Domna, and his son Caracalla both have brown-colored hair, with lighter and darker strokes of paint to indicate waves in her case, and curls for him).

FIGURE 9.6 Mummy portrait of old woman (Roman period: date uncertain). British Museum, 1980.0921.1. © Trustees of the British Museum.

One aspect of hair which the visual arts could not convey was the use of scents and pomades, a habit which, along with curling the hair, was ridiculed by Martial as characterizing the effeminate philanderer.[18]

We tend to rely on the images created by artists for our knowledge of the changing hairstyle fashions of the ancient world without questioning how much the styles shown owe to the imagination of the artist or how far they have been embellished, exaggerated, or misunderstood by him. The hairstyles represented in portraits were probably worn only on special occasions, and are part of the artificial construction of the identity and status of the subject. Thus the elaborate and highly wrought hairstyles seen in the portraits of elite Roman women in the early decades of the second century CE (Figures 9.2a and b; also Figures 3.12 and 8.2) may represent hairstyles worn by real women, but they may also in part be the creation of the artist who made the statue or portrait bust, and not faithful reproductions of the actual hairstyle of the sitter.[19] Nevertheless, artistic representations are essential evidence for the changing styles, and the rate at which change occurred, throughout the period.

Realism vs. pattern

Sculpted and painted hair could look very realistic, almost in defiance of the medium, but artists were also fascinated by the pattern-making potential of hair, and throughout the period pattern vies with naturalism. Artistic exploitation of the pattern-making potential of hair is seen especially in the art of archaic Greece, where rows of identical pin-curls or waves create repetitive rhythms and so a decorative pattern rather than a depiction of real hair. Archaic Greek statues of youths (*kouroi*—see Figures 3.1 and 3.2) show experimentation with the decorative potential of the hair across the brow: for example the statue from Anavyssos has a row of pin-curls while the Volomandra *kouros* has a flame-like fringe.[20] Most elaborately decorative is the Rampin horseman's dreadlocks (Figure 9.7; see also Figure 4.7),[21] and similar interests in patterned representation of hair can also be seen in archaic vase painting (especially Attic black-figure). The Celtic La Tène love of curvilinear shapes was applied to hair (e.g. on coins of the Parisi) to rather different effect.

In the Greek world, artificial patterns gave way to less formal designs, with greater variation in the size, shape, and arrangement of curls and strands of hair, giving a more natural impression. This development can be seen in the early classical period (such as the sculptures from the Temple of Zeus at Olympia—see Figures 1.1, 3.3, and 9.5). By the fourth century BCE artists were less interested in regular patterns, and attempted to represent less structured hair, naturally tousled, no doubt reflecting changes in fashion. More structured hairstyles, however, returned at intervals (as for example with the Roman women's hairstyles of the early second century CE): the artistic representation of hair always involved a balance between the natural and the artificial, and even "natural-looking" hair was to some extent an artifice. Portraits of the emperor Augustus show what looks like a very simple, natural hairstyle, but the locks of hair in his fringe invariably included one pair of forked locks and one pair arranged as crab-claws (see Figures 1.6, 2.2, and 3.8).[22] This arrangement became a way of identifying Augustus, and was adopted for portraits of some other members of his family to stress their connection with him[23]—but was this really a distinguishing feature, or was it an artistic convention?

FIGURE 9.7 Head of the marble statue known as the "Rampin Horseman", detail (ca. 550 BCE). Louvre Museum, Paris. Photo: SuperStock / Alamy Stock Photo MFA.

Representing age: Baldness, receding hairlines, and wigs

Much of the art of Greece and Rome features "ideal" figures (such as gods and heroes) who are in the prime of life, but characters in myth also included both the young and the old, part of whose characterization involved their hair (and beards): portraits, too, although often idealized to some extent, used hair to indicate age. Attitudes to thinning hair, hair loss, and complete baldness were complex and fluid. Baldness (often indicated by receding hairlines or a bald patch on top with a fringe of hair round the sides and back) could be used as a positive sign of venerable old age (as with the "seer" from the Temple of Zeus—Figure 9.5; and see also Figure 8.5),[24] but also represented as balding on Attic vases are satyrs, the half-animal followers of Dionysus, who are usually shown behaving reprehensibly (Figure 9.8).[25]

FIGURE 9.8 Attic red-figure psykter with revelling satyrs by Douris (ca. 500–470 BCE). Brish Museum. ©Trustees of the British Museum.

Complete baldness or sparse hair was frequently represented in portrait images: balding mature and elderly men were represented on Greek gravestones from the mid-fourth century BCE onwards, at first with discreetly receding hairlines and some attempt to cover the bald areas by combing their hair forward,[26] and a degree of hair loss can also be seen on portraits of Greek intellectuals (such as philosophers):[27] here and on marble portraits of Romans of the late republic and early empire baldness appears to be a positive attribute denoting acquired wisdom (see Figure 8.5).[28] Nevertheless, in Greek literature baldness could be regarded as a sign of bad character and a subject of ridicule.[29] Many Roman men were sensitive about their hair loss: best known is Julius Caesar (who wore a wreath to hide his receding hairline according to Suetonius),[30] but Caligula also had receding hair and Domitian, who wrote a treatise on baldness, is shown in his portraits with his hair brushed forward in an attempt to disguise his bald patch.[31] The emperor Otho is also said by Suetonius to have worn a well-made wig, and can clearly be seen wearing one in the portraits on his coins (Figure 9.9).[32]

Portraits of Roman women only rarely show them with thinning hair (let alone bald), but a few do represent very old women with realistically thinning hair.[33] Apuleius declares

FIGURE 9.9 Coin portrait of Otho: obverse of an aureus, 69 CE. © Andreas Pangerl, www.romancoins.info. Published in "Portraits–500 years of Roman Coin Portraits," Munich, 2017.

that: "if you despoil the most outstandingly beautiful woman of her hair, were she Venus herself, bald she would not be able to seduce even her own husband" (*Metamorphoses* 2.8). Abundant amounts of hair would appear to have been desirable and expected for women, and luxuriant hair was a positive attribute for them, even if not entirely their own. Wigs and hairpieces are mentioned in the literature in relation to women, particularly by the satirists.[34] Some portraits appear to show women wearing complete wigs (Figure 3.13), but it would seem that the wig was a fashion choice rather than a necessity caused by hair loss: it was worn on top of the woman's own hair, curls of which can be seen peeping out at the sides.[35] The most obvious examples of this practice date to the late Antonine and Severan periods: such wigs are particularly associated with the empress Julia Domna (early third century CE), and wearing a voluminous wig on top of natural hair may have been a fashionable practice for a limited period only.[36] The more flamboyant hairstyles represented in portraits of the Roman imperial period look as though they would require a lot of very long hair, hence the (contested) suggestion that they may have been complete wigs or have incorporated hairpieces rather than consisting entirely of the woman's own natural hair, but the extent and frequency of such practices is controversial. A small number of marble portraits have been found with the hair carved separately and attached to the statue like a stone wig, but the reasons for this, and whether it bears any relation to the practice of wig-wearing in real life, is debatable.[37]

The aesthetics of body hair

It is noticeable that as far as art is concerned heroes, despite their powerful masculine physiques, have virtually no chest hair.[38] It is possible this was added to marble statues in paint but it does not appear to have been routinely indicated by carving or modeling. On some red-figure vases chest hair is indicated by a delicate brown or black line up the center of the torso (see the satyrs in Figure 9.8).[39] Underarm hair is hardly ever represented, although there is a clear instance of it on the large frieze of the Great Altar of Zeus from Pergamon, Turkey (one of the Giants has a tuft of hair in both armpits).[40] Male pubic hair was more routinely represented on nude figures: it was not generally represented on Greek *kouroi* of the sixth century BCE,[41] but in the classical period and later carved curly pubic hair became the norm for mature male nude figures.[42] Female nudes are much fewer in number, especially those with the pubic area exposed to view, but sculpted versions present them without any indication of pubic hair, and those represented in red-figure vase painting (such as sleeping maenads) have only the merest hint of pubic hair.[43] Clearly ideal figures (male and female) were not supposed to be hairy (with the exception of male pubic hair), and hairiness, if depicted at all, was reserved for alien or outsider figures (satyrs, for example, were sometimes covered in animal hair, as were parts of the body of Pan). Depilation for men (especially Romans) appears to have been a source of anxiety: as several chapters have noted, on the one hand a certain amount of grooming (including the plucking out of unwanted body hair) was expected of the civilized man (as opposed to hairy barbarians), but on the other hand too much attention to body hair removal, resulting in a completely smooth skin, laid one open to charges of effeminacy and ribald jokes.[44]

HAIR AS TEXT, READING HAIR

As several of the examples mentioned above show, hair of various kinds when represented in the visual arts was used to convey messages about the figures depicted, and the viewer was expected to decode the messages when reading the image as a whole. A woman with long hair worn loose, for example, had various connotations according to the context: for a young woman loose hair indicates a virginal, unmarried state whereas for mature women it suggests distress or mourning. Women with hair cropped short are also anomalous and are usually read by modern scholars as slaves: their hair is sometimes represented on vases not only cut short but also of a foreign color and texture.[45]

The language of beards: The beard as sign

It is perhaps beards, however, which best demonstrate the subtle messages to be teased out of the visual material. In early Greek (archaic) art beards were used primarily to distinguish mature men from (beardless) youths (as in Figure 6.1), but the style and length of beard could be further used to distinguish men from each other: for example, when Herakles is represented on vase painting wrestling the giant Antaios (Figure 9.10), Herakles has a full but neatly trimmed beard and a cap of dark hair, whereas his monstrous opponent has a longer, less tidy beard and an unruly mop of ginger-colored hair.[46] Satyrs are frequently represented with long beards, which sometimes jut out suggestively (as in Figure 9.8).

The beard and hairstyles of the male figures on late classical and Hellenistic images (primarily marble portraits and reliefs such as tombstones) have been the subject of recent research. Beards in the fourth century BCE came to be seen as attributes of the good citizen: shorter and neater for mature men, longer (hair and beard) for older men (who may also be shown with a bald pate).[47] Fashions changed under the influence of Alexander the Great, who adopted a clean-shaven appearance in his portraiture (and presumably in life): this new trend was followed by the Hellenistic kings who succeeded him and their courtiers.[48] But the beard was retained for those who identified as Greek citizens, involved in city life, and for soldiers, and longer beards came to be especially associated with philosophers; indeed, slightly different beard styles were adopted by the various philosophical schools. These longer beards went with the lined faces and stooped postures of the elderly philosophers (playwrights like Menander preferred the clean-shaven look of the court).[49] These associations for beards continued in the eastern part of the empire in Roman times.

At Rome the fashion for beards came and went. Early Romans probably wore beards,[50] but in the mid-republic shaving became the norm (possibly as a result of contact with the

FIGURE 9.10 Attic red-figure calyx crater with Herakles wrestling the giant Antaios by Euphronios (ca. 510–500 BCE). Louvre Museum, Paris. Photo: DAIR 54.142R.

Hellenistic Greek world), and most Romans were depicted clean-shaven throughout the first centuries BCE and CE (see Figures 1.6, 2.2, and 3.8 (Augustus); 4.2 (Pompey); 8.5 and 8.6).[51] The main exceptions were young men who had not yet shaved for the first time, and as an ostentatious sign of mourning.[52] The return to beard-wearing is associated with the emperor Hadrian (117–138 CE): there has been much speculation about why he adopted a full beard (plus mustache), and what it should be taken to signify (Greek intellectual interests, a military image, or to hide a blemished chin).[53] Hadrian rapidly established a fashion, and from the mid-second century onwards most Roman men were represented bearded (Figure 9.1; also Figure 3.9): a longer beard seems to have continued to be associated with civilian and philosophical interests, a shorter, more neatly trimmed beard with soldiers. Many emperors during the third century have minimalist beards, often no more than stubble (Figure 9.3), matched with closely cropped hair on the head. Constantine the Great returned to the clean-shaven look (Figure 3.10), perhaps in imitation of the first emperor Augustus, and this remained the norm for emperors for a long time afterwards: the one exception was the emperor Julian (emperor 360–363 CE), who adopted a full beard in defiance of the standard hair code of the day. As with the emperor Hadrian his reasons for doing so, and what can be read into it, have been much discussed.[54]

Hair and beards as expressions of nonconformity and otherness

Julian deliberately used his beard as an expression of nonadherence to the imperial codes of previous emperors and an assertion of difference. He was not the first emperor to do this: Nero's portraits as a boy and youth show him with the standard hairstyle adopted by the Julio-Claudians from the time of Augustus, and without a beard, but as emperor he began to appear with a more distinctive and individual image in both his sculpted portraits and on coins, often with hair that is long at the back, with a stepped fringe and a partial beard in the form of long sideburns which sometimes join up under the chin

FIGURE 9.11 Coin portrait of Nero: obverse of an aureus, 64-66 CE. © Andreas Pangerl, www.romancoins.info. Published in "Portraits–500 years of Roman Coin Portraits," Munich, 2017.

(Figure 9.11).[55] This hairstyle appears to have been associated with charioteers and entertainers: the adoption of a distinctive hairstyle by young circus-racing fans was recorded much later in the eastern Roman empire by Procopius. The style he describes sounds very like the modern mullet, and he associates it with young fans running wild.[56]

Hair and beard styles were also used in art to distinguish those who were foreign, monstrous, or "other" in some way from the true Greek or Roman citizen. This has already been seen in relation to satyrs and giants in Greek art (see Figures 9.8 and 9.10). Chapter Seven has also shown that under the Roman empire hair and beard also became a way of differentiating between Romans and "barbarians" (i.e. non-Romans): they were usually enemies of Rome, although some of the people incorporated into the empire, such as Mauretanians, were represented in art as ethnically different and with distinctive hair.[57] Generic northern barbarians were usually represented with longer, shaggier hair (and beards) than the Romans, but specific groups could also be distinguished by their characteristic hairstyles. On the crenellations of the Tropaeum Traiani monument at Adamklissi, Romania, Dacians are shown with thick straight hair worn in a pudding-basin haircut, whereas those belonging to the Germanic tribes have their hair twisted and tied up in the "Suebian knot" on one side of the head.[58] Long hair and straggly beards continued to be seen as characteristics of uncouth barbarians in late imperial times.

Images of women also use different hair codes to distinguish civilized Greco-Roman women from barbarian women, whose hair is frequently represented hanging loose and disheveled. On the columns of Trajan and Marcus Aurelius this is part of a narrative of capture and mistreatment at the hands of Roman soldiers: such women may even be pulled or dragged by their hair.[59] In both Greek and Roman society adult women are only shown with untamed, unbound hair in specific exceptional circumstances such as when they are in distress or in mourning.[60] Otherwise women's hair was kept under conspicuous control by tying it up in a scarf or some other form of headdress or hat,[61] or by subjecting it to complex hairstyles with the main part of the hair worn as a bun. The treatment of the Roman bride's hair and the hairstyles worn by the Vestal Virgins and the *flaminica dialis* (and also in theory all Roman matrons), involved not only complex hairstyles but also the use of woolen fillets as a way of showing the woman was under control and was capable of controlling herself (see Figure 1.5).[62]

HAIR SYMBOLISM, HAIR AS METAPHOR

In both literature and art, hair was often the part of the body singled out to suggest the quality and nature of the figure concerned: baldness or sparse hair, for example, alluded to a low or bad character such as Thersites (or satyrs), whereas the Olympian gods and heroes have abundant flowing hair. Brief epithets to do with hair further characterize these figures: Jupiter has awe-inspiring locks, Bacchus' hair is dripping with perfume, Apollo has long hair which has never been (and never will be) cut, Aeneas' hair too is long and flowing. Age is also suggested by references to white hair (e.g. Teiresias): when goddesses disguise themselves as old women their hair turns white, and Ovid characterizes Autumn as having hair going gray at the temples, while Winter has no hair or what little he does is white.[63]

Women's hair is represented as worn loose and flowing for a number of reasons, and acts as a code for these situations. Diana and her young female followers (such as Atalanta or various nymphs) are unwed maidens whose hair is worn loose on their shoulders, or at most held by a single ribbon, carelessly arranged.[64] For more mature women such a hairstyle is not appropriate, and for them hair worn loose is a sign of aberration and distress:[65] women let their hair hang loose as suppliants, and in addition tore at their hair in mourning, both in myth (such as Ceres mourning her daughter Persephone) and in real life (relief from Haterii monument).[66]

Molly Levine in a seminal article discussed the use of hair as a metaphor for the contrasted concepts of nature and culture, and the importance of maintaining the right balance between them, in Greek and Roman thought and society.[67] Hair (of various kinds, including beards and body hair) may be left unattended and uncontrolled (according to nature) or elaborately styled and tamed (with culture). Abundant hair for men suggested potency and virility, whereas in women, especially young women, luxuriant hair could be seen as a sign of untamed female sexuality which was a threat to men and proper male control of women. Women's "natural" hair therefore should be contained and controlled by hairdressing or covering, a change which normally occurred on marriage. Medusa can be seen as an illustration or metaphor for these ideas.[68] At the start of her story she had the luxurious locks of the typical beautiful maiden. She attracted the attention of Poseidon who seduced her and took her virginity in the Temple of Minerva, who punished Medusa by turning her hair into snakes: Medusa's usual epithet is "snaky-haired." This not only made her hideous, but she also turned those who looked at her to stone, and the only remedy was the rather radical form of "taming" her hair—decapitation by Perseus.[69] In early Greek art Medusa is a hideous creature with a huge grinning mouth full of animal-like teeth, huge staring eyes and snakes instead of hair. Her frontal head was often represented on its own (Figure 9.12), possibly with apotropaic significance, but in the later classical period onwards the Medusa head loses its hideous aspects: she takes on more of the appearance of a normal woman, albeit one whose wildly tossing hair is interspersed with snakes.[70]

FICTIONAL CHARACTERIZATION

Epithets referring to hair were frequently used in Greek and Roman literature to give a brief indication of the character of the figures involved in myth and epic, and the same was true in art (such as vase painting scenes). Hair similarly contributed to the creation of stereotypes: in the *Satyricon* for example his hair mirrors Trimalchio's changes in fortune and status. When we first meet him he is a bald (or at least sparsely-haired) man past his prime, playing ball with beautiful long-haired slave boys—as he had once been himself.[71] We

FIGURE 9.12 Terracotta antefix with the head of Medusa (mid-5th century BCE): from the Heraion, Samos, in Samos Museum. Photo: D-DIA-STH-Samon 5371.

later hear that he kept the hair from the first time he shaved his beard, a significant moment in his life (*Sat.* 29). Trimalchio's dinner guests are of a similar age and status (freedmen trying to hold on to their youthful looks), as indicated by their use of hair dye and wigs (*Sat.* 38 and 43). Similar attempts to hide the ravages of time and dissolute living are cruelly derided by satirists like Martial. Male attention to grooming (and its corollary, too little attention) was used in epic, historical writing, political invective, and the visual arts to suggest character. Uncouth figures such as giants are shaggy, with uncut hair and untrimmed beard: Ovid's account of the cyclops Polyphemus fits this mold until he falls in love with the nymph Galataea, when he starts to comb his hair (with a rake) and cuts his beard (with a scythe).[72] But, as we have seen in previous chapters, too much attention to such matters was used, especially in Roman political invective, to imply effeminacy and lack of proper manliness.

ISSUES OF SPECTATORSHIP AND IDENTIFICATION

The representation of hair in both the visual and the literary arts had several functions, varying to some extent according to the medium, period, and society that produced it, and the context in which it was viewed. Images and descriptions of hair helped viewers and readers to recognize and understand the figures before them, but such understanding relied on shared values and assumptions which often had judgmental undertones. A scene or image might seem to us to be an uncomplicated image of daily life, or the telling of a simple narrative, but it is not always easy for us to fully comprehend the coded messages or subtexts. Hair, along with facial features, body posture, and clothing, played an important part in communicating status, character, and moral worth. The carefully arranged patterned hair of archaic Greek statues of youths and maidens is a reflection of the aristocratic society they belonged to: they would be viewed and admired in cemeteries and sanctuaries as an expression of the aristocratic ideal. Vases would be viewed above all by the male guests at symposia, though some appear to have been made for use by women: the "purpose" of their decoration and how it relates to everyday experience and attitudes is still imperfectly understood, but again hair plays its part in the communication of a variety of messages, some of them didactic. Roman portraits may often seem to be ruthlessly realistic, but we cannot know for certain that their subjects really looked like this and that their appearance was not manipulated for ideological reasons. Portraits, whether made to be displayed in public as a civic honor, or more privately in the home or at the tomb, were usually made to express, and on occasion boost, the status and (self-)importance of the subject, and they should not be seen as straightforward photographic images without an agenda. Images would be viewed and read in a variety of different circumstances: some of these images offered models for emulation (or on occasion avoidance). But how did one emulate smooth-bodied heroes without slipping into effeminacy? And what was one to do about one's receding hairline?

ROLE IN DISSEMINATION OF STYLE TRENDS

Although art in the Greek and Roman worlds was generally quite widespread and often visible to large audiences, it did not constitute the mass communication we are familiar with. The patrons who commissioned and bought works of art were mostly from the highest and wealthiest sections of society, and art was mostly produced and displayed in urban contexts, especially major centers such as Athens and Rome. It is important to ask therefore who would see works of art, or would have the opportunity to read or hear works of literature; to what extent were fashionable hairstyles and ideas about hair communicated through the arts, and how far within society did they spread? The natural assumption is that trends began at the top of society (with kings, queens, emperors, and empresses) and percolated down to the lower ranks and out to the more remote provincial centers, although this was not always or necessarily the case.[73]

The dissemination of styles is best illustrated by the quite rapidly changing Roman imperial women's hairstyles (first to third centuries CE). Portraits of empresses and some other women from Roman high society were made in a variety of media. Marble statues and busts were displayed in public places in cities and towns throughout the empire, where they could act as models for women living in the provinces or of lower rank.

Heads of empresses with elaborate and detailed hairstyles also appeared on coins which circulated widely, but would only find their way into the hands of the relatively well-off. Representations in other media (such as carved gems) would have an even more limited distribution. The main evidence for the extent and speed at which new hairstyles were copied from these elite models by women of more humble status, or who lived in more far-flung parts of the empire, are honorary or, more often, funerary portraits. Some hairstyles clearly did percolate quite widely: most noticeable is the late Flavian "toupet" style worn by Julia Titi and Domitia Longina.[74] The same hairstyle can also be seen in many images of middle-ranking women (often funerary monuments) such as the wives of a potter and a soldier,[75] and on some provincial monuments.[76] But both lower-class women and women from the provinces also appear with simple generic hairstyles (such as hair drawn back into a bun at the nape of the neck) that do not seem to emulate court styles in any way (see Figure 8.4).[77]

Roman men too mostly adopted the current fashionable look in their portraits (straight hair and clean-shaven in the first century CE; curly hair and beard in the second century CE) in line with the style worn by the emperor, and in the fourth century BCE it seems that ideas of how ideal citizens and their wives should look were communicated by tombstones and portrait statues. But throughout we have to remember that we are seeing hair in all its manifestations through the artist's (or writer's) lens, which may at times distort reality. Did the person represented as a portrait *really* have hair like that of the emperor/empress? Or of an ideal citizen? Or were the hairstyles of emperor and citizen alike artistic constructs, with limited correlation with real life?

CONCLUSION

Hair is the part of the human body that is most easily manipulated and so, as this volume has so often demonstrated, it inevitably became an important medium for the expression of a wide range of human conditions, concepts, and attitudes: individual identity, status, age, gender, ethnicity, beliefs, and more. Hair was consequently also of prime importance for both artists and writers who represented hair in ways that expressed character and enhanced narratives, relying on a shared understanding of contemporary cultural hair codes. The treatment of hair in reality and its representation in art reveal a lot about the societies that produced them but for us, at times, they may need careful decoding.

NOTES

Introduction

1. Synesius, *On Baldness* 1.1. Text and translation by A. Fitzgerald from Jacques Paul Migne's *Patrolgica Graeca* (1168). Available online: http://www.livius.org/sources/content/synesius/synesius-eulogy-of-baldness/ (accessed 17 January 2017).
2. *On Baldness,* Introduction 2.
3. *On Baldness*, Dio's Speech 2–8; Homer, *Odyssey* 6.230–31.
4. *On Baldness*, Dio is too artful 2–4.
5. *On Baldness*, Wild animals are hairy; bald animals are intelligent 3.
6. *On Baldness*, A sphere is perfect 1–5.
7. *On Baldness*, Portraits of hairy gods are incorrect 1–2.
8. *On Baldness*, Bald people are healthier 1–3.
9. *On Baldness*, Bald skulls are stronger 2, 4, 6. Herodotus, *Histories* 3.12.
10. *On Baldness*, Not everyone agrees with Dio that long hair is beautiful 3.
11. *On Baldness*, Not everyone agrees with Dio that long hair is beautiful 5.
12. *On Baldness*, Bald helmets are awe-inspiring 3.
13. *On Baldness*, Vicious people like prostitutes have long hair 1, 3.
14. *On Baldness*, Dio cannot be taken seriously 1, 3.
15. *On Baldness*, Envoi 2.
16. On veiling for Christian women see Aiden Hartney, "'Dedicated Followers of Fashion': John Chrysostom on Female Dress," in *Women's Dress in the Ancient Greek World*, ed. L. J. Llewellyn-Jones (Swansea: Classical Press of Wales, 2002), 246, 252. Mary Rose D'Angelo, "Veils, Virgins, and the Tongues of Men and Angels: Women's Heads in Early Christianity," in *Off with her Head: The Denial of Woman's Identity in Myth, Religion and Culture*, ed. Howard Eilberg and Wendy Doniger (Berkeley: University of California Press, 1995), 131–64; Mary Harlow, "Female Dress, 3rd–6th Century: The Messages in the Media," *Antiquité Tardive* 12 (2004): 213–14.
17. Suetonius, *Domitian* 18, on a lost treatise of that emperor, also on baldness.
18. See Chapter Nine for analysis of visual culture in this period.
19. Some authorities have focused on hair but this work is often less mainstream in that it is read by a relatively small audience of interested classicists, ancient historians, classical art historians, and archaeologists and their students. The works most referenced by authors in this volume are discussed later in the Introduction.
20. See Chapter Nine for a fuller discussion.
21. J. Entwistle, *The Fashioned Body: Fashion, Dress and Modern Social Theory* (Cambridge: Polity Press, 2000), 2.
22. For Sparta see Chapters Three, Six, and Seven.
23. See, for example, categories in Alexandra Croom, *Roman Costume and Fashion* (Stroud: Tempus, 2000), 64, 97.

24. For a concise discussion of Freud's position see Howard Eilberg-Schwartz, "Introduction," in *Off With Her Head! The Denial of Women's Identity in Myth, Religion, and Culture*, ed. Howard Eilberg-Schwartz and Wendy Doniger (Berkeley and London: University of California Press, 1995), 2–4. On Medusa see also Chapter Nine in this volume.
25. Charles Berg, *The Unconscious Significance of Hair* (London: Allen and Unwin, 1951).
26. Eilberg-Schwartz, "Introduction," 3–4.
27. Edward Leach, "Magical Hair," *Journal of the Royal Anthropological Society* 88, no. 2 (1958): 147–64. For commentary see Eilberg-Schwartz, "Introduction," 4–5.
28. Mary Douglas, *Natural Symbols* (New York, NY: Pantheon, 1970), 65–82; C. R. Hallpike, "Social Hair," *Man* 4, no. 2 (1969): 256–64. Eilberg-Schwartz, "Introduction," 5.
29. Gannath Obeyesekere, *Medusa's Hair: An Essay on Personal Symbols and Religious Experience* (Chicago, IL: Chicago University Press, 1981). Eilberg-Schwartz, "Introduction," 5.
30. Anthony Synnott, "Shame and Glory: A Sociology of Hair," *British Journal of Sociology* 38, no. 3 (1987): 382.
31. Synnott, "Shame and Glory," 382–3.
32. See, for example, Sabina Lovibond, "An Ancient Theory of Gender: Plato and the Pythagorean Table," in *Women in Ancient Societies*, ed. L. Archer, S. Fischler, and M. Wyke (London: Macmillan, 1994), 88–101; Holt Parker, "Tetrogenic Grid," in *Roman Sexualities*, ed. J. Hallett and M. Skinner (Princeton, NJ: Princeton University Press, 1997); Chapter Six in this volume.
33. See Chapter Six.
34. See Chapters One and Six.
35. See Chapter Two on Alexander; Chapter Six on the "youthening" effect that artists were attracted to after ca. 500 BCE.
36. On beards see Chapters Three, Six, Seven, and Nine.
37. For depilation see Chapters Three, Four, and Six in this volume; Martin Kilmer, "Genital Phobia and Depilation," *Journal of Hellenic Studies* 102 (1982): 104–12; and David Lavergne, "Lépilation feminine en Grèce ancienne," in *Parures et artifices: le corps exposé dans l'Antiquité*, ed. L. Bodiou et al. (Paris: L'Harmattan, 2011), 99–110.
38. Gal. *On the Usefulness of Parts of the Body* 11.14.
39. See Chapter Six.
40. See Chapter Two for discussions of identity and Chapter Seven for the role of hair in defining Race and Ethnicity.
41. Paul Zanker, *The Power of Images in the Age of Augustus* (Ann Arbor: University of Michigan Press, 1990); chaps. 2, 9.
42. Suet. *Aug.* 79.
43. Andrew Stewart, *Art, Desire and the Body in Ancient Greece* (Cambridge: Cambridge University Press, 1997), 80–2; on hair and homoeroticism see Chapter Six in this volume.
44. Gloria Ferrari, *Figures of Speech: Men and Maidens in Ancient Greece* (Chicago, IL: University of Chicago Press, 2002), 6–9; 27–9.
45. Hegeso monument: Chapters Two and Eight; Neumagen: Chapters Four and Eight.
46. e.g. Ovid, *Ars Amatoria* and *Medicamenta*; Clement of Alexandria, *Paedagogus* 3.
47. Projecta Casket, British Museum, BM 1866, 1229.1; Mosaic from a private bath house in Sidi Ghrib, Tunisia in Bardo Museum, Tunis; cf. Alicia Walker, "Enhancing the Body, Neglecting the Soul," in *Byzantine Women and their World*, ed. Ioli Kalavrazou (New Haven, CT: Yale University Press, 2003), 233–73; Marice E. Rose, "The Construction of Mistress and Slave Relationships in Late Antique Art," *Women's Art Journal* 29, no. 2 (2008): 42–3.
48. Ferrari, *Figures of Speech* 17.

Chapter One

1. Molly Myerowitz Levine, "The Gendered Grammar of Ancient Mediterranean Hair," in *Off with her Head! The Denial of Women's Identity in Myth Religion and Culture*, ed. Howard Eilberg-Schwatrz and Wendy Doniger (Berkeley: University of California Press, 1995).
2. All of these topics are addressed in subsequent chapters of this volume: Spartan brides and ascetics see Chapter Six; slaves see Chapter Eight; head lice see Chapter Five.
3. Levine, "The Gendered Grammar," 85.
4. David Leitao, "Adolescent Hair-Growing and Hair-Cutting Rituals in Ancient Greece: A Sociological Approach," in *Initiation in Ancient Greek Rituals and Narratives*, ed. David B. Dodd and Christopher A. Farrone (London: Routledge, 2003), 112. See Chapters Three and Six in this volume on life course rituals.
5. Leitao, "Adolescent Hair-Growing," 112. On hair cutting rituals and iconography see Evelyn B. Harrison, "Greek Sculpted Coiffures and Ritual Haircuts," in *Early Greek Cult Practice: Proceedings of the Fifth International Symposium at the Swedish Institute at Athens, 26–29 June 1986*, ed. R. Hägg, N. Marinatos, and G. C. Nordquist (Stockholm: P. Åströms Forlag, 1988), 247–54. Harrison gives a brief overview of the evidence for Greek Bronze Age and Egyptian Old Kingdom hair cutting rituals, 247–8.
6. Leitao, "Adolescent Hair-Growing," 112; see also Sarah Hitch, "From Birth to Death: Life-Change Rituals," in *The Oxford Handbook of Ancient Greek Religion*, ed. E. Eidinow and J. Kindt (Oxford: Oxford University Press, 2015), 527–31.
7. See Susan Guettel Cole, "The Social Function of Rituals of Maturation: The Koureion and the Arkteia," *Zeitschrift für Papyrologie und Epigraphik* 55 (1984): 234; Carol L. Lawton, "Children in Classical Attic Votive Reliefs," in *Constructions of Childhood in Ancient Greece and Italy*, ed. A. Cohen and J. B. Rutter (Princeton, NJ: *Hesperia Supplement* 41. The American School of Classical Studies at Athens, 2007), 57–8; Jenifer Neils, "Children and Greek religion," in *Coming of Age in Ancient Greece*, ed. Jenifer Neils and John Oakley (New Haven, CT: Yale University Press, 2003), 145.
8. See Cole, "The Social Function of Rituals of Maturation," 235; and Leitao, "Adolescent Hair-Growing," 114–16 for examples.
9. Leitao, "Adolescent Hair-Growing," 118. For images see G. Van Hoorn, *De vita atque cultu puerum monumentis antiquis explanato* (Amsterdam: in aedibus J. H. de Bussy, 1909); Harrison, "Greek Sculpted Coiffures and Ritual Haircuts," 247–54; Hans Rupprect Goette, "Römische Kinderbildnisse mit Jugend-Locken," *Mitteilungen des Deutschen Archäologischen Instituts, Athenische Abteilung* 104 (1989): 203–17.
10. Plutarch, *Theseus* 5, recalling Homer, *Iliad* 2.542; Harrison, "Greek Sculptured Coiffures and Ritual Haircuts," 248; John Boardman, "Heroic Haircuts," *Classical Quarterly* 23, no. 2 (1973): 196. See also Chapter Three in this volume.
11. Pausanias, *Guide to Greece* 1.37.2.
12. Paus., *Guide to Greece* 2.3.6.
13. Leitao, "Adolescent Hair-Growing," 114–17.
14. Susan Walker, ed., *Ancient Faces: Mummy Portraits from Roman Egypt* (London: British Museum, 1997), 61. On this image see also David Thompson, *Mummy Portraits in the J. Paul Getty Museum* (Malibu, CA: J. Paul Getty Museum, 1982), 40–1.
15. Jane Draycott "Hair Today, Gone Tomorrow: The Use of Real, False and Artificial Hair as Votive Offerings," in *Bodies of Evidence: Ancient Anatomical Votives Past, Present and Future*, ed. Jane Draycott and Emma-Jayne Graham (Abingdon: Routledge, 2017), 79–81. Herodotus, *Histories* 2.65.4.

16. See Chapter Six for fuller discussion. On this image see also Thompson, *Mummy Portraits*, 40–1.
17. Horace, *Ars Poetica* 156–78.
18. Cassius Dio, *Roman History* 48.
19. Suetonius, *Nero* 12.4.
20. Suet. *Nero* 1, cited in Draycott, "Hair Today, Gone Tomorrow," 79.
21. Martial, *Epigrams* 11.39. Mary Harlow and Ray Laurence, *Growing Up and Growing Old in Ancient Rome: A Life Course Approach* (London: Routledge, 2002), 73.
22. Harlow and Laurence, *Growing Up*, 74; Mary Beard et al., *Roman Religion*, vol. 1 (Cambridge: Cambridge University Press, 1998), 47.
23. Ovid, *Fasti* 2. 435–52.
24. Paus. *Guide to Greece* 1.43.4.
25. Propertius, 4.19; Festus 561. For a full discussion of wedding ritual see Karen K. Hersch, *The Roman Wedding* (Cambridge: Cambridge University Press, 2010).
26. See Hersch, *The Roman Wedding*; Susan Treggiari, *Roman Marriage* (Oxford: Clarendon Press, 1991), 163.
27. Sophocles, *Ajax* 1175–81.
28. Albert Henrichs, "The Tomb of Aias and the Prospect of Hero Cult in Sophokles," *Classical Antiquity* 12, no. 2 (1993): 166–7.
29. Henrichs, "The Tomb of Aias," 168, and his references.
30. Levine, "The Gendered Grammar," 86.
31. Aeschlyus, *Libation Bearers* 6–7.
32. Levine, "The Gendered Grammar," 86.
33. Paus. *Guide to Greece* 2.11.6; Draycott, "Hair Today, Gone Tomorrow," 81.
34. Draycott, "Hair Today, Gone Tomorrow," 83–4, with examples of terracotta votives and artificial hair dedicated in similar ways.
35. On the lock of Berenice see Catullus, 66; Kathryn Gutzweller, "Callimachus' Lock of Berenice: Fantasy, Romance and Propaganda," *The American Journal of Philology* 113, no. 3 (1992): 359–85; Dee Clayman, "Bernice and her Lock," *Transactions of the American Philological Association* 141, no. 2 (2011): 229–46. For a political slant on the episode see Lloyd Llewellyn Jones and Stephanie Winder, "A Key to Berenike's Lock? The Hathoric Model of Queenship in Early Ptolemaic Egypt," in *Creating a Hellenistic World*, ed. A. Erskine and L. Llewellyn-Jones (Swansea: Classical Press of Wales, 2011), 247–70. See also Chapter Two in this volume.
36. D. R. Jordan, "*Defixiones* From a Well Near the South-West Corner of the Athenian Agora," *Hesperia* 54, no. 3 (1985): 251.
37. Lucian, *Dialogues with Courtesans* 4.
38. Apuleius, *Metamorphoses* 3.16; John Englebert and Timothy Long, "Functions of Hair in Apuleius' 'Metamorphoses,'" *Classical Journal* 68, no. 3 (1973): 238.
39. *IL* 1737. 26–30; Jordan, "*Defixiones* From the Athenian Agora," 252–3. For other examples see Hendrik S. Versnel, "Prayer and Curse," in Eidinow and Kindt, ed., *The Oxford Handbook of Ancient Greek Religion*, 447–61.
40. See Gary Vikan, "Art, Medicine and Magic in Early Byzantium," *Dumbarton Oaks Papers* 38 (1984): 68–72.
41. Laura Gawlinski, "'Fashioning' Initiates: Dress at the Mysteries," in *Reading a Dynamic Canvas: Adornment in the Ancient Mediterranean World*, ed. Cynthia S. Colburn and Maura K. Heyn (Newcastle: Cambridge Scholars Publishing, 2008), 151–9.
42. Gawlinski, "'Fashioning' Initiates," 156–60; Matthew Dillon, *Girls and Women in Classical Greek Religion* (London: Routledge, 2002), 263–4.

43. See Dillon, *Girls and Women*, 125 on the festival to Demeter in Alexandria; 211–12 on Sparta; 263 on mysteries to Despoina in Arkadia and the Asklepieion at Pergamon.
44. Ov. *Fast*. 3. 257–9.
45. Soranus, *Gynaecology* 2.6.
46. Festus, 454L; Robin Lorsch Wildfang, *Rome's Vestal Virgins: A Study of Rome's Vestal Priestesses in the Late Republic and Early Empire* (London: Routledge, 2006), 11; Laetitia La Follette, "The Costume of the Roman Bride," in *The World of Roman Costume*, ed. Judith Sebesta and Larissa Bonfante (Madison: University of Wisconsin Press, 1994), 56–7, and her discussion of Martial, *Epigrams* 12.32.2–4 where *septem crines* is used to describe a greedy wife.
47. Wildfang, *Rome's Vestal Virgins*, 13; La Follette, "The Costume of the Roman Bride," 57.
48. Varro, *Lingua Latina* 6.21; Wildfang, *Rome's Vestal Virgins*, 13; La Follette, "The Costume of the Roman Bride," 57. Mary Beard, "The Sexual Status of Vestal Virgins," *Journal of Roman Studies* 70 (1980): 12–27; and "Re-reading (Vestal) Virginity," in *Women in Antiquity, New Assessments*, ed. R. Hawley and B. Levick (London: Routledge, 1995), 166–77.
49. Seneca, *Epistles* 14.11; unspun wool was also thought to have protective properties, and brides hung it on the doorposts of their new homes, Pliny, *Natural History* 29.30.
50. Cicero, *On Laws* 2.8.
51. Liza Cleland et al., *Greek and Roman Dress from A-Z* (London: Routledge, 2007), 77.
52. Varro, *Ling*. 8.44.
53. Gellius, *Attic Nights* 15.17.
54. La Folette "The Costume of the Roman Bride," 55f.; Hersch, *The Roman Wedding*.
55. John Scheid, "*Graeco Ritu*: A Typically Roman Way of Honouring the Gods," *Harvard Studies in Classical Philology* 97 (1995): 20, 27.
56. Hom. *Il*. 22. 405–06, 468–72.
57. Hom. *Il*. 18.23–27.
58. Plutarch, *Roman Questions* 14 (*Moralia* 267a–b).
59. See also references in Mary Harlow, ed., *A Cultural History of Dress and Fashion in Antiquity* (London: Bloomsbury, 2017). For the veiling of Greek women see Lloyd Llewellyn Jones, *Aphrodite's Tortoise* (Swansea: Classical Press of Wales, 2003).
60. See Naftali S. Cohn, "What to Wear: Women's Adornment and Judean Identity in the Third Century Mishnah," in *Dressing Judeans and Christians in Antiquity*, ed. Kristi Upson-Saia, Carly Daniel-Hughes, and Alicia J. Batten (Farnham: Ashgate, 2014), 21–36. This volume provides an extensive bibliography on the subject of hair as part of adornment in both Jewish and early Christian texts. Alicia J. Batten, "Neither Gold nor Braided Hair (1 Timothy 2.9; 1 Peter 3.3): Adornment, Gender and Honour in Antiquity," *New Testament Studies* 55 (2009): 484–501.
61. Mary Rose D'Angelo, "Veils, Virgins and the Tongues of Men and Angels: Women in Early Christianity," in Eilberg-Schwatrz and Doniger, ed., *Off with her Head! The Denial of Women's Identity in Myth Religion and Culture*, 131.
62. D'Angelo, "Veils, Virgins and the Tongues of Men and Angels," 131–52, citing Paul 1 Corinthians 11.2–16; Avot de Rabbi Natan A 1, 3; and Tertullian, *On the Veiling of Virgins*; see also Batten, "Neither Gold nor Braided Hair."

Chapter Two

1. "Self," *Oxford English Dictionary* (Oxford: Oxford University Press, 2014). Recent inquiries into the notion of the self in classical antiquity include Richard Sorabji, *Self: Ancient and Modern Insights about Individuality, Life, and Death* (Chicago, IL: University of Chicago Press, 2006); Shadi Bartsh, *The Mirror of the Self: Sexuality, Self-Knowledge, and the Gaze in*

the Early Roman Empire (Chicago, IL: University of Chicago Press, 2006); Christopher Gill, *The Structured Self in Hellenistic and Roman Thought* (Oxford: Oxford University Press, 2006).

2. In most societies, hair plays a role in visually defining aspects of an individual's personal, social, and cultural identities; Geraldine Biddle-Perry and Sarah Cheang, "Introduction: Thinking About Hair," in *Hair: Styling, Culture and Fashion*, ed. Geraldine Biddle-Perry and Sarah Cheang (Oxford: Berg, 2008), 3–12.

3. Anthony Synnott, *The Body Social: Symbolism, Self, and Society* (London: Routledge, 1993), 104–6. See also the Introduction to this volume.

4. Synnott, *The Body Social*, 125. His categories depend upon a binary male/female gender identification. In antiquity, those choosing to negate their gender identities, such as Christian ascetics, would choose an opposite hairstyles to the social norm (men with long hair, women with short), see below.

5. "Hairstyles," in *Greek and Roman Dress from A to Z*, ed. Liza Cleland, Glenys Davies, and Lloyd Llewellyn-Jones (London: Routledge, 2007); Marice Rose and Katherine A. Schwab, in *Hair in the Classical World*, Bellarmine Hall Galleries, Fairfield University Art Museum (Fairfield, CT: Fairfield University, 2015). Exhibition Brochure.

6. Jenifer Neils and John Oakley, *Coming of Age in Ancient Greece* (New Haven, CT: Yale University Press, 2003); Nikolaos Kaltsas and Alan Shapiro, eds., *Worshiping Women. Ritual and Reality in Classical Athens* (New York: Alexander S. Onassis Public Benefit Foundation USA, 2008); John Oakley and Rebecca Sinos, *The Wedding in Ancient Athens* (Madison: University of Wisconsin Press, 1993). Substantial groundwork in the Aegean Bronze Age has been published by Robert Koehl, "The Chieftain Cup and a Minoan 'Rite of Passage,'" *Journal of Hellenic Studies* 106 (1986): 99–110; Ellen Davis, "Youth and Age in the Thera Frescoes," *American Journal of Archaeology* 90, no. 4 (1986): 399–406; and Florence Hsu, "Ritual Significance in Mycenaean Hairstyles," *Chronika* 2 (2012): 92–102. See Patrick Olivelle, "Hair and Society: Social Significance of Hair in South Asian Traditions," in *Hair, its Power and Meaning in Asian cultures*, ed. Alf Hiltebeitel and Barbara Miller (Albany: State University of New York Press, 1998), 11–51, for South Asian treatment of hair in Hinduism and its use as a social control. See also Chapter One in this volume.

7. For examples see G. M. A. Richter, *Korai: Archaic Greek Maidens* (London: Phaidon Press. 1968). For a selection of Acropolis korai, see Cat. No. 109 (Figs. 328–331), Acropolis Museum No. 669; Cat. No.110 (Figs. 336–340), Acropolis Museum No. 681; Cat. No. 111 (Figs. 341–344), Acropolis Museum No. 671; Cat. No. 112 (Figs. 345–348), Acropolis Museum No. 678; Cat. No. 113 (Figs. 349–354), Acropolis Museum No. 679; and Cat. No. 116 (Figs. 362–367), Acropolis Museum No. 682. For examples from the Genelaos dedication at Samos, see Cat. No. 67 Philippe (Figs. 217–220) and Cat. No. 68 Ornithe (Figs. 221–224).

8. David Leitao, "Adolescent Hair-Growing and Hair-Cutting Rituals in Ancient Greece: A Sociological Approach," in *Initiation in Ancient Greek Rituals and Narratives: New Critical Perspectives*, ed. David Dodd and Christopher A. Faraone (London: Routledge, 2003), 109–29, hair-cutting rituals, 111; Neils and Oakley, "Coming of Age," 153. See also Chapter One in this volume.

9. Herodotus, *Histories* 7.209. For Spartan hair see also Chapters Six and Seven in this volume. On "laconizing style" see also Chapter Three in this volume.

10. Maria Wyke, "Women in the Mirror: The Rhetoric of Adornment in the Roman World," in *Women in Ancient Societies: An Illusion of the Night*, ed. Léonie Archer, Susan Fischler,

and Maria Wyke (Basingstoke: Macmillan, 1994), 135; Kelly Olson, *Dress and the Roman Woman: Self-Presentation and Society* (London: Routledge, 2008), 8.

11. Elizabeth Bartman, "Hair and the Artifice of Roman Female Adornment," *American Journal of Archaeology* 105, no. 1 (2001): 5–7. See also Chapters Three and Four in this volume.
12. Dress, including hair, is one of the first communications of gender to others; see Joanne B. Eicher and Mary E. Roach-Higgins, "Definition and Classification of Dress: Implications for Analysis of Gender Roles," in *Dress and Gender: Making and Meaning*, ed. Ruth Barnes and Joanne B. Eicher (New York: Berg, 1992), 17, 23.
13. Alexandra Croom, *Roman Clothing and Fashion* (Stroud: Amberley, 2010), 115.
14. Synesius, *On Baldness* 1.1. Text and translation by A. Fitzgerald from Migne's *Patrologia Graeca* (1168). Available online: http://www.livius.org/sources/content/synesius/synesius-eulogy-of-baldness/synesius-eulogy-of-baldness-1/ (accessed March 17, 2017). See Introduction to this volume for discussion of Synesius' treatise.
15. As did Pompey before him; Paul Zanker, *The Power of Images in the Age of Augustus* (Ann Arbor: University of Michigan Press, 1990), 10. Diana E. E. Kleiner, *Roman Sculpture* (New Haven, CT: Yale University Press, 1992), 61–9, for Augustus' hairstyle types in portraiture.
16. Kleiner, *Roman Sculpture*, 43, 127.
17. A. J. Boyle, "Introduction: Reading Flavian Rome," in *Flavian Rome: Culture, Image, Text*, ed. A. J. Boyle and W. J. Dominik (Leiden: Brill, 2003), 34.
18. Susan Elliott Wood, *Roman Portrait Sculpture, 217–260 AD: The Transformation of an Artistic Tradition*, vol. 12 (Leiden: Brill, 1986), 27–8.
19. Christopher Oldstone-Moore, *Of Beards and Men: The Revealing History of Facial Hair* (Chicago, IL: University of Chicago Press, 2015) 45–8. Nero wore a curly beard on his neck, as did soldiers and middle-class citizens; R. R. R. Smith, "Cultural Choice and Political Identity in Honorific Portrait Statues in the Greek East in the Second Century A.D," *The Journal of Roman Studies* 88 (1998): 89–91. Citizen Roman men did wear facial hair of various lengths and types, see J. J. Arnold, "Theodoric's Invincible Mustache," *Journal of Late Antiquity* 6, no. 1 (2013): 152–83, for descriptions of styles.
20. Leviticus forbids the shaving of the "side-growth of beard" (19:27, 21:5). The practice was interpreted in various ways over time, but a Jewish man's wearing a beard in classical antiquity indicated purity and devotion. Oldstone-Moore, *Of Beards and Men*, 36.
21. Oldstone-Moore, *Of Beards and Men*, 49–62; Caroline Vout, "What's in a Beard? Rethinking Hadrian's Hellenism," in *Rethinking Revolutions through Ancient Greece*, ed. Simon Goldhill and Robin Osborne (Cambridge: Cambridge University Press, 2006), 96–123. On beards see also Chapters Three and Nine in this volume.
22. Paul Zanker, *The Mask of Socrates: The Image of the Intellectual in Antiquity* (Berkeley: University of California Press, 1996), 222–4.
23. Maria E. Doerfler, "Coming Apart at the Seams: Cross Dressing, Masculinity, and the Social Body in Late Antiquity," in *Dressing Judeans and Christians in Antiquity*, ed. Kristi Upson-Saia, Carly Daniel-Hughes, and Alicia J. Batten (Burlington, VT: Ashgate, 2014), 41–3.
24. Bartman, "Hair and the Artifice," 1. On status see Chapter Eight in this volume.
25. Molly Myerowtiz Levine, "The Gendered Grammar of Ancient Mediterranean Hair," in *Off With Her Head! The Denial of Women's Identity in Myth, Religion, and Culture*, ed. Howard Eilberg-Schwartz and Wendy Doniger (Berkeley: University of California Press, 1995), 91–2; Bartman, "Hair and the Artifice," 5.
26. Kristi Upson-Saia, "Hairiness and Holiness in the Early Christian Desert," in *Dressing Judeans and Christians in Antiquity*, ed. Upson-Saia, Daniel-Hughes, and Batten, 170–1.

NOTES 169

27. Elizabeth Bartman, *Portraits of Livia: Imagining the Imperial Woman in Augustan Rome* (New York: Cambridge University Press, 1999), 37. On the *nodus* see also Chapter Three in this volume.
28. Bartman, *Portraits of Livia*, 36–8; Diana E. E. Kleiner *Cleopatra and Rome* (Cambridge, MA: Harvard University Press, 2005), 246.
29. Bartman, *Portraits of Livia*, 38.
30. Myerowitz-Levine, *Gendered Grammar*, 91–6.
31. Lloyd Llewelyn-Jones, *Aphrodite's Tortoise: The Veiled Woman of Ancient Greece* (Swansea: Classical Press of Wales, 2003); Karen Hersch, *The Roman Wedding: Ritual and Meaning in Antiquity* (Cambridge: Cambridge University Press, 2010), 95.
32. Valerius Maximus, *Memorable Deeds and Sayings* 6.3.10.
33. Alicia J. Batten, "Neither Gold nor Braided Hair (1 Timothy 2.9; 1 Peter 3.3): Adornment, Gender and Honour in Antiquity," *New Testament Studies* 55, no. 4 (2009): 484–501; Wyke, "Women in the Mirror," 134–51.
34. Lillian Stoner, "Mourners, Maenads, and Madness: 'Crazy' Hair on Greek Vases," presented at *Hair in the Classical World Symposium*, Fairfield University, November 6, 2015. See also Chapter Six in this volume.
35. Kaltsas and Shapiro, *Worshiping Women*, 156–7, National Archaeological Museum, Athens, Inv. No. 3624.
36. For more on status see Chapter Eight.
37. Zanker, *Mask of Socrates*, 233–42. See Chapter Seven in this volume.
38. Sheila Dillon, "Women on the Columns of Trajan and Marcus Aurelius and the Visual Language of Roman Victory," in *Representations of War in Ancient Rome*, ed. Sheila Dillon and Katherine E. Welch (New York: Cambridge University Press, 2006), 246–9.
39. Jerry Toner, "Barbers, Barbershops and Searching for Roman Popular Culture," *Papers of the British School at Rome* 83 (2015): 99, 101. Livy compares a man's messy hair and beard to that of wild animals; Wyke, "Women in the Mirror," 135.
40. Kristi Upson-Saia, *Early Christian Dress: Gender, Virtue, and Authority* (New York: Routledge, 2011), 80; Upson-Saia, "Hairiness and Holiness," 158.
41. Zanker, *Mask of Socrates*, 262. See also Chapter One in this volume.
42. Charles H. Cosgrove, "A Woman's Unbound Hair in the Greco-Roman World, with Special Reference to the Story of the 'Sinful Woman' in Luke 7:36–50," *Journal of Biblical Literature* 124, no. 4 (2005): 681.
43. Cosgrove, "A Woman's Unbound Hair," 684; Lori Touchette, *The Dancing Maenad Reliefs: Continuity and Change in Roman Copies* (London: University of London Press, 1995). For examples of Amazons, see Guntram Koch and Hellmut Sichtermann, *Römische Sarkophage* (Munich: Beck, 1982). This is a contrast to Greek iconography, where Amazons usually wore helmets, Phrygian caps, or bound hair.
44. Cosgrove, "A Woman's Unbound Hair," 675–92. See also Chapters One and Six in this volume.
45. Levine, "The Gendered Grammar," 104. There is no consensus as to whether this obligation was based in custom or derived from the Torah; Leila Leah Bronner, "From Veil to Wig: Jewish Women's Hair Covering," *Judaism* 42, no. 4 (1993): 467–8.
46. Llewelyn-Jones, *Aphrodite's Tortoise*.
47. Roman texts tended to be prescriptive with regard to dress, including hair; Olson, *Dress and the Roman Woman*, 11.
48. Colin M. Kraay, *Greek Coins* (London: Thames and Hudson, 1966), pl. 176.
49. The authors are grateful to Milexy Torres, professional hairstylist with the *Caryatid Hairstyling Project*, for this observation. On the formation of curls, placement, and keratin

packing of cells, see Kurt S. Stenn, *Hair: A Human History* (New York: Pegasus Books, 2016), 82.

50. Oldstone–Moore, *Of Beards and Men*, 41–8. The clean-shaven fashion gained popularity in the twentieth century with the invention of the disposable razor blade in the 1930s. Beards have regained a prominence and acceptance since the early twenty-first century, whether or not this new trend is associated with masculine authority, as in ancient Greece and Rome, can be debated.
51. Oldstone-Moore, *Of Beards and Men*, 44–5. See also Chapter Nine in this volume.
52. Coin circulation was the fastest means of spreading imagery across the widest geographical expanse in the Greek-speaking world. Both portrait iconography and fashion trends reached a wide audience.
53. British Museum, 1919,0820.1.
54. Andrew Stewart, *Faces of Power: Alexander's Image and Hellenistic Politics* (Berkeley: University of California Press, 1993); Zanker, *The Power of Images*.
55. Stewart, *Faces of Power*; Andrew Stewart, *Art in the Hellenistic World* (Cambridge: Cambridge University Press, 2014); Jerome J. Pollitt, *Art in the Hellenistic Age* (Cambridge: Cambridge University Press, 1986).
56. Stewart, *Art in the Hellenistic World*, 75–83. See Chapter Seven in this volume for further discussion on hair as ethnic differentiator.
57. Hdt. *Histories* 4.64.
58. Densely textured Greek hair, as with the warrior on the Onesimos fragment, compared to the petals of a hyacinth, Homer, *Odyssey* 6.229–231. The authors thank Helaine Smith for this reference.
59. Dyfri Williams, "Onesimos and the Getty Iliupersis," *Greek Vases in the J. Paul Getty Museum 5. Occasional Papers on Antiquities* 7 (1991): 47.
60. Levine, "The Gendered Grammar," 91–6.
61. Curtis E. Montier, "Let Her Be Shorn: Corinthians 11 and Female Head Shaving in Antiquity," (unpublished MA thesis, North Texas State University, 2015), 12–23.
62. David W. J. Gill, "The Importance of Roman Portraiture for Head-Coverings in 1 Corinthians," *Tyndale bulletin* 41, no. 2 (1990): 256; Montier, "Let Her Be," 26–31.
63. Bartman, *Portraits of Livia*, 39.
64. This may be part of a Mediterranean iconographical tradition of victory; the Palette of Narmer, from Predynastic Egypt, ca. 3000–2920 BCE, depicts the king pulling the hair of a defeated foe.
65. Vanessa Rousseau, "Emblem of an Empire: The Development of the Byzantine Empress's Crown," *Al-Masaq: Islam and the Medieval Mediterranean* 16, no. 1 (2004): 6; "Crowns," in Cleland, Davies, and Llewellyn-Jones, ed., *Greek and Roman Dress from A to Z*, 43–44; Ann M. Stout, "Jewelry as a Symbol of Status in the Roman Empire," in *The World of Roman Costume*, ed. Judith L. Sebesta and Larissa Bonfante (Madison: University of Wisconsin Press, 1994), 82.
66. He may also have used it to distract from his baldness. Kleiner, *Cleopatra and Rome*, 127.
67. "Corona," in Cleland, Davies, and Llewellyn-Jones, ed., *Greek and Roman Dress from A to Z*, 40.
68. Pliny, *Naturalis historia* 22:6–13.
69. Stout, "Jewelry as a Symbol of Status," 82.
70. Stout, "Jewelry as a Symbol of Status," 93.
71. Stout, "Jewelry as a Symbol of Status," 83.
72. Rousseau, "Emblem of an Empire," 6.

73. Neils and Oakley, *Coming of Age*, 152. This practice of tonsure, for initiation ceremonies as well as dedications, is found in many cultures and continues through today in some parts of the world, e.g. India. See Emma Tarlo, *Entanglement: The Secret Lives of Hair* (London: One World Publications, 2016), 73–4; see also Olivelle, "Hair and Society."
74. Kaltsas and Shapiro, *Worshiping Women*, 88, 291. Pausanias, *Guide to Greece* 2.11.6, was unable to see Hygieia's cult statue inside her temple at Titane due to the number of hair dedications. Pausanias also remarks on hair dedications by both maidens and youths prior to marriage throughout his travels in Greece (e.g. 2.32.1). See also Jennifer Larson, *Greek Heroine Cults* (Madison: University of Wisconsin Press, 1995). For more on hair dedications see Chapter One in this volume.
75. Marble female head from Argive Heraion, National Museum, Athens, Inv. No. 1571; Nikolaos Kaltsas, *Sculpture in the National Archaeological Museum* (Athens: Kapon Editions, 2002), 115.
76. Levine, "The Gendered Grammar," 81; Plutarch, *Lycurgus* 15.3. See also Chapter Five in this volume.
77. Oakley and Sinos, *Wedding*, 14–16, and fig. 23, an Attic red-figured *lebes gamikos* attributed to the Washing Painter, National Archaeological Museum, Athens, Inv. No. 14790.
78. Oakley and Sinos, *Wedding*, 19–20.
79. For the unique combination of dress and mantle, see Linda Roccos, "The Kanephoros and Her Festival Mantle in Greek Art," *American Journal of Archaeology* 99, no. 4 (1995): 641–66. An example of experimental archaeology led to *The Caryatid Hairstyling Project*, directed by Katherine A. Schwab at Fairfield University in 2009, see www.fairfield.edu/caryatid (accessed March 17, 2017) for resources, images, and a short clip from the film. The experiment proved for the first time that these hairstyles were based in reality and could be reproduced.
80. The Caryatids, statues as columns for the south porch of the Erechtheion, were not the only examples of attention given to hair on Acropolis monuments. Lead locks of hair were attached to the heads of at least two Parthenon south metope figures. Given the quantity of Parthenon metopes badly damaged or entirely destroyed, it is plausible to assume that other heads were equally adorned with lead locks of hair, a technique at once conspicuous and expensive. The idea of this adornment was already in use by the early fifth century BCE, at the Temple of Aphaia at Aegina. See Olga Palagia, "Classical Athens," in *Greek Sculpture: Function, Materials, and Techniques in the Archaic and Classical Periods*, ed. Olga Palagia (Cambridge: Cambridge University Press, 2006), 128, 155 n. 106.
81. Naturally tightly curled to pin straight hair can be arranged in a fishtail braid. Textured hair (wavy to tight curls) is easiest to braid and is ideal for the fishtail. One complete Caryatid hairstyle can be recreated, if the hair is long, thick, and textured, within forty minutes and without modern products or tools. The Erechtheion maidens wear extra thick fishtail braids to strengthen the neck since they supported the roof covering the south porch. The most comprehensive study on these maidens with numerous photographs remains Hans Lauter, *Die Koren des Erechtheion: Antike Plastik*, pt. 16 (Berlin: Walter H. Schuchhardt, Felix Eckstein, 1976).
82. Karl Galinsky, "Introduction," in *Cultural Memories in the Roman Empire*, ed. Karl Galinsky and Kenneth Lapatin (Los Angeles: J. Paul Getty Trust, 2015), 1–22.
83. Vitruvius, *On Architecture* 1:1–5, until Vitruvius, the Erechtheion statues were known as maidens or *korai*; Zanker, *The Power of Images*, 256–7. Katherine A. Schwab and Marice Rose, "Fishtail Braids and the Caryatid Hairstyling Project: Fashion Today and in Ancient Athens," *Catwalk: The Journal of Fashion, Beauty, and Style* 4, no. 2 (2015): 1–24.

84. Leitao, "Adolescent Hair-Growing and Hair-Cutting Rituals," 113–14. See also Chapter One in this volume.
85. Carl A. Roebuck, *The Asklepieion and Lerna. Corinth: Results of Excavations Conducted by the American School of Classical Studies at Athens* XIV (Princeton, NJ: ASCSA, 1951), 118 no. 116.
86. Fragmentary marble relief from Thessaly, British Museum, 1839,0806.4. See also Leitao, "Adolescent Hair-Growing and Hair-Cutting Rituals," 115.
87. Panagiotis Iossif and Cathy Lorber, "Seleucid Campaign Beards," *L'antiquité classique* 78, no. 1 (2009): 87–115, esp. 91.
88. Fragments of a poem, *Coma Berenices*, by Callimachus are preserved in a poem made famous by Catullus (66), written from the point of view of the lock of hair; the queen's beautiful locks of hair, before the dedication are depicted on a garnet intaglio ring ca. 246–222 BCE by Nikandros, in The Walters Art Museum, No. 42.1339. See http://art.thewalters.org/detail/20290/intaglio-ring-with-berenike-ii/ (accessed March 17, 2017).
89. See Chapter One in this volume; "Mourning," in Cleland, Davies, and Llewellyn-Jones, ed., *Greek and Roman Dress from A to Z*, 127.
90. Synnott, *The Body Social*, 126; Cosgrove, "A Woman's Unbound Hair," 682–3.
91. Luke B. T. Houghton, "Death Ritual and Burial Practice in the Latin Love Elegists," in *Memory and Mourning: Studies on Roman Death*, ed. Valerie Hope and Janet Huskinson (Oxford: Oxbow Books, 2011), 68.
92. Maurizio Bettini, *Women and Weasels: Mythologies of Birth in Ancient Greece and Rome* (Chicago, IL: University of Chicago Press, 2013), 71.
93. Cosgrove, "A Woman's Unbound Hair," 685.
94. Toner, "Barbers, Barbershops and Searching for Roman Popular Culture," 97–8. The term *depositio barbae* is a modern phrase used to describe this ritual; Iossif and Lorber, "Seleucid Campaign Beards," 88. See Chapter One in this volume for further discussion of the first shave.
95. Hersch, *The Roman Wedding*, 80–4, 90–1. See also Chapter One in this volume.
96. Textual evidence is spotty, but they are depicted on fifth- and sixth-century Byzantine artifacts that depict couples. The Mishnah records that Jewish grooms and brides were forbidden to wear crowns after the destruction of Jerusalem (perhaps owing to pagan associations), although it is debated whether the prohibition referred to gold or vegetal crowns. Jewish nuptial poems and recordings of customs indicate that crown-wearing was a traditional aspect of weddings in the medieval period; Erwin R. Goodenough, "The Crown of Victory in Judaism," *The Art Bulletin* 28, no. 3 (1946): 158 n. 155; Laura S. Lieber, "The Piyyutim le-Hatan of Qallir and Amittai-Jewish Marriage Customs in Early Byzantium," in *Talmuda de-Eretz Yisrael: Archaeology and the Rabbis in Late Ancient Palestine*, ed. Steven Fine and Aaron J. Koller (Boston, MA: Walter de Gruyter, 2014), 286; Alicia Walker, "Numismatic and Metrological Parallels for the Iconography of Early Byzantine Marriage Jewelry: The Question of the Crowned Bride," *Travaux et Mémoires* 16 (2010): 849–64.

Chapter Three

1. Joanne Entwhistle, *The Fashioned Body* (Cambridge: Polity Press, 2015, 2nd ed.), 7.
2. Mireille Lee, *Body, Dress, and Identity in Ancient Greece* (Cambridge: Cambridge University Press, 2015), 69.
3. Lee, *Body, Dress, and Identity*, 69.
4. Evelyn B. Harrison, "Greek Sculptured Coiffures and Ritual Haircuts," in *Early Greek Cult Practice: Proceedings of the Fifth International Symposium at the Swedish Institute at Athens,*

NOTES

  26–29 June 1986, ed. R. Hägg, N. Marinatos, and G. C. Nordquist (Stockholm: P. Åströms Forlag, 1988), 247.
5. M. E. Irwin, "Odysseus' 'Hyacinthine Hair' in *Odyssey* 6.231," *Phoenix* 44 (1990): 210.
6. Harrison, "Greek Sculptured Coiffures," 248. Conversely, to judge from ancient fresco, "the girls of Thera and the boys of Crete begin with shaved or nearly shaved heads; they are next permitted to grow a few special locks, which can become quite long, and finally, they grow the rest of the hair on their head long." David Leitao, "Adolescent Hair-Growing and Hair-Cutting Rituals in Ancient Greece: A Sociological Approach," in *Initiation in Ancient Greek Rituals and Narratives: New Critical Perspectives*, ed. D. Dodd and C. Faraone (London: Routledge, 2003), 119.
7. Leitao "Adolescent Hair-Growing 119.
8. Plutarch, *Theseus* 5.1; see also Homer, *Iliad* 2.542.
9. Hom. *Il*. 2.542.
10. See R. G. P. Austin, "Hector's Hair-Style," *Classical Quarterly* 22, no. 2 (1972): 199.
11. Harrison, "Greek Sculptured Coiffures," 248.
12. Harrison, "Greek Sculptured Coiffures," 250; see her figures here.
13. Hom. *Odyssey* 1.90; Hom. *Il*., Achilles at 1.197, Hector at 22.401–2, and Paris at 6.509–10.
14. Hom. *Il*. 17.51–2.
15. L. J. Llewellyn-Jones, *Aphrodite's Tortoise: The Veiled Woman of Ancient Greece* (Swansea: Classical Press of Wales, 2003), 136.
16. Hom. *Od*. 6.135. As far as I am aware, there is no mention of wigs or hairpieces in Homer.
17. *Sem*. 7.57–70, in M. L. West, *Iambi et Elegi Graeci*, vols. 1 and 2 (Oxford: Oxford University Press, 1989 and 1992).
18. M. Stieber, *The Poetics of Appearance in the Attic Korai* (Austin: University of Texas Press, 2004), 64; see 63–8 for detailed descriptions of *korai* hair.
19. Stieber, *Poetics of Appearance*, 64.
20. Thucydides 1.6.3; see also Aristophanes, *Knights* 1331, *Clouds* 983; Lucian, *Ship* 3, *Palatine Anthology* [*AP*] 6.156.
21. Larissa Bonfante, *Etruscan Dress*, 2nd ed. (Baltimore, MD: Johns Hopkins University Press, 2003), 74; and Letaio "Adolescent Hair-Growing," 120.
22. Lee, *Body, Dress, and Identity*, 74; P. B. Emery, "Old-Age Iconography in Archaic Greek Art," *Mediterranean Archaeology* 12 (1999): 74.
23. Lee, *Body, Dress, and Identity*, 74; Anakreon fr. 13.358 PMG, 13 Gentili; L. Woodbury, "Gold Hair and Grey, or the Game of Love: Anacreon fr. 13:358 PMG, 13 Gentili," *Transactions of the American Philological Association* 109 (1979): 277–87.
24. Lee, *Body, Dress, and Identity*, 74, with references.
25. Harrison, "Greek Sculptured Coiffures," 250.
26. Plutarch, *Lycurgus* 16.6; see Letaio, "Adolescent Hair-Growing," 119; Ephraim David, "Sparta's Social Hair," *Eranos* 90 (1992): 12–16.
27. Lee, *Body, Dress, and Identity*, 262 n. 173, with references.
28. *Rhetoric* 1.9.26–7.
29. Xenophon, *Spartan Constitution* 11.3, Plutarch, *Lycurgus*, 22. See also Chapter Six in this volume.
30. Lee, *Body, Dress, and Identity*, 72.
31. Lee, *Body, Dress, and Identity*, 72; Ian Jenkins and Dyfri Williams, "Sprang Hair-Nets: Their Manufacture and Use in Ancient Greece," *American Journal of Archaeology* 89, no. 3 (1985): 411–18.
32. Lee, *Body, Dress, and Identity*, 72; Irwin, "Odysseus' 'Hyacinthine Hair,'" 212–13.
33. Lee, *Body, Dress, and Identity*, 69.

34. Letaio, "Adolescent Hair-Growing," 124.
35. Letaio, "Adolescent Hair-Growing," 125; Ar. *Clouds* 14–16, 332, 348–50, 1101, *Knights* 480, 579–80, 1121, *Wasps* 466, 1068–70, *Birds* 1281–2.
36. Letaio, "Adolescent Hair-Growing," 126; Lys. 16.18.
37. Ar. *Wasps* 476, 466; Letaio, "Adolescent Hair-Growing," 124.
38. Lee, *Body, Dress, and Identity*, 70.
39. Xenophon, *Cyropaedia* 1.3.2; Aristophanes, *Thesmophoriazusae* 258.
40. E.g. Aristophanes, *Ecclesiazusae* 24–5, 68–72.
41. James Davidson, *The Greeks and Greek Love* (London: Weidenfeld & Nicolson, 2007), 80–3, with references.
42. Gloria Ferrari, *Figures of Speech: Men and Maidens in Ancient Greece* (Chicago, IL: University of Chicago Press, 2002), 135–7; Lee, *Body, Dress, and Identity*, 76. See Chapter Six in this volume.
43. Davidson, *The Greeks and Greek Love*, 81.
44. Lee, *Body, Dress, and Identity*, 263 n. 186, with references.
45. Bonfante, *Etruscan Dress*, 68.
46. See Lee, *Body, Dress, and Identity*, 78.
47. Lee, *Body, Dress, and Identity*, 72.
48. Bonfante, *Etruscan Dress*, 74, states the *krobylos* style was worn by women in Greece in 480 BCE.
49. Lee, *Body, Dress, and Identity*, 262 n. 164.
50. Lee, *Body, Dress, and Identity*, 71.
51. Llewellyn-Jones, *Aphrodite's Tortoise*, 66.
52. Llewellyn-Jones, *Aphrodite's Tortoise*, 44–5.
53. Llewellyn-Jones, *Aphrodite's Tortoise*, 46–8.
54. Llewellyn-Jones, *Aphrodite's Tortoise*, 56–9.
55. Llewellyn-Jones, *Aphrodite's Tortoise*, 56, 58–9.
56. Llewellyn-Jones, *Aphrodite's Tortoise*, 59–64.
57. Lee, *Body, Dress, and Identity*, 69.
58. *AP* 5.36.
59. Ar. *Eccl.* 904; Lee *Body, Dress, and Identity*, 264 n. 199. On depilation see Chapter Six in this volume.
60. Bonfante, *Etruscan Dress*.
61. Bonfante, *Etruscan Dress*, 67.
62. Bonfante, *Etruscan Dress*, 73 and figs. 79, 110.
63. Bonfante, *Etruscan Dress*, 74.
64. Bonfante, *Etruscan Dress*, 74 and fig. 118.
65. Bonfante, *Etruscan Dress*, fig. 160.
66. Bonfante, *Etruscan Dress*, 78.
67. Bonfante, *Etruscan Dress*, 74–5. See Chapter One in this volume on the image of Alexander.
68. Bonfante, *Etruscan Dress*, 70.
69. Bonfante, *Etruscan Dress*, 70 and figs. 62–3.
70. Bonfante, *Etruscan Dress*, 70.
71. Bonfante, *Etruscan Dress*, 71.
72. Bonfante, *Etruscan Dress*, 71 and fig. 60.
73. Bonfante, *Etruscan Dress*, 75 and fig. 99.
74. Bonfante, *Etruscan Dress*, 75.
75. Varro, *De Lingua Latina*, 7.44.

76. Bonfante, *Etruscan Dress*, 76.
77. Bonfante, *Etruscan Dress*, 77.
78. Bonfante, *Etruscan Dress*, 78.
79. On long male hair see J. L. Butrica, "Clodius the *Pulcher* in Catullus and Cicero," *Classical Quarterly* 52, no. 2 (2002): 507–16; J. Pollini, "Slave-Boys for Sexual and Religious Service: Images of Pleasure and Devotion," in *Flavian Rome: Culture, Image, Text*, ed. A. J. Boyle and W. J. Dominik (Leiden: Brill, 2003), 149–66; Seneca, *Natural Questions* 1.17.7; Juvenal, *Satires* 5.30. On *delicati*, see K. Olson, "Masculinity, Appearance, and Sexuality: Dandies in Roman Antiquity," *The Journal of the History of Sexuality* 23, no. 2 (2014): 185 n. 16.
80. On *capillati*, see Olson, "Masculinity, Appearance, and Sexuality," 188 n. 34.
81. Elizabeth Bartman, "Hair and the Artifice of Roman Female Adornment," *American Journal of Archaeology* 105, no. 1 (2001): 3; and Alexandra T. Croom, *Roman Clothing and Fashion* (Stroud: Tempus, 2002), 66–8.
82. Bartman, "Hair," 3.
83. Paul Zanker, *The Mask of Socrates: The Image of the Intellectual in Antiquity*, trans. A. Shapiro (Berkeley: University of California Press, 1995), 224.
84. Croom, *Roman Clothing*, 67.
85. Croom, *Roman Clothing*, 64.
86. Croom, *Roman Clothing*, 65.
87. Bartman, "Hair," 19.
88. Cicero, *Post reditum in senatu* [*Red. Sen.*] 12, 13, 16; *In Pisonum* 25; *Pro Sestio* 18; see also Plautus, *Asinaria* 627 (*cinaede calamistrate*); Sen. *Ep.* 114.5; Martial, *Epigrams* 10.65. On the *calamistrum*, see Kelly Olson, *Dress and the Roman Woman: Self-Presentation and Society* (London: Routledge, 2008), 73 and 140 n. 132, with references.
89. Suetonius, *Divus Iulius* 45.
90. Caesar 17.2 and 4.9. On the one-finger scratching gesture, see Olson, "Masculinity, Appearance, and Sexuality," 182 n. 2.
91. *myrobrechis ... cincinnos*; Suet. *Divus Augustus* 86; which may not be a reference to literal hair, but to literary style. On Maecenas' effeminacy, see M. Graver, "The Manhandling of Maecenas: Senecan Abstractions of Masculinity," *American Journal of Philology* 119, no. 4 (1998): 607–32; and Olson, "Masculinity, Appearance, and Sexuality," 188 n. 37 for further references.
92. Suet. *Nero* 51.
93. *flexa nitidus coma*; Mart. *Epigrams* 10.65; and see 2.29, 10.72.11.
94. *capillum frangere*; Seneca the Elder, *Controversiae* 1 pr. 8–10.
95. Seneca the Younger, *Letters* 115.2–3.
96. Mart. *Epigrams* 11.39.
97 Tibullus 1.6.39–40; P. Murgatroyd, *Tibullus 1: A Commentary on the First Book of the Elegies of Albius Tibullus* (Pietermaritzburg: University of Natal Press, 1980): 197.
98. Mart. *Epigrams*, 3.63.3–10, 5.61.
99. Propertius 2.4.5; Ovid, *Ars Amatoria* 3.433–48.
100. Cic. *Sest.* 19; Calp. *RE* 90. The Seplasia was the street in Capua where perfumes and unguents were sold. See R. Kaster, *Marcus Tullius Cicero: Speech on Behalf of Publius Sestius*, translated with introduction and commentary (Oxford: Clarendon Press, 2006), 161–2.
101. Horace, *Satires, Epistulae* 1.1.94–7.
102. Horace, *Satires*, 1.3.31–2.
103. Mart. *Epigrams* 10.72 and 2.29. See Chapter Six in this volume for further discussion of effeminacy.

104. Bartman, "Hair," 1.
105. Suet. *Nero* 26, *Calig.* 11.
106. Petronius, *Satyricon* 110.
107. Suet. *Otho* 12.1. See Chapter Four in this volume for further discussion of wigs.
108. *M. Papirius, unus ex iis, dicitur Gallo barbam suam, ut tum omnibus promissa erat*; Livy 5.41.
109. Suet. *Otho* 12.1.
110. A. Bonanno, "Imperial and Private Portraiture: A Case of Non-Dependence," in *Ritratto Ufficiale e Ritratto Privato: Atti della II Conferanza Internazionale sul Ritratto Romano*, ed. N. Binacasa and G. Rizza (Rome: Consiglio Nazionale delle Ricerche, 1988), 159.
111. Bonanno, "Imperial and Private Portraiture," 162.
112. Croom, *Roman Clothing*, 66.
113. *Quod vides istos sequi, qui aut vellunt barbam aut intervellunt, qui labra pressius tondent et adradunt servata et summissa cetera parte*; Sen. *Ep.* 114.21. See also Amy Richlin, "Gender and Rhetoric: Producing Manhood in the Schools," in *Roman Eloquence: Rhetoric in Society and Literature*, ed. W. J. Dominik (London: Routledge, 1997), 94.
114. Suet. *Iul.* 45; Mart. *Epigrams* 2.29, 3.63.3–10.
115. Sen. *Controversiae* 1 pr. 8–10; Mart. *Epigrams* 2.62. In this last, Labienus depilates himself in order to please his girlfriend "gives us an interesting glimpse into women's possible tastes or, rather, into men's ideas about women's tastes" (C. Williams, ed., *Martial Epigrams Book Two* [Oxford: Oxford University Press, 2004], 207). See Chapter Five in this volume for further discussion of depilation.
116. Bartman, "Hair," 12–13.
117. Bartman, "Hair," 5.
118. Diane E. E. Kleiner and S. B. Matheson, eds., *I Claudia: Women in Ancient Rome* (New Haven, CT: Yale University Art Gallery, 1996. Distributed by University of Texas Press), 141.
119. See Diane E. E. Kleiner, "Women and Family Life on Roman Funerary Altars," *Latomus* 46, no. 3 (1987): no. 23, pl. XV.1–2; and Beryl Rawson, *Children and Childhood in Roman Italy* (New York: Oxford University Press, 2003), 47–9 and fig. 1.11. For the inscription, see *CIL* 6.20905.
120. Michele George, "A Roman Funerary Monument with a Mother and Daughter," in *Childhood, Class and Kin in the Roman World*, ed. S. Dixon (London: Routledge, 2001), 181–2.
121. See Kelly Olson, "The Appearance of the Young Roman Girl," in *Roman Dress and the Fabric of Roman Culture*, ed. J. Edmondson and A. Keith (Toronto: University of Toronto Press, 2008), 139–57.
122. Propertius, *Elegies* 4.11.33–4. On *vittae*, see Elaine Fantham, "Covering the Head at Rome: Ritual and Gender," in *Roman Dress and the Fabric of Roman Culture*, ed. J. Edmondson and A. Keith (Toronto: University of Toronto Press, 2008); Olson, *Dress and the Roman Woman*, 36–9; M. Lindner, *Portraits of the Vestal Virgins, Priestesses of Ancient Rome* (Ann Arbor: University of Michigan Press), 100–2, 164–86.
123. Valerius Flaccus 8.6.
124. Nonius 353L.
125. L. Richardson, ed., *Propertius Elegies I–IV* (Norman: University of Oklahoma Press, 1977), 485.
126. George, "A Roman Funerary Monument," 185.
127. H. Gabelmann, "Römische Kinder in Toga Praetexta," *Jahrbuch des Deutschen Archäologischen Instituts* 100 (1985): 522–7.

128. Valerius Maximus, *Memorable Doings and Sayings* 6.3.10; Sen. *Controv.* 2.7.6; Isidore of Seville, *Origines* 19.25.1–3. On veiling in Roman antiquity, see L. Wilson, *The Clothing of the Ancient Romans* (Baltimore, MD: Johns Hopkins University Press, 1938), 148–50; Judith Sebesta, "Symbolism in the Costume of the Roman Woman," in *The World of Roman Costume*, ed. J. L. Sebesta and L. Bonfante (Madison: University of Wisconsin Press, 1994), 48–9; Judith Sebesta, "Women's Costume and Feminine Civic Morality in Augustan Rome," *Gender and History* 9, no. 3 (1997): 534–8; Croom, *Roman Clothing*, 87; Olson, *Dress and the Roman Woman*, 33–6.
129. Croom, *Roman Clothing*, 98–105.
130. L. Furnée-Van Swet, "Fashion in Women's Hair-Dress in the First Century of the Roman Empire," *Bulletin van de Vereeniging tot Bevordering van de Kennis van de Antieke Beschaving* 31 (1956): 4.
131. Furnée-van Swet, "Fashion in Women's Hair-Dress," 4; Diane E. E. Kleiner, *Cleopatra and Rome* (Cambridge, MA: Belknap Press, 2005), 244.
132. S. E. Wood, *Imperial Women: A Study in Public Images, 40 BC–AD 68* (Leiden: Brill, 1993), 93, 94–120, 138–40; and below, n. 142.
133. Furnée-van Swet, "Fashion in Women's Hair-Dress," 8.
134. See Janet Stephens, "Ancient Roman Hairdressing: On (Hair) Pins and Needles," *Journal of Roman Archaeology* 21 (2008): 110–32. See also Chapter Four in this volume.
135. Croom, *Roman Clothing*, 100.
136. Croom, *Roman Clothing*, 101.
137. See K. Fittschen, *Die Bildnistypen der Faustina Minor und die Fecunditas Augustae* (Göttingen: Vandenhoek and Ruprecht, 1982); Bartman, "Hair," 19.
138. Ov. *Ars* 3.135–52.
139. Ov. *Ars* 3.151–2.
140. Bartman, "Hair," 19; Croom, *Roman Clothing*, 98.
141. Croom, *Roman Clothing*, 98.
142. A series of coins issued in Pergamum in Asia Minor between 6 BCE and 2 BCE shows Julia and Livia with the same hairstyle; Kleiner, *Cleopatra*, 247.
143. Although as Wood notes, "the facts, of course, were quite different from the desired political message" (*Imperial Women*, 131).
144. K. Fittschen and P. Zanker, *Katalog der römischen Porträts in den Capitolinischen Museen und den anderen kommunalen Sammlungen der Stadt Rom. Band III: Kaiserinnen und Prinzessinnenbildnisse Frauenporträts* (Mainz am Rhein: von Zabern, 1983), 53–4.
145. See Plaut. *Curculio* 577; Varro, *Ling.* 5.129; Cic. *Orator ad M. Brutum* 78, *Red. Sen.* 16, *Brutus* 262; Tacitus, *Dialogus de oratoribus* 26.1; Petron. *Sat.* 102.15; Lucian, *Amores* 40; Ov. *Ars am.* 2.304, *Amores* 1.14.25–30; Servius, *Aeneid* 12.100. See Chapter Four in this volume for further discussion.
146. Mart. *Epigrams* 12.23: the woman is not ashamed (*nec te pudet*).
147. That is, taken from the head of a captured foreigner; Ov. *Am.* 1.14.45–6; see Bartman, "Hair," 39.
148. T. J. Leary, *Martial Book XIV: The Apophoreta* (London: Duckworth, 1996), 78; and see Mart. *Epigrams* 5.37.8, 68, 14.26; Juv. *Satires* 13.165. On the political significance of such hair ("sent by defeated nations as a token of submission"), see Leary, *Martial*, 79; Ov. *Am.* 1.14.45–6; Claudianus, *De consulatu Honorii* 4.446–7, *Against Eutropius* 1.383.
149. *Dig.* 39.4.16.7.
150. Ov. *Ars* 3.167–8; Mart. *Epigrams* 5.49.12–13; Andrew Dalby, *Empire of Pleasures: Luxury and Indulgence in the Roman World* (London: Routledge, 2000), 241.
151. Mart. *Epigrams* 14.26.

152. Ov. *Ars* 3. 245–6.
153. Ov. *Amores* 1.14.47; see also Tertullian, *De cultu feminarum* 2.7.1.
154. Ov. *Ars* 3.167–8.
155. Varro *Menippeae* 570; Horace, *Satires* 1.8.48; Tert. *de Pallio* 4.10; Arnobius, *Adversus nationes* 6.26; and see Bartman, "Hair," 10.
156. Juv. *Satires* 6.120; see also Tert. *Cult.* 2.7.1.
157. Bartman, "Hair," 10 n. 51. See Chapter Four in this volume.
158. Bartman, "Hair," 7 and nn. 37–8, with references.
159. Lindsay Allason-Jones, *Women in Roman Britain* (London: British Museum Publications, 1989), 137.
160. Bartman, "Hair," 18, of many such busts.
161. Bartman, "Hair," 14 and n. 69, on Egyptian wigs.
162. Kleiner and Matheson, *I Claudia*, 174 and n. 130. Many of these reproduce the coiffures and wigs worn by Julia Domna (Bartman, "Hair," 18).
163. Bartman, "Hair," 18–20; Fittschen and Zanker, *Katalog der römischen Porträts*, 105.
164. Bartman, "Hair," 19.
165. Croom, *Roman Clothing*, 105.
166. Tert. *Cult.* 2.7.1.
167. Tert. *Cult.* 2.7.2.
168. Tert. *de Pallio* 4.9.1.
169. Clement of Alexandria, *Paedogogus*. 2.11.104.
170. Kristi Upson-Saia, *Early Christian Dress: Gender, Virtue, and Authority* (London: Routledge, 2011), 44; Clem. *Paed.* 3.11.63.
171. Claud. *Cons. Hon.* 6.523–9.
172. Jerome, *Letters* 130.7, 130.18, 128.2.
173. Croom, *Roman Clothing*, 104–5.
174. G. Biddle-Perry and S. Cheang, "Introduction: Thinking About Hair," in *Hair: Styling, Culture and* Fashion, ed. G. Biddle-Perry and S. Cheang (Oxford: Berg, 2008), 3, 6.

Chapter Four

1. Suetonius, *Domitianus* 18.2.
2. For methodological problems, see Jerry Toner, "Barbers, barbershops and search for Roman popular culture," *Papers of the British School at Rome* 83 (2015): 91–109, 91–3.
3. This chapter gives citational priority to illustrative primary source material. All literary sources are from the Loeb Classical Library series unless otherwise specified. Technical data about hair biology and chemistry are common knowledge in professional Barber-Cosmetology. For complete technical data, consult Milady, *Standard Textbook of Professional Barber-Styling* (Tarrytown, NY: Milady Publishing, 1983), *Milady's Standard Textbook of Cosmetology* (Albany, NY: Thomson Learning, 2000), and Pivot Point, *Salon Fundamentals: Cosmetology* (Evanston, IL: Pivot Point, 2000). All photographs and diagrams are by the author unless otherwise specified.
4. Aristotle, *Generation of Animals* 1.18; Euripides, *Electra* 521–31.
5. Arist. *Parts of Animals* 2.15.
6. Dio Chrysostom, *Encomium on Hair*.
7. Bowstrings: Appian, *Roman History* 8.1.13.93; *Historia Augusta (HA), The Two Maximini* 33; *Maximinus and Balbinus* 11. Catapult ropes: Dio Cassius, *Roman History* 21; Zonaras 9.26; Caesar, *Civil Wars* 3.9.
8. Shepherd of Hermas, *Visions* 9.5; Plato, *Ion* 535c; Virgil, *Aeneid* 3.47–8.

9. Pliny, *Natural History* [*HN*] 11.94.231.
10. Dio Chrys. *Discourses 35* 11; Tacitus, *Histories* 4.61; as a stereotype, see Suet. *Gaius* 47.
11. Caledonians were noted for their red hair: Tac. *Agricola* 11.2.
12. Manilius, *Astronomica* 715 ff.; Martial, *Epigrams* 5.68; Suet. *Gaius* 47; Tibullus 1.7.12; Claudianus, *Against Eutropius* 1.380, *Against Rufinus* 2, 110; Procopius, *History of the Wars* 3.2.3–4; Ausonius, *Bissula* 3.9–10; Tertullian, *De Cultu Feminarum* 6; Juvenal, *Satires* 13.164–5. See Mark Bradley, *Colour and Meaning in Ancient Rome* (Cambridge: Cambridge University Press, 2009), 141–2.
13. Arist. *Eudemian Ethics* 2.8.1224b.15; Mart. *Epigrams* 4.78.2; Ovid, *Tristia* 8.2; Pliny the Younger, *Panegyricus* 4.7; Plutarch, *Moralia, Old Men in Public Affairs* 9, 10, 11. Ov. *Ars Amatoria* 2.666, 3.75.
14. Dio Chrys. *Encomium on Hair.* Synesius, *On Baldness*, see the Introduction to this volume.
15. Mart. *Epigrams* 9.37.
16. Arist. *Historia Animalium* 8(9).631L.31-632a.5. See also Chapters Five and Six in this volume.
17. See below and Ov. *Amores* 1.14; Nicarchus, *Greek Anthology* 11.398.
18. Hippocrates, *Aphorisms* 5.11–12.
19. Celsus, *De medicina* 6.3; Milady, *Standard Textbook of Professional Barber-Styling*, 373–6.
20. Galen, *Method of Medicine* 13.929K, 13.934K; Lucian, *Dialogues of the Courtesans* 12.5. Headache therapy: Hippoc. *Diseases 3*, 1, *Regimen in Acute Disease (Appendix)*, 9. Today, hair cutting is an accepted therapy for "traction" migraines and neck strain triggered by an excessive weight of long hair. See also Chapter Five in this volume.
21. Arist. *Problems* 4.18.
22. See video recreation, Janet Stephens, "The Hairstyles of Faustina the Younger." Available online: https://www.youtube.com/watch?v=M_HPjg-f8iQ (accessed January 17, 2017).
23. Varro, *De Lingua Latina (s.v. mundus muliebris)* 5.129.ff.; *Digest of Justinian*, 34.2.1.pr.3, 34.2.1.pr.4, 34.2.8.pr.2, 34.2.8.pr.5, 34.2.8.pr.6.
24. Sidonius, *Panegyric on Anthemius* 12.7; Ov. *Ars am.* 3.194–6.
25. Laver bathing: women: red-figured stamnos, Attica (440–430 BCE), Museum of Fine Arts, Boston, MA, Inv. No. 95.21; youth: red-figured cup, Attica (500–450 BCE), Museum of Fine Arts, Boston, MA, Inv. No. 01.8029. Showering: men: black-figured hydria, Attica (550–500 BCE), Rijksmuseum van Oudheden, Leiden, Inv. No. II167; women: black-figured amphora, Attica (525–475 BCE), Berlin, Inv. No. F1843 (lost).
26. *Mishnah Miqvaot* 9.1.
27. Plin. *HN* 28.14.55.
28. Varro, *Ling.* 5.129; "*flexo capillo HA, Hadrian* 26.
29. Mart. *Epigrams* 14.25.
30. Seneca, *Natural Questions* 1.17.8–9.
31. Plin. *HN* 33.45.129.
32. Plin. *HN* 33.46.131.
33. Plin. *HN* 33.45.130; Vitruvius, *On Architecture* 7.3.9.
34. Sen. *QNat.* 1.5.14; Sextus Empiricus, *Outlines of Pyrrhonism* 14.49.
35. Lucian, *Dialogues of the Sea Gods* 323.
36. *HA, Didius Julianus* 7.10; Pausanias, *Description of Greece* 21.12–13, 37.7.
37. Loeb *Greek Anthology* 14.56, 14.108; Sen. *Epistles* 88.27; Arist. *Parva naturalia, On Dreams* 459b; Sen. *QNat.* 1.6.2–4; Lucretius, *De Rerum Natura* 143–68, 269–323; Plato, *Timaeus* 46; regarding Archimedes experiments with mirrors, see Loeb 362: 20 (source Tzetzes,

Book of Histories 2.103–44); Gellius, *Attic Nights* 16.18.3; Diodorus Siculus, *The Library of History* 26.18.

38. Plautus, *Amphitryon* 441–3, *Menaechmi* 1060–5; Alciphron, *Letters of the Courtesans* 6(i. 33).
39. Conceit, arrogance, meretriciousness: Euripides, *Electra* 1071; Mart. *Epigrams* 11.49; Macrobius, *Saturnalia* 3.4; Sidonius, *Panegyric on Anthemius* 2.5.323–4, 2.7.107. Envy and anger: Phaedrus, *Fables* 3.8 [*Brother and Sister*]. Aging: Prop. 3.25.14–5; Loeb *Greek Anthology* 11.266 [Lucilius]; Plautus, *Mostellaria* 250–1. Regret: Loeb *Greek Anthology* 6.L [Plato]. Falsification: *Greek Anthology* 11.370 [Macedonius the Consul]. Self-obsession: Ov. *Ars am.* 3.136; Petronius, *Satyricon* 128L. Mortification: Ov. *Am.* 1.14, *Medicamina faciae* 45–8, *Tristia* 3.38; Dio Cassius, *Roman History* 62.28; Mart. *Epigrams* 2.41.7–8.
40. Hermippus, *Birth of Athena* 6 (Loeb Poets of Old Comedy, 285); Ov. *Ars am.* 3.507–10, *Medicamina faciae* 47–8; Diogenes Laertius, *Lives of the Eminent Philosophers*, Plato 39; Loeb *Greek Anthology* 6.210, 11.54; Ausonius, *Epigrams on various matters* 65; Plut. *Mor.* [*Advice to Bride and Groom*] 25, *On Listening to Lectures* 8, *Lives of the 10 Orators* [*Demosthenes*] 8; Diog. Laert. Socrates 2.5.33; Anacreon, *Anacreontea* 7; Auson. *The Moselle* 10.230–7; Philostratus the Elder, *Letters* 25[55]; Terence, *The Brothers* 415; Augustine, *Letters* 49.16; Horace, *Odes* 4.10; Quintilian, *The Orator's Education* 11.3.68.
41. Oil: Philostratus of Athens, *Apollonius of Tyana* 4.27; butter: Sidonius, *Panegyric on Anthemius* 12.7; pomade: Mart. *Epigrams* 6.74.2, 11.39.11, 12.17.7, 12.38.3, 14.146.
42. Nonnus, *Dion.* 32.9; Plin. *HN* 13.2–3.
43. Petron. *Sat.* 23.
44. Diod. Sic. *Library of History* 5.28.2.
45. Mart. *On Spectacles* 3.9; For technical information and tutorial diagram, see Miranda Aldhouse-Green, *Bog Bodies Uncovered: Solving Europe's Ancient Mystery* (London: Thames and Hudson, 2015), 22–4, 120.
46. For inside and outside braiding techniques see Janet Stephens, "Ornatrix School: Inside Braiding – 2nd ed." Available online: https://www.youtube.com/watch?v=6i-vysel46M (accessed March 11, 2017); and Janet Stephens, "Ornatrix School: Outside Braiding – 2nd ed." Available online: https://www.youtube.com/watch?v=viF2q_8B2FA.
47. Katherine A. Schwab of Fairfield University has convincingly recreated these hairstyles, see Chapter Two in this volume.
48. For analysis and tutorial see Janet Stephens, "Julia Domna: Forensic Hairdressing." Available online: https://www.youtube.com/watch?v=68LEUXw2QJU (accessed February 5, 2017).
49. W. M. Flinders Petrie, *Objects of Daily Use* (London: Publications of the Egyptian Research Account and British School of Archaeology in Egypt, 1927), 2:3 XIX.
50. Part and section: Varro, *Ling.* 5.129; Claud. *Rape of Proserpine* 2.16; fasten: Mart. *Epigrams* 14.24; Lucil. *Satires* 30.1095; Janet Stephens, "Ancient Roman Hairdressing: On (Hair) Pins and Needles," *Journal of Roman Archaeology* 21 (2008): 116; applicator: Stephens "Ancient Roman hairdressing," n. 24; weapon: Petronius, *Satyricon* 21L; Dio Cass. *Roman History* 47.8.4, 51.14.2; experimental archaeology: Stephens "Ancient Roman Hairdressing," 115–16; A. Kern and K. Grömer, "Early Iron Age Headdress in the Central and Eastern Alpine Area," in *Tiarae, Diadems and Headdresses in the Ancient Mediterranean Cultures: Symbolism and Technology*, ed. C. Alfaro (Valencia: Sociedad Española de Matemática Aplicada, 2014), 73–7. For a video tutorial on bodkin use see Janet Stephens, "Ornatrix School: Bodkin Skills – 2nd ed." Available online: https://www.youtube.com/watch?v=krXTfgU9qvE (accessed February 7, 2017).

51. Pearls being particularly prized: *Digest of Justinian*, 34.2.24.10.6.
52. Ov. *Fasti* 2.560; Plut. *Moralia, Roman Questions*, 87, *Romulus*, 15.5.
53. Stephens, "Ancient Roman Hairdressing," 121–4; Janet Stephens, "Recreating the Fonseca Hairstyle," *EXARC Journal Digest*, no. 1 (2013): 21–3. Available online: http://exarc.net/issue-2013-1/ea/recreating-fonseca-hairstyle. For a video tutorial on hair sewing for ancient Roman hairdressing, see Janet Stephens, "Ornatrix School: Needle Skills." Available online: https://www.youtube.com/watch?v=tdgNCCbH4wk (accessed March 22, 2017).
54. Stephens, "Ancient Roman Hairdressing," 132.
55. Pseudo-Lucian, *Affairs of the Heart* 40.
56. Stephens, "Ancient Roman Hairdressing," fig. 5.
57. Ov. *Am.*1.14.
58. Cicero, *Post Reditum in Senatu* 12, *Pro Sestio* 8; Plautus, *The Comedy of Asses* 627; Jerome, *Letters* 22.28, 52.5.
59. Claud. *Epithalamium of Honorius and Maria* 257–8; Anac. *Anacreontea* 16; Pherecrates, *Testimonia and Fragments* 187 (Loeb, 514; Loeb Poets of Old Comedy, 513).
60. Epictetus, *Arrian's Discourses* 3.1.42–3; Auson. *Epigrams* 93; Gell. *Attic Nights* 6.12.4–5. For a longer discussion on hair removal see "Discourses of depilation" in Chapter Six this volume.
61. *Psilothron*: Mart. *Epigrams* 3.74; *dropax*: Auson. *Epigrams* 93; Aelian, *On Animals* 13.27.
62. Mart. *Epigrams* 9.27.
63. Sen. *Ep.* 56.2.
64. Aristophanes, *Knights* 908; Mart. *Epigrams* 14.27; Phdr. *Fables* 2.2; Prop. *Elegies* 3.25.13; Macrob. *Sat.* 2.7.
65. Manlius, *Astronomica* 150.
66. To shape hair and beard: Cic. *De Officiis* 2.25; Plut. *Dion* 9.9.3–4; *Hist. Aug. Commodus Antoninus* 17; to remove leg hair: Suet. *Augustus* 68; to remove pubic hair: Ar. *Women at the Thesmorphoria* 538. See also Chapter Six in this volume.
67. Petron. *Sat.* 94.L; Mart. *Epigrams* 11.58.
68. T. G. E Powell, *The Celts* (London: Thames and Hudson, 1980), 60; the bog body Lindow Man has an intact mustache, see Aldhouse-Green, *Bog Bodies Uncovered*, pl. 9; Caes. *Gallic War* 5.14;
69. Athenaeus, *The Learned Banqueters* 13.565.c–d.
70. Plut. *Sayings of Kings and Commanders* 10.
71. These barbers may have been Greeks: Varro, *On Agriculture* 2.2.10.
72. Egyptians: Herodotus, *Histories* 2.36; Lucian, *On Sacrifices* 15; Isis worshippers: Plut. *Moralia* [*Isis and Osiris*] 3–4; Apuleius, *Metamorphoses* 11.30; *Hist. Aug. Commodus* 9.4–5; slaves: Petron. *Sat.* 103; Achilles Tatius, *Leucippe and Clitophon* 8.5.4–5; Scythians: Ath. *The Learned Banqueters* 524.f.
73. Aldhouse-Green, *Bog Bodies Uncovered*, 150–1.
74. Catholic Encyclopedia 1913 s.v. *tonsure*; Bede, *Ecclesiastical History of the English Nation, Easter Question* 25, *Colman and Eata* 26, *Hadrian and Theodore* 4.1, *Vision of the Next World* 12, *Letter to Egbert* [Duty of a Bishop] 12–3, *Lives of the Abbots* [Benedict Biscop] 2, *Letter to Naitan* 21; Procopius of Caesarea, *Anecdota* B17.38; Sidonius, *Letter* 6.4.
75. E.g. the Fonseca bust: see Stephens "Recreating the Fonseca Hairstyle." See also Chapter Three in this volume.
76. Lucian, *Dialogues of the Courtesans* 8; Menander, *Perikeiromene* [*The Girl with Her Hair Cut Short*]; Ar. *Knights* 373.
77. E.g. a domestic slave: Attic lekythos (ca. 460 BCE), Timokrates Painter, Athens, ARV 12771; *hetaira*: Attic red-figured kylix, (ca. 500 BCE), Onosimos Painter, Getty Villa, Gallery 207.

78. Colossal head of Emperor Constantine, Art Resource: ART319593; Emperor Justinian and his court, Art Resource: ART41700.
79. Attributed to Aristophanes in a fragment by Harpocration, 275.10 (see Loeb: Aristophanes, *Atributed Fragments, Testimonia*).
80. Plut. *Theseus* 5.1.
81. Ath. *The Learned Banqueters* 524.f.
82. Philo. *Contemplative Life* 50–1.
83. Aldhouse-Green, *Bog Bodies Uncovered*: Osterby Man, 22–4; Elling Woman, 21–2.
84. Petron. *Sat.* 67; *HA Elagabalus* 11.7, *Severus Alexander* 41.1, *The Thirty Pretenders* 14.4; *Digest of Justinian*, 34.2.25.10.7 (PHI Latin Texts).
85. Festus, *De Verborum Significatione* 286.67 (PHI Latin Texts).
86. A. Kwaspen, "Features and Analysis of Sprang Hairnets," in *Tiarae, Diadems and Headdresses in the Ancient Mediterranean Cultures: Symbolism and Technology*, ed. C. Alfaro (Valencia: SEMA, 2014), 273–82. For a video demonstration of sprang hairnet construction see Janet Stephens, "Grecian *Sakkos* hairstyle for women." Available online: https://www.youtube.com/watch?v=3zK5P0_XqpI (accessed April 2, 2017).
87. "Poetess" wall painting, Archaeological Museum of Naples, Art Resource: ART7541. Portrait of a woman wearing a sprang hairnet, bronze with silver inlays, Princeton Museum, Princeton, NJ, Fowler McCormick, Class of 1921, Fund y1980–10.
88. Oak: Cassius Dio, *Roman History* [*Caligula*] 59.17.4. Ivy: Ov. *Tr.* 1.7.2. Myrtle: Ael. *Historical Miscellany* 11.4; Ar. *Frogs* 330/1. Olive: Aeschines, *On the Embassy* 46; Eur. *Ion* 1433. Wheat: Gell. *Attic Nights* 7.7.8. Laurel: Suet. *Julius* 45.2; Hor. *Carm.* 2.1.15; Ov. *Ex Ponto* 2.2.90. Flowers: Prop. *Elegies* 3.10.16. Rose petals: Aelian, *Historical Miscellany* 14.39; Mart. *Epigrams* 5.64.4, 11.89, 12.17.7; Tertullian, *Apologeticus* 62.7; Statius, *Silvae* 2.116.
89. Marble bust of the Juno Ludovisi (330–327 BCE), Palazzo Altemps, Rome, Art Resource: ART71650.
90. Gell. *Attic Nights* 7.7.8; Servius, *In Aeneadem* 10.583. Vestal virgin relief, Vatican Museum, Art Resource: AR931818. Video recreation, see Janet Stephens, "Recreating the Vestal Virgin hairstyle." Available online: https://www.youtube.com/watch?v=epz7n8uYXQY (accessed February 26, 2017).
91. Festus, 56.1 L; Catull. 61.6–7.
92. Dio Chrys. *Discourse 72, On Appearance* 3. Head of a young woman, Palmyra, Syria, Kunsthistorishes Museum, Vienna, Inv. No. I 1519, Art Resource: ART205637.
93. Lucian, *The dead come to Life* 35; Philo. *Moses II* 116; Plut. *Artaxerxes* 11.3; Suet. *Nero* 13.2; Xenophon, *Cyropaedia* 8.3.13; Chariton, *Callirhoe* 6.4.2.
94. Sen. *Oedipus* 413; Prop. *Elegies* 4.2.31.
95. Sen. *Hercules* 471, *Hercules on Oeta* 374; Ov. *Heroides* 9.73; Mart. *Epigrams* 2.36, 12.89.1.
96. Petron. *Sat.* 110.2.1.
97. Mart. *Epigrams* 5.68.1; *Tractate Mishna Shabbat* 6.
98. *Digest*, 39.4.16.8.1.
99. Ov. *Ars am.* 3.165–8.
100. Mart. *Epigrams* 12.45.
101. Wefts have been made since at least 3000 BCE. James Stevens Cox, *An Illustrated Dictionary of Hairdressing and Wigmaking* (London: Batsford, 1984), fig. 468.
102. Stevens Cox, "The Construction of an Ancient Egyptian Wig," 67–70.
103. Stevens Cox, "The Construction of an Ancient Egyptian Wig," 67.
104. Mart. *Epigrams* 5.68.

105. W. M. Flinders Petrie, *Objects of Daily Use* (London: Publications of the Egyptian Research Account and British School of Archaeology in Egypt, 1927), 4:5 IV.
106. Ov. *Metamorphoses* 14.655; Mart. *Epigrams* 6.12, 12.23; Lucian, *Alexander the False Prophet* 3, *Dialogues of the Courtesans* 2.3–4; Jer. *Letters* 38; Alciphron, *Letters of Courtesans* 12 [frag. 4]; Juvenal, *Satire* 6.120; Tert. *de Cultu Feminarum* 7.
107. Tractate Mishna Shabbat 6.5.
108. Ov. *Am.* 1.14.
109. Ov. *Am.* 1.14.9–10; Apuleius *Metamorphoses* 2.9.
110. Ov. *Am.* 2.4.39; Mart. *Epigrams* 7.13; Ath. *The Learned Banqueters* 13.568.c.
111. Ov. *Ars am.* 1.513.
112. *Sapo*: Plin. *HN* 28.51.191; *spuma Batava*: Mart. *Epigrams* 8.33.20; *spuma Chattica Teutonicos*: Mart. *Epigrams* 14.26.1; *Pilas Mattiacas*: Mart. *Epigrams* 14.27.
113. Lye and orpiment: Arist. [Pr.] [of the complexion] 38.2; ash water: Val. Max. *Memorable doings and sayings* 2.1.5; Samian earth: Plin. *HN* 31.46.117; stale human urine: Plin. *HN* 28.46.164.
114. Mart. *Epigrams* 6.57.
115. *HA Lucius Verus* 10; *Commodus Antoninus* 17; *The Two Gallieni* 16; Juv. *Satires* 2.93; Ath. *The Learned Banqueters* 13.568.c; Plin. *HN* 33.34.102.
116. Plin. *HN* 15.24.87–8; and Tibullus 1.8.43–4 (walnut); Plin. *HN* 16.71.180 (elderberries); 20.22.49 (leek); 20.83.221 (wild orache); 22.73.153 (bitter vetch); 23.70.135 (mulberry); 23.81.161 (myrtle); 23.53.99 (elate palm); 24.5.10 (gall nut); 24.56.94 (erythrodanum leaves); 24.67.110 (purple and dun acacia). See also Susan Stewart, "Cosmetics and perfumes in the Roman world: a glossary," in *Dress and Identity*, ed. Mary Harlow (Oxford: Archeopress, 2012), 109–16.
117. Plin. *HN* 35.52.183.
118. This is the modern procedure for henna.
119. This is customary for walnut dye.
120. Plin. *HN* 32.23.68; Stevens Cox *An Illustrated Dictionary of Hairdressing and Wigmaking*: s.v. "lead comb."
121. Plin. *HN* 30.46.134.
122. Aelian, *On Animals* 1.48.
123. Plin. *HN* 30.46.134.
124. Some depictions show servants offering ribbons in boxes to the mistress, but not actively dressing her hair, e.g. funerary *stele* of a Woman, Greek (ca. 325–320 BCE), Museum of Fine Arts, Boston, MA, Inv. No. 1979.510. Hom. *Il.* 14.173–177.
125. Quintus Curtius, *History of Alexander* 9.2.6; Cic. *Disputations* 5.20.[58–9]; HA *Elagabalus* 31.7–8; *Corpus Inscriptionum Latinarum* (CIL), 6.07656; 6.08879; 6.08944; 6.08957; 6.08977; 6.09195; 6.37811; 6.33370a; 10.01935; 14.05306; 6.03994; 6.07296; 5.04101; 6.01128; 6.04359; 6.09939; 6.09940; 6.37822; etc.; *Digest* 32.1.65.3.1; Ov. *Met.* 11.180ff.; Mart. *Epigrams* 7.64; enslaved barber: Petron. *Sat.* 41, 95LO, 103, Trimalchio displays his servile nature by considering barbering an appropriate trade for his son (46); Suet. *Nero* 6.3; Plut. *Lives, Caesar* 49.2; Ath. *The Learned Banqueters* 12.520e; Suet. *Claudius* 40.2.4; Loeb *Greek Anthology* 6.307. (PHI Latin Texts)
126. Gell. *Attic Nights* 10.15.12.
127. Augustine, *De Civitate Dei* 6.10.
128. Mart. *Epigrams* 7.61.7–10; Sen. *De brevitate Vitae* 12.3; Jerry Toner, "Barbers, Barbershops and Searching for Roman Popular Culture," *Papers of the British School at Rome* 83 (2015): 94.

129. Mart. *Epigrams* 14.36; Plaut. *Pot of Gold* 316.
130. Varro, *Ling.* 5.129; Catull. 61.131–2; Sen. *Constant.* 14.1.
131. Petron. *Sat.* 94.L.
132. Alciphron, *Letters of Parasites* 3.30 (incompetent); Hor. *Epistles* 1.1.94 (uneven) and *Sat.* 1.3.29 (unstylish): Mart. *Epigrams* 6.52 (good), 7.83 (slow), 8.52 (slow), 11.84 (painful); Ov. *Ars Am.* 1.517; Lucian, *The Ignorant Book-collector* 29–30.
133. Mart. *Epigrams* 11.58.5–10.
134. Josephus, *Jewish War* 1.547–8.
135. Cic. *Disputations* 5.58–9; Plut. *Dion* 9.3–4.
136. Loeb *Mime Fragments* 15.11–14.
137. *HA Commodus* 17; Mart. *Epigrams* 3.74.
138. Self-shaving may have been relatively rare: Plut. *Antony* 1; *HA Elagabalus* 31.7–8.
139. Suet. *Augustus* 79.
140. Keith R. Bradley, *Slavery and Society at Rome* (Cambridge: Cambridge University Press, 1994), 59; Justinian, *Digest* 33.7. 5–6 [PHI Latin Texts].
141. Plaut. *Truculentus* 791; Mart. *Epigrams* 2.17, 7.64, 8.52, 11.84; CIL 6.9493, 6.9941, 6.9949, 12.4514.
142. Plaut. *Mostell.* 863; Apul. *Met.* 10.14; Bradley, *Slavery and Society at Rome*, 159.
143. Ar. *Birds* 1440–5; Plut. *Moralia Concerning Talkativeness* 509[A]; Toner, "Barbers, Barbershops and Searching for Roman Popular Culture," 101–3.
144. Broken hair bodkins found in the drains of public baths indicate only the presence of women, not commercial activity.
145. Dressing hair was degrading even for a eunuch: Claud. *Against Eutropius* 104–9.
146. CIL 6.9731.
147. *Digest* 32.65.3.1 [PHI Latin Texts].
148. Ov. *Am.* 1.11.
149. Whipping: Juv. *Satire* 6.490–1; stabbing: Ov. *Ars. Am.* 7.22, 8.21, 3.240 ff.; biting: Gal. *The diagnosis and Cure of the Soul's Passions*, 8; murdered with a mirror: Mart. *Epigrams* 2.66.4. See further, Chapter Eight in this volume.
150. CIL 6.9493 (=6.33809, =6.2364), 12.4515; Mart. *Epigrams* 7.64.

Chapter Five

1. Date: possibly 430–420 BCE. (E. Craik, *The Hippocratic Treatise On Glands: Edited and Translated with Introduction and Commentary* (Leiden: Brill, 2009), 118). The texts handed down to us under the name Hippocrates are in fact the work of different authors, compiled as a corpus in the Hellenistic period. The medical theories expressed in the different works can therefore differ slightly.
2. Hippocrates, *On the Nature of the Child* 9.
3. We see this example again in Pseudo-Aristotle *Problems* 877a.2–4, who displays familiarity with Hippocratic theories of hair growth earlier in this passage (876b.34-877a.1).
4. Craik, *The Hippocratic Treatise*, 28–9. Galen is aware of this treatise (*Galen's Commentary on Hippocrates "On Joints,"* 18A.379 K).
5. Hippoc. *On Glands* 4.
6. E. Craik, *The Hippocratic Corpus: Content and Context* (London: Routledge, 2015), 48.
7. Hippoc. *On Fleshes* 2.
8. Hippoc. *On Fleshes* 3.
9. Hippoc. *On Fleshes* 10.

NOTES 185

10. Hippoc. *On Fleshes* 11.
11. Hippoc. *On Fleshes* 4.
12. Hippoc. *On Fleshes* 14.
13. Hippoc. *On Fleshes* 14.
14. Hippoc. *Diseases* 4.2. On the authorship of these see Craik, *The Hippocratic Corpus*, 186.
15. Plato, *Timaeus* 75E–76D.
16. Aristotle, *Parts of Animals* 658a.12–b.26. This is not true, giraffes, to take but one example, have eyelashes on both eyelids.
17. Arist. *Parts an.* 658b.15–19.
18. Arist. *Generation of Animals* 728b, 744b, 745a, and 781b–785b.
19. Arist. *Gen. an.* 744b.24.
20. Arist. *Gen. an.* 744b.12–745a.4.
21. A. L. Peck, *Aristotle: Generation of Animals* (Cambridge, MA: Harvard University Press, 1942), lxvi–ii.
22. Arist. *Gen. an.* 735a.5–25.
23. Arist. *Gen. an.* 745a.11–16. These ideas are picked up by the pseudo-Aristotelian author of *Problems* 893a.18–36.
24. Arist. *Gen. an.* 781b.30–785b.15.
25. The importance of porous skin to hair growth is found elsewhere in the peripatetic tradition: Pseudo-Aristotle, *Problems* 867a.5–8.
26. See also Pseudo-Aristotle, *Problems* 867a.24–27.
27. Arist. *Parts an.* 658b.4.
28. Although the brain is the coolest part of the body, it still has some heat (Arist. *Parts an.* 652b.29).
29. See also Aristotle, *History of Animals* 518b.9–10.
30. H. Diller, *Wanderarzt und Aitiologe* (Leipzig: Dieterich, 1934), 115.
31. Arist. *Hist. an.* 517b.18–21.
32. Ps.-Arist. [*Pr.*] 893a.31–4.
33. Arist. *Gen. an.* 783b.25.
34. Arist. *Gen. an.* 784a.11–12.
35. Arist. *Gen. an.* 773a.34.
36. See also Aristotle, *History of Animals* 518b.21–5.
37. Aristotle discusses this in less detail at *History of Animals* 518a.7–18.
38. Arist. *Gen. an.* 782a.6.
39. Arist. *Gen. an.* 784b.7.
40. On concoction see Peck's introduction to the Loeb of Aristotle *Generation of Animals* (1942: lxv-i).
41. Ps.-Arist. *On Colours* 797b.13–35.
42. Ps.-Arist. [*Col.*] 798a.10; b.25; 799a.12.
43. Ps.-Arist. [*Col.*] 797b.13–799b.21.
44. Ps.-Arist. [*Col.*] 798a.4–24.
45. Arist. *Gen. an.* 785b.2–13.
46. Galen, *On the Usefulness of the Parts* 11.14. Galen refers back to this explanation in *Method of Medicine* 10.775K. On the importance of eliminating residues in Galenic medicine see P. Brain, *Galen on Bloodletting: A Study of the Origins, Development and Validity of his Opinions, with a Translation of the Three Works* (Cambridge: Cambridge University Press, 1986): 126.

47. D. Sedley, *Creationism and Its Critics in Antiquity* (Berkeley: University of California Press, 2007): 240.
48. Gal. *de Usu. Part.* 10.7 = G. Helmreich (ed.), *Galen, De Usu Partium* (Amsterdam: A. M. Hakkert, 1968), 2.79–80. For eyelashes as palisades see Gal. *de Usu. Part.* 11.14 = Helmreich 2.157 and Arist. *Parts an.* 658b.19.
49. Gal. *de Usu. Part.* 10.7 = Helmreich 2.80.
50. Gal. *de Usu. Part.* 11.14 = Helmreich 2.158.
51. Gal. *de Usu. Part.* 11.14 = Helmreich 2.159–60.
52. Gal. *The Art of Medicine* 1.310K.
53. Gal. *Ars Med.* 1.315K. See the introduction to Johnston and Horsley's Loeb edition of Galen's *Method of Medicine*, for an introduction to these ideas (2011: lviii).
54. Gal. *Ars Med.* 319K.
55. Gal. *Ars Med.* 1.323K.
56. Gal. *Ars Med.* 1.325K.
57. Gal. *Ars Med.* 1.326K.
58. Gal. *Ars Med.* 1.326K.
59. Gal. *Ars Med.* 1.326K.
60. Gal. *Ars Med.* 1.327K.
61. Gal. *Ars Med.* 1.327K.
62. Gal. *Ars Med.* 1.328K.
63. Gal. *Ars Med.* 1.329K.
64. Gal. *Ars Med.* 1.337, 340K.
65. Gal. *Ars Med.* 1.343K.
66. Gal. *Ars Med.* 10.1015K.
67. See n. 6 above.
68. A. Cameron, "The Date and Identity of Macrobius," *Journal of Roman Studies* 56, no.1 (1966): 25–38.
69. Macrobius, *Saturnalia* 6.10.1. Homer, *Iliad* 8.518.
70. N. Marinone, "Il Medico Disario in Simmaco e Macrobio," *Maia* 25 (1973): 344–5. Symmachus, *Letter* 3.37.
71. Hippoc. *Nat. Puer.* 9; Arist. *Parts an.* 658b.4.
72. Arist. *Gen. an.* 785a.1–2.
73. Arist. *Gen. an.* 785a.11.
74. Galen, *Method of Medicine* 10.1016K.
75. Gal. *Ars Med.* 1.344K.
76. Hippoc. *Epidemics* 4.43; 6.8.11.
77. Hippoc. *Epid.* 6.8.32.
78. On Phaethousa see Helen King, *The One-Sex Body on Trial: The Classical and Early Modern Evidence* (Farnham: Ashgate, 2013), chap. 3.
79. King, *The One-Sex Body on Trial*, 96.
80. See the role of menstruation in Hippocrates, *Diseases of Women* 1 and *Girls*.
81. Gal. *Ars Med.* 1.343K
82. Gal. *Ars Med.* 1.326K.
83. Gal. *Ars Med.* 1.935K.
84. Gal. *Ars Med.* 10.941K.
85. Celsus, *On Medicine*, proem. 54; Gal. *On the Sects* 1.81K. For Methodists theories and history see P. A. Prioreschi, *A History of Medicine, Volume III: Roman Medicine* (Omaha: Horatius Press. 1998), chap. 3.

86. Celsus, *Med.* proem. 56.
87. O. Temkin, *Soranus' Gynecology* (Baltimore, MD: Johns Hopkins Press, 1991), xxxv.
88. Caelius Aurelianus, *Chronic Diseases* 3. 131.
89. Caelius Aurelianus, *Chronic Diseases* 1.12, trans. I. E. Drabkin, *Caelius Aurelianus: On Acute Diseases and On Chronic Diseases* (Chicago, IL: University of Chicago Press, 1950), 447.
90. On Asclepiades of Bithynia see J. T. Vallance, "The Medical System of Asclepiades of Bithynia," *Aufstieg und Niedergang der römischen Welt II* 37, no. 1 (1993): 711–27.
91. Trans. Drabkin, *Caelius Aurelianus*, 5 = Caelius Aurelianus, *Acute Diseases* 1.6.
92. Caelius Aurelianus, *Acute Diseases* 1. 116–17.
93. Caelius Aurelianus, *Acute Diseases* 1. 14; 120.
94. Caelius Aurelianus, *Acute Diseases* 1. 75.
95. Caelius Aurelianus, *Chronic Diseases* 1. 134.
96. Caelius Aurelianus, *Acute Diseases* 1. 118.
97. Caelius Aurelianus, *Chronic Diseases* 4.14–18.
98. On cures for lice see for example Pliny the Elder, *Natural History* 23. 18, 94; 24.18, 73, 74; 25.61; 26. 138; Celsus, *Med.* 6. 15. On the archaeological remains of lice see Harry Kenward, "Pubic Lice (*Pthirus pubis* L.) were Present in Roman and Medieval Britain." *Antiquity* 73, no. 282 (1999): 911–15.
99. Arist. *Hist. an.* 556b.22-557a.4, trans. Peck, *Aristotle: Generation of Animals*, 209.
100. Arist. *Hist. an.* 557a.7–8.
101. M. Waegeman, "The Gecko, the Hoopoe ... and Lice," *L'Antiquité Classique* 53 (1984): 218–25; and J. Bondeson, *A Cabinet of Medical Curiosities* (London: Tauris, 1997).
102. Phthiriasis is often seen as punishment for impiety or tyranny; see T. Africa, 'Worms and the Death of Kings: A Cautionary Note on Disease and History,' *Classical Antiquity* 1 (1982): 1–17; and A. Keaveney and J. A. Madden, "Phthiriasis and its Victims," *Symbolae Osloenses* 57, no. 1 (1982): 87–99.
103. Celsus, *Med.* 6.15.
104. Caelius Aurelianus, *Chronic Diseases* 4.14. Cf. Aristotle, *History of Animals* 557a.5 where he refers to wild-lice that are harder than the normal sort and difficult to get rid of.
105. See p. 5 above.
106. Gal. *Ars Med.* 1.325K.
107. Gal. *Ars Med.* 1.334K.

Chapter Six

1. Hippocrates, *On the Nature of the Child* [*Nat. puer.*] 20–1. Lesley Ann Dean-Jones, *Women's Bodies in Classical Greek Science* (Oxford: Clarendon Press, 1994), 83–5. See Chapter Five in this volume for a longer discussion of the same material.
2. Aristotle, *Generation of Animals* 728a.
3. Arist. *Gen. an.* 728b 26–7.
4. Arist. *Gen. an.* 783b. The Hippocrates also considered the increase in seed production linked to the appearance of body and pubic hair (Hippoc. *Nat. puer.* 20.1–3).
5. Arist. *Gen. an.* 783b25.
6. Arist. *Gen. an.* 784a10.
7. Arist. *Gen. an.* 784a25–784b.
8. O. Temkin, *Hippocrates in a World of Pagans and Christians* (Baltimore, MD: Johns Hopkins University Press, 1991), 47–50.

9. Thomas Laqueur, *Making Sex: Body and Gender from the Ancient Greeks to Freud* (Cambridge, MA: Harvard University Press, 1990), 19.
10. Galen, *On the Usefulness of Parts* 14.6.II.296–299.
11. Marilyn Skinner, "Sex," in *A Cultural History of the Human Body in Antiquity*, ed. Daniel H. Garrison (London: Bloomsbury, 2010), 70–2.
12. There is an extensive bibliography on women in antiquity, for overviews see Janet Tulloch, ed., *A Cultural History of Women in Antiquity* (London: Bloomsbury 2013); Sharon L. James and Sheila Dillon, ed., *A Companion to Women in the Ancient World* (Malden, MA: Wiley-Blackwell, 2012).
13. A theory expounded by Anthony Synnott, "Shame and Glory: A Sociology of Hair," *British Journal of Sociology* 38, no. 3 (1987): 381–413.
14. Mireille Lee, *Body, Dress, and Identity in Ancient Greece* (Cambridge: Cambridge University Press, 2015), 72. On veiling in ancient Greece see L. J. Llewellyn-Jones, *Aphrodite's Tortoise: The Veiled Woman of Ancient Greece* (Swansea: Classical Press of Wales, 2003). See Chapters Two, Three, Eight, and Nine in this volume.
15. On Greek pederasty see most recently Gloria Ferrari, *Figures of Speech, Men and Maidens in Ancient Greece* (Chicago, IL: University of Chicago Press, 2002), 135–61; but also, K. Dover, *Greek Homosexuality* (London: Duckworth, 1978); Craig A. Williams, *Roman Homosexuality* (Oxford: Oxford University Press, 2010).
16. Plato, *Symposium* 181D.
17. *Palatine Anthology* [*AP*] xi.36: Translation from *The Greek Anthology*, vol. 4, trans. W. R. Paton (Loeb Classical Library 85. Cambridge, MA: Harvard University Press, 1918).
18. *AP* xii.30. See commentary on many similar epigrams by Sonya Tarán, "ΕΙΣΙ ΤΡΙΧΕΣ: An Erotic Motif," *Journal of Hellenic Studies* 105 (1985): 90–107.
19. Pl. *Symp.* 217a.
20. Pl. *Symp.* 2176–219d; see Dover, *Greek Homosexuality*, 156–9.
21. Pl. *Protagoras* 309a. Translation from Plato, *Laches. Protagoras. Meno. Euthydemus*, trans. W. R. M. Lamb (Loeb Classical Library 165. Cambridge, MA: Harvard University Press, 1924).
22. *AP* xii.10.
23. Plutarch, *Lycurgus* 22.1. See also Xenophon, *Constitution of the Lacedaemonians* 11.3.
24. Herodotus, *Histories* 7.208; Molly Myerowitz Levine, "The Gendered Grammar of Ancient Mediterranean Hair," in *Off with her Head! The Denial of Women's Identity in Myth Religion and Culture*, ed. H. Eilberg-Schwartz and W. Doniger (Berkeley: University of California Press, 1995), 80–1; Lee, *Body, Dress, and Identity*, 74–5.
25. Alcman, *Partheneion* 1 *PMGF*, lines 50, 100. On blonde hair in antiquity see Chapter Eight in this volume.
26. Alcm. *Partheneion* 3 *PMGF*, lines 5, 70. Extracts from Alcman come from citations in Sarah Pomeroy, *Spartan Women* (Oxford: Oxford University Press, 2002), 6–7.
27. Plut. *Lycurgus* 15.3.
28. J.-P. Vernant, *Mortals and Immortals: Collected Essays*, ed. F. I. Zeitlin (Princeton, NJ: Princeton University Press, 1991), 120, cited in Lee, *Body, Dress, and Identity*, 75; Pomeroy, *Spartan Women*, 42–3. This rather misunderstands notion of homosexuality and heterosexuality in antiquity, for a more nuanced view see Holt Parker, "The Teratogenic Grid," in *Roman Sexualities*, ed. Marilyn Skinner (Princeton, NJ: Princeton University Press, 1997).
29. Euripides, *Hippolytus* 198–202.

30. Apuleius, *Metamorphoses* 2.9. J. Englert and T. Long, "Functions of Hair in Apuleius' 'Metamorphoses,'" *Classical Journal* 68, no. 3 (1973): 236–9.
31. Apul. *Met.* 2.17.
32. Levine, "Gendered Grammar," 96.
33. Karen Stears, "Dead Women's Society: Constructing Female Gender in Classical Athenian Funerary Sculpture," in *Time, Tradition and Society in Greek Archaeology: Bridging the "Great Divide,"* ed. Nigel Spencer (London: Routledge, 2013), 119–20.
34. Ov. *Met.* 4.794–801; Levine, "Gendered Grammar," 92–5. See Chapter Nine in this volume for further discussion.
35. *Numbers* 5: 18; Tosefta Sotah 3:2, MS Vienna, cited in Naftali S. Cohen, "What to Wear: Women's Adornment and Judean Identity in the Third Century Mishnah," in *Dressing Judeans and Christians in Antiquity*, ed. K. Upson-Saia et al. (Farnham: Ashgate, 2014), 30–1.
36. Eur. *Bacchae*, 695, 864–5, 927–31; for Ariadne see Catullus 64.63–70; for witches see Lucian, *The Civil War* 6.607–18; Petronius, *Satyricon* 133; Seneca's Medea loosens her hair when she casts her spells, *Medea* 670–843. See also Charles Cosgrove, "A Woman's Unbound Hair in the Greco-Roman World, with Special Reference to the Story of the 'Sinful Woman' in Luke 7.36–50," *Journal of Biblical Literature* 124, no. 4 (2005): 684–5.
37. Horace, *Epodes* 5.15–16.
38. David Lavergne, "Lépilation feminine en Grèce ancienne," in *Parures et artifices: le corps exposé dans l'Antiquité*, ed. L. Bodiou et al. (Paris: L'Harmattan, 2011), 99. Martin Kilmer, "Genital phobia and depilation," *Journal of Hellenic Studies* 102 (1982): 105.
39. Lavergne argues that in classical Attica at least, women made their whole bodies hairless in order to be more attractive.
40. Aristophanes, *Women of the Assembly* 60–7. Kilmer, "Genital Phobia," 105: considers that this might also include other body hair, and the joke is further emphasized by the fact that in drama all the actors were male. Perhaps those playing female roles depilated in order to stress their characterization?
41. Ar. *Women of the Assembly*, 13–14. See Chapter Four in this volume on more methods for depilation.
42. Ar. *Lysistrata*, 87–9, 151. Lee, *Body, Dress, and Identity*, 79; Kilmer, "Genital Phobia," 105–6.
43. Kilmer, "Genital Phobia," Plates I & II; Lavergne, "Lépilation Feminine," figs. 1–6; Lee, *Body, Dress, and Identity*, 80 and 264 n. 205; while the thought of these activities make a modern reader wince, a quick trawl of the internet identified several sites showing Turkish barbers singeing ear hair, and even one video on how to use a cigarette lighter to remove facial hair for women, see https://www.youtube.com/watch?v=Tyqr0BHC_FQ (accessed January 18, 2017).
44. Lavergne, "Lépilation Feminine,"101–2, figs. 3, 4; Lee, *Body, Dress, and Identity*, 79–80, figs. 3.13, 3.14. See also for context A. J. Paul, "Eros and a Depilation Scene by the Dinos Painter," *American Journal of Archaeology* 97 (1993): 330.
45. Ar. *Women of the Assembly* 723–4.
46. R. R. R. Smith, "Pindar, Athletes, and the Early Greek Statue Habit," in *Pindar's Poetry, Patrons and Festivals: From Archaic Greece to the Roman Empire*, ed. S. Hornblower and C. Morgan (Oxford: Oxford University Press, 2007) 112–16. See also Chapter Nine in this volume.
47. Ar. *Thesmophoriazusae* 31–3, 191, 136–40; Dover, *Greek Homosexuality*, 144.
48. Aulus Gellius, *Attic Nights* 6.12.6–7; Williams, *Roman Homosexuality*, 141.

49. Martial, *Epigrams* 2.62.
50. Seneca, *Epistles* 114.14, cited in Williams, *Roman Homosexuality*, 142–3.
51. Sen. *Ep.* 56.2. See also Chapters Four and Eight in this volume.
52. Pumice: Pliny, *Natural History* [*HN*] 36.154; nut-shells: Suetonius, *Augustus* 68; resin: Sen. *Natural Questions* [*QNat.*] 7.31.2: see Susan Stewart, *Cosmetics and Perfumes in the Roman World* (Stroud: Tempus, 2007): 94–5.
53. Clement of Alexandria, *Paidagogus* 3.3; see Maud Gleason, *Making Men: Sophists and Self-Presentation in Ancient Rome* (Princeton, NJ: Princeton University Press, 1995): 68–9. See also Chapter Eight in this volume.
54. Clem. Al. *Paidagogus* 3.3.
55. Ovid, *Ars Amatoria* 3.193–4.
56. *CIL* 6.37965. See also Chapter Eight in this volume for a full translation of the inscription.
57. Susan Stewart, "Cosmetics and Perfumes in the Roman World: A Glossary," in *Dress and Identity*, ed. Mary Harlow (Oxford: Archaeopress, 2012), 109–16; Stewart, *Cosmetics and Perfumes*, 93–5, 112–18.
58. Plin. *HN* 30.133–4. For other arcane recipes for hair removal see Plin. *HN* 28.249, 255; 24.79; 32.136. See also Amy Richlin, "Making up a Woman: The Face of Roman Gender," in Eilberg-Schwartz and Doniger, ed., *Off with her Head*, 198–9.
59. Mart. *Epigrams* 3.74; 10.90.
60. Apul. *Met.* 2.17.
61. Sen. *QNat.* 1.17.1; see Levine, "Gendered Grammar," 87.
62. Genesis 25–30.43; Levine, "Gendered Grammar," 88.
63. Ov. *Met.* 9. 305–323; 2. 476–85.
64. *Vita Sancta Macarii Romani*, 15, cited in Kristi Upson-Saia, "Hairiness and Holiness in the early Christian Desert," in Upson-Saia et al., *Dressing Judeans*, 164–5. She also lists other examples of excessively hairy ascetics.
65. Upson-Saia, "Hairiness and Holiness," 170–1; see also Mary Harlow, "The Impossible Art of Dressing to Please: Jerome and the Rhetoric of Dress," in *Objects in Context, Objects in Use: Material Spatiality in Late Antiquity*, ed. L. Lavan et al. (Leiden: Brill, 2007), 531–47.
66. Levine, "Gendered Grammar," 88.
67. It was not only the hair that could be read in this way. The head and particularly the face made up with cosmetics, were used as indices to assess female fickleness, potential for deception, desire to seduce men other than their husbands which led, in the ancient mind, to a similar willingness to be free with sexual favors. See Tertullian, *De Cultu Feminarum* 2.2; Richlin, "Making up a Woman," 194–5; Maria Wyke, "Woman in the Mirror: The Rhetoric of Adornment in the Roman world," in *Women in Ancient Societies*, ed. L. Archer et al. (London: Macmillan, 1994).

Chapter Seven

1. Cassius Dio 9.39. Translations by the author unless stated otherwise.
2. Pliny, *Natural History* 34.59, praised Myron's forays into realism but was critical of his representation of cephalic and pubic hair, regarding it as "not free from fault" (*non emendatius fecisse*) and closer to the "rough" (*rudis*) or "unfinished" look of antique works.
3. On *munditia* and *cultus* see P. Watson, "Ovid and Cultus: *Ars Amatoria* 3.113–28," *Transactions and Proceedings of the American Philological Association* 112 (1982): 237–44; R. K. Gibson, "Ovid, Augustus, and the Politics of Moderation in Ars Amatoria 3," in *The Art of Love: Bimillennial Essays on Ovid's Ars Amatoria and Remedia Amoris*, ed. R. K. Gibson, S. Green, and A. Sharrock (Oxford: Oxford University Press, 2006), 121–42;

R. K. Gibson, "Excess and Restraint: Propertius, Horace, and Ovid's *Ars Amatoria*," in *Bulletin of the Institute of Classical Studies*, Suppl. 89 (London: Institute of Classical Studies, 2007).

4. Later styles for men became comparatively flamboyant and thereby reduced the emphasis on authority, might, and machismo. See N. Haas, "Hair over the Ages and in Art: The Culture, and Social History of Hair and Its Depiction in Art," in *Hair Growth and Disorders*, ed. U. Blume-Peytavi, A. Tosti, and R. M. Trüeb (Berlin: Springer, 2008), 528.

5. On race and ethnicity in the ancient Mediterranean see B. Isaac, *The Invention of Racism in Classical Antiquity* (Princeton, NJ: Princeton University Press, 2004), 24–33. Importantly, Isaac's position on racism in antiquity specified the existence of a protoracism, which influenced the racist theories of the Enlightenment and, in turn, those of the nineteenth century.

6. Interspersed with notations of similarities; see R. V. Munson, *Telling Wonders: Ethnographic and Political Discourse in the Work of Herodotus* (Ann Arbor: University of Michigan Press, 2001), 8.

7. Munson, *Telling Wonders*, 8.

8. The ambivalence of Herodotus prompted different interpretations of his attitude to non-Greeks. Plutarch, (*Moralia* 857a) refers to Herodotus as a "barbarian-lover." See P. Cartledge, *The Greeks: A Portrait of Self and Others*, 2nd ed. (Oxford: Oxford University Press, 2002), 68; L. Kurke, *Aesopic Conversations: Popular Tradition, Cultural Dialogue, and the Invention of Greek Prose* (Princeton, NJ: Princeton University Press, 2011), 391 ff. Importantly, Kurke raised the issue of Plutarch's own ethnic gaze on Herodotus: "sneering that he was in no position to be so critical of the Greeks who Medized during the Persian Wars" (391).

9. See J. Redfield, "Herodotus the Tourist," *Classical Philology* 80, no. 2 (1985): 97. See also, M. Liverani, "The Libyan Caravan Road in Herodotus IV.181–185," *Journal of the Economic and Social History of the Orient* 43, no. 4 (2000), 498: "[a] a feature is the presence of extraordinary and fantastic peculiarities: the Garamantes have no weapons (IV.174), the Atarantes have no personal names (IV.184), the Atlantes have no dreams (IV.184) ... and so on."

10. For hair as symbolic of humankind's closeness to, or distance from, nature (versus culture), see Molly Myerowitz Levine, "The Gendered Grammar of Ancient Mediterranean Hair," in *Off with Her Head! The Denial of Women's Identity in Myth*, Religion, *and Culture*, ed. A. Eilberg-Schwartz and W. Doniger (Berkeley: University of California Press, 1995), 88.

11. On structure and sources pertaining to 4.168–99, see Liverani, "The Libyan Caravan Road in Herodotus IV.181–185," 496–520.

12. The use of the present participle κομῶσαι (4.168) has been employed to emphasize that the women actively allowed their hair to grow long; in essence, they did not interfere in the natural process by means of culture. See also κομῶσαι in the passage on the Maxyes (4.191).

13. Levine, "The Gendered Grammar", 88: "Long unbound hair serves as a sign of a state of nature prior to the intrusion of culture."

14. J. Dillery, "Reconfiguring the Past: Thyrea, Thermopylae and Narrative Patterns in Herodotus," *The American Journal of Philology* 117, no. 2 (1996): 230. The reference to the legislation that required Spartiates to grow their hair marked a contrast to Herodotus' accounts of non-Greeks' long hair; again the distinction has been made between Greek hair as a cultural feature (in Sparta subject to law) as opposed to, in the case of the Adurmachidae women, grown in accordance with nature.

15. The Spartiates' long hair, while admired as a cultural signifier of martial prowess and indeed their own Hellenic alterity, was also regarded as anachronistic and even ambiguous in classical

Greece; see Aristotle, *Rhetoric* 1367a (a positive signifier of the elite class); Aristophanes, *Birds* 1282 (a marker of uncleanliness and lack of refinement).

16. Translation based on *Herodotus, The Persian Wars, Volume III: Books 5–7*, 7.208, trans. A. D. Godley (Cambridge, MA: Harvard University Press, 1922). See also Chapter Six in this volume.
17. See Tacitus, *Germania* 38 for a particularly in-depth description of the hair of the Suebi. That Tacitus interpreted hair as an evidential physical characteristic of a certain people's origin, see Tacitus, *Agricola* 11.
18. Tac. *Annales* 14.30.
19. M. Johnson, *Boudicca* (London: Bloomsbury, 2012), 42–3.
20. The hair of the Furies became increasingly monstrous over time and included a particular emphasis on snakes in Latin literature; see Virgil, *Aeneid* 12.848 ff., *Georgics* 4.471; Propertius, *Elegies* 3.5; Ovid, *Metamorphoses* 4.451 ff.; Seneca, *Hercules Furens* 982 ff.; Statius, *Thebaid* 1.46 ff.; Nonnus, *Dionysiaca* 32.100 ff.
21. G. Lloyd-Morgan, "Appearance, Life and Leisure," in *The Celtic World*, ed. M. Green (London: Routledge, 2000), 104. Lloyd-Morgan compared the Celtic noblewomen's hair with "the Japanese appreciation of female beauty during the Heian period (ca. 950–1050), when length of hair and its appearance were not only a woman's crowning glory but could also incite passionate admiration and infatuation."
22. Cass. Dio, *Epitome* 62.2.
23. See J. Ramin, *Le Periple d'Hannon/The Periplus of Hanno* (Oxford: British Archaeological Reports, Suppl. Series 3, 1976). Hanno's journey was cited in late antiquity, and the *Periplus* preserved in a single Byzantine manuscript (*Codex Palatinus Graecus* 398). On the debate concerning the manuscript as a forgery, see P. Kaplan, "Hanno," in *Dictionary of African Biography*, 6 vols., ed. H. L. Gates and E. K. Akyeampong (Oxford: Oxford University Press, 2012), 24.
24. *The Periplus of Hano* 18, trans. W. H. Schoff (Philadelphia, PA: Commercial Museum, 1912).
25. Pliny referenced Hanno's journey, although he referred to the islands as the "Gorgades, which were formerly the habitation of the Gorgons." He mentioned the skins of two of the women having been placed in the Temple of Juno "as proof of the truth of his story and as curiosities, where they were on show until Carthage was taken by Rome" (*Naturalis Historia* [*HN*] 6.200). See also Pompeius Mela's *The Description of the World* (3.93), which mentioned the women, noting that they possessed the ability "to procreate by themselves without sex with men."
26. Mela (*The Description of the World* n. 22) followed the same objective tone concerning the violence committed against the women. For a much later example of hairiness being in the eyes of the beholder, see F. Dikötter, "Hairy Barbarians, Furry Primates, and Wild Men: Medical Science and Cultural Representations of Hair in China," in *Hair: Its Power and Meaning in Asian Cultures*, ed. A. Hiltebeitel and B. D. Miller (Albany: State University of New York, 1998), 51–74. On Chinese responses to hairy Europeans, Dikötter writes: "Giulio Aleni, for instance, was described as a 'man with blue eyes and the beard of a dragon' during his first visit to Fujian province between 1625 and 1639 … The Dutch were commonly referred to as 'red-haired barbarians'" (52–4).
27. Caesar, *De Bello Gallico* 5.14.
28. See Caes. *De Bello Gallico* 5.15–17.
29. For a discussion of the tensions in the writings of both Caesar and Tacitus concerning northern Europeans as both admirable and "barbaric," and the connected ambivalence

associated with civilization and its effete effects, see S. Stroh, "The Long Shadow of Tacitus: Classical and Modern Colonial Discourses in the Eighteenth- and Early-Nineteenth Century Scottish Highlands," in *Transcultural English Studies: Theories, Fictions, Realities, ASNEL Papers* 12, ed. F. Schulz-Engler and S. H. Rodopi. (Netherlands: Rodopi, 2009).

30. See E. Adler, "Boudica's Speeches in Tacitus and Dio," *Classical World* 101 (2008): 190 n. 48 (based on A. O. Lovejoy and G. Boas, *Primitivism and Related Ideas in Antiquity* (Baltimore, MD: Johns Hopkins University Press, 1997 [1935]).
31. Diodorus Siculus, *Bibliotheca Historica* 5.28.
32. Throughout book 5, Diodorus made several overt comparisons between the Gauls and animals; at one point he stated that the Gauls descended to a point below that of animals in their treatment of deceased enemies (5.29).
33. Further on the topic of "barbarians" and food in Roman accounts, see P. C. N. Stewart, "Inventing Britain: The Roman Creation and Adaptation of an Image," *Britannia* 26 (1995): 3.
34. Contra E. S. Gruen, *Rethinking the Other in Antiquity* (Princeton, NJ: Princeton University Press, 2011), 143 (who read the passage as essentially positive). See also Polybius 2.15 for their appealing physiques and bellicosity; see also 2.7, 19, 35, and 78 for negative traits.
35. Further on Diodorus' description, see Miranda Aldhouse-Green, *An Archaeology of Images: Iconology and Cosmology in Iron Age and Roman Europe* (London: Taylor and Francis, 2004b): "His description resonates with certain male images from the Iron Age iconographic record, including the Bohemian stone head from Mšecké Žehrovice which depicts a man, his hair standing up stiffly on his head and a long drooping moustache. Diodorus's remark about the mane-like appearance of male head-hair is confirmed by images on Iron Age Gallic coins that depict riders. with stiff hair sometimes treated identically to the manes of their mounts … What is more, the horses ridden by these coin-men often possess human faces, and call to mind the double maleness of Greek centaurs" (66–7).
36. S. Allen, *Lords of Battle: The World of the Celtic Warrior* (Oxford: Osprey Publishing, 2007), 20. See the sculpture, "The Dying Gaul" as an example of the effects of lime-washed hair.
37. Further, Dionysius of Halicarnassus commented: "Our enemies fight naked. What hurt could their long hair, their wild looks and their clanging arms do to us? These are nothing more than signs of barbarian boastfulness" (14.9). On this passage, see J. N. G. Ritchie and W. F. Ritchie, "The Army, Weapons and Fighting," in *The Celtic World*, ed. M. Green (London: Routledge, 1995), 53, who noted Roman ignorance of Celtic martial corporality in reference to nakedness: "the Celts were fighting naked, not because they were boastful and arrogant, but in accordance with religious and social customs."
38. A. Synnott, "Shame and Glory: A Sociology of Hair," *The British Journal of Sociology* 38, no. 3 (1987): 382.
39. See, for example 24, on hair.
40. The term "Ethiopian" was an ambiguous one in the ancient Mediterranean because it was regularly employed in nonspecific ways. Although used to denote a racial type, it was often geographically vague. See F. M. Snowden, "The Negro in Classical Italy," *The American Journal of Philology* 68, no. 3 (1947): 266–92.
41. See F. M. Snowden, *Blacks in Antiquity: Ethiopians in the Greco-Roman Experience* (Cambridge, MA: Belknap Press, 1970), 101 ff., on the chronology of references to Ethiopians in Greek and Roman writing.
42. Significantly, Herodotus made distinctions between the bodies of the various Ethiopian peoples and the human race in general; the Macrobian Ethiopians, for example, were

described as the tallest and handsomest men on earth (3.20). See also Homer, *Iliad* 1.423, *Odyssey* 1.22–24, on positive references to the Ethiopians. See J. K. Ward, "*Ethnos* in the *Politics*: Aristotle and Race," in *Philosophers on Race: Critical Essays*, ed. J. K. Ward and T. L. Lott (Oxford: Blackwell, 2002), 16. Ward argued that Herodotus' more balanced references to the Ethiopians, in contrast to later classical and Hellenistic writers, "seems to reflect the more complex, cosmopolitan attitude towards non-Greeks found elsewhere in archaic literature."

43. See Aristotle, *On the Generation of Animals* 5.3.782b. Aristotle made other links between climate and various peoples' characteristics, including qualities such as spirit or *thumos* and intellect or *diamoia*; see Arist. *Politics* 1327b.

44. Ptolemy's *Tetrabiblos* 2.2; possibly influenced by Hippocrates, *Airs, Waters, Places* 24. On Roman comments on Ethiopian hair (and other characteristics) and environment, see Strabo, *Geography* 1.2, 15.1; Pliny, *Natural History* 2.189, 6.70.

45. On Memnon, see Snowden, *Blacks in Antiquity*, 151: "A legendary character of divine descent who came to be regarded as Ethiopian and black during the transmission of a myth is Memnon, son of Tithonus and Eos. Though associated with the east and Asia in certain, particularly early, accounts, Memnon was eventually localized unmistakably in Egypt and Ethiopia also." For further examples of Memnon in black-figure amphora, see Snowden, *Blacks in Antiquity*, 48 (figs. 18 and 19).

46. This depiction of Memnon perhaps foreshadowed and complemented the Herodotean reference to the Macrobian Ethiopians as the tallest and handsomest men on earth (3.20) while, importantly, according to J. E. Skinner, it simultaneously reflected "a nexus of ideas in which Homeric Ethiopians and black Africans were variously conflated"; see J. E. Skinner, *The Invention of Greek Ethnography: From Homer to Herodotus* (Oxford: Oxford University Press, 2012), 98. See Hom. *Od.* 11.522, for the beauty of Memnon. On the origins of Memnon and the complex and contested source history, see R. D. Griffith, "The Origin of Memnon," *Classical Antiquity* 17, no. 2 (1998): 212–34.

47. For a discussion of the series, see J. Neils, "The Group of The Negro Alabastra: A Study in Motif Transferal," *Antike Kunst* 23 (1980): 13–23.

48. For Roman/Italian artistic representations of Ethiopians and the depiction of hair, see Snowden, *Blacks in Antiquity*.

49. For a concise discussion, see V. Tsouna, "Doubts about Other Minds and the Science of Physiognomics," *The Classical Quarterly* 48, no. 1 (1998): 175–86.

50. K. L. Wrenhaven, *Reconstructing the Slave: The Image of the Slave in Ancient Greece* (London: Bloomsbury, 2012), 44. Wrenhaven noted the likelihood that the theory of physiognomy emerged much earlier, citing the figure of Thersites in Hom. *Il*. 2.211 ff.

51. See, for example, Ps.-Arist. *Physiognomonic* 806b.

52. μαλακόν also meant effeminate, hence Pseudo-Aristotle combined the quality of the hair with the personality trait it denoted.

53. See Isaac, *The Invention of Racism in Classical Antiquity*, 82 ff.

54. D. Rankin, "The Celts through Classical Eyes," in *The Celtic World*, 28: "[W]hose *tumultus* … they had experienced so often." See Livy, *History of Rome* 38.17 on the terrifying Gallic warriors, replete with tall bodies, flowing hair, great shields, and long swords.

55. See M. A. Sears, *Athens, Thrace, and the Shaping of Athenian Leadership* (Cambridge: Cambridge University Press, 2013), 140–73. See also Xenophanes fr. 16 (Diels) who noted that different nations ascribed their own features to their gods; Thracians, for example, had gods with red hair and blue eyes (and Ethiopians had gods with black faces and broad noses).

56. S. Stewart, *Cosmetics and Perfumes in the Roman World* (Stroud: Tempus, 2007), 44.

57. See M. Johnson, *Ovid on Cosmetics: Medicamina Faciei Femineae and Related Texts* (London: Bloomsbury 2016).
58. See Johnson, *Ovid on Cosmetics*, 95 (with reference to Ovid, *Amores* 1.14.45–52). Greek women of the Hellenistic and Roman periods also dyed their hair and wore hairpieces; see M. M. Lee, *Body, Dress, and Identity in Ancient Greece* (Cambridge: Cambridge University Press, 2015), 70.
59. On the painting, see D. R. Smith, "Inversion, Revolution, and the Carnivalesque in Rembrandt's 'Civilis'," *Anthropology and Aesthetics* 27 (1995): 89–110.
60. M. Aldhouse-Green, "Chaining and shaming: images of defeat, from Llyn Cerrig Bach to Sarmitzegetusa," *Oxford Journal of Archaeology* 23, no. 3 (2004a): 334.
61. For an excellent treatment of Romanization of Gaul, see G. Woolf, *Becoming Roman: The Origins of Provincial Civilization in Gaul* (Cambridge: Cambridge University Press, 2000).
62. See n. 4 above.

Chapter Eight

1. For rites of passage see Chapters One, Two, and Six.
2. See Chapter Four on creating hairstyles and Chapter Nine on the role of visual culture in the creation of ideals.
3. See J. R. Mertens, *How to Read Greek Vases* (New Haven, CT: Yale University Press, 2010); and Chapter Nine in this volume.
4. See, for example, Plautus, *Asinaria* 400. For more on attitudes to red hair in antiquity see Chapter Seven in this volume.
5. Pollux, *Onomasticon* 31.
6. Plaut., *Miles Gloriosus* 923–4. Such a description is, however, not exclusive to the character of the soldier. See further Chapter Three in this volume and Kelly Olson, "Masculinity, Appearance, and Sexuality: Dandies in Roman Antiquity," *The Journal of the History of Sexuality* 23, no. 2 (2014): 182–205.
7. Suetonius, *Julius Caesar* 45.
8. Tacitus, *Agricola* 10–11. See Chapter Seven in this volume.
9. For examples of hair accoutrements see Chapter Four in this volume; Ellen Swift, "The Archaeology of Adornment and the Toilet in Roman Britain and Gaul," in *Dress and Identity*, ed. Mary Harlow (Oxford: Archaeopress, 2012), 47–57.
10. Varro, *De Lingua Latina* 29; Cicero, *Orator ad M. Brutum* 78; Tac., *Dialogues* 26; Quintilian, *Declamationes* 2.512; Virgil, *Aeneid* 12.100; Plaut., *Curculio* 4.421. See also Chapter Four in this volume.
11. A. M. Derks and W. K. Vos, "Wooden Combs from the Roman Fort at Vechten: The Bodily Appearance of Soldiers," *Journal of Archaeology in the Low Countries* 2, no. 2 (2010): 53–77. See also Chapter Four in this volume.
12. Herodotus, *Histories* 7.208.3. For more on Spartans see Chapters Two, Six, and Seven in this volume.
13. Strabo, *Geography* 6.3.2, 13–15. The *demos* was the council composed of all male citizens aged thirty or over.
14. Myron of Priene, *FGrHist* 106 F 2 = Athenaeus 14.657d.
15. For changes in style at Athens see also Chapter Three.
16. See Chapters Two and Three for more on Spartan styles in Athens.
17. Mireille Lee, *Body, Dress, and Identity in Ancient Greece* (Cambridge: Cambridge University Press, 2015), 72. On veiling see Lloyd Llewellyn-Jones, *Aphrodite's Tortoise: The Veiled Women of Ancient Greece* (Swansea: Classical Press of Wales, 2003).

18. On bridal behavior see Chapters Two and Three, and for Spartan brides see Chapter Six.
19. On Spartan women exercising see Aristophanes, *Lysistrata* 79–83; Aristotle, *Politics* 1269b–1270a8; Propertius, *Elegies* 3.14; Horace, *Odes* 2.11. 23–4.
20. Lee, *Body, Dress, and Identity*, 72–3.
21. Cic., *De Officiis* 1.36.130–1.
22. Ov., *Ars Amatoria* 1.505.
23. For more on *cultus* see Chapter Three.
24. Elizabeth Bartman, "Hair and the Artifice of Roman Female Adornment," *American Journal of Archaeology* 105, no. 1 (2001): 1–25.
25. Juvenal, *Satires* 6.502–4.
26. Janet Stephens, "Recreating the Fonseca Hairstyle," *EXARC Journal*, no. 1 (2013). http://exarc.net/issue-2013-1/ea/recreating-fonseca-hairstyle.
27. John R. Crawford, "*Capita Desecta* and Marble Coiffures," *Memoirs of the American Academy in Rome* 1 (1915/1916): 103–19.
28. See Leslie Shumka, "Designing Women: The Representation of Women's Toiletries on Funerary Monuments in Roman Italy," in *The Fabrics of Roman Culture*, ed. Jonathan Edmondson and Alison Keith (Toronto: University of Toronto Press, 2008), 172–91.
29. Andrew Stewart, *Art, Desire and the Body in Ancient Greece* (Cambridge: Cambridge University Press, 1997), 124–9; Llewellyn-Jones, *Aphrodite's Tortoise*, 28–36. See also Marice Rose, "The Construction of Mistress and Slave Relationships in Late Antique Art," *Women's Art Journal* 29, no. 2 (2008): 41–9. See discussion in Chapter Two in this volume.
30. Lena Larsson Loven, "*LANAM FECIT*—Wool Working and Female Virtue," in *Aspects of Women in Antiquity: Proceedings of the First Nordic Symposium on Women's Lives in Antiquity*, ed. Lena Larsson Lovén and Agneta Strömberg (Jonsered: Paul Åströms, 1998), 85–95.
31. Martial, *Epigrams* 2.66.
32. On beards see Chapters Two, Three, and Nine.
33. Cic. *Pro Sestio* 18. See Olson, "Masculinity, Appearance and Sexuality."
34. See Diane E. E. Kleiner, *Roman Sculpture* (New Haven, CT: Yale University Press, 1992), 36–7.
35. See Introduction in this volume on Synesius, *On Baldness*, a late fourth to early fifth century treatise, praising a lack of hair, and n. 3 this chapter.
36. Suet., *Iulius Caesar* 45.
37. Suet., *Otho* 12.
38. Demosthenes, *Against Neaera* 59.122.
39. Propertius, *Elegies* 2.2 5f.
40. Prop., 2.3 13.
41. Ov., *Amores* 1.5.
42. Ov., *Am.* 1.14.
43. The cutting of a captive's hair is a symbol of the dominant status of Rome as a nation over the conquered Germans. Hair like this was sold at various markets across the empire: for example Portico Philippi in Rome: Ov. *Ars Amatoria* 3.168.
44. Ov., *Ars Am.* 3.133–68.
45. Mart., *Epigrams* 3.93 1–2.
46. Mart.,12.31.21. See Chapter Four in this volume for further discussion on hair products.
47. Laura Hackworth Petersen, "Clothes Make the Man: Dressing the Roman Freedman Body," in *Bodies and Boundaries in Greco-Roman Antiquity*, ed. T. Fogen and M. Lee (Berlin: De Gruyter, 2009), 181–214.

48. See Diane E. E. Kleiner and Susan B. Matheson, *I Claudia: Women in Ancient Rome* (New Haven, CT: Yale University Art Gallery, 1996), Cat. 150, 199–200.
49. Diane E. E. Kleiner, "Family Ties: Mothers and Sons in Elite and Non-elite Roman Art," in *I Claudia II: Woman in Roman Art and Society*, ed. Diane E. E. Kleiner and Susan B. Matheson (Austin: University of Texas Press, 2000), 54–5.
50. Translation from Nicholas Horsfall, "CIL VI 37965 = CLE 1988 (Epitaph of Allia Potestas): A Commentary," *Zeitschrift für Papyrologie und Epigraphik* 61 (1985): 251–72.
51. CIL VI 37965.23.
52. Clement of Alexandria, *Paedogogus* 3.2.
53. Petronius, *Satyricon* 32; see Hackworth Petersen, "Clothes Make the Man," 207.
54. Old Oligarch (Pseudo-Xenophon), *Constitution of Athens* 1.10.
55. Appian, *Roman Civil Wars* 2, 17, cited from Thomas Wiedemann, *Greek and Roman Slavery* (London: Croom Helm, 1981), 68–9. Cf. Dio Chrysostom, *Oration* 15, *Slavery and Freedom*.
56. See F. H. Thompson, *The Archaeology of Greek and Roman Slavery* (Reports of the Research Committee of the Society of Antiquaries of London) (Bristol: Bristol Classical Press, 2003), 217–44. Achilles Tatius, *Leukippe and Kleitophon* 5; Apuleius, *Metamorphoses* 9; Petron., *Sat.* 102–3.
57. Petron., *Sat.* 103. See also Michele George, "Slave Disguise in Ancient Rome," *Slavery and Abolition* 23, no. 2 (2002): 41–54.
58. On Hegeso see also Chapter 2 and Figure 2.5.
59. Arezzo, Archaeological Museum. Image available at: http://www.vroma.org/images/mcmanus_images/toilette.jpg (accessed November 1, 2017). Credits: Barbara McManus, 1990.
60. CIL 6.9732; Ov., *Am.* 1.14.16; Juv., *Sat.* 6.491.
61. Ov., *Am.* 2. 7 23–4.
62. Juv., *Sat.* 6.491. The name Psecas is derived from the Greek and refers to her job of anointing her mistress' hair with perfumed oil.
63. Juv., *Sat.* 6.475.
64. On hairdressers see Susan Treggiari, "Jobs in the Household of Livia," *Papers of the British School at Rome* 43 (1975): 48–77. See also Chapters Two and Four in this volume.
65. Mart., *Epigrams* 2. 66.2; Juv., *Sat.* 2.93; Ov., *Am.* 1.14.15. Cassius Dio, *History of Rome* 47.8.1–5.
66. Aulus Gellius, *Attic Nights* 2.26.8–9; see Maria Grazia Sassi, "Erano icapei d'oro a l'aura sparsi," in *Comae. Identità femmimili nelle acconciature di età romana*, ed. Maria Elisa Micheli and Anna Santucci (Pisa: Edizioni ETS, 2011), 4. See also Mark Bradley, *Colour and Meaning in Ancient Rome* (Cambridge: Cambridge University Press, 2009), 1–6, esp. 3, 138–42.
67. Menander, *Fragment* 610.
68. Hor., *Odes* 1.5. 1–4; Juv., *Sat.* 6.120.
69. CIL 6.1520.
70. Virg., *Aen.* 4.698, 12.605.
71. Plutarch, *Sulla* 6.7.
72. *Scriptores Historia Augustae, Verus* 10.7.
73. Ov., *Am.* 2.4.41–2.
74. Juv., *Sat.* 6.120.
75. Suet., *Nero*, 26.1.
76. Mart., *Epigrams* 2.29.9–10.

77. Suet., *Nero*, 28.
78. Aristophanes also describes the forcible removal of pubic hair as a punishment for adultery, *Nubes* 1083.
79. B. K. Gold, "Gender Fluidity and Closure in Perpetua's Prison Diary," *EuGeStA Journal on Gender Studies in Antiquity*, no. 1 (2011): 237–51.
80. Clement of Alexandria, *Paedogogus* 3.2.
81. Clem. Al., *Paedogogus* 3.3.

Chapter Nine

1. The fashion for curly hair with a full beard and mustache was at its height during the reigns of Antoninus Pius to Septimius Severus (138–211 CE): this style was adopted for private portraits of men in this period, many of which show the same virtuoso carving techniques. See Diana E. E. Kleiner, *Roman Sculpture* (New Haven, CT: Yale University Press, 1992), 268–77, figs. 231–34; R. Bianchi Bandinelli, *Rome, the Centre of Power: Roman Art to AD 200* (London: Thames and Hudson, 1970), 285 figs. 319 and 292–5 figs. 328–31. For examples in the Capitoline Museums see Karl Fittschen and Paul Zanker, *Katalog der römischen Porträts in den Capitolinischen Museen und den anderen kommunalen Sammlungen der Stadt Rom Bd. I. Kaiser- und Prinzen Bildnisse* (Mainz am Rhein: von Zabern, 1985) (for emperors) and Klaus Fittschen, Paul Zanker, and Petra Cain, *Katalog der römischen Porträts in den Capitolinischen Museen und den anderen kommunalen Sammlungen der Stadt Rom Bd. II. Die männlichen Privatporträts* (Berlin: De Gruyter, 2010) (for private portraits).
2. This style was favored by the women of Trajan's family, Plotina, Matidia, Marciana, and Sabina. For examples of the hairstyles of Roman empresses at this and other periods see K. Fittschen and P. Zanker, *Katalog der römischen Porträts in den Capitolinischen Museen und den anderen kommunalen Sammlungen der Stadt Rom Bd. III, Kaiserinnen und Prinzessinnenbildnisse Frauenporträts* (Mainz am Rhein: Von Zabern, 1983); Annetta Alexandridis, *Die Frauen des römischen Kaiserhauses: Ein Untersuchung ihrer bildlichen Darstellung von Livia bis Iulia Domna* (Mainz am Rhein: Von Zabern, 2004).
3. Kleiner, *Roman Sculpture*, 363–72. For similar images see also Bandinelli, *Rome, the Centre of Power*, 81 fig. 87 and 99 fig. 107; R. Bianchi Bandinelli, *Rome, the Late Empire: Roman Art AD 200–400* (London: Thames and Hudson, 1971), 7 fig. 8 (Trajan Decius), 24–7 figs. 19–23, 85 fig. 76.
4. E.g. the early classical statues *The Charioteer in Delphi*, *Zeus/Poseidon* from Artemision (see Figure 7.1 in this volume), or statue A from Riace: John Boardman, *Greek Sculpture: The Classical Period* (London: Thames and Hudson, 1985), figs. 34–9; Judith M. Barringer, *The Art and Archaeology of Ancient Greece* (Cambridge: Cambridge University Press, 2014), 190, 221 fig. 4.28 (Zeus), and 215 fig. 4.21 (Charioteer).
5. For the effects achievable see Susan Walker and Morris Bierbrier, *Ancient Faces: Mummy Portraits from Roman Egypt* (London: British Museum Press, 1997); Steven Tuck, *A History of Roman Art* (Oxford: Blackwell, 2015), 269–71 figs. 9.27–30.
6. E.g. the hair of Alexander the Great on the Alexander mosaic from The House of the Faun, Pompeii (in Naples Archaeological Museum): Barringer, *Art and Archaeology*, 307 fig. 5.37b.
7. Black-figure's use of incision was better suited to patterned than textured effects, but see Ajax and Achilles playing dice by Exekias (Barringer, *Art and Archaeology*, 165 fig. 3.32) and by the Andokides Painter (Boardman, *Athenian Red Figure Vases: The Archaic Period* [London: Thames and Hudson, 1975] = *ARV*, fig. 2.1.2). For several different effects, including Herakles with textured hair created by a thick slip, see Figure 9.10: Boardman, *ARV*, fig. 23 (Euphronios); also figs. 10 (the Andokides Painter) and 146 (the Berlin Painter).

8. For illustrations see Bernard Ashmole, *Olympia: The Sculptures of the Temple of Zeus* (London: Phaidon, 1967); Boardman, *Greek Sculpture: The Classical Period*, 40–50.
9. E.g. the marble statue of Hermes with infant Dionysus by Praxiteles at Olympia: Barringer, *Art and Archaeology*, 290 fig. 5.2; the bronze Antikythera Youth: Mark D. Fullerton, *Greek Art* (Cambridge: Cambridge University Press, 2000), 126 fig. 92.
10. See Chapter Seven in this volume. For the dying Gaul see Barringer, *Art and Archaeology*, 351 fig. 6.31; for North African hair see F. M. Snowden, Jr., "Iconographical Evidence on the Black Populations in Greco-Roman Antiquity," in *The Image of the Black in Western Art. Volume 1: From the Pharaohs to the Fall of the Roman Empire*, ed. D. Bindman and H. L. Gates (Cambridge: Cambridge University Press, 2010), 141–250; Ben Russell, "A sculpted Head of an African Woman in the British Museum," *Römische Mitteilungen* 121 (2015): 507–32.
11. Recent work on recovering the color on statues has been carried out by the Tracking Colour Project. http://trackingcolour.com/ (accessed December 9, 2016). Also: Mark B. Abbe, "Polychromy," in *The Oxford Handbook of Roman Sculpture*, ed. Elise A. Friedland, Melanie Grunow Sobocinski, and Elaine K. Gazda (Oxford: Oxford University Press, 2015), 173–88, fig. 1.5.1 shows a reconstruction of the color used on the statue of an Amazon from Hadrian's Villa: she has blonde hair—light brown seems to have been favored for many sculpted figures of the classical period.
12. Kelly Olson points out that although blonde and auburn hair were perceived as foreign and could be associated with slaves these colors were still considered beautiful and worth achieving by dyeing or wearing a hairpiece or wig. Kelly Olson, *Dress and the Roman Woman. Self-presentation and Society* (London: Routledge, 2008), 73 and 79. See also Chapter Eight in this volume on the attraction of blonde hair for the Romans.
13. The painting is reproduced in Tuck, *History of Roman Art*, 52 fig. 3.3. D. H. Lawrence in *Etruscan Places* (1932; repr., London: Penguin, 1950, 1965) identifies these women as *hetaerae* or prostitutes "chiefly because they have yellow hair," but he would appear to be projecting assumptions of his own day without any justification.
14. Some emperors may have worn gold dust in their hair in real life (Suetonius, *Gaius Caligula* 52; *Historia Augusta, Commodus* 1.7.5).
15. E.g. a fourth-century BCE terracotta head from Greek south Italy or Sicily (now in the Getty Museum) which may represent Hades or Zeus: Vinzenz Brinckmann, "The Polychromy of ancient Greek Sculpture," in *Color of Life: Polychromy in Sculpture from Antiquity to the Present*, ed. Roberta Panzanelli (Los Angeles: J. Paul Getty Museum, 2008), 136 no. 20: the beard is bright blue, though the hair on the head is a more conventional brown. The beards of the three heads of the triple-bodied monster on a pediment on the Acropolis, Athens were also painted blue: John Boardman, *Greek Sculpture: The Archaic Period* (London: Thames and Hudson, 1978), fig. 193.
16. See Walker and Bierbrier, *Ancient Faces*, nos. 78, 83, and 97 for gray-haired men, and no. 79 for a woman.
17. Illustrated in Tuck, *History of Roman Art*, 275 fig. 10.1.
18. Martial, *Epigrams* 2.29 oily hair that can be smelled all over the Theatre of Marcellus; 3.63 a "pretty fellow" who curls his hair, arranges it carefully, and smells of balsam or cinnamon; 12.38 the seducer whose hair is black with pomade. See also Chapters Three and Six in this volume.
19. Discussed by Elizabeth Bartman in "Hair and the Artifice of Roman Female Adornment," *American Journal of Archaeology* 105, no. 1 (2001): 1–25. The question of how the styles represented in art were achieved is considered in Janet Stephens, "Ancient Roman

Hairdressing: On (Hair) Pins and Needles," *Journal of Roman Archaeology* 22 (2008): 110–32. See also Chapters Three and Four in this volume.

20. Both *kouroi* are in the Athens National Museum: Boardman, *Greek Sculpture: The Archaic Period*, figs. 104 (Volomandra, ca. 570–60 BCE) and 107 (Anavyssos, ca. 530 BCE): the illustrations throughout this book show many other examples of patterned hair on both male and female figures.
21. The Rampin head (ca. 550 BCE) is in the Louvre: see Boardman, *Greek Sculpture: The Archaic Period*, fig. 114.
22. For portraits of Augustus created at different times in his life see Kleiner, *Roman Sculpture*, 61 fig. 37, 62 fig. 39, 64 fig. 40, 65 fig. 41, 66 fig. 42, 68 figs. 43 and 44.
23. Especially his grandsons and heirs Caius and Lucius Caesar: see Kleiner, *Roman Sculpture*, 72–4 figs. 48, 50, and 51. For similar hairstyles worn by Tiberius and Caligula see 125 fig. 100 and 127 fig. 102. See also Chapter Two in this volume.
24. Priam on a red-figure amphora by Euthymides in Munich has a bald pate with long hair at the sides and back of his head (Boardman, *ARV*, fig. 33.1); Nereus and Erechtheus were also represented this way: Bessie Ellen Richardson, *Old Age among the Ancient Greeks: The Greek Portrayal of Old Age in Literature, Art and Inscriptions* (New York: Greenwood Press, 1933), 78 and 95–6.
25. Satyrs: For the psykter by Douris (fig. 9.8) see Boardman, *ARV*, fig. 299; for a cup by Brygos Painter with satyrs attacking goddesses: Boardman, *ARV*, fig. 252; Centaurs were also often represented balding (see Boardman, *ARV*, fig. 196). Balding men were also represented revelling (Boardman, *ARV*, fig. 47) and with prostitutes (figs. 222 and 302).
26. Dillon traces this development in the late classical and Hellenistic periods: Sheila Dillon, *Ancient Greek Portrait Sculpture: Contexts, Subjects and Styles* (Cambridge: Cambridge University Press, 2006), 69–70 fig. 74 and pp. 86 and 118. An older man with a bald head is also shown taking part in a footrace on a Panathenaic amphora attributed to the Berlin Painter, ca. 480–70 BCE: Richardson, *Old Age*, 107–8.
27. E.g. Chrysippus: R. R. R. Smith, *Hellenistic Sculpture* (London: Thames and Hudson, 1991), figs. 33, 1–2. See also Paul Zanker, *The Mask of Socrates. The Image of the Intellectual in Antiquity*, trans. A. Shapiro (Berkeley: University of California Press, 1995); Dillon, *Portrait Sculpture*, 114.
28. For Republican portraits of men with very little hair see Kleiner, *Roman Sculpture*, 35 fig. 11, 38 fig. 16; Bandinelli, *Rome, the Centre of Power*, 70 fig. 80, 81 fig. 87, also 98 fig. 106. The Republican look was revived by Vespasian (emperor 69–79 CE): Kleiner, *Roman Sculpture*, 173–4, figs. 138, 139, and 140; Bandinelli, *Rome, the Centre of Power*, 212 figs. 234–5. For painted mummy portraits of men with hair receding at temples or on top see Walker and Bierbrier, *Mummy Portraits*, 46 no. 20 and 104 no. 97.
29. See Richardson, *Old Age*, 9 (Thersites in Homer, *Iliad* II, 218); baldness was a characteristic of the parasite in comedy and Aristophanes was teased over his own baldness; 183: bald characters on stage were usually buffoons, jesters, and parasites, and baldness was often associated with low cunning.
30. Suet., *Julius Caesar* 45.2. Portraits of Julius Caesar (most made after his death) show him with varying amounts of hair: see Kleiner, *Roman Sculpture*, 22, 45–6, and 61 figs. 26, 27, 28, and 38 (coin portrait wearing wreath).
31. Suet., *Domitian* 18. For a portrait of Domitian with his hair obviously combed forward to cover his bald patch see Kleiner, *Roman Sculpture*, 177, fig. 145.

32. Suet., *Otho* 12. J. P. C. Kent, *Roman Coins* (London: Thames and Hudson, 1978), nos. 216 and 217, pl. 62; Kleiner, *Roman Sculpture*, 169, fig. 136. See the Introduction to this volume for a discussion of Synesius' *On Baldness*.
33. E.g. a portrait of an old woman in the Museo Nazionale Romano, ca. 30 BCE: the *"nodus"* hairstyle did not require the masses of hair needed for many later women's fashionable hairstyles. Kleiner, *Roman Sculpture*, 39, fig. 18; Bandinelli, *Rome, the Centre of Power*, 97 fig. 105.
34. Martial refers to bought, captured, and manufactured hair (6.12, 9.37, 13.26): he implies the hair of the women in question was thin or even nonexistent. Wigs might also be worn as a disguise. See Olson, *Dress and the Roman Woman*, 74, and Chapters Three, Four, and Eight in this volume.
35. See portrait of an unknown woman in the Capitoline Museum illustrated by Olson, *Dress and the Roman Woman*, 74, fig. 2.2. Stephens, "Ancient Roman Hairdressing," 132 and n. 47; and Chapter Four in this volume argues that even the most complex and voluminous hairstyles can be reconstructed using the sitter's own hair alone, and Bartman in "Hair and the Artifice" argues that wig-wearing was not as common as some scholars have imagined. She discusses whether the "toupet" (mass of curls above the forehead) of the Roman hairstyles of the late first/early second centuries CE was constructed of the sitter's own hair or was made separately from "artificial" hair (p. 9), and points out that just because such styles *could* be made using the natural hair alone, this does not necessarily mean that they always *were* (p. 13).
36. For Julia Domna's wig-like hairstyle see Bartman, "Hair and the Artifice," 14; Kleiner, *Roman Sculpture*, 326–8, figs. 290–2.
37. See Kelly Olson, *Dress and the Roman Woman*, 72 fig. 2.1: a Severan hairstyle made to fit onto a portrait statue like a wig. Where the "wig" is in a darker-colored marble the intention might simply have been to produce a more permanent and effective color contrast than was possible with paint. That the detachable wig allowed for changes to hairstyles as fashions changed has been rejected for various reasons. See Olson, *Dress and the Roman Woman*, 71–2; Bartman, "Hair and the Artifice," 19 and Fittschen and Zanker, *Katalog der römischen Porträts in den Capitolinischen Museen*, III, 105; Olson, Chapter Three in this volume; Stephens, Chapter Four in this volume.
38. E.g. Theseus in a painting from the House of Gavius Rufus in Pompeii: Bandinelli, *Rome, the Centre of Power*, 112, fig. 116.
39. For mature male figures with chest hair see Boardman, *ARV*, fig. 230 (Onesimos); 245 and 246 (the Brygos Painter). A vase in the British Museum by the Clinic Painter unusually shows Herakles, Dionysos, and a satyr all with chest hair represented by a series of dots liberally scattered over the chest (Boardman, *ARV*, fig. 376).
40. Barringer, *Art and Archaeology*, 354, fig. 6.36; Smith, *Hellenistic Sculpture*, fig. 196.4. The Gaul shown killing himself in the Ludovisi group also has underarm hair: Fullerton, *Greek Art*, 70 fig. 50. The *Barberini Faun*, on the other hand, who might be expected to show underarm hair clearly does not have any. See Barringer, *Art and Archaeology*, 320 and 334 fig. 6.16.
41. This may in part be because of the supposed age of these youths. It does appear in stylized form (in the shape of a star) on the late archaic *kouros* of Aristodikos: Boardman, *Greek Sculpture: The Archaic Period*, fig. 145.
42. Numerous examples of nude male statues without visible chest hair but with quite copious pubic hair are illustrated in Boardman, *Greek Sculpture: The Classical Period*; and Christopher H. Hallett, *The Roman Nude: Heroic Portrait Statuary 200 BC—AD 300* (Oxford: Oxford University Press, 2005).
43. E.g. sleeping maenad being crept up on by a satyr on a cup by the Epidromos Painter, and a naked flute girl by the Kleophrades Painter: Boardman, *ARV*, figs. 113 and 129.2.

44. For attitudes to (male) depilation in the Roman imperial period see Maud Gleason, *Making Men* (Princeton, NJ: Princeton University Press, 1995), 68–70 and 74–6; Chapter Six in this volume.
45. See Chapters One, Six, and Eight in this volume.
46. Calyx crater by Euphronios in the Louvre: Boardman, *ARV*, fig. 23. The same contrast can be seen in scenes where Theseus (neat hair and beardless) fights opponents with long shaggy hair and beards (Sinis/Skiron/Procrustes): Boardman, *ARV*, figs. 115, 137, 223.2, 319.
47. Dillon, *Portrait Sculpture*, 1–10 and 67–88, discusses and elaborates on the earlier work of J. Bergemann on the grave reliefs. Also Johannes Bergemann, "Attic Grave Reliefs and Portrait Sculpture in Fourth-Century Athens," in *Early Hellenistic Portraiture. Image, Style, Context*, ed. Peter Schultz and Ralf von den Hoff (Cambridge: Cambridge University Press, 2007), 34–48.
48. For a coin portrait of Alexander see Figure 2.1 in this volume. Smith, *Hellenistic Sculpture* figs. 6–9 (Alexander) and 10–20 (kings and others). Dillon, *Portrait Sculpture*, 73–4. See also Chapter Two in this volume.
49. Smith, *Hellenistic Sculpture*, figs. 23–37 (bearded philosophers and other intellectuals), 42 (beardless Menander); Ralf von den Hof, "Naturalism and Classicism: Style and Perception of Early Hellenistic Portraits," in Schultz and von den Hoff, ed., *Early Hellenistic Portraiture*, 49–62; and Stefan Schmidt, "Fashion and Meaning: Beardless Portraits of Artists and Literati in the Early Hellenistic Period," in Schultz and von den Hoff, ed., *Early Hellenistic Portraiture*, 99–112. See also Chapter Three in this volume.
50. The bronze head known as "Brutus" in the Capitoline Museums is bearded (Kleiner, *Roman Sculpture*, 25, fig. 2). For the introduction of shaving ca. 300 BCE see Jerry Toner, "Barbers, Barbershops and Searching for Roman Popular Culture," *Papers of the British School at Rome* 83 (2015): 96; and Caroline Vout, "What's in a Beard? Rethinking Hadrian's Hellenism," in *Rethinking Revolutions through Ancient Greece*, ed. Simon Goldhill and Robin Osborne (Cambridge: Cambridge University Press, 2006), 117.
51. Although men are shown in Roman sculpture with completely smooth chins it is debatable how achievable this was in practice: see Toner, "Barbers." A bronze head in Paris shows designer stubble as a series of dots all over the chin, which may be a more accurate representation of the shaven look: Bandinelli, *Rome, the Centre of Power*, 73 fig. 81. See Chapter Six in this volume.
52. Both Octavian (later Augustus) and Mark Antony are shown with light beards when mourning the death of Julius Caesar (Kleiner, *Roman Sculpture*, 61–2 figs. 37 and 39).
53. Susan Walker, "Bearded Men," *Journal of the History of Collections* 3, no. 2 (1991): 265–77; more recent arguments are summarized and evaluated in Vout, "What's in a Beard?" See also Chapters Three and Six in this volume.
54. Nicholas Baker-Brian and Shaun Tougher, ed., *Emperor and Author: The Writings of Julian the Apostate* (Swansea: Classical Press of Wales, 2012), 193–7, 266, and 323–5. Julian's response to public ridicule of his beard was to write the *Misopogon*.
55. Kleiner, *Roman Sculpture*, 135–9, figs. 110 and 111 (youthful) and 112–13 (older); Tuck, *History of Roman Art*, 164 fig. 6.18. For coin portraits: Kent, *Roman Coins*, nos. 188–205, pl. 54–8.
56. Procopius, *Secret History* VII, 8–10.
57. See Chapter Seven in this volume. For Mauretanian cavalry on Trajan's Column see Bandinelli, *Rome, the Centre of Power*, 243, fig. 268.
58. Bandinelli, *Rome, the Late Empire*, 312 fig. 292.

59. For the column of Marcus Aurelius see Bandinelli, *Rome, the Centre of Power*, 327 fig. 367; Tuck, *History of Roman Art*, 258 fig. 9.15; Sheila Dillon, "Women on the Columns of Trajan and Marcus Aurelius and the Visual Language of Roman Victory," in *Representations of War in Ancient Rome*, ed. Sheila Dillon and Katherine E. Welch (Cambridge: Cambridge University Press, 2006), 244–71. An earlier representation of a woman dragged by her hair can be seen on the lower register of the Gemma Augustea: (Figure 2.6 in this volume).
60. E.g. the woman mourning Ajax on a red-figure cup tondo by the Brygos painter: Boardman, *ARV*, fig. 246, or the mourners on a relief from the Roman tomb of the Haterii (ca. 100 CE): Kleiner, *Roman Sculpture*, 166 and 196 fig. 64; Tuck, *History of Roman Art*, 205 fig. 7.27. See Chapters One and Six in this volume.
61. Women in Roman Italy are not usually represented wearing hats or turbans, though they are frequently shown "veiled" (with their mantle covering the top of the head), but women in various provinces did wear turban-like headgear that covered their hair almost completely (e.g. at Palmyra: Tuck, *History of Roman Art*, 252, fig. 9.8) or hats and bonnets of various shape (in northern provinces: Bandinelli, *Rome, the Late Empire*, 126 figs. 114–16 and 162 fig. 151). See Fig. 4.11, this volume.
62. Laetitia La Follette, "The Costume of the Roman Bride," in *The World of Roman Costume*, ed. Judith Lynn Sebesta and Larisa Bonfante (Madison: University of Wisconsin Press, 1994), 56–60. See Chapters One and Six in this volume.
63. Such epithets abound in the epic literature. For the characterization of Autumn and Winter see Ovid, *Metamorphoses* 15.209–13.
64. E.g. Ov. *Met.* 1.477 and 497 (Daphne); 2.411–13 (Callisto); 3.169–70 (Diana herself); 9.89–9 (one of Diana's attendants); 10.592 (Atalanta). Virgil, *Aeneid* 1.319 (Venus disguised as a young woman).
65. Cassandra being dragged from Minerva's Temple (Virg. *Aen.* 2.403–4), or Medea going out at night to perform terrible magic (Ov. *Met.* 7.179–85).
66. Ov. *Met.* 5,472 (Ceres mourning); 13.583–6 (Aurora mourning); 13.686–9 (women proclaiming their grief). For the Haterii relief see note 60.
67. Molly Myerowitz Levine, "The Gendered Grammar of Ancient Mediterranean Hair," in *Off with her Head! The Denial of Women's Identity in Myth, Religion and Culture*, ed. Howard Eilberg-Schwartz and Wendy Doniger (Berkeley: University of California Press, 1995), 76–130.
68. For example as told by Ovid in *Met.* 4.790–804.
69. Discussed by Levine, "Gendered Grammar," 92–4: Medusa's hair "encodes both the lure and the threat of female sexuality to patriarchy" (94).
70. For archaic versions see John Boardman, *Athenian Black Figure Vases* (London: Thames and Hudson, 1974), figs. 69 (Medusa mask—coils of hair rather than snakes) and 80 (running Medusa with snakes in hair), both also with beards. Boardman, *ARV*, fig. 153 (Medusa running, by the Berlin Painter—she has normal hair for the period, and no beard, but her head is surrounded by a row of small snakes); running Medusa also forms the centerpiece of the pediment in Corfu (J. Boardman, *Greek Sculpture: The Archaic Period* (London: Thames and Hudson, 1978), fig. 187.1), and the head appears on Athena's breast (Boardman, *Archaic Sculpture*, fig. 205.3). For an early example of the new beautiful type of Medusa head see Boardman, *Greek Sculpture: The Classical Period*, fig. 241 (her hair is otherwise normal but has wings in it, and there are snakes tied under the chin).
71. Petronius, *Satyricon* 27, 32, 63; see Chapter Eight in this volume for further discussion.
72. Ov. *Met.* 13.764–7. Later, Polyphemus gives a spirited defense of his hairiness, concluding that "a beard and shaggy hair on a body well become a man" (13.844–50).

73. Roman women's hairstyles did not necessarily originate with the styles created for empresses: other elite women might also be leaders of hair fashion: Klaus Fittschen, "Courtly Portraits of Women in the Era of the Adoptive Emperors (98–180) and their Reception in Roman Society," in *I Claudia. Women in Ancient Rome*, ed. Diana E. E. Kleiner and Susan B. Matheson (New Haven, CT: Yale University Art Gallery, 1996), 42–51.

74. Discussed by Eve D'Ambra, "Mode and Model in the Flavian Female Portrait," *American Journal of Archaeology* 117, no. 4 (2013): 511–25. The best known and finest example is the Fonseca head ("the Flavian Beauty": Figures 3.12 and 8.2 in this volume), now thought to be a comparatively late example (Trajanic or even Hadrianic): there is no consensus about who it represents. Bandinelli, *Rome, the Centre of Power*, 102 fig. 110; Kleiner, *Roman Sculpture*, 181 fig. 149.

75. Funerary altars made in Rome with portraits of nonelite women with the toupet hairstyle: Kleiner, *Roman Sculpture*, 195 figs. 162–3; Eve D'Ambra, *Roman Women* (Cambridge: Cambridge University Press, 2007), 79 fig. 3. For the potter's wife (a relief in Virginia Museum of Art, Richmond) see D'Ambra, *Roman Women*, 25, fig. 11 and for the soldier's wife: gravestone from Nimes, France: D'Ambra, *Roman Women*, 171, fig. 94.

76. Two statues from Aphrodisias, Turkey: D'Ambra, *Roman Women*, 19, figs. 7 and 8; stucco reliefs from Carthage (D'Ambra, *Roman Women*, 123 figs. 67 and 68); a portrait bust from Ampurias, Spain (Bandinelli, *Rome, the Late Empire*, 188–9 figs. 179–81). An abbreviated version of the style can also be seen on Egyptian mummy portraits: e.g. D'Ambra, *Roman Women*, 90 fig. 40.

77. Relief of a saleswoman from Ostia, her hair in a simple bun: Bandinelli *Rome, the Centre of Power*, 63 fig. 69; D'Ambra, *Roman Women*, 139 fig. 80.

BIBLIOGRAPHY

Abbe, M. B. "Polychromy." In *The Oxford Handbook of Roman Sculpture*, edited by E. A. Friedland, M. Grunow Sobocinski, and E. K. Gazda. Oxford: Oxford University Press, 2015.
Adler, E. "Boudica's Speeches in Tacitus and Dio." *Classical World* 101 (2008): 173–95.
Africa, T. "Worms and the Death of Kings: A Cautionary Note on Disease and History." *Classical Antiquity* 1 (1982): 1–17.
Aldhouse-Green, M. *An Archaeology of Images: Iconology and Cosmology in Iron Age and Roman Europe*. London: Taylor and Francis, 2004.
Aldhouse-Green, M. "Chaining and Shaming: Images of Defeat, from Llyn Cerrig Bach to Sarmitzegetusa." *Oxford Journal of Archaeology* 23, no. 3 (2004): 319–40.
Aldhouse-Green, M. "Crowning Glories: Languages of Hair in Later Prehistoric Europe." *Proceedings of the Prehistoric Society* 70 (2004): 299–325.
Aldhouse-Green, M. *Bog Bodies Uncovered: Solving Europe's Ancient Mystery*. London: Thames and Hudson, 2015.
Alexandridis, A. *Die Frauen des römischen Kaiserhauses: Ein Untersuchung ihrer bildlichen Darstellung von Livia bis Iulia Domna*. Mainz am Rhein: von Zabern, 2004.
Allason-Jones, L. *Women in Roman Britain*. London: British Museum Publications, 1989.
Allen, S. *Lords of Battle: The World of the Celtic Warrior*. Oxford: Osprey Publishing, 2007.
Archer, L., S. Fischler and M. Wyke, eds. *Women in Ancient Societies*. London: Macmillan, 1994.
Arnold, J. J. "Theodoric's Invincible Moustache." *Journal of Late Antiquity* 6 (2013): 152–83.
Ashmole, B. *Olympia: The Sculptures of the Temple of Zeus*. London: Phaidon, 1967.
Austin, R. G. P. "Hector's Hair-Style." *Classical Quarterly* 22, no. 2 (1972): 1.
Baker-Brian, N. and S. Tougher, eds. *Emperor and Author: The Writings of Julian the Apostate*. Swansea: Classical Press of Wales, 2012.
Barnes, R., and J. B. Eicher. *Dress and Gender: Making and Meaning in Cultural Contexts*. New York: St. Martin's Press, 1992.
Barringer, J. M. *The Art and Archaeology of Ancient Greece*. Cambridge: Cambridge University Press, 2014.
Bartman, E. *Portraits of Livia: Imagining the Imperial Woman in Augustan Rome*. New York: Cambridge University Press, 1999.
Bartman, E. "Hair and the Artifice of Roman Female Adornment." *American Journal of Archaeology* 105 (2001): 1–25.
Bartsh, Shadi. *The Mirror of the Self: Sexuality, Self-Knowledge, and the Gaze in the Early Roman Empire*. Chicago: University of Chicago Press, 2006.
Batten, Alicia J. "Neither Gold nor Braided Hair (1 Timothy 2.9; 1 Peter 3.3): Adornment, Gender and Honour in Antiquity." *New Testament Studies* 55 (2009): 484–501.
Beard, M. "The Sexual Status of Vestal Virgins." *Journal of Roman Studies* 70 (1980): 12–27.

Beard, M. "Re-reading (Vestal) Virginity." In *Women in Antiquity, New Assessments*, edited by R. Hawley and B. Levick. London: Routledge, 1995.

Beard, M., J. North and S. Price. *Religions of Rome. Volume 1: A History*. Cambridge: Cambridge University Press, 1998.

Bergemann, J. "Attic Grave Reliefs and Portrait Sculpture in Fourth-Century Athens." In *Early Hellenistic Portraiture: Image, Style, Context*, edited by P. Schultz and R. Von Den Hof. Cambridge: Cambridge University Press, 2007.

Bettini, M. *Women and Weasels: Mythologies of Birth in Ancient Greece and Rome*. Chicago: University of Chicago Press, 2013.

Bianchi Bandinelli, R. *Rome, the Centre of Power: Roman Art to AD 200*. London: Thames and Hudson, 1970.

Bianchi Bandinelli, R. *Rome, the Late Empire: Roman Art AD 200–400*. London: Thames and Hudson, 1971.

Biddle-Perry, G., and S. Cheang. "Introduction: Thinking About Hair." In *Hair: Styling, Culture and Fashion*, edited by G. Biddle-Perry and S. Cheang, 3–12. Oxford: Berg, 2008.

Biddle-Perry, G., and S. Cheung, eds. *Hair: Styling, Culture and Fashion*. Oxford: Berg, 2008.

Boardman, J. "Heroic Haircuts." *Classical Quarterly* 23, no. 2 (1973): 196.

Boardman, J. *Athenian Black Figure Vases*. London: Thames and Hudson, 1974.

Boardman, J. *Athenian Red Figure Vases: The Archaic Period*. London: Thames and Hudson, 1975.

Boardman, J. *Greek Sculpture: The Archaic Period*. London: Thames and Hudson, 1978.

Boardman, J. *Greek Sculpture: The Classical Period*. London: Thames and Hudson, 1985.

Bodiou, L., F. Gherchanoc, V. Huet, and V. Mehl, eds. *Parures et artificies: le corps exposé dans l'Antiquité*. Paris: L'Harmattan, 2011.

Bonanno, A. "Imperial and Private Portraiture: A Case of Non-Dependence." In *Ritratto Ufficiale e Ritratto Privato: Atti della II Conferenza Internazionale sul Ritratto Romano*, edited by N. Binacasa and G. Rizza, 157–64. Rome: Consiglio Nazionale delle Ricerche, 1988.

Bondeson, J. *A Cabinet of Medical Curiosities*. London: Tauris, 1997.

Bonfante, L. *Etruscan Dress*, 2nd ed. Baltimore, MD: Johns Hopkins University Press, 2003.

Boyle, A. J. "Introduction: Reading Flavian Rome." In *Flavian Rome: Culture, Image, Text*, edited by A. J. Boyle and W. J. Dominik, 1–68. Leiden: Brill, 2003.

Bradley, K. R. *Slavery and Society at Rome*. Cambridge: Cambridge University Press, 1994.

Bradley, M. *Colour and Meaning in Ancient Rome*. Cambridge: Cambridge University Press, 2009.

Brain, P. *Galen on Bloodletting: A Study of the Origins, Development and Validity of his Opinions, with a Translation of the Three Works*. Cambridge: Cambridge University Press, 1986.

Bronner, L. L. "From Veil to Wig: Jewish Women's Hair Covering." *Judaism* 42, no. 4 (1993): 465–77.

Butrica, J. L. "Clodius the *Pulcher* in Catullus and Cicero." *Classical Philology* 52 (2002): 507–16.

Butterworth, A., and R. Laurence. *Pompeii*. London: Weidenfeld and Nicholson, 2006.

Cameron, A. "The Date and Identity of Macrobius." *Journal of Roman Studies* 56, no. 1 (1966): 25–38.

Cameron, A. and A. Kuhrt, eds. *Images of Women in Antiquity*. London: Routledge, 1983.

Canter, H. V. "Personal Appearance in the Biography of the Roman Emperors." *Studies in Philology* 25, no. 3 (1928): 385–99.

Cartledge, P. *The Greeks: A Portrait of Self and Others*, 2nd ed. Oxford: Oxford University Press, 2002.

Clayman, D. "Bernice and Her Lock." *Transactions of the American Philological Association* 141, no. 2 (2011): 229–46.

Cleland, L., G. Davies, and L. Llewellyn-Jones. *Greek and Roman Dress from A to Z*. London: Taylor and Francis, 2007.

Cohen, A., and J. B. Rutter. *Constructions of Childhood in Ancient Greece and Italy*. Hesperia Suppl. 41. American School of Classical Studies at Athens, 2007.

Cohen, N. S. "What to Wear: Women's Adornment and Judean Identity in the Third Century Mishnah." In *Dressing Judeans and Christians in Antiquity*, edited by K. Upson-Saia, C. Daniel Hughes, and A. Batten. Farnham: Ashgate, 2014.

Colburn, C. S., and M. K. Heyn. *Reading a Dynamic Canvas: Adornment in the Ancient Mediterranean World*. Newcastle: Cambridge Scholars Publishing, 2008.

Cole, S. G. "The Social Function of Rituals of Maturation: The Koureion and the Arkteia." *Zeitschrift für Papyrologie und Epigraphik* 55 (1984): 234.

Cosgrove, C. H. "A Woman's Unbound Hair in the Greco-Roman World, with Special Reference to the Story of the 'Sinful Woman' in Luke 7: 36-50." *Journal of Biblical Literature* 124, no. 4 (2005): 675–92.

Craik, E. *The Hippocratic Treatise On Glands: Edited and Translated with Introduction and Commentary*. Leiden: Brill, 2009.

Craik, E. *The Hippocratic Corpus: Content and Context*. London: Routledge, 2015.

Croom, A. T. *Roman Clothing and Fashion*. Stroud and Charleston, SC: Tempus, 2002 (2010).

Dalby, A. *Empire of Pleasures: Luxury and Indulgence in the Roman World*. London: Routledge, 2000.

D'Ambra, E. *Roman Women*. Cambridge: Cambridge University Press, 2007.

D'Ambra, E. "Mode and Model in the Flavian Female Portrait." *American Journal of Archaeology* 117, no. 4 (2013): 511–25.

D'Ambra, E. "Statuesque Hair in the Roman Empire." Paper presented at *Hair in the Classical World Symposium*, Fairfield University, Fairfield, CT, November 6, 2016.

D'Angelo, M. R. "Veils, Virgins, and the Tongues of Men and Angels: Women's Heads in Early Christianity." In *Off with Her Head! The Denial of Woman's Identity in Myth, Religion and Culture*, edited by H. Eilberg and W. Doniger. Berkeley: University of California Press, 1995.

David, E. "Sparta's Social Hair." *Eranos* 90 (1992): 11–21.

Davidson, J. *The Greeks and Greek Love*. London: Weidenfeld & Nicolson, 2007.

Davis, E. "Youth and Age in the Thera Frescoes." *American Journal of Archaeology* 90 (1986): 399–406.

Dean-Jones, L. A. *Women's Bodies in Classical Greek Science*. Oxford: Clarendon Press, 1994.

De La Bedoyere, G. *The Real Lives of Roman Britain*. New Haven, CT: Yale University Press, 2015.

Derks, A. M., and W. K. Vos. "Wooden Combs from the Roman Fort at Vechten: The Bodily Appearance of Soldiers." *Journal of Archaeology in the Low Countries* 2, no. 2 (2010): 53–77.

Dikötter, F. "Hairy Barbarians, Furry Primates, and Wild Men: Medical Science and Cultural Representations of Hair in China." In *Hair: Its Power and Meaning in Asian Cultures*, edited by A. Hiltebeitel and B. D. Miller, 51–74. Albany, NY: State University of New York Press, 1998.

Diller, H. *Wanderarzt und Aitiologe*. Leipzig: Dieterich, 1934.

Dillery, J. "Reconfiguring the Past: Thyrea, Thermopylae and Narrative Patterns in Herodotus." *American Journal of Philology* 117, no. 2 (1996): 217–54.

Dillon, M. *Girls and Women in Classical Greek Religion*. London: Routledge, 2002.
Dillon, S. *Ancient Greek Portrait Sculpture: Contexts, Subjects and Styles*. Cambridge: Cambridge University Press, 2006.
Dillon, S. "Women on the Columns of Trajan and Marcus Aurelius and the Visual Language of Roman Victory." In *Representations of War in Ancient Rome*, edited by S. Dillon and K. E. Welch, New York: Cambridge University Press, 2006.
Dodd, D. B., and Christopher A. Faraone, eds. *Initiation in Ancient Greek Rituals and Narratives*. London: Routledge, 2003.
Doerfler, M. E. "Coming Apart at the Seams: Cross Dressing, Masculinity, and the Social Body in Late Antiquity." In *Dressing Judeans and Christians*, edited by K. Upson-Saia, C. Daniel-Hughes, and A. J. Batten. Burlington, VT: Ashgate, 2014.
Douglas, M. *Natural Symbols*. New York: Pantheon, 1970.
Dover, K. *Greek Homosexuality*. London: Duckworth, 1978.
Drabkin, I. E. *Caelius Aurelianus: On Acute Diseases and On Chronic Diseases*. Chicago: University of Chicago Press, 1950.
Draycott, J. and E-J. Graham, eds. *Bodies of Evidence: Ancient Anatomical Votives Past, Present and Future*. Abingdon: Routledge, 2017.
Dyck, A. "Dressing to Kill: Attire as a Proof and Means of Characterization in Cicero's Speeches." *Arethusa* 34 (2001): 119–30.
Edmondson, J., and A. Keith, eds. *Roman Dress and the Fabric of Roman Culture*. Toronto: University of Toronto Press, 2008.
Ehrhardt, C. "Hair in Ancient Greece." *Echos du Monde Classique* 15 (1971): 14–19.
Eicher, Joanne B., and M. E. Roach-Higgins. "Definition and Classification of Dress: Implications for Analysis of Gender Roles." In *Dress and Gender: Making and Meaning*, edited by R. Barnes and J. B. Eicher. New York: Berg, 1992.
Eidinow, E., and J. Kindt, eds. *The Oxford Handbook of Ancient Greek Religion*. Oxford: Oxford University Press, 2015.
Eilberg-Schwartz, H., and W. Doniger, eds. *Off with Her Head! The Denial of Women's Identity in Myth, Religion and Culture*. Berkeley: University of California Press, 1995.
Emery, P. B. "Old-Age Iconography in Archaic Greek Art." *Mediterranean Archaeology* 12 (1999): 17–28.
Englebert, J., and T. Long. "Functions of hair in Apuleius' *Metamorphoses*." *Classical Journal* 68 (1973): 236–39.
Entwhistle, J. *The Fashioned Body: Fashion, Dress and Modern Social Theory*. Cambridge: Polity Press, 2015 (2nd ed.).
Evans, E. C. "Physiognomics in the Ancient World." *Transactions of the American Philosophical Society* 59, no. 5 (1969): 1–101.
Fantham, E. "Covering the Head at Rome: Ritual and Gender." In *Roman Dress and the Fabrics of Roman Culture*, edited by J. Edmondson and A. Keith. Toronto: University of Toronto, 2008.
Ferrari, G. *Figures of Speech: Men and Maidens in Ancient Greece*. Chicago: University of Chicago Press, 2002.
Fittschen, K. *Die Bildnistypen der Faustina Minor und die Fecunditas Augustae*. Göttingen: Vandenhoek and Ruprecht, 1982.
Fittschen, K. "Courtly Portraits of Women in the Era of the Adoptive Emperors (98-180) and their Reception in Roman Society." In *I Claudia. Women in Ancient Rome*, edited by D. E. E. Kleiner and S. B. Matheson. New Haven, CT: Yale University Art Gallery, 1996.

Fittschen, K., and P. Zanker. *Katalog der römischen Porträts in den Capitolinischen Museen und den anderen kommunalen Sammlungen der Stadt Rom*. Volume III: Kaiserinnen und Prinzessinnenbildnisse Frauenporträts. Mainz am Rhein: von Zabern, 1983.

Fittschen K., and Paul Zanker. *Katalog der römischen Porträts in den Capitolinischen Museen und den anderen kommunalen Sammlungen der Stadt Rom Bd. I. Kaiser- und Prinzen Bildnisse*. Mainz am Rhein: von Zabern, 1985.

Fittschen, K., P. Zanker, and P. Cain. *Katalog der römischen Porträts in den Capitolinischen Museen und den anderen kommunalen Sammlungen der Stadt Rom Bd. II. Die männlichen Privatporträts*. Berlin: De Gruyter, 2010.

Fless, F. *Opferdiener und Kultmusiker auf stadtrömischen historischen Reliefs: Untersuchungen zur Ikonographie, Funktion, und Benennung*. Mainz: Bücher, 1995.

Fullerton, M. D. *Greek Art*. Cambridge: Cambridge University Press, 2000.

Furnée-Van Zwet, L. "Fashion in Women's Hair-Dress in the First Century of the Roman Empire." *Bulletin van de Vereeniging tot Bevordering der Kennis van de Antieke Beschaving* 31 (1956): 1–22.

Gabelmann, H. "Römische Kinder in Toga Praetexta." *Jahrbuch des Deutschen Archäologischen Instituts* 100 (1985): 517–41.

Galinsky, K. "Introduction." In *Cultural Memories in the Roman Empire*, edited by K. Galinsky and K. Lapatin, 1–22. Los Angeles: J. Paul Getty Museum, 2015.

Galinsky, K., and K. Lapatin, eds. *Cultural Memories in the Roman Empire*. Malibu, CA: J. Paul Getty Museum, 2015.

Gawlinski, L. "Fashioning Initiates: Dress at the Mysteries." In *Reading a Dynamic Canvas: Adornment in the Ancient Mediterranean World*, edited by C. S. Colburn and M. K. Heyn, 146–69. Newcastle: Cambridge Scholars Publishing, 2008.

George, M. "A Roman Funerary Monument with a Mother and Daughter." In *Childhood, Class and Kin in the Roman World*, edited by S. Dixon. London: Routledge, 2001.

George, M. "Slave Disguise in Ancient Rome." *Slavery and Abolition* 23 (2002): 41–54.

George, M. "Family Imagery and Family Values in Roman Italy." In *The Roman Family in the Empire: Rome, Italy, and Beyond*, edited by M. George. Oxford: Oxford University Press, 2005.

Gibson, R. K. "Ovid, Augustus, and the Politics of Moderation in Ars Amatoria 3." In *The Art of Love: Bimillennial Essays on Ovid's Ars Amatoria and Remedia Amoris*, edited by R. K. Gibson, S. Green, and A. Sharrock, 121–42. Oxford: Oxford University Press, 2006.

Gibson, R. K. "Excess and Restraint: Propertius, Horace, and Ovid's *Ars Amatoria*." *Bulletin of the Institute of Classical Studies*, Suppl. 89. London: Institute of Classical Studies, 2007.

Gill, C. *The Structured Self in Hellenistic and Roman Thought*. Oxford: Oxford University Press, 2006.

Gill, D. W. J. "The Importance of Roman Portraiture for Head-Coverings in 1 Corinthians." *Tyndale Bulletin* 41, no. 2 (1990): 245–60.

Gleason, M. W. *Making Men: Sophists and Self-representation in Ancient Rome*. Princeton, NJ: Princeton University Press, 1995.

Goette, H. R. "Römische Kinderbildnisse mit Jugend-Locken." *Mitteilungen des Deutschen Archäologischen Instituts, Athenische Abteilung* 104 (1989): 203–17.

Gold, B. K. 2011. "Gender Fluidity and Closure in Perpetua's Prison Diary." *EuGeStA Journal on Gender Studies in Antiquity* 1: 237–51.

Goodenough, E. R. "The Crown of Victory in Judaism." *The Art Bulletin* 28, no. 3 (1946): 139–59.

Graver, M. "The Manhandling of Maecenas: Senecan Abstractions of Masculinity." *American Journal of Philology* 119 (1998): 607–32.

Griffith, R. D. "The Origin of Memnon." *Classical Antiquity* 17, no. 2 (1998): 212–34.

Gruen, E. S. *Rethinking the Other in Antiquity*. Princeton, NJ: Princeton University Press, 2011.

Gutzweller, K. "Callimachus' Lock of Berenice: Fantasy, Romance and Propaganda." *The American Journal of Philology* 113, no. 3 (1992): 359–85.

Haas, N. "Hair over the Ages and in Art: The Culture, and Social History of Hair and Its Depiction in Art." In *Hair Growth and Disorders*, edited by U. Blume-Peytavi, A. Tosti, and R. M. Trüeb, 525–37. Berlin: Springer, 2008.

Hackworth Petersen, L. "Clothes Make the Man: Dressing the Roman Freedman Body." In *Bodies and Boundaries in Greco-Roman Antiquity*, edited by T. Fogen and M. Lee, 181–214. Berlin: De Gruyter, 2009.

Hallett, C. H. *The Roman Nude: Heroic Portrait Statuary 200 BC – AD 300*. Oxford: Oxford University Press, 2005.

Hallpike, C. R. "Social Hair." *Man* n.s. 9 (1969): 256–64.

Harlow, M. "Female Dress, 3rd–6th Century: The Messages in the Media." *Antiquité Tardive* 12 (2004): 203–15.

Harlow, M. "The Impossible Art of Dressing to Please: Jerome and the Rhetoric of Dress." In *Objects in Context, Objects in Use: Material Spatiality in Late Antiquity*, edited by L. Lavan, E. Swift, and T. Putzeys. Leiden: Brill, 2007.

Harlow, M., ed. *Dress and Identity*. Oxford: Archaeopress, 2012.

Harlow, M. and Ray Laurence. *Growing Up and Growing Old in Ancient Rome: A Life Course Approach*. London: Routledge, 2002.

Harrison, E. "Greek Sculptured Coiffures and Ritual Haircuts." In *Early Greek Cult Practice: Proceedings of the Fifth International Symposium at the Swedish Institute at Athens, 26–29 June 1986*, edited by R. Hägg, N. Marinatos, and G. C. Nordquist, 247–54. Stockholm: P. Åströms Forlag, 1988.

Hartney, A. "'Dedicated followers of fashion': John Chrysostom on Female Dress." In *Women's Dress in the Ancient Greek World*, edited by L. J. Llewellyn-Jones. Swansea: Classical Press of Wales, 2002.

Henrichs, A. "The Tomb of Aias and the Prospect of Hero Cult in Sophokles." *Classical Antiquity* 12, no. 2 (1993): 165–80.

Hersch, K. K. *The Roman Wedding: Ritual and Meaning in Antiquity*. Cambridge: Cambridge University Press, 2010.

Hitch, S. "From Birth to Death: Life-Change Rituals." In *The Oxford Handbook of Ancient Greek Religion*, edited by E. Eidinow and J. Kindt. Oxford: Oxford University Press, 2015.

Horsfall, N. "CIL VI 37965 = CLE 1988 (Epitaph of Allia Potestas): A Commentary." *Zeitschrift für Papyrologie und Epigraphik* 61 (1985): 251–72.

Houghton, L. B. T. "Death Ritual and Burial Practice in the Latin Love Elegists." In *Memory and Mourning: Studies on Roman Death*, edited by V. Hope and J. Huskinson. Oxford: Oxbow Books, 2011.

Hsu, F. "Ritual Significance in Mycenaean Hairstyles." *Chronika* 2 (2012): 92–102.

Iossif, P., and C. Lorber. "Seleucid Campaign Beard." *L'antiquité classique* 78 (2009): 87–115.

Irwin, M. E. "Odysseus' 'Hyacinthine Hair' in *Odyssey* 6.231." *Phoenix* 44 (1990): 205–18.

Isaac, B. *The Invention of Racism in Classical Antiquity*. Princeton, NJ: Princeton University Press, 2004.

James, S. L., and S. Dillon, eds. *A Companion to Women in the Ancient World*. Malden, MA: Wiley-Blackwell, 2012.

Jenkins, I., and D. Williams. "Sprang Hair-Nets: Their Manufacture and Use in Ancient Greece." *American Journal of Archaeology* 89 (1985): 411–18.

Johnson, M. *Boudicca*. London: Bloomsbury, 2012.

Johnson, M. *Ovid on Cosmetics: Medicamina Faciei Femineae and Related Texts*. London: Bloomsbury, 2016.

Johnston, I., and G. H. R. Horsley. *Galen: Method of Medicine, Volume I: Books 1–4*. Cambridge, MA: Harvard University Press, 2011.

Jordan, D. R. "*Defixiones* from a Well Near the South-West Corner of the Athenian Agora." *Hesperia* 54, no. 3 (1985): 251.

Kaltsas, N. *Sculpture in the National Archaeological Museum*. Athens: Kapon Editions, 2002.

Kaltsas, N., and A. Shapiro. *Worshiping Women: Ritual and Reality in Classical Athens*. New York: Alexander S. Onassis Public Benefit Foundation, 2008.

Kampen, N. *Image and Status: Working Women in Ostia*. Berlin: Mann, 1981.

Kaplan, P. "Hanno." In *Dictionary of African Biography*, edited by H. L. Gates and E. K. Akyeampong, 3: 24–26. Oxford: Oxford University Press, 6 vols, 2012.

Kaster, R. *Marcus Tullius Cicero: Speech on Behalf of Publius Sestius*. Translated with introduction and commentary. Oxford: Clarendon Press, 2006.

Keaveney, A., and J. A. Madden, "Phthiriasis and Its Victims." *Symbolae Osloenses*, 57, no. 1 (1982): 87–99.

Kent, J. P. C. *Roman Coins*. London: Thames and Hudson, 1978.

Kenward, H. "Pubic lice (Pthirus pubis L.) Were Present in Roman and Medieval Britain." *Antiquity* 73 (1999): 911–15.

Kern, A., and K. Grömer, "Early Iron Age Headdress in the Central and Eastern Alpine Area." In *Tiarae, Diadems and Headdresses in the Ancient Mediterranean Cultures: Symbolism and Technology*, edited by C. Alfaro. Valencia: SEMA, 2014.

Kilmer, M. "Genital Phobia and Depilation." *Journal of Hellenic Studies* 102 (1982): 104–12.

King, H. *Hippocrates' Woman: Reading the Body in Ancient Greece*. London: Routledge, 1998.

King, H. *The One-Sex Body on Trial: The Classical and Early Modern Evidence*. Farnham: Ashgate, 2013.

Kleiner, D. E. E. "Women and Family Life on Roman Funerary Altars." *Latomus* 46 (1987): 545–54.

Kleiner, D. E. E. *Roman Sculpture*. New Haven, CT: Yale University Press, 1992.

Kleiner, D. E. E. "Family Ties: Mothers and Sons in Elite and Non-elite Roman Art." In *I Claudia II: Woman in Roman Art and Society*, edited by D. E. E. Kleiner and S. B. Matheson. Austin: University of Texas Press, 2000.

Kleiner, D. E. E. *Cleopatra and Rome*. Cambridge, MA: Belknap Press, 2005.

Kleiner, D. E. E., and S. B. Matheson, eds. *I Claudia: Women in Ancient Rome*. New Haven, CT: Yale University Art Gallery; Austin, TX, distributed by University of Texas Press, 1996.

Koch, G., and H. Sichtermann. *Römische Sarkophage*. Munich: Beck, 1982.

Koehl, R. B. "The Chieftain Cup and a Minoan Rite of Passage." *Journal of Hellenic Studies* 106 (1986): 99–110.

Kraay, C. M. *Greek Coins*. London: Thames and Hudson, 1966.

Kurke, L. *Aesopic Conversations: Popular Tradition, Cultural Dialogue, and the Invention of Greek Prose*. Princeton, NJ: Princeton University Press, 2011.

Kwaspen, A. "Features and Analysis of Sprang Hairnets." In *Tiarae, Diadems and Headdresses in the Ancient Mediterranean Cultures: Symbolism and Technology*, edited by C. Alfaro. Valencia: SEMA, 2014.

La Follette, L. "The Costume of the Roman Bride." In *The World of Roman Costume*, edited by J. L. Sebesta and L. Bonfante. Madison: University of Wisconsin Press, 1994.

Laqueur, T. *Making Sex: Body and Gender from the Greeks to Freud*. Cambridge, MA: Harvard University Press, 1990.

Larson, J. *Greek Heroine Cults*. Madison: University of Wisconsin Press, 1995.

Larsson Lovén, L. "*LANAM FECIT* – Wool Working and Female Virtue," in *Aspects of Women in Antiquity*, edited by L. Larsson Lovén and A. Strömberg, 85–95. Jonsered: Paul Åströms, 1998.

Lauter, H. *Die Koren des Erechtheion. Antike Plastik* 16. Berlin: Walter H. Schuchhardt, Felix Eckstein, 1976.

Lavergne, D. "Lépilation feminine en Grèce ancienne." In *Parures et artificies: le corps exposé dans l'Antiquité*, edited by L. Bodiou et al. Paris: L'Harmattan, 2011.

Lawton, C. "Children in Classical Attic Votive Reliefs." In *Constructions of Childhood in Ancient Greece and Italy, Hesperia Supplement* 41, edited by A. Cohen and J. B Rutter. Athens: American School of Classical Studies at Athens, 2007.

Leach, E. "Magical Hair." *Journal of the Royal Anthropological Society* 88, no. 2 (1958): 147–64.

Leary, T. J. *Martial Book XIV: The Apophoreta*. London: Duckworth, 1996.

Lee, M. M. *Body, Dress, and Identity in Ancient Greece*. Cambridge: Cambridge University Press, 2015.

Leitao, D. "Adolescent Hair-Growing and Hair-Cutting Rituals in Ancient Greece: A Sociological Approach." In *Initiation in Ancient Greek Rituals and Narratives: New Critical Perspectives*, edited by D. Dodd and C. Faraone, 109–29. London: Routledge, 2003.

Levine, M. M. "The Gendered Grammar of Ancient Mediterranean Hair." In *Off with Her Head! The Denial of Women's Identity in Myth, Religion, and Culture*, edited by A. Eilberg-Schwartz and W. Doniger, 76–130. Berkeley: University of California Press, 1995.

Lewis, S. "Barbers' Shops and Perfume Shops: 'Symposia without wine.'" In *The Greek World*, edited by A. Powell, 432–41. London: Routledge, 1995.

Lieber, L. S. "*The Piyyutim le-Hatan of Qallir and Amittai: Jewish Marriage Customs in Early Byzantium*." In *Talmuda de-Eretz Yisrael: Archaeology and the Rabbis in Late Ancient Palestine*, edited by S. Fine and A. J. Koller, 275–99. Boston, MA: Walter De Gruyter, 2014.

Lindner, M. *Portraits of the Vestal Virgins, Priestesses of Ancient Rome*. Ann Arbor: University of Michigan Press, 2015.

Liverani, M. "The Libyan Caravan Road in Herodotus IV.181–185." *Journal of the Economic and Social History of the Orient* 43, no. 4 (2000): 496–520.

Llewellyn-Jones, L. *Aphrodite's Tortoise: The Veiled Woman of Ancient Greece*. Swansea, Wales: Classical Press of Wales, 2003.

Llewellyn-Jones, L., and S. Winder, "A Key to Berenike's Lock? The Hathoric Model of Queenship in Early Ptolemaic Egypt." In *Creating a Hellenistic World*, edited by A. Erskine and L. Lewellyn-Jones, 247–70. Swansea: Classical Press of Wales, 2011.

Lloyd-Morgan, G. "Appearance, Life and Leisure." In *The Celtic World*, edited by M. Green. London: Routledge, 2012.

Lovejoy, A. O., and G. Boas, *Primitivism and Related Ideas in Antiquity*. Baltimore, MD: Johns Hopkins University Press, 1997 [1935].

Lovibond, S. "An Ancient Theory of Gender: Plato and the Pythagorean Table." In *Women in Ancient Societies*, edited by L. Archer, S. Fischler, and M. Wyke. London: Macmillan, 1994.

Marinone, N. "Il medico Disario in Simmaco e Macrobio." *Maia*, 25 (1973): 344–5.

McClure, L. "Courtesans Reconsidered: Women in Aristophanes' Lysistrata." *Eugesta* 5 (2015): 54–84.
McNiven, T. J. "Behaving Like a Child: Immature Gestures in Athenian Vase Painting." *Hesperia Supplements* 41 (2007): 85–99.
Mertens, J. R. *How to Read Greek Vases*. New Haven, CT: Yale University Press, 2010.
Micheli, M. E., and Santucci, A. *Comae: identità femminili nelle acconciature di età romana*. Pisa: Edizioni ETS, 2011.
Milady. *Standard Textbook of Professional Barber-Styling*. Tarrytown, NY: Milady Publishing, 1983.
Milady. *Milady's Standard Textbook of Cosmetology*. Albany, NY: Thomson Learning, 2000.
Montier, C. E. "'Let Her Be Shorn': 1 Corinthians 11 and Female Head Shaving in Antiquity." MA thesis, University of North Texas, 2015.
Munson, R. V. *Telling Wonders: Ethnographic and Political Discourse in the Work of Herodotus*. Ann Arbor: University of Michigan Press, 2001.
Murgatroyd, P. *Tibullus I*. Edited with introduction, notes, and vocabulary. Bristol: Bristol Classical Press, 1980.
Neils, J. "The Group of The Negro Alabastra: A Study in Motif Transferal." *Antike Kunst* 23 (1980): 13–23.
Neils, J., and J. Oakley. *Coming of Age in Ancient Greece*. New Haven, CT: Yale University Press, 2003.
Nicholson, F. W. "Greek and Roman Barbers." *Harvard Studies in Classical Philology* 2 (1891): 41–56.
Oakley, J., and R. Sinos. *The Wedding in Ancient Athens*. Madison: University of Wisconsin Press, 1993.
Obeyesekere, G. *Medusa's Hair: An Essay on Personal Symbols and Religious Experience*. Chicago: Chicago University Press, 1981.
Oldstone-Moore, C. *Of Beards and Men: The Revealing History of Facial Hair*. Chicago: University of Chicago Press, 2015.
Olivelle, P. "Hair and Society: Social Significance of Hair in South Asian Traditions." In *Hair, Its Power and Meaning in Asian Cultures*, edited by A. Hiltebeitel and B. Miller, 11–51. Albany, NY: State University of New York Press, 1998.
Olson, K. "*Matrona* and Whore: The Clothing of Women in Roman Antiquity." *Fashion Theory* 6, no. 4 (2002): 387–420.
Olson, K. *Dress and the Roman Woman: Self-Presentation and Society*. London: Routledge, 2008.
Olson, K. "The Appearance of the Young Roman Girl." In *Roman Dress and the Fabrics of Roman Culture*, edited by J. Edmondson and A. Keith. Toronto: University of Toronto Press, 2008.
Olson, K. "Masculinity, Appearance, and Sexuality: Dandies in Roman Antiquity." *Journal of the History of Sexuality* 23 (2014): 182–205.
Palagia, O. "Classical Athens." In *Greek Sculpture: Function, Materials, and Techniques in the Archaic and Classical Periods*, edited by O. Palagia, 119–62. Cambridge: Cambridge University Press, 2006.
Parker, H. "Tetrogenic Grid." In *Roman Sexualities*, edited by J. Hallett and M. Skinner. Princeton, NJ: Princeton University Press, 1997.
Paul, A. J. "Eros and a Depilation Scene by the Dinos Painter." *American Journal of Archaeology* 97 (1993): 330.
Peck, A. L. *Aristotle: Generation of Animals*. Cambridge, MA: Harvard University Press, 1942.

Petrie, W. M. Flinders. *Objects of Daily Use*, 42. London: Publications of the Egyptian Research Account and British School of Archaeology in Egypt, 1927.
Pivot Point. *Salon Fundamentals: Cosmetology*. Evanston, IL: Pivot Point, 2000.
Pollini, J. "Slave-Boys for Sexual and Religious Service: Images of Pleasure and Devotion." In *Flavian Rome: Culture, Image, Text*, edited by A. J. Boyle and W. J. Dominik, 149–66. Leiden: Brill, 2003.
Pollitt, J. J. *Art in the Hellenistic Age*. Cambridge: Cambridge University Press, 1986.
Pomeroy, S. *Spartan Women*. Oxford: Oxford University Press, 2002.
Potter, P. *Hippocrates: Generation, Nature of the Child, Diseases 4, Nature of Women, and Barrenness*. Cambridge, MA: Harvard University Press, 2012.
Powell, T. G. E. *The Celts*. London: Thames and Hudson, 1980.
Prioreschi, P. A. *A History of Medicine, Volume III: Roman Medicine*. Omaha: Horatius Press, 1998.
Ramin, J. *Le Periple d'Hannon: The Periplus of Hanno*. Oxford: British Archaeological Reports, 1976.
Rankin, D. "The Celts through Classical Eyes." In *The Celtic World*, edited by M. Green. London: Routledge, 1995.
Rawson, B. *Children and Childhood in Roman Italy*. New York: Oxford University Press, 2003.
Redfield, J. "Herodotus the Tourist." *Classical Philology* 80, no. 2 (1985): 97–118.
Richardson, B. E. *Old Age among the Ancient Greeks: The Greek Portrayal of Old Age in Literature, Art and Inscriptions*. New York: Greenwood Press, 1933.
Richardson, L., Jr., ed. *Propertius Elegies I–IV*. Norman: University of Oklahoma Press, 1977.
Richlin, A., "Making Up a Woman: The Face of Roman Gender." In *Off with Her Head! The Denial of Women's Identity in Myth, Religion and Culture*, edited by H. Eilberg-Schwartz and W. Doniger. Berkeley: University of California Press, 1995.
Richlin, A. "Gender and Rhetoric: Producing Manhood in the Schools." In *Roman Eloquence: Rhetoric in Society and Literature*, edited by W. J. Dominik. London: Routledge, 1997.
Ritchie, J. N. G., and W. F. Ritchie. "The Army, Weapons and Fighting." In *The Celtic World*, edited by M. Green. London: Routledge, 1995.
Roccos, L. "The Kanephoros and Her Festival Mantle in Greek Art." *American Journal of Archaeology* 99 (1995): 641–66.
Roebuck. C. A. *The Asklepieion and Lerna. Corinth: Results of Excavations Conducted by the American School of Classical Studies at Athens* XIV. Princeton, NJ: ASCSA, 1951.
Rose, M. E. "The Construction of Mistress and Slave Relationships in Late Antique Art." *Women's Art Journal* 29, no. 2 (2008): 41–9.
Rose, M., and K. A. Schwab, eds. *Hair in the Classical World*. Bellarmine Hall Galleries, Fairfield University Art Museums, Exhibition Brochure, Fairfield University, 2015.
Rosellini, M., and S. Saïd. "Women's Customs Among the 'savages'." In *Herodotus: Volume 2: Herodotus and the World*, edited by R. V. Munson, 213–44. Oxford: Oxford University Press, 2013.
Rousseau, V. "Emblem of an Empire: The Development of the Byzantine Empress's Crown." *Al-Masaq: Islam and the Medieval Mediterranean* 16 (2004): 5–15.
Russell, B. "A Sculpted Head of an African Woman in the British Museum." *Römische Mitteilungen*. 121 (2015): 507–32.
Sassi, M. G. "Erano icapei d'oro a l'aura sparsi." In *Comae. Identità femmimili nelle acconciature di età romana*, edited by M. E. Micheli and A. Santucci, 4. Pisa: Edizioni ETS, 2011.
Scheid, J. "Graeco ritu: A Typically Roman Way of Honouring the Gods." *Harvard Studies in Classical Philology* 97 (1995): 15–31.

Schmidt, S. "Fashion and Meaning: Beardless Portraits of Artists and Literati in the Early Hellenistic Period." In *Early Hellenistic Portraiture. Image, Style, Context*, edited by P. Schultz and R. Von Den Hof. Cambridge: Cambridge University Press, 2007.

Schoff, W. H. *The Periplus of Hanno*. Philadelphia: The Commercial Museum, 1912.

Schwab, K. A., and M. Rose. "Fishtail Braids and the Caryatid Hairstyling Project: Fashion Today and in Ancient Athens." *Catwalk: The Journal of Fashion, Beauty, and Style* 4 (2015): 1–24.

Sears, M. A. *Athens, Thrace, and the Shaping of Athenian Leadership*. Cambridge: Cambridge University Press, 2013.

Sebesta, J. L. "Symbolism in the Costume of the Roman Woman." In *The World of Roman Costume*, edited by J. L. Sebesta and L. Bonfante, 46–53. Madison: University of Wisconsin Press, 1994.

Sebesta, J. L. "Women's Costume and Feminine Civic Morality in Augustan Rome." *Gender and History* 9, no. 3 (1997): 529–41.

Sedley, D. *Creationism and Its Critics in Antiquity*. Berkeley: University of California Press, 2007.

Shapiro, H. A. "The Iconography of Mourning in Athenian Art." *American Journal of Archaeology* 95, no. 4 (1991): 629–56.

Sherwin-White, A. *Racial Prejudice in Imperial Rome*. Cambridge: Cambridge University Press, 1967.

Shumka, L. "Designing Women: The Representation of Women's Toiletries on Funerary Monuments in Roman Italy." In *The Fabrics of Roman Culture*, edited by J. Edmondson and A. Keith, 172–91. Toronto: University of Toronto Press.

Skinner, J. E. *The Invention of Greek Ethnography: From Homer to Herodotus*. Oxford: Oxford University Press, 2012.

Skinner, M. B. "Sex." In *A Cultural History of the Body. Volume 1: Antiquity*, edited by D. H. Garrison. London: Bloomsbury, 2010.

Smith, D. R. "Inversion, Revolution, and the Carnivalesque in Rembrandt's 'Civilis'." *Anthropology and Aesthetics* 27 (1995): 89–110.

Smith, R. R. R. *Hellenistic Sculpture*. London: Thames and Hudson, 1991.

Smith, R. R. R. "Cultural Choice and Political Identity in Honorific Portrait Statues in the Greek East in the Second Century A.D." *The Journal of Roman Studies* 88 (1998): 56–93.

Smith, R. R. R. "Pindar, Athletes, and the Early Greek Statue Habit." In *Pindar's Poetry, Patrons and Festivals: From Archaic Greece to the Roman Empire*, edited by S. Hornblower and C. Morgan. Oxford: Oxford University Press, 2007.

Snowden, F. M. "The Negro in Classical Italy." *The American Journal of Philology* 68, no. 3 (1947): 266–92.

Snowden, F. M. *Blacks in Antiquity: Ethiopians in the Greco-Roman Experience*. Cambridge, MA: Belknap Press, 1970.

Snowden, F. M. *Before Color Prejudice: The Ancient View of Blacks*. Cambridge, MA: Harvard University Press, 1983.

Snowden, F. M. Jr. "Iconographical Evidence on the Black Populations in Greco-Roman Antiquity." In *The Image of the Black in Western Art. Volume 1: From the Pharaohs to the Fall of the Roman Empire*, edited by D. Bindman and H. L. Gates. Cambridge, MA: Belknap Press, 2010.

Sorabji, R. *Self: Ancient and Modern Insights about Individuality, Life, and Death*. Chicago: University of Chicago Press, 2006.

Spencer, N., ed. *Time, Tradition and Society in Greek Archaeology: Bridging the "Great Divide."* London: Routledge, 2013.

Stears, K., "Dead Women's Society: Constructing Female Gender in Classical Athenian Funerary Sculpture." In *Time, Tradition and Society in Greek Archaeology: Bridging the 'Great Divide'*, edited by N. Spencer. London: Routledge, 2013.

Stenn, K. S. *Hair: A Human History*. New York: Pegasus Books, 2016.

Stephens, J. "Ancient Roman Hairdressing: On (Hair) Pins and Needles." *Journal of Roman Archaeology* 21 (2008): 110–36.

Stephens, J. "Recreating the Fonseca Hairstyle." *EXARC Journal Digest* (2013): 21–3. http://exarc.net/issue-2013-1/ea/recreating-fonseca-hairstyle.

Stevens Cox, J. "The Construction of an Ancient Egyptian Wig (c. 1400 B.C.) in the British Museum." *Journal of Egyptian Archaeology* 63 (1977): 67–70.

Stevens Cox, J. *An Illustrated Dictionary of Hairdressing and Wigmaking*. London: Batsford, 1984.

Stewart, A. *Faces of Power: Alexander's Image and Hellenistic Politics*. Berkeley: University of California Press, 1993.

Stewart, A. *Art, Desire and the Body in Ancient Greece*. Cambridge: Cambridge University Press, 1997.

Stewart, A. *Art in the Hellenistic World*. Cambridge: Cambridge University Press, 2014.

Stewart, P. C. N. "Inventing Britain: The Roman Creation and Adaptation of an Image." *Britannia* 26 (1995): 1–10.

Stewart, S. *Cosmetics and Perfumes in the Roman World*. Stroud: Tempus, 2007.

Stewart, S. "Cosmetics and Perfumes in the Roman World: A Glossary." In *Dress and Identity*, edited by M. Harlow. Oxford: Archaeopress, 2012.

Stieber, M. *The Poetics of Appearance in the Attic Korai*. Austin: University of Texas Press, 2004.

Stoner, L. "Mourners, Maenads, and Madness: 'Crazy' Hair on Greek Vases." *Hair in the Classical World Symposium*, Fairfield University, November 6, 2015.

Stout, A. "Jewelry as a Symbol of Status in the Roman Empire." In *The World of Roman Costume*, edited by J. Sebesta and L. Bonfante, 77–100. Madison: University of Wisconsin Press, 1994 (2001).

Stroh, S. "The Long Shadow of Tacitus: Classical and Modern Colonial Discourses in the Eighteenth- and Early-Nineteenth Century Scottish Highlands." *Transcultural English Studies: Theories, Fictions, Realities*, edited by F. Schulz-Engler and S. H. Rodopi, 339–56. *ASNEL Papers* 12. Netherlands: Rodopi, 2009.

Synnott, A. "Shame and Glory: A Sociology of Hair." *British Journal of Sociology* 38 (1987): 381–413.

Synnott, A. *The Body Social: Symbolism, Self, and Society*. London: Routledge, 1993.

Tarán, S. L., "ΕΙΣΙ ΤΡΙΧΕΣ: An Erotic Motif." *Journal of Hellenic Studies* 105 (1985): 90–107.

Tarlo, E. *Entanglement: The Secret Lives of Hair*. London: One World Publications, 2016.

Taylor, J. "Judean Priestly Dress: The Berne Josephus and Judea Capta Coinage." In *Dressing Judeans and Christians*, edited by K. Upson-Saia, C. Daniel-Hughes, and A. J. Batten, 195–212. Burlington, VT: Ashgate, 2014.

Temkin, O. *Hippocrates in a World of Pagans and Christians*. Baltimore, MD: Johns Hopkins University Press, 1991.

Temkin, O. *Soranus' Gynecology*. Baltimore, MD: Johns Hopkins Press, 1991.

Thomas, R. *Herodotus in Context: Ethnography, Science and the Art of Persuasion*. Cambridge: Cambridge University Press, 2002.

Thompson, F. H. *The Archaeology of Greek and Roman slavery*. Reports of the Research Committee of the Society of Antiquaries of London, 217–44. Bristol: Bristol Classical Press, 2003.

Thompson, P. *Mummy Portraits in the J. Paul Getty Museum*. Malibu, CA: J. Paul Getty Museum, 1982.
Toner, J. "Barbers, Barbershops and Searching For Roman Popular Culture." *Papers of the British School at Rome* 83 (2015): 91–109.
Touchette, L. *The Dancing Maenad Reliefs: Continuity and Change in Roman Copies*. London: University of London Press, 1995.
Treggiari, S. "Jobs in the Household of Livia." *Papers of the British School at Rome* 43 (1975): 48–77.
Tsouna, V. "Doubts about Other Minds and the Science of Physiognomics." *The Classical Quarterly* 48, no. 1 (1998): 175–86.
Tuck, S. L. *A History of Roman Art*. London: Wiley Blackwell, 2015.
Tulloch, J. ed. *A Cultural History of Women in Antiquity*. London: Bloomsbury, 2013.
Upson-Saia, K. *Early Christian Dress: Gender, Virtue, and Authority*. London: Routledge, 2011.
Upson-Saia, K. "Hairiness and Holiness in the Early Christian Desert." In *Dressing Judeans and Christians in Antiquity*, edited by K. Upson-Saia, C. Daniel-Hughes, and A. J. Batten, 155–72. Burlington, VT: Ashgate, 2014.
Vallance, J. T. "The Medical System of Asclepiades of Bithynia." *Aufstieg und Niedergang der römischen Welt* II 37, no. 1 (1993): 711–27.
Van Hoorn, G. *De vita atque cultu puerum monumentis antiquis explanato*. Amsterdam: J.H. de Bussy, 1909.
Vernant, J. P. *Mortals and Immortals: Collected Essays*. Edited by F. I. Zeitlin. Princeton, NJ: Princeton University Press, 1991.
Versnel, H. S. "Prayer and Curse." In *The Oxford Handbook of Ancient Greek Religion*, edited by E. Eidinow and J. Kindt. Oxford: Oxford University Press, 2015.
Vikan, G. "Art, Medicine and Magic in Early Byzantium", *Dumbarton Oaks Papers* 38 (1984): 68–72.
Von Den Hof, R. "Naturalism and Classicism: Style and Perception of Early Hellenistic Portraits." In *Early Hellenistic Portraiture. Image, Style, Context*, edited by P. Schultz and R. von den Hof. Cambridge: Cambridge University Press, 2007.
Vout, C. "What's in a Beard? Rethinking Hadrian's Hellenism." In *Rethinking Revolutions through Ancient Greece*, edited by S. Goldhill and R. Osborne. Cambridge: Cambridge University Press, 2006.
Waegeman, M. "The Gecko, the Hoopoe … and Lice." *L'Antiquité Classique* 53 (1984): 218–25.
Walker, A. "Enhancing the Body, Neglecting the Soul." In *Byzantine Women and their World*, edited by I. Kalavrazou. New Haven, CT: Yale University Press, 2003.
Walker, A. "Numismatic and Metrological Parallels for the Iconography of Early Byzantine Marriage Jewelry: The Question of the Crowned Bride." *Travaux et Mémoires* 16 (2010): 1–14.
Walker, S. "Bearded Men". In *Plaster and Marble*, edited by Glenys Davies. *Journal of the History of Collections* 3, no. 2 (1991): 265–77.
Walker, S. *Ancient Faces: Mummy Portraits from Roman Egypt*. London: British Museum Press, 1997.
Ward, J. K. "*Ethnos* in the *Politics*: Aristotle and Race." In *Philosophers on Race: Critical Essays*, edited by J. K. Ward and T. L. Lott, 14–37. Oxford: Blackwell, 2002.
Watson, P. "Ovid and *Cultus: Ars Amatoria* 3.113–28." *Transactions and Proceedings of the American Philological Association* 112 (1982): 237–44.
Wiedemann, T. *Greek and Roman Slavery*. London: Croom Helm, 1981.

Wildfang, R. L. *Rome's Vestal Virgins: A Study of Rome's Vestal Priestesses in the Late Republic and Early Empire*. London: Routledge, 2006.
Williams, C. A., ed. *Martial* Epigrams *Book Two*. Oxford: Oxford University Press, 2004.
Williams, C. A. *Roman Homosexuality*. Oxford: Oxford University Press, 2010.
Williams, D. "Onesimos and the Getty Iliupersis." *Greek Vases in the J. Paul Getty Museum 5. Occasional Papers on Antiquities* 7 (1991): 41–64.
Wilson, L. M. *The Clothing of the Ancient Romans*. Baltimore, MD: Johns Hopkins University Press, 1938.
Wood, S. E. *Roman Portrait Sculpture, 217–260 AD: The Transformation of an Artistic Tradition*. Columbia Studies in the Classical Tradition. Vol. 12. Leiden: Brill, 1986.
Wood, S. E. *Imperial Women: A Study in Public Images, 40 BC– AD 68*. Leiden: Brill, 1999.
Woodbury, L. "Gold Hair and Grey, or the Game of Love: Anacreon fr. 13:358 PMG, 13 Gentili." *Transactions of the American Philological Association* 109 (1979): 277–87.
Woolf, G. *Becoming Roman: The Origins of Provincial Civilization in Gaul*. Cambridge: Cambridge University Press, 2000.
Wrenhaven, K. L. *Reconstructing the Slave: The Image of the Slave in Ancient Greece*. London: Bloomsbury, 2012.
Wyke, M. "Woman in the Mirror: The Rhetoric of Adornment in the Roman World." In *Women in Ancient Societies*, edited by L. Archer et al. London: Macmillan, 1994.
Zanker, P. *The Power of Images in the Age of Augustus*. Ann Arbor: University of Michigan Press, 1990.
Zanker. P. *The Mask of Socrates: The Image of the Intellectual in Antiquity*. Translated by A. Shapiro. Berkeley: University of California Press, 1995.

CONTRIBUTORS

Glenys Davies is now retired and an Honorary Fellow in the School of History, Classics and Archaeology at the University of Edinburgh, UK, where she taught classical art and archaeology for many years. She has published several articles on Roman dress, gender, and body language, but has also written on other aspects of Roman art (especially funerary art) and on eighteenth-century collecting of antiquities. Her monograph, *Gender and Body Language*, was published in 2018 and she continues to work on other aspects of body language in classical art. Hair is a new topic for her, but one she has enjoyed working on.

Mary Harlow recently retired from her post of Associate Professor of Ancient History at the University of Leicester, UK (2013–20). From 2011 to 2013 she was Guest Professor at the Centre for Textile Research at the University of Copenhagen, Denmark. Her research interests include the study of dress and appearance, and the history of families, age and ageing, and gender in the Roman world. She has edited/co-edited and contributed to (among many other publications) *A Cultural History of Childhood and the Family* (2010), *Greek and Roman Dress and Textiles, An Interdisciplinary Anthology* (2014), *A Cultural History of Dress and Fashion* (2017), *Textiles and Gender in Antiquity* (2020) and *A Cultural History of Shopping* (forthcoming, 2022).

Marguerite Johnson is Professor of Classics at the University of Newcastle, New South Wales, Australia. She is an interdisciplinary cultural historian of the ancient Mediterranean, and a comparative cultural analyst. She is the coauthor (with Terry Ryan) of *Sexuality in Greek and Roman Society and Literature: A Sourcebook* (2005), coeditor (with Harold Tarrant) of *Alcibiades and the Socratic Lover-Educator* (2012), and author of *Sappho* (2006), *Boudicca* (2012), and *Ovid on Cosmetics: Medicamina Faciei Femineae and Related Texts* (2016).

Lena Larsson Lovén is Associate Professor in Classical Archaeology and Ancient History at the Department of Historical Studies, University of Gothenburg, Sweden. Her main research focus lies with studies on dress and textiles, visual cultures, gender studies, and aspects of socioeconomic history in the Roman world, with a particular emphasis on the Roman West. She is founder of the network *ARACHNE* and has edited several volumes from *ARACHNE* conferences. Some recent publications include "Visual Representations" in *A Cultural History of Dress and Fashion* (ed. M. Harlow, 2017), "Gender and Textile Production in Roman Society and Politics", in *Textiles and Gender in Antiquity* (eds. M. Harlow, C. Michel & L. Quillien, 2020), "Male and Female Work in Images and Inscriptions" in *Il Mediterraneo e la storia* III (ed. L. Chioffi *et.al.*, 2021).

Lydia Matthews is a researcher in Ancient History at the University of Oxford, UK. Her research interests include Roman history, ancient sexuality and gender, ancient medicine, and ancient ethnography. She is also a sculptor whose work draws on ancient models, especially Roman funerary sculpture.

Kelly Olson holds a PhD from the University of Chicago, Illinois, USA, and is currently Associate Professor in Classical Studies at the University of Western Ontario, Canada, with cross-appointments in the Faculty of Law and the Department of Women's Studies and Feminist Research. Her research focuses on Roman society, sexuality, and appearance, as well as fashion history more generally. She is the author of several articles on clothing in Roman antiquity, published in *Mouseion, Fashion Theory, The American Journal of Ancient History, Classical World*, and *The Journal of the History of Sexuality*. She has recent chapters and articles on gender and appearance in various publications, and is author of *Dress and the Roman Woman: Self-Presentation and Society* (2008) and *Masculinity and Dress in Roman Antiquity* (2017). A volume co-edited with Alicia Batten, *Dress in Mediterranean Antiquity: Greeks, Romans, Jews, Christians*, was published by Bloomsbury in 2021.

Marice Rose is Associate Professor of Art History and Visual Culture at Fairfield University in Fairfield, Connecticut, USA. Her research focuses on art and gender in late Roman domestic contexts, as well as on classical reception and art history pedagogy. Her publications include several journal articles and chapters and comprised the collected volume *Receptions of Antiquity, Constructions of Gender in European Art, 1300–1600* (2015), co-edited with Alison Poe. With Katherine Schwab, she co-curated the 2015 exhibition *Hair in the Classical World* at the Fairfield University Art Museum, which comprised artworks and hair implements from the sixth century BCE to late antiquity, from Greece, Cyprus, and the Roman Empire. The exhibition examined practical aspects of hair's arrangement and adornment, its role in divine and royal iconography, and its styling as evidence of cultural exchange, to elucidate the critical role that hair played in identity formation in the ancient Mediterranean. In addition to the exhibition, she collaborated with Katherine Schwab on an article on fishtail braids in ancient Greece and today for *Catwalk: The Journal of Fashion, Beauty, and Style* (2015).

Katherine A. Schwab is Professor of Art History and Visual Culture in the Department of Visual and Performing Arts, Curator of the Plaster Cast Collection, and Director of the Program in Classical Studies. Her research focus concerns the Parthenon metopes, the short film *Caryatid Hairstyling Project* (www.fairfield.edu/caryatid), and restoration work on the plaster cast collection. Her publications include several book chapters and journal articles on the Parthenon metopes. A national touring exhibition of her original Parthenon drawings, *An Archaeologist's Eye: The Parthenon Drawings of Katherine A. Schwab*, launched at the Greek Consulate General in New York City in January 2014, and travelled to several university and college art galleries and museums concluding at the Nashville Parthenon in 2018. Grayscale scans of her east and north metope drawings are permanently installed in the Parthenon Gallery of the Acropolis Museum. In 2015 she organized an exhibition, *Photographs of the Caryatid Hairstyles*, for the Greek Consulate General in New York City and the Greek Embassy in Washington, DC. In the same year, she cocurated (with Marice Rose) the exhibition *Hair in the Classical World* for the Fairfield University Art Museum (formerly Bellarmine Museum of Art), and coorganized a symposium on the same topic. She coauthored (with Marice Rose) "Fishtail Braids and the *Caryatid Hairstyling Project*: Fashion Today and in Ancient Athens," for *Catwalk: The Journal of Fashion, Beauty and Style* (2015).

Janet Stephens is a professional hairdresser and self-trained experimental archaeologist, specializing in the technical recreation of ancient Roman hairstyles. She was a 2012 Rome Prize finalist (Design) and American Institute of Archaeology travelling lecturer in 2014/15 and 2016/17. She is published in the *Journal of Roman Archaeology* and *EXARC—the Journal of Experimental Archaeology*. She has a popular YouTube channel devoted to historical hairdressing from antiquity through the nineteenth century. Her research has been featured by the *New Yorker Magazine*, *Wall Street Journal*, BBC, and National Public Radio.

Susan Stewart is an independent scholar and librarian. Studying part-time with The Open University, Susan gained her PhD in 2003. Her thesis was entitled "From Ovid to the Price Edict: Women under the Roman Empire, their use of Cosmetics and Perfumes and its Significance." Her first book, *Cosmetics and Perfumes in the Roman World* (2007), is based on the findings explained in detail in her thesis. Susan went on to publish widely in journals and magazines on the meaning of cosmetics and their place in everyday life in the classical world. She has given papers at conferences in the UK and abroad and taken part in both the Edinburgh International Book Festival and the Edinburgh International Science Festival. In 2017, Susan published a broader history of make-up entitled *Painted Faces: A Colourful History of Cosmetics*. The book, which is aimed at a general reader, stresses the importance of cosmetics as a social, political, and economic marker not only in antiquity but throughout history. A companion book on the social and cultural history of perfume is due for publication in 2022. Susan is also working on a joint paper with Kirsty Stewart on the late antique and byzantine cosmetics commissioned by Ghent University. Her current ideas for new projects include work on new perspectives on Roman cosmetics in the light of recent academic interest in reception studies and sensory history as well as a study of the objects on a lady's dressing table (mirror, combs etc).

INDEX

Achilles 27, 28, 29
Aeneas 158
Aeschylus 22
African hair 148, 157. *See also* Ethiopians, representations of
Agamemnon 22
age, hair as marker of 16–22, 31–2, 41, 47, 49, 52, 55, 58, 69, 93, 99. *See also* rites of passage
Agrippina Maior 59
Ajax 22
Alcman 102
Alexander the Great 2, 8, 10, 32, 33f, 38, 43, 54, 76, 155
Allia Potestas 107, 140
Amazons 119–21, 120f, 121f, 126, 126f
Andania, cult regulations 24
Andromache 28
Antaios 155, 156f
Apatouria, festival of 16
apex 27
Aphrodite 23
Apollo 16–18, 20, 27, 32, 41, 50–1, 148, 158
Appian 141
Apuleius 23, 102–3, 107, 153–4
Ara Pacis 26–7, 59
Archaic Greek art 151, 155, 160
aristocratic society/ideals 49, 160
Aristophanes 49, 50, 54, 104–5, 106, 130, 141
Aristotle 49, 87–90, 92, 93, 96, 98, 119
armpit hair. *See* underarm hair
asceticism 15, 34, 108–9, 143. *See also* celibacy
Athenian hair rituals for boys 16–17
Attic black-figure vase painting 29, 148, 151
Attic red-figure vase painting 148, 149, 154–5, 156f
Augustus 10, 11, 20, 26, 32, 33f, 34, 38, 43, 44, 106, 113, 151, 156

Bacchus 158
baldness 1, 2, 3, 4, 16, 34, 49, 69, 75, 89, 92, 97, 98, 102, 131, 136, 137, 145, 152–3, 155, 158 (sensitivity to) 153
Dio Chrysostom *On Baldness* 1–3
Synesius *On Baldness* 1, 3, 32
barbarians 36, 40, 68, 115, 155, 157
barbers 2, 23, 49, 76, 82–3
Bartman, Elizabeth 7, 55, 58, 62–3
baths 131
beards 8, 9, 20, 32, 38, 50, 54, 58, 76, 91, 104, 143, 145, 155–7, 158, 161. *See also* facial hair
blue beard 159
first appearance of 8, 9, 20, 50, 58, 99, 101–2
first shave 20, 44
Julian (Emperor) 156
in women 93–4
Berenik(c)e, locks of 23, 44
Berg, Charles 7, 9
body hair 4, 8–9, 31, 69, 70, 86, 88, 118, 145, 154–5, 158. *See also* depilation
female 9, 54, 94, 97, 98, 104, 107, 140
male 51, 58, 97, 104, 106, 143, 144
body language 134, 141, 160
Boudicca 115–16, 117
bride's hair
Athenian 41
Roman 22, 25, 44, 74, 77–8, 157
Spartan 8, 15, 41, 102
British hair 124–6. *See also* Boudicca

Caelius Aurelianus 94–5, 96
Caligula 34, 44, 153
Callimachus 23, 44
capite velato 26
Caracalla 34
care of the self 11, 106. *See also cultus*
Caryatids 41, 43, 113
Catullus 23, 44
Celsus 96
Celtic art 151
Celts/Celtic hair 4, 73, 76, 77, 111, 115, 117, 123, 126
Ceres 23
Ceres and Persephone 158
charioteer/circus fan hairstyle 157

chest hair (represented in art) 154
children's hair 4, 20, 41, 82, 91, 95, 98, 99, 103
Christianity/Christian attitudes to hair 24, 34, 36, 38, 44, 63, 108–9, 143–4
Cicero 132, 136
clean shaven 8, 20, 32, 34, 38, 44, 50, 54, 55, 58, 76, 106, 117, 145, 155–6
Clement of Alexandria 63, 106, 143–4
climate and hair 118–19
Clytemenestra 22
coins 145, 151, 153–4, 154f, 156–7, 157f, 161
Columns of Trajan and Marcus Aurelius 40, 157
combs 49, 71, 81, 131, 138, 139, 141
comedy 9, 103, 123, 130, 131, 136, 141. *See also* Aristophanes
Constantine the Great 34, 41, 77, 156
corona 40–1. *See also* crowns; wreaths
courtesans (prostitutes) 9, 11, 23, 104, 107, 129, 132, 138–9, 143
Croom, Alexandra 55, 59
cropped hair. *See* hair styles
crowns 21, 41. *See also* polos
cult regulations 24
cultus 2–3, 5, 11, 32, 34, 36, 40, 63, 106, 108, 109, 113, 130, 135
curling tongs/wands (*calamistrum*) 55, 60, 69, 70, 75, 131, 134, 138
curses, curse tablets 22, 23–4

Dacians 157
Daedalic style 47
defixiones. *See* curse tablets
Demeter and Kore 21
Demosthenes 138
depilation 8, 58, 75–7, 103–7, 117, 118, 139, 145, 155. *See also* epilation
designer stubble 145, 156
diadems 40–1, 78, 134
Diana 158
Dionysos/Dionysus 16, 76, 152
Domitian 153
Douglas, Mary 7
dragging by the hair 40, 125, 125f, 157
Draycott, Jane 19, 30
Dying Gaul 39, 39f, 73, 148

effeminacy 2, 9, 34, 55, 57, 68, 75, 104, 106, 108, 132, 136, 144, 151, 155, 159
Eilberg-Schwartz, Howard 7

epilation 75–7. *See also* depilation
epithets 158
eroticism/homoeroticism 7, 9, 11, 20, 34, 47, 49, 50, 55, 99, 100, 101, 102–3, 104, 107, 113, 132, 138, 142
Ethiopians, representations of 119–21, 120f, 121f. *See also* African hair
ethnicity 4, 5, 15, 111–27, 148, 157
Etruscans 54–5, 73
    Etruscan art (tomb of the Leopards, Tarquinia) 149
eunuchs 70, 89, 98
Eurysaces, son of Ajax 22
eyebrows 10, 54, 75, 78, 81, 87, 88, 90, 91, 141

facial hair 8, 20, 31, 32, 34, 39, 50, 51, 58, 75, 99, 106, 136. *See also* beards
false hair 57, 59, 60, 62, 63, 78, 80, 81, 141. *See also* wigs
fashion 5, 10, 31, 32, 41, 42, 47–63, 71, 77, 111, 134, 140, 145, 151, 154, 155, 156, 160, 161
Faustina 59
Faustina the Younger 59, 60f, 71
Ferrari, Gloria 12
fillets. *See* woolen fillets
flamen dialis 27
flaminica dialis 27, 157
flammeum 20, 22, 25, 27, 44
"Flavian Lady". *See* Fonseca Bust
Fonseca Bust 60–1, 61f, 133, 134
freedmen/women 34, 139–40, 159
Freud, Sigmund 7, 9
Fulvia 59

Galen 9, 90–3, 98
galerus 27, 57, 60
    albogalerus 27
garlands 78. *See also* crowns; wreaths; diadems
Gauls 115, 117, 123. *See also* Dying Gaul
Gemma Augustea 36, 37f, 40
gems 59, 145, 161
gender 4, 8, 9, 10, 15, 29, 31, 32, 36, 81, 83, 97–109, 129, 132, 143, 144, 145, 161. *See also* effeminacy; sexuality
German hair and hairstyles 40, 69, 73, 75, 123, 124, 131, 157
    use in wigs 60, 75, 123, 138
giants 154, 157, 159
gilding 150
gods/heroes 1, 4, 15, 16, 20, 23, 30, 32, 47, 78, 142, 152, 158

Greek funerary monuments 153, 155, 161. *See also* Hegeso, monument of
Greek vase painting 11, 28, 31, 47, 49, 50, 51, 104, 129, 145, 150, 160. *See also* Attic-black figure; Attic-red figure painting
grooming 3, 32, 35, 65, 81, 101, 104, 106, 108, 113, 155, 159. *See also* hair care, care of the self; *cultus*

Hadrian 34, 38, 58, 76, 156
hair
   artistic representation of 145, 151, 155, 160–1 (*see also* Greek vase painting; sculpture; mummy portraits)
   as disguise 142–3
   as expression of emotion 16, 29, 32, 66, 103, 115
   loose, unbound, uncontrolled 24, 29, 34, 35, 36, 38, 40, 44, 102, 103, 109, 115, 155, 157, 158
   luxuriant/abundant hair 32, 64, 154, 158
   physiology of (ancient) 85–93 (modern) 65–70
   power of 8, 16, 22–4, 28, 30, 38–40, 112–13, 115, 117, 122, 124, 132
   as racial signifier Chapter 7, esp. 118–24
   as sign of resistence/oppression 124–6
   as sign/treatment of illness/disease 93–6
   as social organisation/control 4, 7, 16, 34, 42, 47, 103, 132, 157, 158
   structure of (biology) 65–70
   as symbol 7, 8, 9
   washing 41, 71–3
hair bodkins 74
hair color and coloring 69, 80–1, 89, 121, 123, 124, 138, 145, 148–50, 155
   blond(e)/yellow 67, 71, 91, 102, 115–16, 123, 140, 142, 149
   brunette/brown 67, 148, 150
   dark/black 91, 93, 142, 143, 148
   gray/white 16, 49, 69, 75, 80, 89–90, 92, 93, 98, 138, 150, 158
   red 67, 89, 91, 92, 116, 122–3, 124, 131, 138, 142, 155
hair cutting 77. *See also* ritual hair behaviour
hair dyes/colorants 60, 80–1, 107, 123, 136, 138, 143, 159
hair modification 114, 116–17
hair oil 2, 23, 71, 73, 102, 107, 135, 141. *See also* unguents
hair pins 74, 131, 134, 142
hair/head covering 9, 35. *See also capite velato*; veiling
hairdressers (*ornatrix/ornatrices*) 54, 65, 83, 135, 141–2
hairiness 4, 8, 89, 93, 106, 108, 155
   as characteristic of barbarians 155. *See also* barbarians
   as symptom of disease 94
   in women 116
hairloss/thinning hair 58, 69, 70, 80, 152
hairnets 77–8, 78*f*. *See also sakkos*
hairstyles
   apskuthisthai 77
   artistic representations of Roman women's 145–7, 151, 154
   bowl-cut 77
   braids, braiding 25, 41–4, 47, 49, 54–5, 57, 58, 59, 69, 70, 73, 77, 80, 99, 103, 112, 135, 143
   as a control of women 16, 40, 42, 157
   cropped hair 2, 36, 38, 113, 127, 132, 140, 141, 145, 155, 156
   curls/curly hair 1, 10, 31, 32, 34, 38, 42, 47, 54–5, 57–8, 59, 62, 68, 69, 71, 73, 75, 77, 80, 88, 90, 91–2, 93, 101, 112, 119–27, 131, 141, 143, 145, 148, 150–1
   dissemination of 133, 160–1
   fishtail braid 41–4, 73
   Flavian 'toupet' style 161
   ganymede 77
   lime-washed 73, 117–18
   melon 58
   mullet 157
   nodus 34, 35*f*, 59, 60
   pudding basin haircut 157
   sewn 70, 70*f*, 74
   Suebian knot 73, 77, 157
   Theseis 18, 77
   tutulus 27, 55
Hallpike, C. R. 7
Haterii monument 158
headbands 24, 73
headdresses 21, 26, 63, 143, 157
Hecabe 28
Hector 27, 47
Hegeso, monument of 11, 35–6, 37*f*, 136, 141
Hellenistic Kings 155
helots 132
Herakles 38, 51, 148, 155, 156*f*
   Hercules 27

hercules knot 74, 74f
Herodotus 1–2, 10, 19, 39, 113–15, 119, 132
Hippocratic writings 85–7, 93, 97, 119
Homer 2, 27, 28, 47–9, 93
Homeric heroes 1–2, 18, 117
Horace 57, 103, 132, 142
Horus lock 19
Hygiene 85–96, 131, chapter 5

identity 5, 7, 8, 10, 29, 31–4, 40, 41, 42, 45, 47, 58, 60, 119, 124, 129, 145, 151
infula 26, 78

jewels 41, 59, 63, 103. *See also* gems
Jewish, attitudes to hair and hair practices 29, 34, 38, 71, 80, 103, 108
Julia, daughter of Augustus 59, 75
Julia Domna 73, 134, 150, 154
Julian the Apostate 156
Julius Caesar 20, 40, 55, 113, 117, 131, 136–7, 153
Jupiter 158
Juvenal 133, 141, 142

Kilmer, Martin 103, 104
konnos 17
Kore 21
kouros/kouroi/korai 32, 41, 42, 43, 45, 47, 49, 112, 151, 154
kredemnon 136
krôbylos 17, 49, 50, 54–5

"laconizing" hair styles 32, 49–50, 132
Laqueur, Thomas 98
Lavergne, David 103–4
Leach, Edward 7
Lee, Mireille 7, 52, 104–5, 132
Leitao, David 7, 16, 18, 50
Levine, Molly Myerowitz 7, 22, 108, 158
Libya/Libyans 113–14
lice (head, body, pubic) 15, 95–6, 113
Livia, wife of Augustus 34, 59, 60, 113
Livy 26
Llewellyn-Jones, Lloyd 54
Lucian 23
Lupercalia, *luperci* 20

Macrobius 93
maenads 35–6, 36f, 38, 155
magic 7, 15, 22, 23–4, 30
maidens 32, 41–2, 58, 102, 158, 160. *See also* young girls, virgins

mallos 17
Marcus Aurelius 36, 55, 145–6, 146f
marriage 7, 8, 20, 21, 22, 23, 31, 32, 41–2, 101, 103, 132, 138, 158
Martial 20, 57, 58, 106, 107, 139, 142, 143, 151, 159
masculinity 4, 8, 34, 50, 101, 102, 106, 108, 112, 113, 131
Mauretanians 157
Medusa 7, 73, 103, 158, 159f
Menander 142, 155
Messalina, Empress 60, 142
metaphor (hair as) 117, 133, 158
Minerva 158
mirrors 11, 49, 71–3, 72f, 108, 131, 136, 143
mosaics 77, 129, 133, 145, 148
mourning 7, 27–9, 31, 38, 44, 132, 143, 155, 156, 157, 158
moustaches 39, 51, 58, 76, 117, 156
mummy portraits 78, 148, 148f, 150, 150f
mythological figures 11, 35, 41, 129, 145, 158

nature vs culture 36, 107–9, 113–14, 115, 158
negative modelling 145, 147f
Nero 20, 44, 57–8, 143, 144, 156–7, 157f
Neumagen Relief 11, 135–6, 141
nonconformity 156
nymphs 158

Obeyesekere, Gannath 8
Octavia, sister of Augustus 34, 59
Octavian 20, 26. *See also* Augustus
old age 4, 10, 86, 87, 88, 89, 90, 92, 93, 152–3, 155, 158
Orestes 22–3
Otho 58, 138, 153, 154f
Ovid 20, 24, 59, 60, 75, 103, 107, 108, 123, 132, 138, 142, 158, 159

paint on sculpture 44, 63, 104, 129, 133, 149
painted representation of hair 119, 129, 148, 148f, 150, 150f. *See also* specific vase painting
Pan 155
Pausanius 18, 21, 23
perfume/perfumed hair 2, 23, 57, 73, 102, 131, 141, 151, 158
Pergamene monument 39
Pergamon, Great Altar of Zeus 154
philosophers 31, 34, 36, 153, 155
physiognomy 121–3
Plato 70, 87, 99, 100–1, 106

Pliny the Elder 41, 71, 81, 95, 96, 107, 116
Plutarch 18, 21, 23, 29, 47, 55, 101, 142
  Life of Theseus 18, 47
Pollux catalogue 131
polos 21
Polyphemus 159
portraits (Greek) 38, 155, 161
  (Roman) 32, 34, 41, 55, 58, 62, 63, 145, 146f, 147f, 149, 151, 152, 153, 154, 161. See also mummy portraits
Poseidon 32, 103, 158. *See also* Artemision bronze
Procopius 157
Propertius 44, 58, 123, 132, 138
puberty 16, 47, 69, 70, 85, 89, 97, 98, 101
pubic hair 65, 69, 70, 85, 86, 87, 89, 90, 91, 92, 97, 98, 104, 107, 143. See also depilation
  representation of in art 4, (male) 154
  (female) 54, 154–5

Rampin horseman 151, 152f
razors 70, 76–7, 82
rites of passage 7, 15, 16–17, 20, 41–2, 102
  (Sparta), 129
ritual hair behaviour 15, 16–22, 19, 22, 23, 32, 41, 114, 129
  dedications 17–21, 22–3, 31, 32, 43–4, 114
  of girls/women 21, 22, 24
  koreion 16, 17, 21
Roman matron 38, 157

sakkos 35, 52, 55, 77
satyrs 152, 153f, 154–5, 157, 158
scalping 39, 40f
scents and pomade 151. See also perfumes; hair oil; unguents
sculpture 4, 10, 112–13. See also hair, artistic representations
  bronze sculpture 112–13, 112f, 147f, 148
  marble sculpture 145, 146f, 147f, 154, 160
  representation of body hair on 154
Seneca the Elder 57, 58
Seneca the Younger 57, 58, 75, 106, 107–8
sex crines 25, 26
sexuality 7, 9, 20, 23, 32, 34, 40, 97, 99, 103, 123, 138, 158. See also Gender; effeminacy
sexual desire 7
shaved heads 7, 8, 15, 19, 20, 40, 76–7, 94, 102, 132, 141, 143. See also bride's hair; Spartan

eyebrows 141
  as remedy for disease 94–5, 96
  shaving 19, 20, 34, 38, 50, 76–7, 82–3, 104, 114, 118, 141, 143, 155–6, 159. See also beards; depilation; epilation
shears 77
sideburns 58, 156
skollos 17
slaves 4, 15, 40, 54, 55, 58, 76, 77, 78, 81, 82, 83, 104, 131, 132, 134, 135, 136, 139, 141–2, 143, 149, 155, 159
Soranus 24, 44, 95
Sparta 5, 12, 99, 101, 102, 131. See also bride's hair; Spartan
  female hair 8, 102, 132
  male hair 2, 32, 49, 50, 101, 114–15, 132
Suebian knot 73, 77, 157
Suetonius 10, 57, 58, 131, 136, 137, 143, 153
suffibulum 26
Synesius of Cyrene 1–4, 32, 69
Synnott, Anthony 8, 9, 31, 45, 118

Tacitus 40, 115, 122, 124, 126, 131
Teiresias 158
Temple of Zeus at Olympia (pedimental sculpture) 148, 149, 149f, 151
Tertullian 30, 63, 123
texture 31, 32, 65–6, 70, 75, 121
  representation of 34, 39, 42, 120, 145, 148, 155
theatre masks 123, 130
Thersites 158
Theseus/*Theseis* 18, 47, 77
Thucydides 49
tondo of Septimius Severus and family in Berlin 150
tonsure 77
Trimalchio 140, 158–9
Tropaeum Traiani (Adamklissi) 157
turbans 78

underarm hair 65, 75, 86, 90, 104, 106
  represented in art 154
unguents 57, 73, 136

Valerius Maximus 35
veiling 2, 9, 22, 25–6, 27, 29, 30, 31, 35, 38, 41, 44, 49, 52, 54, 59, 103, 108, 113, 132, 135. See also hair/head covering; *capite velato*; *flammeum*; *suffibulum*
Vespasian 34
Vestal Virgins 22, 25–6, 78, 157
vittae 22, 26, 58–9

wigs/hairpieces 47, 49, 50, 55, 57–8, 60, 62–3, 62f, 78–80, 134, 136, 137, 138, 143, 145, 152, 153–4, 154f, 159
   German hair for wigs 40, 60, 123
witches 23, 103
women's hair in opposition to male hair 2, 4, 8, 9, 29, 31, 99
woolen fillets 26, 58, 73, 157
wreaths 24, 40, 44–5, 78, 131

youth (young men and women) 4, 17, 19, 20, 32, 47, 49, 58, 63, 99, 100–1, 102, 151
   in Greek vase painting 11
youthful looks 8, 10, 16, 20, 34, 38, 100–1, 112, 142, 151, 155, 156, 159, 160

Zeus 32, 41

www.ingramcontent.com/pod-product-compliance
Ingram Content Group UK Ltd.
Pitfield, Milton Keynes, MK11 3LW, UK
UKHW052225260326
469398UK00011B/183